Praise for IF YOU REALLY LOVED ME:

'Those of us addicted to true crime tales can't wait for Ann Rule's books. We count on her for powerful stories brilliantly investigated and beautifully told. With *If You Really Loved Me*, she has fulfilled our expectations once again.'   Jerry Bledsoe, author of *Bitter Blood*

'Rule has triumphed again. In this vivid account, a monster to whom every other human being was a "throwaway person" is masterfully portrayed.' *Publishers Weekly*

'*If You Really Loved Me* expresses a nearly perfect murder and dissects the diabolical criminal mind behind it, while putting a sad new twist on the psychology of victims. Ann Rule is simply the best.' Carla Norton, co-author of *Perfect Victim*

'This is a truly frightening book, informed by the depth and incisive writing we have come to expect from Ann Rule.'   Jonathan Coleman, author of *Exit the Rainmaker* and *At Mother's Request*

'Shocking and juicy.'   *Kirkus*

ANN RULE

If You Really Loved Me

A True Story of Desire and Murder

A *Time Warner* Paperback

First published in Great Britain in 1992
by Warner Books
Reprinted 1992 (twice), 1993, 1994, 1995, 1996, 1998, 1999, 2001
Reprinted by Time Warner Paperbacks in 2003

ISBN 0 7515 0339 8

Printed in England by Clays Ltd, St Ives plc

Time Warner Paperbacks
An imprint of
Time Warner Books UK
Brettenham House
Lancaster Place
London WC2E 7EN

www.TimeWarnerBooks.co.uk

Ann Rule is a former Seattle policewoman and the author of over ten best-selling books, including *If You Really Loved Me*, a chilling chronicle of a millionaire's murderous secret life; *Everything She Ever Wanted*, the terrifying story of a sociopathic Georgia belle and her fatal allure; *The Stranger Beside Me*, the fascinating account of Rule's dawning horror as she realised her friend and co-worker, Ted Bundy, was a serial killer; *Dead by Sunset*, the extraordinary cautionary tale of a charmingly deadly misogynist; and seven volumes of her unrivalled 'Crime Files': *A Rose for Her Grave*, *You Belong to Me*, *A Fever in the Heart*, *In the Name of Love*, *The End of the Dream*, *A Rage to Kill* and *Empty Promises*. All of these are available in paperback from Time Warner Paperbacks.

When she is not attending trials and researching new books, Ann Rule lives near Seattle, Washington.

*This book is dedicated to the memory of
J. D. Newell and C. R. Stackhouse,
the best of fathers—who gave their love
with no strings attached.*

Contents

If You Really Loved Me

If a child lives with criticism, he learns to condemn.
If a child lives with hostility, he learns to fight.
If a child lives with ridicule, he learns to be sharp.
If a child lives with shame, he learns to feel guilty.
If a child lives with tolerance, he learns to be patient.
If a child lives with encouragement, he learns to be confident.
If a child lives with praise, he learns to appreciate.
If a child lives with fairness, he learns justice.
If a child lives with security, he learns to have faith.
If a child lives with approval, he learns to like himself.
If he lives with acceptance and friendship, he learns to find love and warmth.

—DOROTHY LAW NOLTE, QUOTED BY JEOFF ROBINSON IN HIS FINAL ARGUMENTS.

Prologue

T H E   P H O E N I X is a mythic bird of surpassing beauty, large as an eagle, that soars triumphant, reborn, from the ashes of defeat and destruction. It can neither be diminished nor destroyed. With its plumes of brilliant scarlet and glowing gold, it represents new life in numerous cultures. Ancient tombs unearthed in Egypt have images of the phoenix rising from a bed of flames. A phoenixlike creature appears throughout Oriental mythology, and it is found in the coat of arms of King James, Queen Elizabeth I, and Mary, Queen of Scots.

The rebirth of the phoenix symbolizes the resurrection of man. Down through the ages, it has also come to represent divine power, royalty, and survival against all odds. Over and over and over again, the magnificent bird bests its enemies and takes flight, whole again, from the embers of ruin.

And yet the phoenix *is* only a dream, a myth, born of the imagination and of wishful thinking. It lives somewhere with the unicorn, the centaur, Pegasus, and all the mythic creatures of the mind. Even so, there are some for whom the image of the phoenix is an invisible cloak of armor, an escape hatch, a sure promise that no matter what sin a man may commit, he will always survive to fly free of his tormentors.

It was so for David Arnold Brown. . . .

PART ONE

• • •

The Crime

LONG BEFORE Walt Disney saw his dream blossom into Disneyland, Orange County, California, was a spot much sought after. Independent, perhaps even a bit feisty, Orange County seceded from Los Angeles County a century ago. The area known as the Santa Ana Valley became a whole new county, eventually the third most populated in California. Orange groves thrived, vineyards proliferated, and the new county beckoned to those who would come west to begin a new life. But a prickly distrust lingered between Los Angeles and Orange counties. Los Angeles County is bigger, glitzier, smoggier, and its meaner streets are statistically more dangerous. The stargazers and the starlets, the baby moguls and the legends, live there, clawing for fame and fortune, at least according to those south of the "Orange Curtain." Conversely, Orange County residents are deemed priggish, plastic, conservative—even "nerdy" by some of the more urbane Los Angelenos. Richard Nixon was born in Yorba Linda in northeast Orange County, and some of the L.A. contingent contend that says it all.

In reality, Orange County is wealthy and high tech, predominantly Republican, with a population so young and upwardly mobile that many who live there cannot possibly envision what it must have been like when citrus groves and vineyards spread out endlessly. The boom hit after 1950. Anaheim, now home to Disneyland, huge convention centers, and the California Angels, had fewer than fifteen thousand residents forty years ago; today, there are a quarter million. In the last twenty years, Orange County's overall population has mushroomed to 2,280,400. There is precious little true "country" left. City lines simply merge. The same streets run through Anaheim and Santa Ana, through Huntington Beach and Irvine. Only the changing colors of street markers indicate city borders.

Orange County is rife with diverse lifestyles existing side by side. The poor live among and between the rich. In a matter of blocks, neighborhoods change. Three-room houses give way to lovely homes with flourishing gardens and then to walled estates. Santa Ana, the county seat, was once sedate and graciously upper-middle class. Now, it is a melting pot.

Young Hispanic parents walk along Santa Ana's streets, carrying their proudest possessions—beautiful babies and children, oddly bundled against the heat. Cinco de Mayo is a major holiday, albeit a noisy one, in Orange County.

The old Orange County Courthouse, its red-rock exterior burnished by sunlight, exists only as a museum, dwarfed and outdated by the near-skyscrapers in the Civic Center Plaza. Lovely old homes along Broadway house attorneys' offices, and one—a bank. The grounds of the Orange County Civic Center Plaza draw the movers and the shakers, the attorneys and politicians, but the plaza is also a dwelling place for the homeless, young druggies, middle-aged dropouts, and the elderly poor, all attracted to Orange County by the moderate climate or simply for their own ethereal reasons. Their shopping carts, overflowing with possessions, are parked in militarylike lines in the shade of the courthouse—Building 30.

Drive-by shootings occur almost daily in Santa Ana, and exquisite small parks reverberate with curses and fights far into the night. Police wryly call convenience stores "stop and robs". But other Santa Ana parks are safe and serene, and state-of-the-art shopping malls rival any in America.

Life can be good in Orange County; the median household income is close to $50,000 a year. The median-priced home sells for close to $250,000. Even the most rudimentary house with two bedrooms and one bathroom will bring $150,000.

Orange County smells of eucalyptus and dusty olive trees, of orange blossoms, jasmine, wild plum, Mexican food, the Pacific Ocean (when the wind is right), suntan lotion, the sweat of runners, and freeway exhaust. Geraniums and impatiens bloom year-round, along with the fuzzy red pokers of bottlebrush trees. The violet billows of the jacaranda tree last for months. The median strips of every freeway bloom with scarlet, pink, and white oleander bushes, ten feet high. Yellow daylilies crowd the sidewalk near the Orange County Jail, and the entrance to the Coroner's Office is like a garden with feathery ferns, salvia, lobelia, and the majestic stalks of light-blue allium.

In 1985, 13,031 deaths were recorded by the Orange County Coroner's Office. That office investigated 6,047 of those deaths and determined that 112 were homicides.

One of those homicides occurred on Ocean Breeze Drive on March 19 in the city of Garden Grove.

• • •

Ocean Breeze Drive is a one-block street, minutes from police headquarters, a charmingly misnamed street where any wafting of sea wind would be highly unlikely short of a major storm; the Pacific Ocean is a dozen miles away. Ocean Breeze is a pretty street, sandwiched between Pleasant Place and Jane Street. There are six houses on either side, all constructed in the sixties on large lots. All have shake roofs and stucco-and-brick exteriors, and some are identical save for color, trim, and landscaping. Each would sell today for a quarter million dollars.

The yard on the southwest end of the block has pink cabbage-rose bushes behind a curving, white picket fence. Another front lawn features a circular fountain edged with pansies, and colored lights play over it at night. Lawns are always mowed, but trees and bushes have grown tall in the last twenty-five years, and the houses on Ocean Breeze are shaded from the sun and reassuringly private. The residents are mostly professional people, middle-aged. Family people.

A weeknight in March in such a neighborhood was usually a quiet time for police, especially as the hours crept toward morning. Garden Grove patrol officer Darrow Halligan was nearing the end of his "evening's" watch at 3:26 A.M. on March 19, 1985. After a heavy daytime rain, the weather was cold and clear, somewhere near forty to forty-five degrees, and Halligan kept his heater going. Winding down from his eight-hour shift, he was driving near Brookhurst and Lampson Avenue when he heard the radio call directing him to a "possible 187" (homicide) at 12551 Ocean Breeze Drive.

He knew the street well. The north end abutted Lampson; he was only a few blocks away.

The street had no streetlights, and it was very dark as he inched along, shining his spotlight on the houses to find "12551." Bushes grew so high around many of the homes that Halligan couldn't even see the numbers. The house numbers had been painted on the coved curbing, but not recently and the ciphers were pretty well worn off. Finally, he made out the "12551" on a green stucco and brick bungalow on the west side of the street.

It was so quiet, so unlike the usual homicide call. No shouting or screaming, and nobody out in the street to wave him in. Odd. Quiet enough to make the muscles tighten in the back of Halligan's neck. Maybe it was only a prank call, but "possible 187" was not a call any California cop wants to hear, especially at three-thirty in the morning with no backup in sight. Halligan had arrived so rapidly that he knew that the suspect, if any, might very well still be nearby.

His radio crackled with the information that the victim was inside the house with a gunshot wound, but that the dispatcher had no further information, and no description at all of a suspect.

"The suspect is not in the residence," the Garden Grove Communications Center updated. "I have the informant on the phone with me now."

"Well, have the informant meet me at the front of the house, would you?" Halligan responded, with some relief.

The porch light was out, but he could see lights on in the front window. A man, short and heavyset, opened the door. He stood, silhouetted, in the backlighting from the living room.

Halligan stepped in—alone—to a situation about which he had precious little information. The man was clearly tense and distraught, his face streaked with tears. Nearby, a young blond woman held a crying baby in her arms and sobbed hysterically.

"I think my wife's been shot," the man said, stuttering with emotion. "She's in the bedroom. I'm afraid to go look, Officer. Would you?"

He hadn't *looked?* Maybe that did mean a false alarm. Halligan asked where the bedroom was and the stocky man pointed toward the southwest corner of the house.

The young woman sobbed even louder, and the man seemed frightened. His voice trembled when he asked Halligan to check on his wife. Halligan had no time to ask him why he believed she'd been shot when he hadn't seen her. But whatever his reasons, the guy was getting more and more agitated.

"Sit there on that couch, both of you," Halligan instructed. "I'll check the bedroom."

He moved in the direction the man was pointing and found himself in a den or office. He switched on his flashlight as he moved deeper into the house. The hall beyond the den was very dark. He moved the beam of his flashlight along the corridor until he spotted a half-closed door to the left of the den.

As he nudged the door open with his shoulder, he heard some sound, a gasp—no, a gurgle. He knew better than to touch a light switch and contaminate any fingerprint left there. He could make out a bed opposite the door. His flashlight swept over a figure lying there, feet toward the door.

Halligan moved swiftly toward the person on the bed, the cone of light fixing on a female with longish light hair. He could see a massive amount of still-wet blood on her chest. She lay on her back with her right arm trailing off the side of the bed and her left hand raised to her ear.

She could not be dead. He rejected that because he could still hear the choking gurgle in her throat as she struggled to draw in air. Halligan put his fingertips to the carotid artery where it ran up the side of her neck. He felt nothing. No reassuring pulse where there should have been a steady beat.

He leaned toward the young woman, who lay on flowered sheets, placing his left ear next to her nose. He felt no breath. He looked to see if her breasts rose and fell with any intake of air.

They did not.

Blood stained the woman's lips and chin, blood that had almost certainly come up from her lungs. Halligan saw that the blue blanket covering her from the waist down was smooth and flat; there could have been no struggle. It was quite possible that she had not even wakened to see a gun pointed inches away from her breasts.

Almost simultaneously other Garden Grove police officers and paramedics began to arrive at the green bungalow. If there was a chance that the victim still lived, they had to act. Conversation with the couple who huddled on the couch in the living room would have to wait. Who they were or their relationship to the victim would come later. The man had said that the injured woman was his wife. He looked much older than she, but then he was under tremendous stress. Grief and fear change people.

Officer Scott Davis, Patrol Sgt. Dale Farley, who would take over control of the crime scene, and Halligan stood near the bed, helpless. Patrol Officers Alan Day and trainee Andy Jauch joined them as they watched the victim for some sign of life. The woman was so desperately injured that no one short of paramedics could treat her.

The police had to have a picture of the woman on the bed; it might be the only tangible proof they had later of how she had been found. It might appear uncaring, but it was not. Day had brought a Polaroid camera in with him, and although the memory of that moment haunts Sergeant Farley today, he handed it to Halligan and said, "The light's not good, but get as many exposures as you can before she's moved."

She seemed young, and so vulnerable.

Halligan had time to take only two. Two Polaroid shots of a pretty young woman with her eyes half open, her face bloodied but eerily serene. Her left hand was still flung up next to her ear as it must have been while she slept. The officers estimated her age as late teens to early twenties.

Paramedics Chris Esser and Ruben Ruvalcaba from the Garden Grove Fire Department Engine 4–1 rushed into the southwest bedroom. They thought they heard the woman gasp for air. It was hard to tell. A death rattle sounds almost the same. They lifted the comatose victim from the bed and carried her to the closest hard surface where they could administer cardiopulmonary resuscitation—the den/office floor. She wore a knit shortie nightgown—black and white and red with laughing penguins in top hats parading across the front until they disappeared into the solid red of blood. They placed her on the tan carpet and quickly cut away the silly little nightie, leaving her nude except for a pair of fuzzy blue nightsocks.

As the paramedics worked, inserting an airway, and then an intravenous line with a solution of D5W, they compressed the young woman's chest rhythmically, urging her heart to start beating effectively.

The walls of this room were covered with family pictures. A huge studio portrait of a man and a woman, smiling and obviously in love, hung over the red-brick fireplace. They seemed to gaze down at the activity on the floor. It was difficult to tell if the woman in the picture and the woman on the floor were the same person. There was a definite similarity, but then the sobbing woman in the living room *also* resembled the portrait. And a shooting victim, in extremis, would look nothing at all like herself. Her skin was pallid, her eyes unfocused. The paramedics' LifePak heart monitor showed erratic response to their CPR, but no normal sinus rhythm. She would need surgery to have any chance of survival, but they dared not move her until she was stabilized.

So many people were now coming and going that Farley placed Jauch at the front door to maintain scene control. A log marked the arrival and departure times of all personnel. Davis and Day were instructed to separate the man and girl in the living room—and to begin preliminary interviewing.

Halligan finally had time to glance around the bedroom where the injured woman had been found. A revolver with a two-inch barrel lay on the carpet between the door to the hall and the bed, but no one knew yet if that was the murder weapon. He left it there, waiting for the primary investigators to arrive. Only now did he notice a small bathroom just off the bedroom, the door closed. Cautiously, he pushed the door open, half-expecting to see someone hiding there.

There was no one.

For any policeman, anywhere, there is a clearly defined list of priorities, and the first item on that list is that life must be preserved. On down the roster are things such as keeping the peace and arresting the guilty. Time hung frozen in the den as the paramedics tried to help the victim live. Finally, she was carried out to a Southland ambulance and rushed with sirens screaming toward the Fountain Valley Community Hospital trauma unit. The ambulance was packed with medical personnel; there was no room for Halligan, so Farley instructed him to follow behind in his squad car and stay with the victim as she was treated in the emergency room.

Dr. Michael Safavian was working the early-morning shift in the emergency room. When the ambulance pulled up, he needed just a glance to see that only heroic measures might bring the victim back.

It was five minutes after four in the morning when Safavian and the ER crew began to work on the young woman. No air could reach her right lung; clotted blood blocked the way. Safavian inserted a trocar into that lung to release blood, hoping the organ would reinflate. At the same time, he ordered three units of blood to be transfused into the patient.

No response.

Halligan watched as the emergency room surgeon tried one final, heroic measure. Without anesthetic—she needed none—Safavian cut into the young woman's left chest and reached in so that he could massage her heart, but it lay leaden and still in his hands.

At twenty-six minutes past four, she was pronounced dead. Cause of death, or rather *manner* of death, was apparent. There were two bullet wounds of entry in her chest.

Joe Luckey, an Orange County deputy coroner, arrived at Fountain Valley Community Hospital at five A.M. Luckey found a perfectly formed body still warm to the touch; there was no rigor, no lividity.

Luckey began to list the hospital appliances: the IV points, a right chest tube, a sutured left chest incision, an airway, and EKG monitor pads. He collected the bloodied nightie and the pair of blue bootie socks, a wedding-engagement ring set, and a gold bracelet, placing them in paper bags. He bagged the victim's hands in case there was some trace evidence caught there.

And then the dead woman, tentatively identified as Linda Marie Brown, twenty-three, was taken to the sally port entry behind the Orange County coroner's office in Santa Ana. The gurney-scale in the floor just inside the door showed her weight to be 127 pounds.

Less than two hours after the first call for help came in to 911, Linda Brown rested on a shelf in the cold room, awaiting postmortem examination.

It had begun—as it does with all homicide investigations. A human being who had been alive only hours before was now dead, deliberately dead by someone else's hand. It was more difficult to deal with somehow when the victim had died in her own home where she had every reason to feel safe. At that point, Garden Grove police investigators had just a peephole into the wall that surrounded the private lives of the people who lived at 12551 Ocean Breeze Drive. There were questions to be answered, and with luck, the truth would emerge. In this case, however, the truth would be a long time coming.

A long, long time.

G A R D E N Grove homicide investigator Fred McLean was sound asleep shortly before 4:30 A.M. on the morning of March 19, 1985. But after eighteen and a half years with the department, a phone shrilling in the night was far from unusual. As always, McLean woke instantly alert. It was second nature. His career demanded that he deal with the aftermath of the human emotions, aberrations, and bad judgment that often lead to violent death. An uninterrupted night's sleep was a luxury.

Lt. Larry Hodges, the Garden Grove watch commander, was on the phone. He instructed McLean to respond to 12551 Ocean Breeze Drive to take over as the primary investigator into the gunshot murder of a young woman who had just been pronounced dead at the Fountain Valley trauma facility. Patrol officers had been called to the house within the past hour, had done preliminary interviews of the occupants, and cordoned off the crime scene.

McLean stopped at Garden Grove Police Headquarters on Acacia Parkway to pick up Det. Steve Sanders and a homicide kit. He saw that Sgt. John Woods and Det. Bill "Bugs" Morrissey had been rousted out of bed too and were preparing to go to the homicide scene. It was still dark as they pulled up in front of the green stucco and brick bungalow on Ocean Breeze Drive. The street was alive with police cars now. Andy Jauch listed their names and arrival time as Sanders and McLean passed into the brightly lit living room.

The room was jam-packed with furniture, and it all looked new. In fact, it looked as if someone had gone to a mall and overdosed at Levitz, K Mart, Toys-R-Us, and Video-Land. There were two Early American–style couches upholstered with beige and brown bursts of flowers, two matching brown velour recliners, two rocking chairs— one a child's—two maple end tables, a playpen full of toys, a baby's walker, a gun case with six rifles neatly in place, a coffee table, a number of lamps with their shades still wrapped in plastic, a large console television set, a VCR, and remote controls within arm's reach in every corner of the room. The furnishings were all good, solid, unimaginative stuff, expensive but uninspired, and far too much for this smallish living room.

Beyond that, every flat surface was covered with knickknacks. Some were tasteful—a brass clock, a small cut-crystal vase—but some of it looked like carnival prizes. The lamp-clock in a hard plastic case with vibrating metal fronds and constantly changing colors, and the bouquets of feathers and artificial ferns, could have been won in a three-pitch-for-a-dollar booth on the midway.

The walls and tabletops were covered with family pictures and otherworldly paintings featuring unicorns. Knickknack shelves held dozens of ceramic unicorns. The living room was crowded, but it was neat, the thick brown carpet vacuumed, the furniture dusted, and the walls freshly painted. Whoever had decorated this room had worked carefully to keep a brown, beige, white, and yellow color scheme.

It was a homey-looking room. Whatever had happened to summon police here in the middle of the night had not touched this area of the home. McLean glanced around and saw a pair of man's scuff slippers in front of one of the recliners, a woman's blue Reeboks in the middle of the floor, a zigzagged afghan over the larger rocking chair. A baby's bottle, two-thirds empty, still rested on a lampstand.

The television was on, but muted. McLean noted idly that it was tuned to MTV; as he glanced over, The Cars were singing "Why Can't I Have You?" Then he looked at the stereotypical print of a clipper ship coursing through rough waves in its frame over the cold fireplace and subconsciously summed up the room. The people who lived here either had enough money to buy whatever they liked, or the credit to charge it. At the same time McLean wondered why *everything* was brand-new. It was as if this were a home without a history, as if it had just sprung up overnight. How many families can afford to replace every piece of furniture, every gewgaw and lamp, at the same time?

The rest of the house was the same. A cursory look showed McLean that the family living here denied themselves nothing material. Every single room of the three-bedroom, two-bathroom house was crowded with new furniture. Where one dresser would have served, there were two—or three. Furniture and toys and *things* were everywhere. It was as if teenagers had been given permission to buy whatever they wanted.

McLean strolled through the kitchen into the little back hall that doubled as a laundry room. On the dryer, he saw an empty glass and three empty prescription pill bottles. The pill vials lay on their sides, their caps off. He read the labels as he carefully slipped the bottles into evidence bags and initialed them. The first one had held Darvocet-N, 100 mg, #60, issued 11-28-84; the second one Dyazide

#100, issued 6-29-82; and the third container—Darvocet-N too, also #100, number 2s, issued 11-24-83.

McLean wasn't an expert on pharmaceutical matters, but whatever this stuff was meant to do—if the vials had been full to begin with —it looked as if someone had taken an awful lot of it. Beyond that, empty pill bottles seemed out of place in a laundry room.

McLean lifted the drinking glass cautiously from the dryer, preparing to slip it into a bag and label it. The glass had a trace of clear liquid in the bottom, probably water. It was one of those premiums that fast-food restaurants give away, a *Star Trek III* glass with a picture of one of the series' villains on the side—Lord Kruge. He examined the glass, curious. The face embossed on the side was that of a glowering man, balding with straight dark hair, a mustache, and a pock-marked face. It was probably only a weird coincidence, but Lord Kruge looked startlingly like the man he had just seen sitting on the couch in the living room, chain-smoking.

Back in the living room, Sergeant Farley briefed Fred McLean and Steve Sanders on what he knew so far. It wasn't much. The woman who had just died was Linda Marie Brown, the twenty-three-year-old wife of the man who sat on the brown-and-beige-flowered couch. She had apparently been shot sometime after midnight while she lay in her bed in the master bedroom. The most likely weapon still lay on the floor in that bedroom.

"Who was here?" McLean asked.

Farley gestured toward the nervous man on the couch. "The husband was out someplace and got back here after the shooting occurred. He's the reporting party. The blond girl with the baby is Patricia Bailey. She's seventeen."

"The baby's hers?"

Farley shook his head. "No, the child is his—David Brown's—and the dead woman's—Linda Brown's."

"Anyone else live here?"

"Cinnamon."

"*Cinnamon?*"

"Cinnamon Brown. She's fourteen, Brown's daughter by an earlier marriage. They think she did it."

McLean stared at the patrol sergeant. "*Who* thinks?"

Farley inclined his head in David Brown's direction. "Him—and Bailey. Cinnamon's gone."

Farley said that Patricia Bailey had told Officer Scott Davis that she thought she had seen Cinnamon after hearing gunshots, and that someone who looked like Cinnamon went out the back door after the shooting. Davis and Farley had searched the house, and the backyard and a small travel trailer that was pulled up next to the house, for any sign of a suspect or suspects.

"We didn't find anyone."

Farley said he had checked the yard thoroughly for the missing teenager, gone through the detached garage, and shone his flashlight into the dog pen behind the garage. There had been no sign of Cinnamon Brown.

McLean walked to the southwest bedroom, pondering the information he had just received about a likely suspect. He had been a homicide detective long enough to know that anything was possible. Still. Fourteen-year-old girls rarely used guns to get their way. If the kid—*Cinnamon*—had killed Linda Brown, what had gone on to lead up to it? Temper tantrums and teenage girls went together. But not this.

What kind of a violent kid were they looking for?

Or had Patricia Bailey been mistaken? She seemed on the edge of hysteria now; it was quite possible that she didn't know *whom* she had seen as a gun roared in the dark house.

The gun was there where the shooter had apparently dropped it. A chrome-plated, .38-caliber Smith & Wesson revolver with a two-inch barrel. Without moving it, McLean could see that it appeared to be loaded with silver-tip bullets, and that two or three of those bullets had been fired.

Bill Morrissey would work the case as the crime scene investigator. McLean would do the "people part." Morrissey would look for tangible support for the developing case. He would collect physical evidence and photograph everything within the yellow cordon ribbons. If the shooter proved to be Cinnamon—or any other member of the family or regular visitor to this house—Morrissey's job would be more difficult. Trace evidence is more meaningful in a stranger-to-stranger homicide. Everybody who lived here could be expected to leave fingerprints, hairs, fibers, body secretions. Nevertheless, Morrissey would retrieve what might be meaningful later.

McLean asked Alan Day and Andy Jauch to diagram the scene. Darrow Halligan, back from observing the fruitless efforts to save the victim at Fountain Valley Hospital, was assigned to heel-and-toe it up and down Ocean Breeze Drive—to canvass the neighbors to see if anyone had heard or seen anything unusual during the night.

Where there had been chaos, there was now a sense of order,

stunned and disbelieving as the survivors might be. Each member of the Garden Grove investigative team was painstakingly carrying out his assigned task.

There was no need to hurry any longer.

The investigators knew now that two adults, two teenagers, and a baby girl had lived in this house up to the wee hours of the morning, apparently in a family unit of some kind, although their connections to one another were not clear. Linda Brown was dead. Cinnamon Brown was missing. Patricia Bailey sobbed as she sat in the dining room with Linda's baby in her arms. David Brown chain-smoked, visited the bathroom frequently, and paced, his face a study of worry and pain.

Officer Scott Davis radioed the Dispatch Center with a description for Cinnamon Brown. Patricia thought she had been wearing a sweatshirt and pants. Brown hair, brown eyes. A little over five feet, maybe 120 pounds.

David Brown, trembling with stress, inhaled deeply and then snubbed out a half-smoked cigarette as he waited in his living room to talk to Fred McLean. Brown's family had evaporated. He had lost his wife; his daughter was somewhere out there in the night.

What had gone wrong?

McLean observed David Brown. The man looked forty-five or fifty, but Day, who had done an initial interview with him, said that he was only thirty-two. McLean asked him his birthdate—just to be sure.

"November sixteenth, 1952."

That made him only thirty-two, all right. He was short, not more than five feet seven or so, and thick in the middle, his skin and muscle tone that of a man who rarely went out in the sun and seldom exercised. Brown's hair was dark brown and lank, thinning, and his eyes an oddly variegated mixture of colors. Scars from teenage acne marred his skin. There was a sheen of perspiration on his face, and his hands shook as he lit yet another cigarette.

Well, hell, the man's world had just exploded. How was he supposed to look? The picture of health and vigor?

At first glance, David Arnold Brown seemed a man without power, a man who had lost his grip on the reins of his existence. His very posture was limp, his narrow shoulders dragged down by the impact of his wife's violent death. But when he spoke, in response to McLean's questions, his voice was startling. He could have been a radio or television announcer. David Brown had a deep baritone speaking voice, and he answered McLean's questions easily and with authority. He was not vague about what had happened. Painful as it was, he had apparently accepted the fact that his daughter was the shooter. He repeated to Fred McLean the sequence of events he had given to Day, adding a bit of information here and a speculation there.

He did not seem surprised that Cinnamon had done something so inexplicably cruel. Not at all. It was almost as if he had seen disaster coming and yet been incapable of heading it off. Now, he was trying determinedly to arrange the frayed ends of his life, and the strain was profound.

"My head aches," Brown murmured to McLean.

"Do you need some aspirin?"

"No . . . never mind."

Fred McLean led David Brown through the twenty-four hours that had just passed. It was apparent that Brown was a man who had spent most of his time working and the rest of it with his extended family, a family in which he seemed to function as the head. He explained that he lived with Linda, their eight-month-old baby, Krystal, and with Linda's sister, Patricia Bailey, seventeen. He added that Patti's mother was a "chronic alcoholic," so he and Linda had taken her sister in.

"And Cinnamon?"

"Cinnamon's mother and I were divorced ten years ago. Cinny's been back and forth between us. She's been with us this time since last fall."

David Brown described himself as a beleaguered parent, torn between his wife and young baby and his teenage daughter. The picture he painted of Cinnamon revealed an angry girl who did not fit in with the family and resisted his attempts to get help for her. "I've talked to her about counseling, but she threatened to commit suicide if I forced her into counseling."

"Did anything special happen today—yesterday—that might have escalated the situation?"

Brown shook his head slowly, as he reached for another cigarette, and tried to form his thoughts. He recalled that his parents, Manuela and Arthur Brown—who lived in Carson—had come over and spent most of the day with them. It was a Monday, but David Brown ran his own business: Data Recovery. He had invented a "process" that enabled him to retrieve lost data from computers. He had worked, he said, for a number of major corporations as well as the Pentagon.

"Linda and I ran my business. The phones rang all day long."

But he could work the hours he wanted, take a day off in the middle of the week to make up for working all weekend. On Monday—only yesterday—they had all planned to go out to the desert for a picnic excursion, but rain made them change their plans.

McLean noted that Brown remembered some events of the day before precisely, and then there were times his clear recall suddenly became vague and fuzzy. Shock. McLean had seen it before.

Brown continued his recollections. They had spent most of Monday playing a card game: Uno. They often did. It was a favorite of his whole—extended—family. And his parents were over to visit a lot. Linda had refused to play Uno the day before.

"She was irritable yesterday. Cinny played for about half a game. Then she left—she might have gone out to her trailer."

"Trailer?" McLean prompted.

David Brown explained that Cinnamon had been living in a little Terry travel trailer in the backyard for about three weeks. There had been problems between Cinnamon and Linda. His wife had "kicked Cinnamon out" of the house and said she had to stay in the trailer.

"They just didn't get along," Brown said, sighing. "There were continual problems between them. About two weeks ago, I spoke to her mother—to my first wife, Brenda—about having Cinny move back to her. But we compromised by having Cinny live in the trailer. Cinny was having problems at school too, so I transferred her out of Bolsa Grande in Garden Grove and she just started at Loara High School in Anaheim."

Brown explained that Cinnamon refused to help with the household chores and didn't get along with either Linda or her younger sister, Patti. Although Cinnamon slept in the trailer, she usually came into the house for meals and to watch television, so it wasn't as if she had been completely banished.

Asked to home in on the evening before, Brown strained to remember. He had an appointment with his chiropractor sometime between five and six, and he had taken Cinnamon and Patti with him. The trio had been in an automobile accident months earlier and were all being treated. On the way back home, Cinnamon had begun to cause trouble again and had verbally abused Patti, treating her "very badly," as Brown recalled.

David Brown had certainly been a man pulled in many directions. His parents were still at the home on Ocean Breeze, his wife was "irritable," and he was driving home on a rainy day with two arguing teenagers. He said he had stopped to pick up some fast food—Mexican food for Cinnamon and his father, and pizza for the others—so everyone would be happy, and they'd returned to the house about six-thirty. They all ate the food and decided to play a second game of Uno.

Brown recalled there had been some friction between his mother, Manuela, and his young wife over Linda's care of Krystal. Manuela was of the old school—where babies were not allowed to cry themselves to sleep—and Linda was trying to get Krystal on a regular schedule. Linda had been hurt that anyone would question her care of her beloved baby. Manuela had finally rocked Krystal to sleep, but Linda was angry and hurt about that.

"My folks must have left about nine," Brown said, and he had noticed that Cinnamon had already changed into her sweat pants and shirt, the outfit she commonly wore to bed.

Then Brown ruefully recalled that he and Linda had had an argument, about, he thought, the same subject Linda had disagreed on with her mother-in-law. He just didn't want her to let Krystal cry; he wanted Linda to pick her up right away. The argument had disturbed him.

David Brown admitted he was a very sensitive man, and he certainly looked as if the tiff with his wife had troubled him. Of course, it would trouble him; it was the last evening he would ever have with her. "We made up, and we went to bed together. But I was upset, and I couldn't get to sleep."

Brown's solution to insomnia, he told McLean, was usually to take a drive. He had gotten out of bed, dressed, and driven to the Circle-K twenty-four-hour market at the corner of Central and Brookhurst, not far from his home. He had bought a Dr Pepper and a Hostess apple pie. "Then I went back in. I bought three or four comic books. The clerk thought it was funny for an adult to be buying comic books."

McLean was noncommittal about that. Brown's taste for comic books was the least of his concerns.

Still disturbed about his argument with Linda, Brown said he had headed for the beach, for a quiet spot where he could sit and think. He recalled getting on the Garden Grove Freeway westbound, and then veering off southbound to the Newport Freeway, headed toward the ocean.

"I stopped in a Denny's Restaurant in Newport Beach—to use the rest room. I didn't buy any food—the place was full of Hispanics. I do recall seeing a heavy-built waitress with curly red hair and glasses."

David Brown, so distressed over a minor argument with his wife that he could not sleep, had been away from his home for only an hour or so. Ocean Breeze Drive was dark and still as he pulled up into his own driveway in his Honda Prelude. There would be hours yet to sleep, his emotions soothed by the sight and sound of the waves rolling in as the Pacific Ocean hit the shore at Newport Beach.

Instead, he found stark horror inside the dark house. Patti Bailey, holding Krystal, met him. "She was shaking, crying, almost hysterical.

"She said Cinny had tried to kill her."

D A V I D Brown described his daughter as difficult, stubborn, adamant about not seeing a counselor. He told both Day and McLean that Cinnamon, "Cinny" as he called her, fought with his wife, with his sister-in-law Patti, and with her own mother, that she didn't get along in school. He was clearly a man with tremendous problems, apparently dealing with a child who was not only out of control, but dangerous. Everything he said enhanced that picture.

But Brown hadn't been home when the shooting took place. He was not the best source of what had happened after he left the house and headed for the ocean beach to think.

Patricia Bailey *had* been there. Patti had talked at length to Officer Davis, and to Detective Sanders, and she was willing to talk with Fred McLean, even though the ordeal of the long night was becoming more real to her with each retelling.

She had known David Brown well, she said, since she was a child. Later, after David and Linda married, they all moved to Yorba Linda. "We all got along, and we had no problems in 'the family,'" she said. They had moved often and had lived in Brea on Branch Lane before they moved to Garden Grove.

Patti Bailey was seventeen years old, and she had grown up as much with David and Linda as she had with her mother, Ethel. Cinnamon had been like family to her too, although they weren't really related.

Patti was a pale, pretty girl, with straight ash-blond hair that hung halfway down her back. She was small, but she had wide shoulders and hips and full breasts. She spoke softly, shyly, her hair partially covering her face as she ducked her head. She seemed somehow older than seventeen, and she held her dead sister's baby on her hip as easily as most teenagers might balance an armful of schoolbooks. Her eyes were red and swollen from crying now, and she shivered in remembered terror.

She began by trying to orient McLean to the rather unusual makeup of the household. Cinnamon had moved in and out of her father's home. Patti recalled that Cinnamon had lived with them in Brea, but she had left in June of 1984 to move back with her mother in Anaheim. "She left because she wasn't getting along with Linda or David," Patti said. "She just argued constantly about doing chores and the household rules. I don't think she got along with her mom either—and I guess that's why she moved back with us."

Cinnamon had been living with "the family" this time since school started in the fall of 1984. There hadn't been an extra room for Cinnamon in Garden Grove. Patti had the bedroom at the front of the house, and Krystal had the middle room, but Patti had agreed to let Cinnamon share her room.

"She didn't talk that much about anything," Patti recalled. "But everyone else got along fairly well. I don't know though. Right after Christmas—during vacation—Cinnamon just started drawing away from the family, and she didn't get along with anyone. Linda made a special effort to be nice to Cinnamon, but Cinnamon didn't respond to her."

Patti said that Cinnamon Brown had become very moody, so moody that she didn't talk to any of the rest of the family. "She started talking about killing herself in January. She was going to use a gun, she said. I tried to talk her out of moods like that. I would tell her that I loved her very much and that I would always love her. That seemed to cheer her up."

The teenager that Patti Bailey described to detectives sounded like a very disturbed youngster indeed. Cinnamon had a father who loved her and a stepmother who bent over backward to accept her, and Patti herself was trying to help her.

But, Patti emphasized, nothing got through to Cinnamon.

Things got so bad in January and February of 1985 that Cinnamon had, according to Patti, become "very rebellious and sarcastic toward Linda and David." In late February, Patti said that Linda, who was usually so patient and kind, had had enough and she "kicked Cinnamon out" and made her stay in the trailer in the backyard. It was true that she came in to eat and to watch television, but Patti said she wouldn't talk to anyone.

Cinnamon *had* slept inside both Sunday, March 17, and Monday, the eighteenth. "She asked me if I minded if I had company, and if she could sleep on the cot that rolls out from under my bed. I said fine and I really thought that Cinnamon wanted to talk about something. There was something wrong, I felt, but she didn't want to talk about anything."

Monday morning—the last day of Linda's life—Cinnamon ate breakfast with them. They all ate off trays in the living room. "She didn't talk to us. The only thing she said was could she have the last two pieces of sausage—and Linda gave them to her."

They had all taken turns watching Krystal. They had planned to go to the desert, Patti remembered, to visit friends and have a barbecue. "David invited Cinnamon to come with us, but she didn't feel like going. David just about insisted. He said it would be 'nice to get reacquainted and be a family again.' "

But the rain pelted down, and by the time Manuela and Arthur Brown arrived, they decided to call off the trip. Yes, they had played Uno most of the day, but Cinnamon had gotten angry because she was losing.

It had been such an ordinary day. Patti remembered the argument about whether to pick up Krystal or not when she cried. David had sided with his parents, but he had apologized to Linda later. None of it was a big deal.

Despite her grief and fright, Patti Bailey proved to have a meticulous memory for details. She recalled that Cinnamon had been watching a movie called *Wife for Sale* when the elder Browns left. Linda had taken a shower around nine or nine-thirty and then gone to bed. But she had come out to get a soft drink in the kitchen an hour later and said, "Cinnamon, remember you have to go to school tomorrow."

Cinnamon had snapped back sarcastically, "I *know*."

"We went to bed in my room; David went to his and Linda's room. But Cinnamon wanted to watch more television. Something was *wrong* with her and I thought she wanted to talk. So I went out with her to the living room. It was about eleven-fifteen, and we watched MTV— but she still wouldn't talk to me."

Patti had been very tired, and at a quarter to midnight, she had begged off and got up to go to bed. And it was at that point that Cinnamon made an odd request. "Cinnamon followed me and said, 'Okay—but could you show me something first?' "

Patti said she had turned to look at Cinnamon and was a little startled to see a small gray gun in Cinny's right hand. She asked Patti how it worked.

"I asked her, 'Why?' "

"Just in case."

"Just in case *what?*" Patti had asked.

"In case someone breaks in."

"No way—the alarm is too good."

But Cinnamon had not been convinced. Patti thought that Cinnamon might have been planning to sleep in her trailer, which was not wired into the security alarm system. At any rate, Cinnamon had seemed anxious that an "emergency" might come up and wanted to know how to shoot the gun.

" 'I'm not positive how to work it,' I told her. 'I've just seen it on TV—but you just cock it back and pull the trigger.' "

"She just said, 'Oh . . . okay,' and then, 'Good night.' "

McLean asked if she had been concerned to see Cinnamon with the gun, and Patti shook her head. She really hadn't thought much about it. Guns were not unusual for the family; they often went target shooting out in the desert.

"I went to sleep about midnight," Patti said. "Cinnamon was in the living room watching TV. I was asleep and I woke up with a gunshot in my room! It was very loud and it echoed. I looked toward the door and I saw Cinnamon standing there next to my bed, and then she ran out."

Patti had instinctively looked at the clock beside her bed. It said 2:23.

Somewhere in the house, she had heard a baby crying. Less than a minute later, Patti heard a second shot. She was sure it was inside the house. She had been immobilized with terror.

And then the gun had sounded again.

After the third shot, Patti told detectives she had lain in her bed, petrified with fear, for about a minute. But then she heard Krystal, wailing in her crib in the nursery. "I ran into the nursery, picked the baby up, and ran back to my room."

"Did you look in the house for someone who'd been shot, or to see where the shots came from—or for Cinnamon?" McLean asked.

"No. I was freaking. I hadn't heard anyone leave the house. I thought Cinnamon was still in the house and she might shoot me or the baby. I didn't have a phone in my room, so I sat on the floor with my back to the door. The baby was screaming and I tried to turn the radio on to calm her. I began pacing back and forth. The baby screamed until three or a quarter after."

"And then I heard a very quiet knock on the front door. I thought it was Cinnamon and I wouldn't answer it. Then I heard another quiet knock, and I went into the living room, by the entry, and I listened. I heard a key in the lock and I knew it had to be either David or Linda—because Cinnamon didn't have a key."

Patti, clutching the baby and her bottle, ran toward the door, filled with relief that someone had come to save them.

It was David.

"He asked me what was wrong, and I told him about hearing the gunshots and seeing Cinnamon with the gun. He said, *'God, no!'* "

Patti Bailey told McLean that David Brown had questioned her carefully about *where* she had heard the shots, but she wasn't sure because the sound seemed to be everywhere. "He said, 'It's important that you tell me.' But I couldn't tell him, because all I knew was that it was close to my bedroom because of the loud noise and the echoing."

David Brown had then checked the entire house—with the exception of the master bedroom. He'd come back to Patti and told her that everything looked okay.

"Did you check Linda's room?" Patti had asked.

"No."

Patti told McLean that she had been afraid that Cinnamon might have shot Linda first and then committed suicide. "I begged David to check the back bedroom. He said, 'Don't say that!' because he knew what I was afraid of and he couldn't face it."

For an instant, Fred McLean's face betrayed surprise, and Patti explained almost matter-of-factly that David Brown couldn't handle the sight of blood—everyone who knew him knew that.

"But I asked him again to please go and look so that we would know what happened."

If anything, David Brown had been more frightened than his wife's sister. He told Patti he just couldn't look; he was incapable of facing what he might find back in the bedroom he shared with his wife.

"He sent me outside to look for Cinnamon," Patti said. She had looked around the backyard, with the baby in her arms, but she hadn't located Cinnamon, not in her trailer nor farther back where the shadows swallowed up the light from the kitchen window.

"When I came in, David was on the phone talking to his father, asking him what to do, telling him to come over because he needed help. I guess Grandpa Brown told David to hang up and call the police, because that's what he did."

Patti Bailey recalled hearing two periods of gentle knocking at the front door. David Brown said he never knocked at his own front door; he had a key. He said he always set the security alarm. But it hadn't gone off that night. It was controlled with both a key and a code to punch in each time it was either armed or disarmed. How did Cinnamon get out of the house without setting off the alarm? Or, if Brown had forgotten to set the alarm, why would he have had such a lapse? He said he was "religious" about setting it. But he had left for the beach; his wife, his baby daughter, Krystal, his teenage daughter,

Cinnamon, and seventeen-year-old Patti were alone in the dark, possibly without the alarm's protection.

McLean pondered the tragic synchronicity that had left the home unprotected at the very moment it had been so vital. The man seemed devastated at the loss of his wife, and he had to be blaming himself for forgetting the alarm. But then Brown had said over and over how upset he had been by the day-long family bickering, and then the argument with his wife. That could have been enough to make him forget the alarm on this one, terribly important night.

Fred McLean studied Patti Bailey. It was clear she put all of her trust in David Brown, and she didn't seem disturbed that David had not had the courage to go back and check on her sister. That was just the way David was.

Routinely, Sgt. John Woods and Bill Morrissey conducted GSR (gunshot residue) tests on David Brown and Patricia Bailey. Davis asked Patti if she had handled the little silver gun when Cinnamon asked her how to shoot it, and she said she had not.

"When's the last time you fired a gun?" Officer Davis asked as Woods swabbed her palms, fingers, and the back of her hands with a Q-Tip, and Morrissey carefully inserted the swabs in plastic vials.

"Over a year ago."

Even as the Garden Grove police investigators tried to piece together the events leading up to the shooting of Linda Marie Brown, patrol units all over the area were looking for Cinnamon Brown. Her father had given officers her mother's address. He wracked his brain to come up with other suggestions about where she might have gone. She didn't have a gun anymore, as far as anyone knew. But then no one had any inkling that she hated her stepmother enough to shoot her. If she was as disturbed as her father and Patti Bailey described, she could be very, very dangerous to anyone who encountered her.

Patricia Bailey had attended Bolsa Grande High School with Cinnamon and gave officers the names of one or two of her friends, stressing that Cinnamon talked more to her *imaginary* friends than to real people. Patti was emphatic about the other "friends" Cinnamon Brown had. Invisible friends. "Maynard" and "Oscar" and "Aunt Bertha."

"Sometimes, I'll walk into the room and she's actually *talking* to them."

Perhaps that was the answer to the puzzle of a fourteen-year-old girl who would shoot her stepmother as she slept. Possibly Cinnamon Brown lived in her own fantasy world, with imaginary friends, friends who seemed more real to her than anything else. She apparently didn't talk to her family unless pressed. She talked to people nobody else could see. Adolescent schizophrenia?

None of the investigators had yet *seen* Cinnamon Brown. They had no way to judge what her motivations had been.

They couldn't even be positive that Cinnamon Brown was the shooter. For all they knew, Cinnamon could be a victim too. It was second nature for them to question what seemed obvious. In a homicide investigation—more than any other police action—nothing can be taken for granted. There were aspects of the events of that night that didn't quite match up, and the yard—the whole street—was so dark. Cinnamon could be out there, dead.

Patti Bailey had furnished them with the names of Cinnamon's friends—Krista Taber, and a "Jamie" and "Joanne"—but said she didn't know if Cinnamon would have run to their houses.

Det. Steve Sanders recalled that he had taken a report on an indecent exposure complaint from Cinnamon Brown in October of 1984—some "lily-waver" who had beckoned to the teenager. He asked the records section to check for any witness names on that report. They came up with one; a girl named Rebecca had heard Cinnamon gasp and seen her run away from the man.

Phones rang in the homes of her teenage friends at five A.M. Was Cinnamon there? Had anyone heard from her? Where might she be?

No one contacted had the slightest notion where Cinnamon might be. It was soon apparent that Cinnamon had very few friends. She was not encouraged to make a lot of friends according to her best pal, Krista Taber.

"She was grounded a lot," Krista said when she was questioned. "The slightest thing and her dad would ground her. She wasn't allowed to give out her address, and most people didn't know her phone number. I haven't even heard from her for more than a week 'cause she's grounded again."

Some of the other girls contacted said they knew Cinnamon Brown only slightly. They could not imagine she would run to them if she was in trouble.

Krista, the only friend with whom Cinnamon shared secrets, denied vigorously that the missing girl had a boyfriend.

Odd—because Patti Bailey had mentioned an older boyfriend of

Cinnamon's, but she didn't know his name. All she knew was that he went by the nickname Steely Dan.

The Garden Grove Dispatch Center checked the nickname through their computers and came up with a case where a junior high school girl had been harassed by a twenty-three-year-old male known as Steely. His real name was Jamie Guiterrez*, and he lived on Juno Avenue in Anaheim, the same street where Cinnamon's mother lived.

Woods and Sanders headed for Anaheim to check Guiterrez's apartment. That scenario might make sense. A teenage girl besotted with a guy nine years older than she, furious because she had been grounded. Maybe even furious enough to kill? If she had shot her stepmother, she might well run to Guiterrez.

Officers canvassing Ocean Breeze Drive had no luck finding witnesses. The one exception was when Darrow Halligan contacted the Sugarmans' residence, which was obliquely across the street from the Browns' to the east. Alvin Sugarman had heard something heavy thud against his garage sometime between three and three-thirty that morning, something heavy enough to wake him from a sound sleep. He had investigated, but found no one, and could see no damage to his property.

Halligan walked with Sugarman, searching his house and yard with flashlights, but they found nothing. The crash against the attached garage had sounded like something—or some*one*—hitting the siding. This opened up new possibilities. Perhaps there was some *outside* force that had caused the havoc in the Brown household—someone prowling in the neighborhood who had watched David Brown drive away after midnight, then entered the house where the sleeping young women were unprotected.

Or perhaps someone had struck the Sugarman garage deliberately to make it appear that way.

*The names of some individuals in the book have been changed. Such names are indicated by an asterisk (*) the first time each appears in the book.

4

A L T H O U G H the neighbors along Ocean Breeze Drive had slept—at least for the most part—undisturbed through the night of March 18–19, Andy Jauch's roster of people in and people out of 12551 Ocean Breeze was fairly lengthy. Arthur Brown, sixty-five, a bald, nervous man, and his wife, Manuela, fifty-nine, had rushed from their home in Carson, California, to comfort their son. There had been two paramedics, six firefighters (emergency medical technicians whose proximity almost always gets them to the scene of trauma before the medics), two ambulance drivers, and nine investigators.

Nevertheless, the bedroom where Linda Brown had been shot was kept sacrosanct; once she had been removed by the paramedics, the crime scene was protected. The gun that had killed her still lay on the gold shag carpet next to a brown pillow and a damp pile of towels near the door to the hall.

There had to be a combination here that would unlock a tragic sequence of events. CSI expert Bill Morrissey worked at preserving and marking every conceivable piece of physical evidence, deliberately shutting out the questioning, the weeping, the palpably raw emotions that hung in the rooms of this house as heavily as the pall of cigarette smoke.

Linda Marie Brown's life had become a case with a number: 85-11342. Beside the Smith & Wesson, Morrissey left a rectangle of white paper with a printed two-inch scale, and his penned directional sign "N" (arrow), his initials, the date—"TUE 3-19-85"—and the gun's serial number: "R304915."

He took pictures of everything in the bedroom. If there is one immutable axiom of crime scene investigation, it is the sure knowledge that you don't get a second chance. The murder scene itself will never again be the same. Pictures, diagrams, measurements, notes, had cemented dozens of scenes in Morrissey's mind and in his case files. When he left this room, this house, he would know every square foot better than he knew his own house.

More important, he would be able to reconstruct what he found now a month, a year, or even a decade later.

"Bugs" Morrissey was a wiry, sardonic man who kept his sense of humor carefully masked. His wisecracks always took people by surprise. At the moment, he had no reason to find humor in anything. He worked steadily as the first rays of dawn began to light the street outside. He could have no way of knowing that daylight had arrived. The bedroom he worked in had both blinds and drapes.

The room was yellow, a bright daffodil shade that carried out the home's color scheme. There was little leeway for Morrissey to work in because every bit of wall space was taken up with massive golden oak furniture, all new. Although one wall of the room already had floor-to-ceiling customized built-in drawers and cupboards painted the same sunny yellow, the Browns had added three full-size chests of drawers, two double-drawered bedside tables, and a massive matching entertainment center that faced the bed.

Morrissey saw that the legs of the expensive television/entertainment console rested on four large cans of Hunt's chili beans to raise it just enough to enable viewers in bed to watch comfortably. David Brown was obviously no handyman—but certainly inventive.

Morrissey glanced at the rows of video cassettes on the shelves beneath the TV. Pretty average home viewing, it appeared. Nothing kinky—at least not in plain sight: *Poltergeist, Star Wars,* a lot of fantasy, ghost-story stuff. Camera in hand, he worked his way around the room, snapping frame after frame, beginning with the east wall. Human beings' secrets can sometimes emerge from the most mundane accoutrements of their lives.

She had slept on this side of the bed. That was easy. The bedside table held the mother's stuff: the remote listening device to the baby's room, a picture of a newborn encased in a ceramic frame and baby shoe, a delicate-chimneyed lamp of milk glass, cigarettes in a case—next to a "How to Quit Smoking" pamphlet—a half-empty Dr Pepper, a speakerphone. A poster had been tacked to the wall above—a rainbow and a poem about "A Friend Is—"

A sentimental woman.

The bed itself was king-size, an ornate white iron frame with touches of brass that looked as if it were about to take wing. New too—like everything else. No scratches. There was no blood easily visible on the sheets; the victim had bled copiously, but internally.

The opposite bedside stand had another speakerphone, two full ashtrays, a box of Kleenex, the controls to the television and VCR. On the floor, there was a paper bag overflowing with Kleenex and a wastebasket embossed with Garfield's grinning face.

There were themes in this house. Someone collected unicorns and rainbows, someone collected bald eagles and other bird statuettes, and someone collected expensive dolls.

Garfield the cat's image was everywhere.

Pictures of the west side of the room indicated that the man of the house was unwell. His chests of drawers were rife with pill bottles, elixirs, cough syrups, antacids, antidiarrheals, vitamins. Many of the pill bottles were prescription, and a lot of the over-the-counter stuff was designed for those with bronchitis or asthma. Paradoxically, there were also cigarettes, lighters, boxes of imported cigars.

The camera snapped again. Again. A Rolex watch, a solid-gold cross on a chain. Chunky gold men's rings set with huge diamonds. The oval Victorian mirror over the chest held a snapshot of a woman sitting on the couch in the living room, wearing a white robe and nuzzling a newborn. Morrissey guessed it was the dead woman, only months before, smiling radiantly as she held her baby girl.

A full message pad, a beeper, pink Post-It notes marked "Please call, important" and "Please call." And in the center of the crowded top of the chest of drawers, two greeting cards: "For You, Daddy" and a bold black, red, and gold card, "This birthday card can only be opened by THE GREATEST DAD IN THE WORLD!!"

As Morrissey aimed his camera around the yellow room, Andy Jauch and Alan Day worked diagramming all the rooms in the house. Measuring, sketching—precise calculations to back up the photographs.

David Brown and Patti Bailey still sat woodenly in the living room, waiting to leave, to go somewhere where the tragedy did not seem so omnipresent. Occasionally, Patti walked the floor absently with Krystal, soothing the infant who had just lost her mother. Finally, Arthur and Manuela Brown took the baby to their house in Carson.

Out in the streets of Garden Grove, patrolmen watched for a short brunette girl in sweatpants—for a killer on the run.

In their search of the house and grounds, Dale Farley and Scott Davis had encountered a number of dogs. There was a puppy of some miniature breed in the blue and white trailer where Cinnamon had been living. The cramped interior was a jumble of Cinnamon's clothes, books, records, stuffed dolls, and blankets—and the floor was rapidly being covered with defecation by the little dog.

"What'll we do with the puppy in the trailer, Sarge?" Davis asked Farley.

"Let's put it with the others back in the pen behind the garage for now."

Fred McLean went outside with the patrol officers, curious to see the trailer where Cinnamon Brown had been banished, and to take a look at the backyard. Davis retrieved the crying puppy and moved through the dark yard, past the lowering form of a huge, ivy-draped maple tree, and around behind the garage where there was a low chain-link fence forming a dog run.

McLean began moving around the house, looking for some sign of forced entry at any of the doors or windows; all the windows were locked tight, save for those with air conditioners. He was checking for some disturbance in the dust and dirt of the sills, some obviously recent attempt at jimmying or prying. Nothing. Then he checked the trailer and the garage. No points of entry showed any indication at all that someone had tried to force his or her way in.

Had David Brown been so upset when he left the house that he not only forgot to set the alarm, but also forgot to lock the doors? If Cinnamon Brown was, indeed, the shooter, that would be a moot question. But if some outsider got into David Brown's house, then the lack of signs of forced entry might be very meaningful.

Fred McLean was not at all convinced that the killer had been identified; he always worked under the assumption that nothing can be presumed.

McLean worked his way around to the backyard and strolled over to the little dog pen. It was full Tuesday now, the sky washed with sunlight, the air still chilled, and he could hear the sounds of commuters' cars headed for the freeway.

He glanced at his watch: ten minutes to seven.

McLean idly watched the four barking dogs in the pen. Two blond cocker spaniels, a white Pomeranian, and the puppy from the trailer, which was so tiny it kept squeezing through a space in the gate. They barked at him and then skittered back to their doghouses. They were all nervous breeds, the kind that would have raised a hell of a racket during the night if a stranger *had* been around.

The doghouses were painted barn red and placed so their rear walls were against the garage. There was a rack for firewood beyond them, and an empty water dish on the near side. McLean grabbed the pup for the third time and stepped over the thirty-inch-high fence to put it back inside.

Once inside the dog pen, McLean gazed toward the doghouses, and he felt a tightening in his neck. The larger doghouse was not empty.

Something was inside. He had to hunker down to get a better look.

There was a figure jammed into the doghouse. It was a small human being, curled into a fetal position, the head bent. Silken brown hair made a veil over the face.

Almost whispering, McLean called out, "Cinnamon . . . Cinnamon?"

He wasn't sure she was alive.

"Cinnamon," he called again, moving closer to the doghouse. Daylight had not yet filtered through the thicket of fig trees shrouding the dog pen.

Suddenly, the form in the doghouse shifted slightly and made a sound the detective couldn't understand. Whoever it was, it was alive.

McLean held out his hand and a small hand grasped his. Awkwardly, her muscles cramped from being so long in one position, a young girl crawled out of the doghouse.

He looked at her in the morning light. It *was* Cinnamon Brown. He had studied pictures of her inside. She wore a sweatshirt and sweatpants, both stained now with reddish vomit and urine.

McLean glanced down into the doghouse as he steadied the girl with his arm. The floor was covered with vomit, and he could see perhaps three dozen orangey capsules still intact in the reddish pool on the floor.

Cinnamon Brown was a very small girl, still carrying a soft cushion of baby fat. She clung to Fred McLean, a perfect stranger, as if he were her savior. She said nothing. It was clear that she was very, very sick, very, very cold, and drowsy. She looked nothing like the crazed teenaged desperado the whole Garden Grove Police Department was combing the streets for.

McLean held the girl's hand and steered her toward a squad car parked beside the house. He instructed Davis to take her at once to police headquarters.

She was not what he had expected. But then, *what* had he expected? Somebody bigger, maybe. Tougher looking.

Fred McLean had arrested a number of killers in his years on the force. He knew all too well that in police work even more than in ordinary life, things are seldom what they seem. But this little girl, who had clearly lain for hours in the icy pitch dark in a pool of her own vomit had to be the most pathetic suspected felon he had yet encountered.

Smelling now of vomit himself, McLean unrolled the piece of pink cardboard that Cinnamon had been clutching in her right hand as he removed her from the doghouse; he had practically had to pry her fingers apart to get her to release it. He untied the purplish ribbon that encircled it. In the light, McLean could make out laborious printing on the cardboard:

"Dear God, please forgive me. I didn't mean to hurt her."

5

L O N G   B E F O R E Woods and Saunders got to Juno Avenue in Anaheim, they heard the radio transmittal that told them they could stop their search for Cinnamon.

"We have the juvenile suspect in custody," Davis's voice sounded on their radio, giving his odometer reading. "I'm transporting her to the station. Time check? I have oh seven sixteen hours. I am leaving one two five five one Ocean Breeze Drive." Female subjects are never transported by male officers without time and mileage checks.

Sanders and Woods turned around and headed toward the Garden Grove Police Station, spotting Davis's patrol unit ahead of them. The two police cars arrived together.

Cinnamon Brown was first taken into the holding-cell area on the lower level.

"Do you remember me?" Steve Sanders asked.

The girl looked up, and nodded. "Yes."

"Can you tell me where you remember me from?"

"From last fall—at Bolsa Grande High School. You came out when I saw the flasher."

That was right. The kid looked terrible and smelled worse, but she was oriented enough to remember a detective she had seen once five months ago.

"I have a terrible headache," Cinnamon Brown murmured. "And I'm afraid I'm going to throw up."

They quickly handed her a wastebasket and the girl leaned over it, vomiting bright orange material.

Woods administered a GSR test on Cinnamon to see if *she* had fired a gun. The swabs from her hands would go to the lab along with the GSR tests from Patti Bailey and David Brown.

Sanders turned to Halligan and Davis. "Has she been Mirandized?"

"No, we didn't question her or talk to her at all."

At twenty minutes after seven, paramedics examined Cinnamon. They found her pulse normal, her blood pressure slightly low, and although her pupils were sluggish in reacting to light, they didn't think she was in immediate danger. She was in stable condition, but they warned that that could change at any time. She had clearly been vomiting a lot, ridding herself naturally of whatever she had ingested.

"Do you know what she's taken?"

"No. McLean just found her."

"Well, since you don't know what she's taken, she should be seen by a doctor."

The medics questioned Cinnamon about what she had ingested. She told them she had taken three bottles of pills—one might have been a tranquilizer prescription—and then she started throwing up while she was in the doghouse.

"When did you take the pills?"

"Maybe two-thirty . . . maybe about three. I'm really tired, and my head hurts, and I feel kind of light-headed," Cinnamon responded. "Is my dad all right?"

Sanders looked up sharply. The kid was sick as a dog and she was more worried about her father than herself. He answered carefully, "Your father's all right and Patti's all right."

"How about Linda? How's Linda?" Cinnamon asked.

Sanders looked away and said nothing. McLean was going to do the questioning.

Fred McLean arrived a few minutes later and handed the paramedics the list of the medications he had bagged into evidence. They winced as they read the list. Darvocet-N was a painkiller. The medics checked their *PDR* (*Physicians' Desk Reference*). The 100-mg dosage came in large orangey-red capsules, containing 100 mg of propoxyphene napsylate and 650 mg of acetaminophen. Dyazide was a diuretic, usually prescribed for high blood pressure, to rid the tissues of excess fluid.

McLean nodded his head when the medics asked if the bottles had been completely empty.

If Cinnamon Brown had taken all the pills that had originally been in those bottles, she would have swallowed 260 capsules. If she hadn't vomited, she might well have been dead by now. But she was on her feet and making pretty good sense; the bottles must not have been full. Still, she was one miserably sick girl.

She continued to gag and throw up and complain of a headache. Lab technicians were requested to take blood samples that would give them a more accurate picture of the concentration of propoxyphene and Dyazide in her blood. The paramedics stood by watchfully; at the first sign that she was deteriorating, they would transport her to a hospital.

At 7:38 that Tuesday morning, Steve Sanders asked Jail Matron Barbara Gordon to accompany Cinnamon Brown to a cell area where she changed her vomit-stained clothes. Cinnamon removed her sweat pants and shirt, her undergarments, the thin gold chain with the star charm holder from around her neck, her earrings, and handed them to Gordon, who put each item into a separate bag and labeled them.

Sanders had asked the matron to check Cinnamon carefully for any bruises, abrasions, or scratches. She did, but she reported back to Sanders, "There's not a mark on the girl's body."

Gordon mentioned that Cinnamon was menstruating and brought her fresh tampons and pads. Dressed in a clean jail jumpsuit, Cinnamon walked down the police station hallway with Detective Sanders, and up the flight of stairs to the east interview room on the second floor. She seemed terribly weary, and her face was void of all expression.

At eight A.M., Fred McLean sat across the table from the girl he had led from the dog pen. He saw a pretty girl with brown hair, lightened with one peroxided blond blaze across her bangs. There was still a bit of childhood roundness in her cheeks. Her deep brown eyes had lost all light; she might have been fifty—eighty, even—if he stared only at those eyes. She looked at him stoically, almost hopelessly.

"Cinnamon," McLean said softly. "Cinnamon?"

"What?"

"I need to talk to you now."

She stared back at him silently.

"I need to talk to you. I'm Fred McLean. I'm a detective with the Garden Grove Police Department, and this is Officer Steve Sanders. You've met him before?"

"Yes—at school."

"Okay. Right now, you're at the Garden Grove Police Department. You know that?

"Do you know why you're here?" McLean asked.

" 'Cause I hurt Linda."

"Because you hurt Linda," McLean echoed. "How did you hurt Linda?"

"I shot her."

"All right, Cinnamon. I've got to advise you of your rights."

"What do you mean?"

"Okay. I'll just explain to you some things, and then we'll talk. Today is March the nineteenth, 1985, it's Tuesday morning, and right now, it's oh eight oh one hours in the morning. Cinnamon, your last name is Brown?"

"Yes."

"Cinnamon Darlene Brown, and you're fourteen years old?"

"Right . . . yes."

"Okay. You've been taken into custody, Cinnamon—"

"*I have?*" For the first time, the girl's voice was full of disbelief.

"By me . . . I've taken you into custody because of what you did to Linda. Now, Linda is dead—"

"*She's dead?*" Again, Cinnamon Brown seemed genuinely shocked.

"Yes."

"*Oh . . . no!*"

"So you've been taken into custody for murder, and I want you to listen to me right now."

McLean quickly advised Cinnamon of her rights under Miranda and explained them to her, reading from the Garden Grove Police Department's standard Miranda-warning card. She nodded and said "I think so" each time he asked her if she understood. But she seemed to falter in understanding, and McLean explained the Miranda warning in more detail. And when he asked her again if she understood, she said "Yes" firmly. Steve Sanders sat nearby, watching silently.

It was hard to tell if the girl was truly drugged, or if she was only exhausted from a night without sleep. She seemed to drift in and out. When McLean could keep her attention, she responded quickly and intelligently. She didn't appear to need time to form her answers.

"With those rights in mind," he said, "are you willing to talk to me about the charges against you, Cinnamon? Do you understand that you don't have to talk to me?"

"Yes."

"Do you want to tell me what happened last night—yesterday?"

"Yes."

"All right, Cinnamon—you were living at your father's residence at one two five five one Ocean Breeze?"

"We were moving around a lot too."

"Uh-huh. When did you move in with your father?"

"The first day of school."

Cinnamon explained to McLean that she had attended the ninth grade at Loara High School during the fall of 1984.

"Why weren't you living with your mother?"

"Oh, because she yells too much. It made me nervous."

"Why does your mother yell at you?"

"Because I'm a brat."

"What do you do to be a brat?"

"I go to the beach every day."

"What do you do at the beach?"

"Get a tan."

"Do you go with anyone?"

"My best friend . . . Krista Taber."

So far, McLean could not see the rebellious teenager he'd expected. Playing hooky at the beach was hardly a major felony. He saw that Cinnamon was getting drowsier, drifting away from him, and he frequently had to repeat her name to bring her back.

"Cinnamon, can you hear me?" McLean repeated.

She waved her arm at him impatiently, as one would shoo a fly.

"Cinnamon? *Cinnamon!*"

"What?"

"Can you hear me?"

"Yes."

"How many times did you fire the gun?"

She did not respond.

"Cinnamon? The gun. Do you remember how many times you fired the gun?"

"Three . . . times. Once in Patti's bedroom . . . and twice . . . at Linda in her room."

"Do you ditch school?" McLean asked, backing off from the danger area for the moment.

"Only during the summer. This week I didn't go because I wasn't feeling good. I started feeling better yesterday, but—"

"Well, we know why you're not feeling good now. Okay, what happened yesterday . . . *Cinnamon?*"

"I'm here."

"Okay. What happened between you and Linda yesterday?"

". . . Me and my father get along pretty good—but Linda said a while back that she didn't want me in the house. So we moved me out to the trailer. . . . It still didn't work out. She wanted me to move far away from them. She said, 'If you don't leave the house by the time I wake up, I'm going to kill you,' and . . . everything."

"Linda said she was going to kill you?"

"Yes. Me and her were in a big fight and I don't know why she was—why she started it."

"You have no idea why there was a fight between you and Linda—*Cinnamon?*"

"I'm here—I don't feel good."

"Why did Linda want you to leave?" McLean hated having to press on with the questioning—the kid was pale green with nausea—but he also felt she was evading his questions. He needed to find some motive for such a seemingly senseless crime.

"She was tired of me, and she didn't want me around. She just doesn't like me."

"Why?"

"I guess because I'm my daddy's daughter—she's jealous. I don't know. We never did get along . . . because one day my dad went to the post office with Patti, and I was in Patti's room drawing a picture and Krystal was choking, and all she did was sit there. She didn't even try to help her, and when my dad gets home, she never hugs him. She never says, 'Hi, dear.' She just ignores him. She's been acting real weird lately."

"When Krystal was choking, did you help her?"

"I tried to, but when she would see me going in, she goes, 'It's my baby—I'll take care of her,' and I go, 'Fine.' "

"When Krystal was choking, did you actually pick her up to help her? *Cinnamon?*"

"*What?*"

"Did you pick Krystal up to help her?"

"No . . . but I wanted to. . . . She like sometimes *bits* Krystal, and it makes me so mad when Daddy isn't home. One time, my dad saw her do it, and Linda didn't know he was home."

"You didn't like her treating the baby badly? Cinnamon—?"

"I'm here." And then under her breath, she murmured, "*Please don't let them get away with murder.*"

"Well, you've got to answer my questions then," McLean said gently, puzzled by the way the girl's answers didn't always match up to his questions.

"I'm trying to—but I can't keep my eyes open."

"You don't have to keep your eyes open to talk to me. I just want you to concentrate on what you're telling me. Yesterday, Linda said she was going to kill you if you didn't leave?"

"Yes. That's the first time she ever said that. I thought she loved me. She told me she hated my guts, and I go, 'Well, I guess I hate you too.' We started arguing."

"Did Linda *say* why she hated you?"

"No, she wouldn't tell me."

Cinnamon seemed unaware that she had just contradicted herself. McLean had to drag answers out of her, but she repeated that Linda had hated her, wanted her out of the house, and was cruel to the baby, Krystal. She could not, however, give specific responses when McLean asked her what she and Linda argued about.

"Just little things—I don't know."

"Cinnamon, what little things?"

"Uh?"

"Cinnamon?"

"Uh?"

"CINNAMON?"

"Huh? I'm . . . here."

McLean asked her about the gun, and she remembered that she had found it in a drawer in her father's office, that it was there for anyone to use "in case of emergency." She insisted that she had asked no one how to use it.

"I shot three shots."

". . . Three shots?"

"Uh-huh. One was in the room with Patti, and the other two were with . . . with Linda."

"Why did you shoot a bullet in Patti's room?"

"The gun got stuck . . . or something in it . . . the thing got stuck—that trigger thing—the thing you pull back. I couldn't turn on the light or she would have seen it."

"Did you ask anyone how to use the gun? Cinnamon? *Cinnamon?*"

"Uh-huh. No. Uh-uh . . ."

"Cinnamon. Cinnamon."

"I'm *here*. Would you just stop saying my name?"

McLean realized that he had very little time left with her. She was sleepy, and she was annoyed with his constant questions. Yes, she answered, yes, she knew how to fire a gun. They went out shooting guns in the desert.

"Cinnamon?"

"I'm here."

"Cinnamon?"

"I'm here. . . ."

But she really wasn't. She muttered that they used little guns in the family " 'cause they don't do much harm."

"Where did you shoot those little guns?"

"What do you mean?"

"Those little guns—where did you shoot them?"

"I was watching TV, and then I was asleep."

McLean stopped the interview. He wanted to have a reading on the proportion of drugs in the girl's bloodstream before he continued. He looked at her and saw her eyelids drooping.

She seemed to him a very little girl. Not fourteen. Not even twelve. And yet she had just told him she had shot her stepmother.

This time around, he was almost sorry he had found his suspect.

It was eight-twenty when Edith Gwinn of the Golden Coast Lab arrived to take a blood sample from Cinnamon. Over the next eight minutes, three vials were filled. One read #8015, one #8020, and the third was to type in case Cinnamon needed a transfusion later.

Cinnamon seemed to rouse and become more alert during the blood drawing, but only because she was frightened. She had never had blood drawn before.

When McLean attempted to talk to her again at 8:40, her condition had changed radically. Her head lolled, and her eyes were not focusing. She was unable to respond to his questions in anything more than a mumble.

He stopped the interview at once and summoned the paramedics.

Cinnamon's blood pressure had dropped to a point where it would not register on the cuff and had to be palpated. Her pulse was eighty. The paramedics hooked her up to a heart monitor and started an IV as they raced her to the Garden Grove Medical Center. Police Officer Pamela French rode with Cinnamon in the aid car. The girl appeared to be unconscious or asleep during the trip, and there was no conversation.

French remained with Cinnamon in her hospital room from 9:18 until noon, and during that time, Cinnamon Brown did make some statements. But they sounded robotlike to the policewoman—almost as if they had been programmed into the teenager's subconscious. Cinnamon would blurt them out from time to time, with virtually no continuity. Although she vomited almost continuously, she was barely awake.

Some of her ramblings were clear enough for Pam French to understand, and some were garbled.

"Haven't slept for twenty-four hours . . . had an accident . . . killed my stepmother . . . didn't do it on purpose, didn't mean to."

Still, despite all the disjointed mumbling, some sentences hung in the air as clearly as if they were written there.

"She was hurting me . . . she hated me . . . she wanted to kill me . . . she wanted me out of the house."

French had not questioned Cinnamon, and she made no response to the girl's words, although she jotted them down in her notes.

"I got the gun out of the office drawer in the house—I was angry with her . . . she hurt my little sister . . . I couldn't ignore her choking her."

French had no way of knowing that she was hearing almost exactly the same words that Cinnamon had said to McLean. The girl tossing on the bed beside her seemed bone tired—no, more than that—absolutely exhausted as she fought the effect of the pills she had taken, but she also seemed coherent.

"She hated me . . . wanted me out of the house . . . I was angry at her."

And then, finally, Cinnamon Brown could no longer fight the medication's creeping sedation, and she slipped into unconsciousness.

It seemed a classically simple case. The suspect herself had admitted the crime. Although the thought appeared to break his heart, her own father presumed she had done it. Cinnamon had asked Patti Bailey to show her how to shoot the .38 only hours before Linda was shot. What other answer could there be? A jealous teenager, resenting her stepmother, chafing at rules, regulations, orders to do chores, and believing that she was the object of hatred and rejection, had struck back.

With a gun. She was sorry now, horrified to hear that Linda had died.

But it was far too late.

If the events of March 19, 1985, had been a movie and not tragically real, it would have been over. But a confession is never enough to take into court. It is only a part of the *body of the crime;* the corpus delicti is not—as so many people believe—the *actual* corpse, but is, instead, all the components that make up each crime itself.

Back at the house on Ocean Breeze Drive, Bill Morrissey continued to take pictures, gather evidence, and supervise the measurement of each room of the house. If, as Cinnamon Brown had now admitted, she had shot Linda, he needed the evidence that would substantiate her confession. More of the body of the crime, as it were.

McLean had reported to Morrissey that Cinnamon said she had shot the gun three times—twice at Linda, and once in Patti Bailey's room. And Patti herself said she had been awakened by gunfire. Morrissey moved to the front bedroom. Patti's room.

Morrissey's photographs showed that, like the rest of the house, Patti Bailey's room was crammed with new furniture. It seemed a room any teenage girl would love. The walls were papered in beige, yellow, and brown. and there were crisply starched white sheers over the window, topped with lacy valances. Patti's furniture was heavy maple with brass drawer pulls, and her bed was a smaller version of the white iron bed where her sister had died. The covers were turned back, as if someone had leapt out in a hurry.

There was a trundle bed in the room, pulled from beneath Patti's bed; it had not been slept in.

Patti had her own stereo, her own television set. And she had a profusion of dolls and teddy bears and stuffed animals. The dolls were "collector's items," the kind offered to viewers of television shopping networks. Any one of them would cost a hundred dollars or more. There were books—the only books in the house beyond a *Reader's Digest* condensed-book series and the Bible on one of David Brown's chests. Patti's books were teen romance novels. Innocent puppy love books, much beloved by pubescent girls, the precursors to Harlequin romances—without the sex scenes.

David Brown had not only taken his wife's sister into his home, he had given her a room that any girl would envy. And she kept it in immaculate condition, with all of her treasures neatly arranged and all her furnishings polished.

Morrissey scanned the walls, looking for some sign that a bullet might have pierced them. He gazed around the room, taking it in in segments, his camera dispassionately recording everything. The mirrors, TV, stereo, window, were all intact. The dolls and teddy bears sat undisturbed, as did Patti's large jewelry case, and the gold and crystal display case above it. There were golden chains tumbling out of the crammed drawers.

Just over the head of Patti's bed there was a little sconce holding teddy bears and a framed picture, an etching in pale silvery tones. Morrissey bent closer. It was a bird of some sort taking flight. He had seen similar birds in David Brown's office. Eagles or—what were they?—*phoenix* birds. Like in that old movie with Jimmy Stewart and his crew who crashed in the desert and rebuilt their shattered plane, *The Flight of the Phoenix*.

Morrissey was a no-nonsense man, not given to musing over the deeper meaning of mythical birds. His eyes were grainy from lack of sleep, and he had hours to go as he methodically preserved the olive-green bungalow and its contents with photographs and measurements. But at the moment, he wanted most to find the single missing bullet that would validate Patricia Bailey's firm belief that Cinnamon had stood in the door of her room and deliberately fired a gun at her.

And then he saw it. He had been staring right at it without registering what he saw. There was a large wall hanging over Patti Bailey's bed—about three feet by five feet. It was the kind of tapestry often sold at roadside stands, along with cement lawn statues, birdbaths, and wooden whirligigs. This was a familiar staple in the tapestry medium—tigers playing with their cubs against the bright yellow earth, green palm trees, and a red sky.

One tiger had taken a bullet right through its plush heart.

Morrissey figured the slug had to be embedded deep in the wall behind the hanging. That meant the tapestry would come down, and if the bullet was not resting just behind it, the wall was coming down too. As luck would have it, the wall had to be carefully sawed in a large rectangle, removed, and there, between the studs, Morrissey found one battered .38 slug.

Beyond that slug, Bill Morrissey's roster of evidence removed from the Ocean Breeze Drive house the morning of March 19 included:

1. Gunshot-residue evidence kit with swabs from two tests—David Arnold Brown and Patricia Bailey;

2. One Smith & Wesson .38 revolver, serial #R304915 (initialed by officer), from floor of . . . master bedroom;

3. One Smith & Wesson, Model 19-4, .357 magnum revolver, serial #6F8K783, with six live rounds, in holster in plastic bag, from master bedroom;

4. One box Winchester .38 Special silvertip ammunition—from beneath bed in master bedroom;

5. One box Winchester .357 magnum silvertip ammunition—from beneath bed in master bedroom;

6. Bloodstained bed sheet, multifloral pattern, pillows and cases, blanket;

7. One black leather "Liberty" holster for .38 Smith & Wesson, with chrome metal belt clip, in drawer in master bedroom;

8. Drinking glass with Star Trek character;

9. Sample of clear liquid in glass;

10. Three empty prescription vials;

11. One 56½" by 38½" tiger wall tapestry.

In combination, or separately, these items might make salient physical evidence in a murder case. Certainly, the murder gun would. But what about the rest of it?

The crime scene investigators stayed at the house hours after David Brown and Patricia Bailey left at seven A.M. The grieving family fled to Arthur and Manuela's home with only a suitcase filled with items for the baby. They could not bear to stay in the house—not yet. The investigators found it difficult to work around them and were relieved to see them go.

Alan Day suggested that David Brown return in an hour; he would be able to give him a better idea then of how long it might be before they could occupy the house. When David and Patti Bailey returned, Day told them it would be several hours more, maybe even a few days. They were allowed in to collect toys and diapers, which they loaded into David's van.

David was concerned about some jewelry that he had left in the master bedroom and asked if he could retrieve it. Day said that wouldn't be possible, but he offered to get it if Brown could describe what he wanted.

"My wristwatch—a Rolex—and my cross, on a chain. I took them off last night and put them on my chest of drawers."

Day located the items in a jewelry box and brought them to Brown. Once again, David and Patti drove off.

When the investigators were finished, Morrissey would oversee the locking of the residence with a police lock; he had obtained the code for the security alarm system from David Brown. They had not yet begun to search the Terry travel trailer, and they would need to come back to the house itself.

The investigators left at the shooting scene on Ocean Breeze Drive worked through the morning, their night's sleep lost forever. By 12:22, the house was empty. The yellow ribbons whipping in the March wind cordoned off the crime search area and told passersby that something unusual had happened there. Neighbors gathered in knots to stare, and to try to remember something—anything—that might have forewarned them that things were not well in the Brown household.

But they were hard put to come up with anything. Nobody had really known David and Linda Brown, and the teenagers who lived with them. They were the only renters on the street, and the Browns had seemed an extremely close-knit family who had little time to talk with neighbors. With their extended family visiting so often, they appeared sufficient unto themselves. Later, upon reflection, neighbors would have more to say to reporters from the *Orange County Register* and the *Los Angeles Times*. Encouraged—entreated—to search their minds for something, *anything*, that might be important, they came forth with blurry remembrances.

Within hours of Linda Brown's murder, police investigators believed that they knew *who* had done the shooting; they even had a motive that seemed plausible, if simplistic. Still, they suspected they might never know the real reasons Cinnamon Brown had killed her stepmother. The designated shooter had lapsed into a comatose state from which she might never awaken.

6

W H E N G A R D E N Grove homicide investigator Fred Mc-
Lean's steel-blue eyes first met the warm brown eyes of Orange
County coroner's deputy Bernice Mazuca, the ambiance was hardly
idyllic for romance. "Bernie," the more talkative of the pair, smiled
as she recalled their meeting. "We were in Little Saigon at a triple
murder scene, and Fred and I were trying to identify shoe impressions
in blood. I said, 'Nike,' and he said, 'New Balance,' and we looked
at each other and suddenly realized we had more in common than a
mutual interest in death investigation. We were both runners." The
initial attraction long outlasted that murder. They got married.

Fred McLean, compactly muscled at fifty-three, a ruddy-cheeked
blend of Scotch and German ancestry, was the one obsessed with
running. He began each day by traversing a brisk five- to seven-mile
course. He was what you might expect if you took a career Marine
and turned him into a street cop, tough and taciturn at first glance,
a softie when his veneer was peeled away. He did not peel easily.

"My folks came to L.A. from Kansas in the thirties to find gold;
they found the Depression instead, and I was born in the Salvation
Army hospital in Los Angeles. Back in Wellington, Kansas, my grandfather owned half the businesses in town and had a verbal contract
with the Santa Fe Railroad to ice their produce cars. The Santa Fe
built a spur to Wellington right up to Heinrich Wilhelm Glamann
and his enterprises. The old man gave my dad a job when L.A. fizzled
on him, paid him eighty-five cents a day—good wages in 1937."

And so began McLean's sporadic "commute" between Kansas and
California. His love of sports stemmed from the glory years of football
in Kansas when his team was first in the state. He joined the Marine
Corps in 1956 where he played guard and blocking back on the football
team in the single-wing formation. Young McLean soared high and
fast in the Marine Corps. He became a first lieutenant when he was
barely twenty-one, flying 119s, Panther jets, and any aircraft the
Marine Corps used. He wasn't thirty when he was one of the "old
guys" who shepherded five thousand young Marines to stand by off
the Bay of Pigs during the Cuban missile crisis. "They never got to
fight. They were too young to appreciate that; they were so revved
up they damn near tore up a town."

McLean learned a lot about human behavior, and a great deal about discipline and commitment, in the Corps. He loved it all. When he said, "The Marine Corps was my life," you know he meant it and could sense what it cost him to walk away. But McLean's first wife gave him an ultimatum after he had been with the Corps for a decade. He seldom had stateside duty; his son rarely saw his father. The choice was simple. The Marine Corps or the marriage.

McLean chose the marriage.

Police work was the only civilian career that appealed to him, and it began as a grudging second choice. McLean's wife was dubious about it, suspecting—correctly—that it might be as dangerous and as time-consuming as being in the Marine Corps. She agreed only after he promised he would stay away from Los Angeles County and sign on with some sleepy Orange County department.

Garden Grove fitted that description when McLean joined the force on August 26, 1966.

But not for long.

The marriage foundered, but McLean's fascination with police work bloomed. To counteract the fine edge of tension that walks with a policeman always, McLean ran and played football. He was forty-eight when he hung up his shoulder pads for the last time. He was out in the field on training maneuvers with his Marine Corps reserve unit until he was fifty. And to celebrate his fiftieth birthday, he ran fifty miles. Over the years, McLean survived shoot-outs and dicey encounters, and his skill with people moved him steadily up through the ranks from patrol into the detective unit.

He had found his niche.

As the primary investigator into Linda Marie Brown's murder, McLean was present at her autopsy. The postmortem examination began at nine-thirty A.M., five hours after the young mother had been pronounced dead.

From the "cold room," in the Orange County Forensic Center, the gurney carrying Linda's body turned right and trundled perhaps twenty feet down the hallway to the entrance of the autopsy room. It was L-shaped, bright with overhead lights, as clean as constant scrubbing with floral-scented disinfectant could make it, and equipped with a half dozen stainless steel tables. Depending on the weather, the phase of the moon, or any number of conditions that seemed to serve as catalysts for violent death, the tables might all be occupied or there might be only a single postmortem in progress.

Sly irreverence, the black humor that makes constant exposure to tragedy bearable to those who must deal with it every day, revealed itself impishly in the Orange County coroner's autopsy room. The light-switch plates bore likenesses of tiny, naked cartoon men. When the switches were on, the little men had erections. The switch plates had been there so long that only a visitor noticed anymore.

Dr. Richard I. Fukomoto performed the autopsy, witnessed by McLean and his fellow investigator Steve Sanders; Joe Luckey and Bill Lystrup of the Orange County Coroner's Office; Rob Keister, a criminalist with the Orange County Sheriff's Office; and Mary De Guelle, a forensic specialist with the Sheriff's Office. All had attended numerous postmortems, and they gathered around the table with interest, but with a dispassion achieved over long time. Experience had taught them to suspend emotion in this room.

But sometimes this removal from what was before them was difficult to maintain. Linda Brown had been a beautiful young woman with a perfect figure. Her skin was pale as snow now and marred with two bullet wounds of entry between her full breasts.

Rob Keister began the procedure by retrieving evidence *on* the body. The Orange County criminalist placed a sheet of clear acetate over the stippling pattern on Linda Brown's chest, then marked the pattern of the gun-barrel debris. He plucked three unburned kernels from her breast and retained them for evidence.

Linda's hands also had several unburned powder kernels, and these were removed before GSR tests were done. Routine—the position of the wounds and the gun made it well nigh impossible for Linda to have shot herself, but she might have held her hands up in a vain gesture of protection. More likely, the shooter had simply been very close to her as the gun was fired.

Fingernail scrapings were collected, and the victim's pubic hair was combed for alien hairs or fibers. None were collected.

Dr. Fukomoto began dictating as he approached his subject. Pathologists measure precisely, and Fukomoto adhered to that as he described the first wound as "upper midchest wall, located forty-nine and a half inches from the sole of the foot, and thirteen inches from the top of the head, slightly to the right of the midline—approximately one-half inch."

This wound just inside the right breast measured 1.1 centimeters and was circled with a concentrated "tattooing" of gunpowder and barrel debris with a diameter of one inch. There was less tattooing extending over another two inches. Fukomoto detected no burning of the tissues and found the angle of fire was from below, traveling slightly upward and left to right. The fact that the tissue was not actually burned ruled out a contact wound, but the gun would have had to be six inches or less from the victim when fired.

The second wound was located forty-seven and a half inches from the sole of the foot and fifteen inches from the top of the head. The wound itself was the same size as the first, but the tattooing affect sprayed over a much wider radius—up to nine inches—with debris from the gun apparent all the way up to the chin and left side of the face. To the layman, the tattooing of gun-barrel debris means little; to the criminalist, it can pinpoint the distance the shooter stood from the victim. The second of Linda's wounds had resulted from a bullet fired from twelve to twenty inches away.

There was no way to determine which had come first; they had been sustained within minutes of each other.

Fukomoto turned the body over and saw an area of hemorrhaging on the back. With the flick of a scalpel, he removed a slightly deformed large-caliber slug from just beneath the skin near the midline of the back. A second, similar slug was removed near the upper right shoulder. Rob Keister took possession of the two battered slugs and bagged them, noting that no trace evidence was found on either.

Fukomoto executed the usual Y-shaped incision—down obliquely from each shoulder, meeting at midline. Autopsy means "to see for one's self," and the procedure can give up unfathomable secrets. There is irony in the study of the dead. So many postmortems reveal ravaged organs, hardened arteries, systems that should have long since shut down and still have worked remarkably well for decades. Only misadventure or violence ended the lives of the subjects.

And in the young, as in the examination of Linda Brown, the body so recently an efficient machine, the heart's arteries pink and glistening with no deposits of fatty plaque, the lungs light pink despite Linda's continual worry that she could not seem to quit smoking, the kidneys healthy. Everything healthy.

But she was dead.

One bullet had merely grazed her right lung, but had pierced the superior vena cava; the other had entered the right lung. The superior vena cava is a large vein that returns blood to the right atrium of the heart. Vital. Linda Bailey Brown could not have survived more than fifteen minutes—on the outside—with a hole in the vena cava, unless she had immediate medical care. She might have lived for some time with the wound to the right lung alone.

Linda Brown had bled to death. She was only very tenuously alive when Officer Darrow Halligan bent over her to see if she breathed, and she was still clinically alive when she reached the hospital. At this point, it was too late to be sure how long she might have been alive and bleeding internally in gushing freshets of blood from her vena cava and her lung before help was summoned.

Her husband had been afraid to check on her. He had been terrified about what he should do, and in his panic, he had called his father for advice before he called 911. Would the sequence of his calls have made any difference? Probably not. Linda had been so terribly injured.

Still, it made Fred McLean wonder. He himself was a man of action. He could not fathom the thought that a man would not rush to check on a wife he loved, how he could wait until a policeman got there to find out if she was dead or alive.

Cinnamon had admitted to the shooting—to "hurting Linda." It was difficult to disbelieve her. And McLean could see the destruction the bullets had wrought. Hell, it probably wouldn't have made any difference if Brown had rushed in and carried Linda out and driven her to the hospital the minute Patti Bailey told him she had heard shots in the house while he was away. People bleed to death in hospitals with a team of surgeons standing by.

But still . . .

Even after the postmortem, tests would be done on blood and tissue samples, on body fluids and stained clothing. Blood from the right pleural cavity, stomach contents, liver tissue, urinary bladder tissue, brain tissue, vitreous fluid from the eyes. Heart blood was retained, along with the pretransfusion blood retained by Joe Luckey, muscle and marrow samples, vaginal, anal, and oral swabs and slides, and the bloodstained nightshirt with the dancing penguins.

All of it neatly packaged and labeled.

And then Linda's body was released to the Dimond and Sons Mettler Mortuary for burial arrangements. She was cremated at the Coastal Crematory in Pasadena on March 25, 1985.

Her ashes were not immediately inurned; her widower wanted everything to be "as perfect for her as I could make it."

A long time later, David Brown recalled that he had agonized over what to do with Linda's ashes. "Linda and I both believed in cremation. We agreed that whichever one of us was left behind would scatter the other's ashes off of Diamond Head in Hawaii—because we were so happy there. But that was before Linda was a mother. I couldn't do that to our child. I couldn't deny Krystal a place to go where she could be close to her mother. I instructed the cemetery in Newport Beach to allow Krystal to take Linda's ashes to Diamond Head if that's what Krystal chose to do when she was old enough to decide.

"Linda's in a fountain, right in the base of the fountain, where she can hear the water cascading down twenty-four hours a day. She's way up where she can see the ocean—if it isn't a smoggy day. I loved her enough that I wanted her to have everything the way we discussed it."

Employees at the memorial park recalled David Brown. He bought *two* niches, and two dark verdigris antique-bronze plaques. He was not satisfied with the first chiseling of an inscription and ordered the job redone. His manner was so unyielding and arrogant that he was not remembered fondly.

For his own reasons, he had that first plaque removed and destroyed.

7

THE GARDEN Grove investigators spread out in a half dozen directions, racing their own arbitrary twenty-four-hour deadline, aware that the most vital and pertinent information and evidence can only be retrieved during the first day and night following any murder. Just as physical trauma victims must be treated within that first "golden hour" to forestall deadly shock, homicide detectives have a "golden twenty-four hours." After that, people and things evaporate. Witnesses can rethink their stories, alter their perceptions, all unaware. Witnesses can be deliberately contaminated. Inexorable, invisible mutations of fact occur. The chances of an arrest's being made lessen.

A homicide investigation is, always, a race against time and change.

Fred McLean would begin with interviews of those who knew and/ or were related to the David Brown family. He had heard only from David Brown and Patricia Bailey at this point, and they were in complete agreement about the dangerousness of Cinnamon Brown. With the confession from Cinnamon herself, the follow-up investigation did not seem to be a matter of finding a suspect.

Cinnamon Darlene Brown, fourteen, *was* the suspect.

Steve Sanders headed to the Manchester Building, the Juvenile Court building on The City Drive in Orange, part of an aging complex that housed the district attorney's juvenile offices in 1985—along with the Juvenile Court, Public Defender's Office, and the Department of Probation. The DA's Juvenile Division occupied offices on the third floor of the Manchester Building. Within a few hundred yards on either side of the building are the University of California (Irvine) Medical Center and the Sitton-Orangewood Children's Home.

Juvenile Hall loomed behind the Juvenile Court building, outdated as were all the juvenile facilities in the mid-eighties. There was then, and is today, an irony in the cluster of buildings. Abused children shout and laugh in the play yard of the Sitton-Orangewood Children's Home, so close to the Juvenile Hall where teenagers peer through bars. Too late, perhaps, to save the older kids—possibly too late for some of the babies.

Sanders knew it was time to confer with Deputy DA Dick Fredrickson, give him a synopsis of the case so far and see if charges could be filed against Cinnamon Brown for the murder of her stepmother.

From all the investigators could discern, Cinnamon's crime was murder without extenuating circumstances. The code in California was PC-187. The admitted shooter was only fourteen, but she had confessed to pulling the trigger three times. *She* was a juvenile, but her crime was adult.

Dick Fredrickson was no neophyte when it came to juvenile homicide suspects. Without intending to, Fredrickson had become the resident expert on teenage killers—a phenomenon that was becoming disturbingly commonplace in Orange County. Although Fredrickson usually served as an administrator, he had recently prosecuted two particularly ugly murders involving teenagers.

Kathy Sloane* was fourteen and her boyfriend, Sean Conley*, sixteen when they beat and stabbed Kathy's mother, Debbie Newton, thirty-six, to death on February 16, 1984. Ironically, the victim was a former chairwoman of the Orange County Coalition Against Domestic Violence and ran a shelter for female incest victims. She had allowed Sean Conley to live in the garage of her Fullerton residence—until she became alarmed over the sexual intensity of her fourteen-year-old daughter's romance and attempted to break the couple up.

The teenage lovers killed her for interfering.

Fredrickson had prosecuted Kathy and Sean for the murder as violent as any he had seen an adult commit. Physical evidence verified that *each* of them had used the weapon in the murder. Kathy was convicted of first-degree murder in an Orange County Superior Court in September of 1984 and sentenced to twenty-six years to life. Sean received the same sentence when he was convicted two months later.

Fredrickson had also prosecuted Alan Coates*, sixteen, for the sadistic murder of his mother, a woman he despised. His writings, found in school papers in his desk, revealed the depth of his hatred.

It was a growing problem for law enforcement all over America; when is a kid *not* a kid—at least in the eyes of the law? What is the cutoff point where a teenager should be prosecuted in adult court? Can such arbitrary decisions *ever* be made when one is dealing with human beings?

Now, Fredrickson studied the Linda Brown case synopsis Sanders handed him, then silently passed it over to the man sitting across the desk from him. Assistant district attorneys and investigators are paired off in twos. And on the morning of March 19, 1985, Dick Fredrickson was lucky enough to draw Jay Newell as his investigator.

Newell, thirty-nine, was a big, broad-shouldered man who *looked* like an athlete. In fact, he was a grudging—but habitual—runner. He was also a scuba diver because he reveled in the beauty and mystery far beneath the water's surface. He didn't play golf; he didn't bowl. Nevertheless, he ran in the Challenge Cup, a 120-mile relay from Baker, California, to Las Vegas each year to earn pledges for the policemen's widows and orphans fund. "I always run my ten K in the dark," he said. "When it's cooler."

Athletics came to Jay Newell with no encouragement from him; he would far rather sit on a stakeout. He coached and managed a Youth Soccer League team for nine years, but only because of his kids. One daughter was a volleyball star, and he was extremely proud of that. He was proud of both his daughters, and of his wife, Betty Jo, a highly successful businesswoman. Newell was totally disinterested in watching sports on television. The outcome of the Super Bowl or the World Series meant little to him, but the outcome of a homicide case walked with him constantly.

Newell was a *detective* with fourteen years of law enforcement behind him. This was what he did. This was what interested him. He was immensely talented at reading people, at judging their veracity by the way they shifted their bodies, averted their eyes, cleared their throats, breathed, smelled, gulped, smoked, drank.

A craggily attractive man with dark hair, soft eyes, and a strong chin, Newell could look like a country preacher, a slick real estate salesman, a biker, or a tough cop. He was an interrogator with a deceptively easy manner who lay in wait for one misstep.

He was a dogged pursuer. He never quit.

He was a dangerous enemy for a felon to have.

At eleven in the morning on that Tuesday in March, Jay Newell heard the name Cinnamon Brown for the first time. He read over the synopsis, noted the address on Ocean Breeze Drive, and headed out the door. "The first thing I do is to go to the scene. I'm not looking for anything in particular—I just want to get a feel, a sense of the place. It's a jumping-off point for me."

And so Newell drove to the Brown's rented bungalow. Morrissey and his crew were still picking up evidence as he approached the strangely quiet house.

Newell walked around the property first, noting the three vehicles still parked in the driveway after the Browns had left. There was an older, classic MG, a Ford Mustang, and a Chevy Monte Carlo. He ducked under the huge old maple tree, its trunk entwined with ivy. Even with the sun out, the backyard was dark, dappled with shadows. He saw the dog pen back of the garage and stared at the two red doghouses. The family had left the four little dogs behind, and they yapped hysterically.

Newell turned away, wondering what it must have been like for a fourteen-year-old girl, sick from a massive overdose, to wait the night out in a doghouse in the pitch-black chill. His oldest daughter wasn't much younger than Cinnamon Brown, and he had always tried to protect his girls from anything hurtful or frightening. It was hard not to compare.

The little trailer, its aqua and white paint rusting, dented here and there, was backed in so that it nudged the double glass doors between the two rear wings of the house, only a few steps from the back door that led to a utility porch. The hitch was propped on a brick and a slab of wood. Newell peered in the door and stepped back quickly to get away from the odor. The floor was dotted with dog feces.

The Terry trailer was a compact unit, maybe fourteen feet long with a built-in stove, refrigerator, and bunks. It would have been fun for kids to camp out in on a summer night, but it seemed a bit bleak in March—when the rest of the Brown family lived inside the house. Cinnamon had been provided with a portable television, a radio, and a heater. A large, well-worn teddy bear occupied the top bunk, and there was a Cabbage Patch doll on the bottom bunk.

Newell stepped into the house, nodding to Bill Morrissey and his crew. He padded down the hallways, memorizing the location of the rooms. The place looked normal, as if a family had just scattered to go to work and school. The kitchen was sunny, and someone—probably the victim—had had a green thumb. Vines and houseplants bloomed on shelves and tables. It was a "Donna Reed" kind of kitchen, cozy, immaculate, and welcoming.

Like the other investigators, Newell noted the proliferation of new, expensive furniture. The middle room along the south hallway was the most startling study in excess—especially when Newell contrasted it with the shabby trailer he had just seen.

It was a nursery—but what a nursery. The furniture was top of the line, just as in the rest of the house. There were enough toys for a dozen babies. Newell stopped counting at three dozen teddy bears, most of them Care-Bears in every color of the rainbow. There were a half dozen mobiles, toy chests, Sesame Street characters on the wall, an automated baby swing, a car seat, and a small herd of porcelain unicorns. Krystal's name was spelled out on one wall in giant letters.

Krystal Brown had obviously been a much-wanted baby, if you could judge by earthly possessions.

And now she had no mother.

Newell turned away.

The motive given in the police synopsis made sense. Fourteen-year-old child of a first marriage in the way. Stepmother—and maybe father—favor new baby. Teenager relegated to crummy trailer.

But something niggled. Newell paused to watch Morrissey sawing away at the wall in Patricia Bailey's room. Bailey had a lovely room too. His mind registered a question.

Where did Patti Bailey fit in, and why was she apparently held in more favor than David Brown's own older daughter?

Jay Newell talked to Patti Bailey the next day. She was a quiet, almost phlegmatic girl. Her lack of animation made her more plain than pretty. She had obviously been crying, and her face was blank as she explained to the DA's investigator why she had come to live with her sister and brother-in-law.

Things had been tough at home, she said, without elaborating. "I visited every weekend, and then Linda said, 'If you're really having trouble, I don't mind if you come and live with me until you and Mom straighten things out, or until you're eighteen. I'd love to have you.' I said, 'Fine.' "

Whatever problems she might have saddled him with before, David Brown was fighting to save his teenage daughter now. Even as she lay unconscious, he had hired an attorney to see to her interests.

Al Forgette had eighteen years experience as an attorney, and fifteen years of criminal law. He was a most respected attorney in Orange County, as much for his reputation for fair play as for his expertise. He had the face of a kindly prizefighter, broad shoulders, and wavy gray hair.

Al Forgette listened as David Brown stressed that he would do anything he could to look out for Cinnamon. The man seemed grief stricken. He didn't understand why the tragedy had happened, but he didn't want Cinnamon going to jail.

Forgette agreed to take the case. It piqued his interest.

He went immediately to the Garden Grove Medical Center to see his client. But Cinnamon Brown was comatose. Forgette left his card and asked to be notified when she regained consciousness.

· · ·

Officer Pamela French turned over her chair beside Cinnamon Brown's bed to Officer Kurt Roudybush at noon on Tuesday. "Gus" Ortiz took over the shift at eight that night. If Cinnamon should say anything, they would note it.

Medical personnel came and went, and one female medical student spent a good deal of time caring for Cinnamon.

Most of the treatments administered to Cinnamon had been—and continued to be—hideously unpleasant. On the way to the hospital, Garden Grove paramedics had administered Narcan intravenously—to attempt to reverse, at least partially, the respiratory depression that follows the ingestion of narcotics.

Sick as she was, the treatment of choice was to encourage *more* vomiting, and she was given syrup of ipecac. Cinnamon vomited again and again—until physicians were assured that no more Dyazide or Darvocet remained in her stomach. She was also given magnesium citrate to hasten the evacuation of any colon contents. What the medical experts could not yet know was exactly how much medication was already in her system and liver.

There was still the possibility that Cinnamon might die, although that was the worst-case scenario. Her vitals had been nearly normal when she began the interview with Fred McLean, but she had deteriorated with shocking suddenness.

Officers back at the house had had the distasteful task of counting the undigested capsules left in the vomit in the doghouse. They estimated there were twenty-four to thirty-six intact capsules and evidence of undigested time-release granules. Had Cinnamon *not* become violently sick to her stomach, it was doubtful that she would still be alive. The combination of Darvocet and Dyazide was deadly.

An overdose of Dyazide alone can be fatal when it throws the electrolyte balance in the body out of synch because of excessive depletion of fluids. Deep muscle reflexes are compromised, heart rhythm is disturbed, and death may ensue. One of the other side effects of overdose is, fortunately, nausea and vomiting.

Darvocet-N is a pain reliever and a central nervous system depressant. In a study on deaths by overdosage, 20 percent of those deaths occurred within *the first hour after ingestion*. Breathing is repressed, convulsions may occur, and the lungs fill with fluid. The heart loses normal sinus rhythm and all body systems fail. Again, nausea and vomiting may occur.

Cinnamon Brown had swallowed enough pills to be dead several times over, but her body had rejected them. She had either been very serious about committing suicide or unaware of the toxicity of what she had taken.

If she regained consciousness, there were other dangers ahead. She might develop pneumonia from fluid in her lungs, and there was a strong possibility that her liver would be damaged from the assault of chemicals.

At five-thirty on that long, long Tuesday afternoon, Cinnamon regained consciousness, fighting for air. She was being given Muco-myst with a face mask. It was another torturous treatment, an un-pleasant-smelling vapor designed to clear her lungs of excess mucus. She would receive Mucomyst treatments for two days—until doctors were sure that her lungs were clear. It would take longer than that to ascertain if she had permanent liver damage.

Al Forgette returned to the hospital and spoke very briefly with Cinnamon. He left, saddened. Whatever he would learn from his young client, her story was a tragedy. He reported to her father that he would talk to her more when she was feeling better.

At eight-thirty that evening, Cinnamon was moved by Southland Ambulance to the University of California Medical Center in Orange. Under a written order from Judge James Franks, Cinnamon was booked in absentia into the Orange County Juvenile Hall. She would remain under twenty-four-hour guard. Her official incarceration began at fifteen minutes after midnight on March 20, 1985.

Cinnamon Darlene Brown, fourteen, had entered the justice system of the State of California, County of Orange. She slept fitfully through the night, unaware of what that would mean to her.

8

H E A D L I N E S in the *Orange County Register* and the *Los Angeles Times* trumpeted out the most salient aspect of Linda Brown's murder: "Girl, 14, Held in Fatal Shooting of Stepmother."

Neighbors along Ocean Breeze Drive were hounded by reporters anxious to unearth details, something more about Cinnamon Brown and the woman she was accused of murdering. The police press release had contained nothing but the stark facts. For the most part, the press came up empty, or in many cases, misinformed. Articles added two years to David Brown's age and mistakenly said Linda Brown had suffered two bullet wounds to the abdomen—not the chest. Cinnamon Brown was reported to be suffering "from an unspecified illness" in a hospital.

The few neighbors who had had any dealings with the Brown family were at a loss to explain what had happened, not because they had known the family well and been shocked at the tragedy, but because they really didn't know the Browns at all. One sixteen-year-old schoolmate of Patti's and Cinnamon's told reporters that Cinnamon was strange, a girl who had "invisible friends and stuff like that." The girl, feeling somehow important because she had even a slight connection to the Browns, said she thought Cinnamon had come to live with her father because she couldn't get along with her mother. She also pointed out that she thought it was "weird" that Cinnamon and Patti had dressed in costumes for Halloween and gone trick-or-treating. "Patti was a witch, and Cinnamon was an old man—I thought that was rather immature for somebody that age."

Pickings were slim indeed for reporters aching for sinister portents.

Another neighbor had found Cinnamon the only member of the family "who would talk to you. My husband and I both went over and talked to her just a couple of days ago after she got a new miniature dachshund. She was friendly."

No one knew Linda. She hadn't made friends with anyone. "The only time I'd see her would be when she was out mowing the lawn," one neighbor said.

Reporters realized they weren't going to get much more than that. The families who lived around the Browns had seen them coming and going, noticed that they had a new baby in the summer of 1984, and that was about it. They didn't mingle; they didn't talk over the fence, and they surely had not shared any family problems.

The avocado-green bungalow stood empty. Yellow police ribbons reading "Police Barrier—Do Not Cross" stretched across every access to the property, and even the photographer who dared to step over one and creep up to the house found nothing in his lens; the windows were all covered with opaque curtains.

The family was not there. With Linda dead and the terrible memories associated with this rented house, David and Patti and Krystal had gone to live temporarily with Arthur and Manuela Brown. His mother could help with the baby; Patti was useless—all she did was sob.

Soon, David would have to think about moving back into the house where Linda had died. His career was essential to so many. His office was there, and his clients depended on him. David would have to take care of business. Some things could not wait. He would also have to contact the insurance companies that had issued policies on Linda.

David Brown barely slept those first few days. He was a bad sleeper anyway. Anybody who knew him well was used to David's insomnia.

Cinnamon, who had regained consciousness, lay in her hospital bed, listless and pale. She watched her police guards come and go and spoke once in a while to the medical personnel who tended to her. Her medical file grew thicker.

Although Cinnamon had been told she was under arrest, and that she had been booked into Juvenile Hall—in absentia—she didn't seem to comprehend what that really meant. She slept a good deal of the time and spoke briefly with her attorney, Al Forgette.

Up in Garden Grove and Anaheim, detectives were working backward through Cinnamon Brown's life, trying to connect the girl herself with the crime she had admitted. In this painstaking, often tedious area of investigation, homicide detectives come to know both their victims and their killers far better than anyone else ever has. Because they cannot know *which* information will prove to be vital, they collect minor details and the most intimate secrets about people they had not heard of the day before. They will *never* know the victim—except through others' eyes and recall; they will know the killer better than they know their own wives.

The dead, even long buried, live in the minds of the detectives who work—if not to avenge—to *validate* their demises. The accused killers are paint-by-numbers to be filled in. Motive, means, opportunity—

those were the easiest factors to figure out. *Why* someone resorts to deliberately effecting the violent death of another human being goes far beyond mere motive.

Now Steve Sanders and Fred McLean began to fill in the portrait of Cinnamon Darlene Brown.

Who *was* she?

Sanders had the names of three girls who had attended school with Cinnamon at Loara High School in Anaheim: Jamie Williams, Lauri Ann Hicks, and Krista Taber.

He arrived at the school at two P.M. on March 19 and spoke with the vice principal. Sanders's questions did not surprise him; the news that Cinnamon Brown had shot her stepmother was all over school. "She just transferred over here from Bolsa Grande on March sixth," the vice principal said, checking his records. "And she's been absent half the time since then—so we hardly knew her. I do know there were no referrals to my office about her."

Sanders asked to see Cinnamon's locker but was told she had none. She hadn't been in school at Loara long enough to be assigned a locker. Sanders needed a sample of Cinnamon's handwriting—to compare with the suicide note she had clutched in her hand when Fred McLean found her in the doghouse. Her home economics teacher came up with a quiz, the only test Cinnamon had taken at Loara High School. It asked questions on the uses of fats in cooking; as in the suicide note, her answers to the quiz were printed—not written—in bold, fat letters.

Later, Fred McLean would obtain a search warrant for the Ocean Breeze Drive residence and the trailer and bring back many examples of Cinnamon's writing, along with a handful of red pens. The printing was all the same. Cinnamon *had* printed the suicide note.

At Sanders's request, Krista Taber was called to the vice principal's office, and she immediately said, "I know why you're here. The police were at our house at four this morning. I don't know why Cinny's father thought she'd be with me. I haven't seen her since last Monday—the eleventh. She hasn't been to school since."

Krista said that she had been Cinnamon's best friend since they were in kindergarten, and that Cinny had transferred into the freshman class to Loara High so they could be together.

"Have you noticed that Cinnamon's been upset lately?" Sanders asked.

Krista shook her head, baffled. "No, she's been like always. Maybe she was a little uneasy being at this new school, starting in the middle of the year after she was going to Bolsa Grande. But nothing major. She's been on restriction—but that's nothing new."

"For what?"

"For coming home late on Friday—on the eighth of March. We went to see a boy she knows in the tenth grade—Len*. She went steady with him last summer. We get out of school at two thirty-two P.M., and she's supposed to go right home. She rides her bike to school. Well, she called home at three-thirty to ask if she could stay a little longer. She talked to her stepmother, I think. Linda was upset with her and told her to get home right away. Cinnamon left right then."

"How often is Cinnamon on restriction?" Sanders asked.

Krista sighed and rolled her eyes. "Well, right now, she's on restriction for *three months*—for talking back. Every time she talks back, she gets another restriction. No visits. No phone calls. I don't know if she's lost her TV privileges or not."

"Would you say that Cinnamon is a troublemaker?" Sanders asked.

"*Cinnamon?*" Krista seemed incredulous, searching her mind for something rebellious her friend might have done. "Maybe a *little* bit—at school," she finally said. "Cinny pulls pranks, just silly stuff. But she really minds at home. She gets—got—along fine with her stepmother, and with Patti. The only thing that ever gets her in trouble at home is she argues with her dad about little things."

Krista was baffled by the rumors about her best friend. If anyone knew Cinnamon, she thought it was herself. They had missed each other a lot when Cinnamon started at Bolsa Grande High in September, but they had written letters, and Cinnamon had been allowed to call her on Thursday evenings, and visit—until she got grounded. "I guess I've seen her about six times in the last month. She never mentioned *any* problems. Just arguments with her dad."

"Do you know where she slept?"

"In Patti's room, I think. Sometimes, when she got mad at her dad, she'd go out to the trailer to sleep. And when she's on restriction on the weekends, her dad would lock her in the backyard where the trailer is. There's a Cyclone fence all around the yard."

"Okay. Has Cinnamon *ever* talked about using a gun to hurt anyone—or to kill anyone?"

Krista drew back. "No! Never anything at all. Cinnamon would be the last person to ever harm anyone. The *only* way she would ever have killed anyone would be because she was defending herself or something threatened her. I can't believe Cinnamon did it."

The other two girls mentioned as Cinnamon's friends were as stunned as Krista was. They had never seen a trace of violence or discontent in Cinnamon. They all denied that Cinnamon ever used drugs or drank alcohol. "She's not that type."

Sanders asked about the older man called Steely Dan whom Patti had mentioned. The girls exchanged looks.

"We know who you mean," Krista admitted. "Cinnamon and I used to stop by and see him once in a while when we had nothing else to do—but we had a pact that one of us would never go there alone."

"Why?"

"We didn't trust him. One time he bought a whole bunch of beer and tried to get us to drink it with him. We wouldn't—we thought he was going to take advantage of us."

"Did Cinnamon feel the same way?"

"Absolutely. We stopped going there after that. That was way last summer anyway."

Len Miller, Cinnamon's former steady boyfriend, agreed that she had gotten into trouble for visiting his house after school. "It wasn't even three-thirty yet, and she called for permission to stay longer—her and Krista and Lauri—but it was her father she talked to. I heard him shout, 'You get your butt home,' and she left right away."

Len described the most innocent of "going steady" arrangements during the summer of 1984. He had met Cinnamon at the pool at school, and they had dated only during the daytime—going to Disneyland or to the Dairy Queen. "We broke up two weeks before school started last fall. I've seen Cinnamon about five times since then."

The picture emerging was of a teenager who lived under suffocatingly strict rules. "We couldn't call her," Jamie said. "She wasn't allowed to give out her phone number, and we didn't know her address. We only saw her on weekends when she visited Krista."

If there were any hidden areas of Cinnamon Brown's life, her friends didn't know about them. They had never seen her get angry, they had never seen her on anything more than an afternoon date, and the only problems she ever seemed to have were with her father.

"She didn't think he liked her," Lauri said.

Fred McLean visited Brenda Sands, Cinnamon's mother, that same afternoon. Understandably, she was very distraught. He was patient as the small woman, who looked so much like Cinnamon, struggled to calm herself so she could answer his questions.

Brenda said she had divorced David Brown a decade earlier because she first suspected—and then verified—that he was engaging in extramarital affairs. Cinnamon was their only child, and over the years, she had sometimes lived with one of them, sometimes the other.

Brenda Sands had dark memories of her first marriage, which was brief and ended in a bitter divorce. Even now, she seemed to vacillate between recrimination and fear. She recounted for McLean an incident where she said David had threatened her with a gun. "It was just after I left him. One day, he came to my apartment to get his rifle that he'd left under the cedar chest, and my rings. He was going to give them to Lori, his new girlfriend."

Brenda told McLean she was afraid to let David have the gun and followed him out to his car where they struggled over it. "He was inside the car, and I was holding on to it. He got hold of the other end and revved the car so that I got knocked up against a telephone pole—and I let go of the gun."

She was still afraid of her former husband. "I think Linda was afraid of him too," Brenda mused softly.

That was news to McLean. Brown seemed such a Milquetoast kind of guy without a trace of violence in him. And he professed such grief over his murdered wife. So far, all the police investigators had heard was that Linda and David Brown were so in love that they had practically been joined at the hip.

"They were just here," Brenda commented, unaware that she had injected a new element into the probe.

"*Who* was just here?" McLean asked.

"David and Patti. David told me that Cinny had overdosed on some of his prescription drugs. He told me not to tell you detectives that Cinny was always a good, behaved girl."

McLean's antenna went up again on that one, and he was annoyed that David Brown had beaten him to Brenda, but he said only, "I want you to tell me the truth—and not let anyone influence you."

"I will. I'll tell you everything I know."

Brenda told McLean that she was surprised to find David and Patti taking the tragedy so quietly. Her ex-husband could be a very emotional man, but she had found him quite controlled.

That was another revelation for McLean. Even so, he figured Brenda didn't understand what profound shock could do to people. To check her perceptions, he questioned her. "Patti wasn't crying when she was here?" he asked. "David wasn't chain-smoking, hands shaking?"

Brenda shrugged. "David always chain-smokes," she answered. "But he wasn't shaking. He was pretty calm. I asked him where the gun had come from, but he said he didn't know. Then he said it must have been Linda's gun. Patti was positive it was Linda's gun."

McLean asked Brenda to evaluate her daughter's state of mind in recent months. She seemed mystified at Cinnamon's actions, including the attempted suicide.

"We're close," she said. "She shares her feelings with me, and secrets—things that worry her. I know Cinnamon believed that Linda was afraid of David."

"Has Cinnamon ever spoken to you about suicidal thoughts?"

Brenda looked up at McLean through disbelieving eyes and shook her head. "Oh, you know—how teenagers can be dramatic. If she was mad, or if her feelings were hurt, she might say, 'I wish I was dead!' She wasn't serious. I know she wasn't."

"When was the last time you saw Cinnamon?" McLean asked.

"Yesterday. Just yesterday. My grandmother, Ruby, and my aunt were here visiting from Salt Lake City. We went over to David's house so they could visit with Cinnamon. David even came out— after Cinnamon begged him to—and he acted glad to see my relatives. *I* know him, and I knew he was faking it, but they didn't. They thought he was just charming."

"And how was Cinnamon?" McLean interrupted.

"She was fine, but she wanted to come home with us and visit. I couldn't take her then because my car was just jam-packed with their suitcases. I told her I'd come over after I'd unpacked the car. But when I called later to tell her I'd be over, David answered the phone. He said everyone had settled down for the night, and he didn't want to wake her."

Brenda looked at her hands, shredding a piece of Kleenex. "That's what bothers me so much. If I'd just made room in the car, or if I'd gone over last night to get her, it wouldn't have happened. I keep going over that in my mind."

No matter how many times he approached the question of Cinnamon Brown's emotional stability, McLean got essentially the same answer. She was, her mother said, a completely normal teenager. The only time she was down was when she had a cold or suffered from menstrual cramps.

Why then would David Brown insist that Cinnamon was flaky, suicidal, out of control? He had said it. Patti Bailey had said it, and David had even asked Brenda to describe Cinnamon that way. Maybe he was trying to protect his daughter by building an image that would suggest a "not guilty by reason of insanity" motive. If a normal, rational girl committed murder, she might get a stiffer sentence than one who was clearly insane. That could explain David's scurrying ahead of the police to be sure that image was created.

Brenda struggled to recall what frame of mind Cinny had been in over the few days preceding the shooting. Cinnamon *had* suffered from menstrual cramps a few days before. Her mother was not aware that Cinny had ever before taken an overdose of drugs or medication.

"Would Cinnamon lie?" McLean asked.

"I suppose she was capable of stretching the truth, but I can always get the facts out of her."

"How about drugs—any problem with that?"

"Never. She always puts down drug users."

"How about school? How was she doing?"

"Well, she got poor grades last spring, so she was going to summer school—"

"Summer of 1984?"

Brenda nodded. "She got a B in U.S. Government and History, but she still only got a D in Math 8 in summer school. I know she cut some classes to go to the beach."

When McLean asked how Brenda felt about Cinnamon's living at her father's house, she repeated what David had explained to her. She really had no choice but to let Cinny live with her dad. "He said Cinny said she would run away if she was forced to come back and live with me."

Brenda told McLean that she and Cinnamon had had a doozy of a blowup, and she had been more than glad to have her daughter go live with her father for a while. But they weren't still angry. They talked all the time.

"Cinnamon wanted to go to school here in Anaheim—back at Loara. She didn't feel safe at Bolsa Grande, not after that man exposed himself to her and then there was a drive-by shooting near the school. She missed her friends at Loara too.

"Cinny never told me she thought of running away. Oh, she complained. Sometimes, she said she felt like a slave at David's house. She said she had to do so much housework, and Patti didn't do her share."

"That's kind of par for the course," McLean offered.

"No, something was wrong there. Cinnamon said that Linda and David weren't getting along. And she said one time she, David, and Patti came home and they overheard Linda and her twin brother—Alan—talking about getting rid of David."

"Getting rid of David?"

"That's what she said. 'Getting rid of David.' "

"What was David's reaction when he heard them say that? Did Cinnamon say?"

"No. I just know Cinnamon said the three of them backed out of the house and left without letting Linda and Alan know they'd heard their conversation."

"Why would Linda and her brother want to get rid of David?" McLean asked.

"I have no idea. Something was going on. Cinnamon told me that Linda was afraid David might leave her for Patti, and that David told her he might hire a detective to follow Linda."

McLean wondered if Cinnamon had an overactive imagination. It seemed unlikely that so much intrigue had been going on behind the bland green walls of the house on Ocean Breeze Drive. "Patti's only sixteen or seventeen, isn't she?" he asked Brenda.

"David likes them young. Linda was younger than that when he started with her," Brenda said with a touch of bitterness. "So was I."

Asked to recall what David Brown had told her of the events leading up to Linda's murder, Brenda repeated almost word for word the familiar story detectives had heard several times now. David had told his ex-wife that he was upset over an argument with Linda, went for a drive to calm his nerves, and returned home to find his wife shot.

"Patti told me Cinnamon shot at her and missed—because Patti ducked," Brenda said, her voice heavy with disbelief. "That just doesn't sound like Cinny. None of it does."

"Let me throw out some names," McLean said. "Tell me if you're familiar with them?"

"Okay."

"Oscar . . . Maynard . . . Aunt Bertha?"

Brenda half-smiled for the first time. "Maynard was Cinnamon's make-believe friend. Kids have them. She'd tease us, and say, 'Well, we will go tell Maynard.' There wasn't really a Maynard—she knew it, and we knew it. David made up Maynard a long time before Cinnamon was even born. There isn't any Aunt Bertha either—Cinnamon makes jokes about her."

"And Oscar?"

"That's new. I've never heard of Oscar."

Just before five on March 19, Fred McLean returned to the Garden Grove Police Department where Alan Bailey waited to talk to him.

The wiry man with straight reddish-blond hair and a number of missing teeth had obviously been crying. He introduced himself as "Linda's twin."

Alan said he had last seen Linda around the first of March and had spoken to her on the phone only four days ago. There had been nothing unusual, nothing in her voice that alarmed him. And they were close—as close as twins often are. He would have known.

But Alan said that there had been some change in Cinnamon's attitude toward Linda. "That included me. She used to call me 'favorite uncle'; now, suddenly, she can't stand me."

Alan Bailey felt that Cinnamon Brown had been allowed to live "more or less where she wanted. If she was in the trailer, it would have been because she asked to be there."

As for Cinnamon and Patti's relationship, they had never been close. "Patti has no sense of humor—none. She gets ticked when Cinnamon has fun and jokes with Oscar and Maynard, her imaginary friends. Patti can't see anything funny about it."

As far as Cinnamon's being unstable, that characterization surprised Alan Bailey. He hadn't heard about that or any suicide threats from her. He thought that *David* might have attempted suicide in the past—when he was being divorced from Brenda. And Alan recalled that Patti "was very disturbed for a while."

But not Cinnamon.

Alan felt that Patti had caused a lot of friction in the Brown marriage, although he didn't believe the story that David was interested in Patti. He knew that Patti had a teenage crush on David, and that she was jealous of Linda's position in the household and with David.

Alan Bailey viewed David Brown as a very dominant personality, and very protective about his immediate family and their privacy. David had often had go-rounds with Ethel Bailey, Linda and Patti's mother. Patti liked living with David and Linda, Alan thought, because she had more freedom and because she was able to have nice things.

"Did you know Patti was no longer in school—that David hired a tutor for her at home?" McLean asked.

"No . . . ," Alan said, surprised. "I didn't know that."

Alan said that David had started dating Linda when she was around fifteen, and that they had been married, divorced, remarried.

"Did they argue?"

"Oh, yeah. But she usually gave in. He always convinced her he was right. David can turn things around with his words."

"You don't like him?"

Alan Bailey shrugged. "We had a falling out over a paycheck. I took the matter to the Labor Board. I work landscape gardening now with my brother."

"Did you ever threaten David's life?"

"*What?*"

McLean's voice was casual, despite the questions he was throwing at Alan. "Maybe you and Linda were angry at David? Even kidding, did you ever say anything about getting rid of him?"

"No way." Linda's twin seemed genuinely surprised at the question. "I don't kid like that."

McLean switched gears. "Would you have thought your sister and David were happily married?"

"Yeah . . . I think so. Especially since the baby. David is so proud of that baby. They've both seemed happy since Krystal was born."

So far, no one, beyond her father and Patti Bailey, had described Cinnamon as anything but a normal, overdisciplined, sometimes rebellious teenager. If there was some pathology working in Cinnamon Brown, she had kept it well hidden from most of the people she was close to.

Steve Sanders moved on to Bolsa Grande High School in Garden Grove, hoping he might find some information there that would either confirm or deny what he and McLean had been told about Cinnamon. This wasn't the way a homicide investigation was supposed to evolve. Almost always, background checks on the suspect elicited witnesses who firmed up the charges—not the other way around.

Cinnamon and Patti had both attended Bolsa Grande High from September of 1984 until March 6—two weeks before the murder. They were well-known at Bolsa Grande. The school counselor, Bill Reynolds, was as stunned as everyone else about Linda Brown's murder. He had never had occasion to meet Linda—or David, for that matter. Cinnamon and Patti had occasionally come to his office to have a "typical sibling problem" settled, but never anything major, and they seemed to him to get along very well. Even though Patti was actually Cinnamon's step-aunt, they interacted more like sisters. Cinnamon was the spunky one, the mischievous one—and Patti was the quiet one.

Bolsa Grande principal Don Wise *had* talked to Linda Brown and Patti and Cinnamon about two weeks before they withdrew from school. It was to have been a family conference, but David Brown had said he was too busy to come in.

Cinnamon and Patti said they had both had radios stolen from their lockers, that some students had weapons in the classroom, that some of their teachers did not know how to teach, and that they allowed dope dealing in the classroom. Wise perceived at once that the girls wanted to transfer from Bolsa Grande, and that they were simply making up outrageous complaints to effect their withdrawal.

In retrospect, the principal felt that Linda, Cinnamon, and Patti got along well with each other, and he had seen no hostility at all among them. Linda had brought her baby with her to the conference. If anything, it seemed to Wise that it was the *father* who was blowing incidents all out of proportion, and that David Brown seemed to be the catalyst in the group—even though he was not physically present at the conference.

Two weeks later, David Brown *did* appear—to remove Cinnamon and Patti from Bolsa Grande High School. School officials recalled a short, florid man who seemed extremely hostile. Brown had shouted, "*This one* [pointing to Patti] is going to Nebraska!" and "*That one* [indicating Cinnamon] is going to Loara High School!" With much huffing and puffing, David Brown had unceremoniously withdrawn his two charges from Bolsa Grande on March 6, 1985, leaving behind school personnel puzzled by his anger.

The girls themselves had been compliant and easy to get along with, and until the conference with Linda two weeks earlier, there was no reason to think they were unhappy in school. Sanders found that they both had good attendance records, and that Cinnamon had only two minor incidents that had brought her to the vice principal's office: she had "disrupted the class" with her antics on Halloween, and she had been truant from two class periods.

Sanders talked to several of Cinnamon's teachers, and he got reviews as mixed as the teachers' own personalities. Cinnamon's food-services teacher found her "a sweet kid, nonaggressive, nondisruptive, well liked, and never foulmouthed. . . . We had a blind girl transfer in, and Cinnamon went out of her way to help her."

Cinnamon's math teacher had negative views. "Everyone knows they cannot be excused from my fourth-period class to go to the rest room. Cinnamon insisted she had to go, and she left. I sent her to the office. The next day, she brought a note from home saying she had weak kidneys and had to be excused whenever she asked. I think she did it only to get attention."

Sanders frowned to himself. Hardly the stuff of vicious killers.

But one teacher *had* noticed a distinct change in Cinnamon Brown's behavior *midway* through the year. Cinnamon had been a strong B student—until after the Christmas holidays. Something or some*one* in her life had changed then, because Cinnamon's work and attitude disintegrated. "She no longer paid attention in class, she talked, she wrote notes. I had to change her seating arrangements. She was even worse in February. I have no idea why she changed so drastically. I wondered what might have happened at home during the Christmas break to make her so different in class."

Even so, this teacher commented on how well Cinnamon got along with her peers. As for insolence or bad language, the teacher said with a smile, "The only foul word I ever heard Cinnamon Brown say was *sheep dip*—which isn't exactly profanity."

The worst thing any teacher could say about Cinnamon Brown was that she was sometimes full of mischief, enjoyed attention, and was easily distracted. She was a chatterbox, and one teacher said Cinnamon's constant banter "drove me crazy." She laughed as she said it, recalling that she had mentioned Cinnamon's volubility once to Patti, who happened to be the teacher's student aid.

"I *know*," Patti agreed. "Me too! She's like that a lot."

Patti Bailey was quieter, shyer. Where Cinnamon was quick, Patti was slow and seldom smiled. She confided to one teacher that her real father was in a hospital somewhere but that no one would tell her where. Later, she came in with an address in Oregon, and she asked the teacher to help her write a letter to him. "I corrected her spelling and punctuation, but I didn't pry into Patti's reasons for writing. I don't know if she even mailed the letter."

Neither Patti nor Cinnamon ever talked about their home life in school.

Detectives found that extended family relationships seemed more strained. Ethel Bailey, Linda's mother, and Alan Bailey, her twin, thought David was overbearing and controlling. Mary Bailey, one of Linda's sisters-in-law, didn't like him, and all of the Baileys thought Patti had a crush on David. Brenda Sands didn't trust her ex-husband and thought Linda had been afraid of him—just as she once was. David thought the Baileys and Brenda were just jealous because he was far wealthier than they were.

Who knew? And where did Cinnamon fit in?

9

FRED MCLEAN interviewed David Brown for the second time on March 20, twenty-four hours after the shooting. He noted that Brown was nervous and appeared to have slept little.

David reconstructed once more the evening before the murder, with only minor changes for the most part. His parents had visited all day, and they had played board games. "Both Linda and Cinnamon played. Linda quit to get ready for bed. Cinnamon quit for some reason."

The argument *had* been about whether or not to let Krystal cry. Linda said it was sometimes good to let a baby cry, and David disagreed. Arthur Brown had settled it by declaring flatly that Linda was right.

Now Krystal cried all the time.

David remembered *exactly* the sequence of his drive to the beach. To the letter: the kind of pie, the brand of soft drink. When he returned home and opened the front door with his key, he said he found Patti and the baby just inside the doorway. Patti was stuttering, repeating that something was wrong, that Cinnamon had tried to kill her. "When I took the baby and started to go into my bedroom, Patti grabbed me and said, *'Don't!'*"

McLean's clear blue eyes blinked. Patti had said that she had *asked* David to check the master bedroom, but *David* had refused because he was afraid. Now, David described his response to danger in a more macho, take-charge way—completely opposite to Patti's version.

Even so, David said he hadn't gone farther than the bedroom door, where he saw his wife lying in "an unnatural position" and backed away.

"Did you kill your wife?" McLean said suddenly.

". . . No. No, of course not."

"Do you think Patti Bailey did?"

"No . . . I don't. I don't even know why Cinnamon did."

David leaned forward. "You know, Cinny took an overdose of aspirin—about two weeks ago. I called her mother about it."

"Does—*did*—Linda use any drugs, any prescriptions?"

"No—only some suppositories that Dr. Ogden prescribed."

McLean asked Brown about his business, how much his wife had been involved in it, about any insurance she might have had. David said that Linda was the one person who knew *everything* about his business. He had attempted to train Alan Bailey in some facets of Data Recovery, but he had fired him because he was unreliable.

"He once threatened my life." David threw the remark away almost casually. "There was a witness—Sam, who owns the coin shop on Brookhurst and Ball, heard him say it."

David seemed to have little affection for Linda and Patti's family. He said he had never been close to any of the Baileys—only to his deceased wife and her little sister.

As for any insurance, David struggled to remember. Yes, he thought he once had about a million-dollar policy on Linda, but he had dropped it sometime earlier. "About a month ago, I got a new— small—policy on her."

Asked why he had taken Patti out of school, David said she had been having trouble with the special ed program at Bolsa Grande, and that he felt she would do better with tutoring at home. "I've made arrangements for it."

McLean didn't ask David Brown why he had told school authorities that Patti was moving to Nebraska.

David Brown was agitated about newspaper reports of his wife's murder. One reporter had said that there had been people coming and going at the Brown residence at all times of the day and night, hinting that it was "suspicious activity." That was not true, David said; the activity mentioned occurred in the house across the street, and he felt the faulty reporting reflected badly on him. (Indeed, the paper would later print a retraction of this facet of the case.)

Fred McLean wanted to talk once again to Patti Bailey, but David Brown asked him not to—he was concerned that Patti was too upset, that her grief was deepening and he didn't want her bothered. McLean told Brown that Patti *had* to be questioned, and that he would be as gentle and tactful as he could. Brown had finally, reluctantly, backed off.

Patti seemed a little tired—not almost cheerful as Brenda Sands had described, but not devastated either. She answered McLean's questions without tears. Her recounting, like David's, was essentially the same as she had given just after the shooting. She now recalled that she had found the back door unlocked when David sent her outside to look for Cinnamon.

That was new—and would surely mean that David had left the house for his drive without setting the alarm.

Patti offered further information that Cinnamon was growing hostile to the family. "She was jealous of Krystal. She was never close to the baby, and she only called her 'little sister' because David wanted her to."

Patti also said that Cinnamon had tried to overdose on aspirin after she had argued with Brenda Sands. "Then she moved out to the trailer because she got in an argument with Linda and me."

McLean shot the question out at Patti Bailey too: "Did you kill your sister?"

"No . . . I didn't."

Patti didn't even blink.

Al Forgette, Cinnamon's attorney, wanted to get a psychiatric evaluation of his client as soon as possible. He arranged for Dr. Seawright Anderson to interview Cinnamon on March 20. Anderson, a 1950 Harvard graduate and a practicing psychiatrist since 1952, had testified in some five hundred cases, usually as a defense witness.

Seawright Anderson saw Cinnamon Brown for the first time as she lay in her hospital bed at the University of California Medical Center in Orange. She was doing much better than she had been, but was being carefully monitored.

Dr. Anderson wanted to establish Cinnamon's general mental status to see if she was capable of testifying in her own behalf in any court action to come. He found the teenager coherent and relevant, quite forthcoming in her recounting of the night of the shooting. "Her account was spontaneous and set off on a long narrative on what she did," Dr. Anderson would testify later. "When she talked about that night, she really went on."

Her stepmother had forced her to live outside in the trailer, she told the psychiatrist. It had made her feel bad, but she told people she didn't mind—that it would better for her new puppy for them to live together out there.

Still, it *had* mattered to her, she said, but she had kept her feelings to herself.

When she described the crime itself to Dr. Anderson, Cinnamon seemed unable to respond to questions that required her to separate her feelings from the scenario she recited. "Breaking down the interview—when you break it down bit by bit and ask her why she did it—what she *thought*—she didn't know."

Cinnamon denied that she wanted to kill Linda, a bizarre response considering that she admitted shooting her twice.

When asked if she thought she needed to be in a mental hospital, Cinnamon shook her head. No, she did not. Her biggest concern was whether or not her father would still love her. She feared that he would no longer want her around him because she had shot Linda.

She could not bear to lose her daddy.

Dr. Anderson searched for a diagnosis. Cinnamon Brown did not fit easily into any of the standard classifications of the *Diagnostic and Statistical Manual*. She was too oriented to be psychotic, and she seemed too sincerely contrite and sad to be an antisocial personality. If she was truly a human being without any conscience at all, she was a superlative actress.

As she gave her life's history—albeit a short history over only fourteen years of life—Dr. Anderson asked Cinnamon if she could remember ever being sad for two weeks or more. She recalled that her dog had died when she was nine. Looking back, she thought she probably *had* cried for more than two weeks. It seemed her tears would never stop, and she could never love another dog.

That recounting might allow Cinnamon to be wedged—if not cleanly fitted—into a diagnostic slot. Five years since the first lengthy depression. And now—another. Dr. Anderson found Cinnamon to be in the grip of a "major clinical depression," a *recurrent* major depression—another episode quite like the one she had suffered when she was nine.

After speaking with Cinnamon for two hours, and taking other factors into account, Dr. Anderson decided that she was so depressed that she did not know the nature or the quality of the act of murder she had committed. That is, under the M'Naughton rule, Cinnamon had not known the difference between right and wrong at the time of the murder.

It was a diagnosis that a defense attorney could run with.

Al Forgette cared about the girl in the hospital bed, and a diagnosis that would allow him to invoke M'Naughton would probably ensure that Cinnamon Brown would go into a mental hospital—and not to prison.

Still, Forgette had an uneasy feeling that his case was incomplete. There were things he didn't know. With absolutely nothing but instinct to go on, the defense lawyer believed that there was someone besides Cinnamon involved in Linda Brown's murder. He didn't know who, and he didn't know why—but there it was.

And it bothered him.

Forgette talked with David Brown, pointing out that it was Cinnamon—and only Cinnamon—that he represented. "For instance, I do not represent you, Mr. Brown. If our investigation should indicate to us that there was someone else involved—*even you*—we would go after that person—*even you.*"

Al Forgette, who looked all-Irish although his name is French, sat at his desk with his football shoulders straining at his suit jacket, his Knute Rockne face solemn as he gazed unflinchingly at David Brown. He explained that detectives always look closely at all members of a murder victim's family. Forgette had discussed the case with Fred McLean; he had a good grasp of the facts as they had come forth the night of the murder.

"It's conceivable that *you* might be charged with murder, Mr. Brown. If that were to happen, I would still be representing your daughter and only your daughter. Is that clear to you? Would you still want to retain me as Cinnamon's attorney?"

David Brown shifted nervously in his chair and seemed concerned, even stunned, to hear that he might be considered a suspect. He lit a cigarette and pondered Forgette's words.

Then Brown's tension eased. As he absorbed the unsettling news, he was still adamant that he would protect Cinnamon. He agreed totally with Forgette. No matter how the cards fell, David Brown was prepared to continue to retain Forgette as Cinnamon's attorney.

Cinnamon had looked forward to being home with everyone within a week or two and was hopeful at a detention hearing on March 26 that the judge would let her out of "jail." But Juvenile Court judge Betty L. Lamoreaux ordered that she be returned to Juvenile Hall. For the first time, perhaps, Cinnamon Brown realized that she might not be going home soon.

It mattered little to her that she could not be tried as an adult because she was under sixteen. All that mattered was that she was alone in a world she had never even imagined.

David was a frequent visitor for his daughter—first in the hospital and then in Juvenile Hall where she was transferred when she was fully recovered from the effects of her suicide attempt. Her daddy had not deserted her. Cinnamon depended on him and on his advice. She listened raptly to David's voice and searched his face to see how he was bearing up under the strain.

And at some time while Cinnamon Brown moved through her days in the strange new world she had been plunged into, her mind closed over. She no longer talked about the reasons for the murder of her stepmother, or about how it had taken place.

When Dr. Seawright Anderson examined Cinnamon for the second time in July of 1985, he found that his patient did not recognize him; he might have been a complete stranger. Moreover, she had completely blocked all memory of the murder.

"She knew it all the first time, and the second time she didn't even remember *me*. All she would say was, 'If they said I killed Linda, I want to be in a mental hospital. If I'm convicted, I'd go crazy. If I didn't do it, I want to go home with my father and my sister.' "

Dr. Anderson now had a different diagnosis for Cinnamon Brown. He found her to be suffering from amnesia—psychogenic amnesia, originating in the *mind*, rather than due to physical trauma—and dissociative disorder, along with recurrent depression.

Cinnamon just didn't remember any longer, she said. She only knew that she wanted desperately to go home again.

During the spring and summer of 1985, "home" as Cinnamon Brown remembered it had begun to change. With Linda gone, things were not the same—nor would they ever be. Neither David nor Patti had realized how much Linda had done to make the place home. Without her, things began to fall apart.

The week that followed Linda Bailey Brown's death had passed in a dull blur. Patti Bailey went to her sister's funeral, "but I still couldn't believe she was dead. If I was riding in a car, it still seemed as if she was there."

Through it all Krystal wailed steadily. She was too young to know that her mother was dead. But old enough to sense some profound change around her. When Krystal cried, Patti sobbed. She seemed utterly bereft. At the same time she refused to accept that Linda was dead, she knew down deep that her sister was gone. David told people that no one seemed able to help Patti cope with her loss. Ethel Bailey was so caught up in her own grief that she had no emotion left for Patti. Alan, Linda's twin, was inconsolable.

Both David and Patti were spooked. They heard sounds in the night, strange crying and wailing they could not explain rationally. They had been afraid at first to go back to the house where Linda was shot. It was as if Linda were still somewhere in the house.

Patti and David prevailed upon friends and relatives to move back into the house with them so that they would not have to be alone with their imaginings. One of the friends who had come in and out of Linda and David's life was a pretty twenty-one-year-old woman named Denise Summers*, who lived in Riverside. Denise was originally a friend of Alan Bailey's, and through him, she had met and become close to Linda and David Brown when they were living in Yucca Valley, and subsequently, when they moved to Brea.

"David told me about this company he was going to form, and that I could have a job," Denise recalled. "The commute for me would have been a long way—so I moved in with David and Linda in Brea."

It was a full house in 1983. During that period, Patti and Cinnamon both lived there too, plus Ethel Bailey *and* Alan. Denise lived with the Browns and the Baileys until three months before they moved into the house on Ocean Breeze Drive. Ethel had not lasted as long.

"I would say that Linda was my best friend—but that I was good friends with Patti and Cinnamon," Denise explained. "After they all moved to Garden Grove, I kept in touch with them—mostly by phone."

During the summer of 1984, when Linda was pregnant with Krystal, she had confided to Denise that she suspected that her sixteen-year-old sister, Patti, and her husband, David, "had an affair going." When Denise asked her why on earth she would think such a thing, Linda said that David was devoting more of his time and attention to Patti—and very little to his pregnant wife.

At one point, Linda told her friend she had blown up and told David that she wanted him to take Patti back home to Riverside and leave her there. He and Patti left the house on Ocean Breeze with suitcases full of Patti's things. But when David reached Riverside, he called Linda and said, "I'm not coming back without her. That's the way it's going to be."

Denise Summers recalled that Linda tried, in vain, to get Patti out of her home and her marriage. As always, David prevailed. Her friend knew that Linda had always deferred to him, that he won every argument. Linda told Denise she had let him bring Patti home, but she had screwed up her courage and confronted him, asking him if there was anything "funny" going on between him and her sixteen-year-old sister.

"David finally admitted to Linda that Patti had a crush on him," Denise said. "He said he didn't want to mention it—that it wasn't important. But Patti made a pass at him. He said he just told her to back off, that nothing happened, that she was a kid."

Linda told Denise that she had had to let it drop. She wanted to believe David. But she had been very hurt—to think that David would choose Patti over her when it came to either-or. Even if nothing had been going on, she felt diminished.

This was, Denise Summers said, the beginning of a distinct change in Linda Brown. Linda, who had always been warm and friendly, became distant. It was as if she was disillusioned—no *distrustful*—even with Denise. Linda's alienation grew more intense after the Christmas holidays. Their phone conversations seemed cold and stilted.

"Part of the problem might have been that David was listening in," Denise told police. "They had these speakerphones all over the house, so every conversation was heard by anybody nearby. David had a lot of conference calls in his business."

Denise seemed as dumbfounded as everyone else that it had apparently been Cinnamon who pulled the trigger of the gun that killed Linda. She had seen the family up close, *lived* with all of them, and she had never noticed the slightest problem between Linda and Cinnamon.

The last time Denise had seen the Browns before the tragedy was after Linda's baby shower in November 1984. "Everything seemed to be okay." The last time Denise *talked* to anyone in the Brown household had been at the end of February 1985. "David called me—just to see how I was. It was a short conversation because he was on his way somewhere."

Denise Summers talked to Patti Bailey on the phone after the shooting. She told Sgt. John Woods what Patti had told her about the night of March 18–19. The story was almost identical to the versions the investigators had heard earlier—except Patti had told Denise that she was hiding in her bedroom when David Brown came home and was not waiting for him in the front hallway. She said she had refused to come out, arguing, "There's shooting out there!"

"She said David asked her, 'Who?' and she said she didn't know, and then he just *ordered* her to come out, and she said for him to look around first. She said that David looked into the bedroom and saw Linda *hanging* over the bed. . . .

"Then David came into the room and caught her on the phone with me, and she couldn't talk anymore."

Compared to the other versions of the night of the shooting, it was still another variation. No one had said that Linda's body had been *hanging* over the bed; in fact, she had been found lying as if asleep—with one arm flung up. And David had always described Patti, with the baby in her arms, waiting for him in the front hall when he arrived home.

Probably the slight variations meant nothing.

Denise Summers had returned to the house on Ocean Breeze Drive with the family after the funeral on Friday, March 22. She sat with David and Patti in the master bedroom, and they discussed having her help clean up the house and assist them in moving out the things that had to go. They all agreed that it would be too painful to see some of Linda's things every day.

"Patti pointed to a robe and asked David what he wanted done with it. It was David's robe—but Patti said Linda had been wearing it during the evening she was shot. I picked it up real carefully because I expected it to have bullet holes and blood on it—but it was clean. I guess she only wore it before she went to bed. David said he didn't want to talk about it. He couldn't stay there that night either. We all went over to his parents' house in Carson. He said he was going home later that night, but he didn't.

"I talked to him the next day, and he said he was definitely moving back home. I told him to call me if he needed anything."

David Brown and his baby girl did move back into the house on Ocean Breeze Drive, and Patti came along to care for Krystal. Manuela Brown moved in temporarily to help.

David couldn't sleep on the bed where he had made love to his wife the night she died. Instead, he dragged a mattress onto the floor of his office and tried to sleep there. Manuela slept on the couch in the living room.

There were reminders of Linda everywhere. A beautiful stained-glass hanging of a woman, with Leo astrology symbols for Linda, still rested against the wall in Krystal's nursery. Nobody to hang it up now. The teddy-bear calendars in the kitchen had notations of events-to-be, written in Linda's hand. God, there were even leftovers in the refrigerator that Linda had carefully stored in Tupperware containers, but it had been five days and a dusting of green mold covered the food. The little plants she had coaxed to root were all over the kitchen, drying out now.

The fragrance of L'Air du Temps, Linda's favorite perfume—which David had given her in huge decorative decanters—seemed to drift in the air.

Dust gathered, laundry piled up, and it was all Manuela and Patti could do to keep halfway caught up. It didn't help that Patti had always suspected that Arthur and Manuela Brown didn't like her and were always asking David why she lived with David and Linda. David wasn't well enough to do much physically to help his mother and Patti; all his ailments had flared up with the terrible stress he was living under.

The dogs that Cinny loved so much became infested with fleas and other parasites in the muggy, shady pen out behind the garage—the pen she had shared with them for a night. Mary Bailey recalls that the fleas were so bad that, one by one, the animals died, neglected.

And in the night, when the shrubs and the big ivy-shrouded maple tree blocked out even the moon, David and Patti still heard someone crying.

They couldn't wait to move out; there were too many memories and too many tears here.

David hadn't been back in his house twenty-four hours before he called Denise Summers for help. "He called about one-thirty A.M. on Sunday and he told me the baby was crying and Patti was crying."

Denise knew that David Brown was never a man to come out directly and ask for anything. He had a way of letting his needs be known and making her feel guilty if she did not respond with help. She knew he wanted her to drive over to Garden Grove and help with the baby.

"But I'd just taken a tranquilizer—what with the funeral and everything being so rough—and I was afraid to drive. Sunday morning, he called again and kind of talked around the subject. He wanted me to come and help them. He told me I could use Linda's car."

It was David's way of doing things, she knew. He offered rewards for requests he never truly voiced.

Denise told him she couldn't come that day, but promised to come over to spend the night with them Monday after she got off work. She kept her promise, arriving around eight-thirty.

She saw a mattress on the floor of David's office. The house had an air of thinly muffled anxiety—as if something awful were about to happen; the occupants all seemed to be camping out, prepared to escape if need be.

David Brown was too frightened, it seemed, to sleep alone. He suggested that he and Patti and Denise sleep together on one of the mattresses. He would sleep between the two girls. "I told him I didn't like that arrangement," Denise said. "We ended up with Patti sleeping in the middle—next to David."

Even though David Brown was a bereaved widower, there was still a sexual energy about him. He said things that could be taken two ways. He could suggest sleeping with two women without thinking it at all unusual. His comforters were almost exclusively female, just as his household was. Apparently he had no male friends.

Denise spent several nights with David, Patti, Manuela, and Krystal. On one evening, Patti's friend Betsy Stubbs* visited from Brea. David and Denise drove Betsy home at the end of the evening while Patti stayed with Krystal. "On the way back, I came right out and told David I thought that Patti was in love with him," Denise said. "He said he didn't want to hear that.

"When we got home, Patti started asking David why we were gone so long. She always gave him the third degree when he was with me. She never said she was jealous—but there was a tone in her voice . . . you could just feel that she was."

Denise told Sergeant Woods that she actually began to be *afraid* of Patti Bailey. Maybe it was just the general feeling in the house—fear, suspicion, the strange sounds in the night—but Patti spooked Denise, and she moved back home long before she had planned to. There was a tone in Patti's voice that made Denise wonder how far Patti might go to assure that she could stay with David Brown.

"I think Patti did it. I think Patti shot Linda," Denise Summers blurted to John Woods.

Woods stared at Denise. *"Why?"*

"Cinnamon is not capable of doing that. She got along with Linda; she looked upon Linda as a mother figure. Patti and Linda always had problems."

Denise went further. She said that Patti had begun to replace Linda—totally. "Linda's chair is her chair now. Patti's wearing Linda's clothes."

Detectives wondered at what point a teenage crush could metamorphose into possessive jealousy and even murder. Patti Bailey seemed so mild, and so sincerely grief stricken at the death of her sister. Besides that, the investigators had nothing to go on. It was *Cinnamon* who had confessed. It was Cinnamon who had swallowed an overdose, and it was Cinnamon's handwriting on the suicide note that admitted the shooting.

Despite gossip and assumptions made by people who knew the family, there was no way to make a case against Patti Bailey.

While Cinnamon was surrounded by strangers, she was essentially alone. She talked to the medical personnel and to Al Forgette and to her police guards—but she spoke less and less. Her world had become very small. Everything she had counted on before had vanished. She had become more of a number than a human: "Garden Grove Police Department case 85-11342, Penal Code 187."

David Brown could not bear to be alone. He seemed to need a crowd around him twenty-four hours a day, or to be doing something all the time. He resented the police and district attorney's investigators poking into his life, and so he continued to contact anyone he could think of that the probers might seek out. He apparently needed to assess what his family, friends, and associates might say to detectives; if their recall seemed unfortunate to him, he either suggested, cajoled, or downright ordered a new version. Since most of the people in his world either admired or feared him, David was able to plug a number of worrisome leaks.

It was not as if he had anything to hide, really; it was just that he had always detested any invasion of his privacy. He hadn't even allowed Linda to talk to her family about their personal business, he had mightily resented school officials who wanted to draw him into discussions about Cinny and Patti, and he most certainly did not want Garden Grove and Orange County snoops asking so many questions. He had suffered a tragedy, he was not a well man, and they wouldn't even let him grieve in private.

There had been enough publicity right after the shooting to make privacy almost impossible. While David had always enjoyed being the center of attention in certain circles and reveled in his position of a much sought-after data-retrieval expert, he did not relish being recognized on the streets of Orange County.

David didn't mind, however, being greeted at his bank—Home Savings of America, Branch #86, in Garden Grove. He was a welcome customer, keeping checking, savings, and a limited checking/savings accounts there. His checking account was always at least $100,000, far more than the bank's average depositors.

Ellen Gilbert*, eighteen, had come to know the Browns through their many transactions at her teller's window. Ellen found David Brown's manner "charming," but privately, she thought he seemed too old to be married to Linda. Linda always came in with her husband when they banked, and Ellen grew to enjoy talking to the pregnant blond woman. She felt a little sorry for Linda though, because she seemed to have no friends or social life outside her immediate family. Linda talked with Ellen as if she were starved for friendship.

Linda's world seemed narrow to the young bank teller. All she did was follow her husband around.

Although the Browns maintained three accounts at the bank, almost all their transactions were done with cash. Once, when Ellen asked David what his business was, he explained that he recovered data from damaged computers for large firms and for the United States government, confiding, "I'm the only one in America who can provide this service."

In fact, David said his business was doing so well that he needed more help. "You should quit Home Savings and come to work for me," he offered.

She demurred.

From time to time, other family members came in with the Browns in the almost daily banking: Alan Bailey and Patti Bailey and sometimes an older couple that Ellen thought were David's parents.

After Krystal was born in July 1984, Ellen left her post at the bank for a moment to see the new arrival in her car bed in David's van. Linda seemed very happy, and the marriage stronger than ever.

When the bank manager announced the tragedy to all employees on March 19, Ellen Gilbert was shocked speechless. She cried for her friend who had seemed to live such a dull, subservient life, who only came alive with her delight at her new baby. She had been so happy to have Krystal, and so proud. Now, she would never have a chance to break free and be young. Never have a chance to see her baby grow up.

Ellen was surprised to see David himself come into the bank that very day. He explained that the automatic teller machine wasn't working and that he needed cash to pay for Linda's funeral services. He returned later to make another withdrawal. "He looked like he was carved of stone," Ellen remembered. "There were tears in his eyes though."

Ellen offered to take care of Krystal during the funeral services, but then her own grandmother died suddenly that same day, and she had to renege. She sent a sympathy card to the Brown family.

As spring gave way to summer, David was in the Home Savings bank often. He always asked for Ellen and waited until she was free to handle his banking.

Despite his personal tragedy, his financial picture grew brighter than ever. David Brown deposited several insurance checks, and one was for a *large* amount, somewhere well over $200,000—closer to $350,000.

Curious that Linda Brown, a housewife, had been insured for so much, Ellen asked David why that should be. David answered that Linda had known all about his data recovery business, and she had been essential to it. The insurance was to help him rebuild his staff. He would have to find several people to replace Linda. Even so, he would never be able to find anyone as brilliant.

Ellen had always found Linda sweet—and friendly. But she would never have called her "brilliant" or pictured her as the indispensable person in a sophisticated computer firm.

David was seldom alone when he came into the bank. Patti Bailey was usually with him—just as Linda had once followed quietly behind him. Patti cashed checks each week, checks signed by David in amounts ranging from $300 to $500.

Her younger sister resembled the dead woman so much it was spooky. Moreover, Ellen noticed that Patti was wearing clothes and jewelry that she had once seen on Linda. Patti carried Linda's baby as if it were *her* baby.

It was almost as if Linda had never existed at all.

Despite Patti's omnipresence, the bank teller was startled to realize that David Brown's attitude toward her was changing. He began to speak to Ellen in a more familiar—somehow intimate—manner. Incredulous, Ellen realized that the tubby little man who looked old enough to be her father was "coming on" to her. He even asked her to come to his home at night and visit—and she quickly refused.

She was vastly relieved when Brown moved from Garden Grove and seldom visited her bank branch anymore. Nevertheless, she ducked out of sight every time he *did* come in, and she asked other tellers to handle his cash transactions.

Much of the private speculation about David Brown would not reach the ears of either the Garden Grove police or the Orange County District Attorney's Office for a long time. David Brown frightened some people, and he convinced others that they were only imagining demons where there were none. All in all, there was a reluctance to become involved in his life.

David and Patti and the baby packed up and left Ocean Breeze Drive. David's pattern of living only a short time in one spot continued. The first move was to a rental house at 2041 Breckenridge in Orange. It sat on a one-block street, a hundred yards from the freeway, a nice little house, shrouded by shrubs and trees just as David's last house had been. They would not live there long.

10

E V E N   T H O U G H the very detectives who were gathering evidence and witnesses against Cinnamon Brown all felt "hinky" about the case—nagged by a chill presentiment that they were hunting down a rabbit when a coyote lurked nearby—they knew their jobs were never meant to be ruled by feelings.

They had virtually nothing tangible that might lead them anywhere *but* to Cinnamon Brown as the killer of Linda Marie Brown.

There was one element, however, that seemed curious. Antimony is the primer used in the cartridge of a bullet. When a gun is fired, the nitrocellulose that creates the accompanying gases *also* releases the component of the primer; 90 to 100 percent of it exits the muzzle. Linda Brown, for instance, had significant deposits of antimony on her hands. That was to be expected; she took the full blasts from the muzzle of the gun. A small percentage of antimony may escape through the mechanical openings of the gun. If it does, it is deposited on the shooter's hands.

There are two tests criminalists use to determine the presence of antimony, barium, and lead, both with names so esoteric that they boggle the layman's mind: "atomic absorption test" and the "scanning electron microscopy examination" (SCMEDX). To do a proper test for antimony, two tests must be done in sequence—tape lifts first, and then swabbing. Sgt. John Woods and Crime Scene Investigator Bill Morrissey had correctly performed the tests on the living subjects—David Brown, Patti Bailey, and Cinnamon Brown. GSR tests *had* proved positive for the presence of antimony (albeit at low levels) on both David Brown and Patti Bailey, and *negative* on Cinnamon.

But any criminalist who knew his stuff could explain that away in a courtroom. Cinnamon had lain all night in vomit and urine; any gunshot residue on her hands would have been obliterated. Patti didn't *remember* handling the gun that Cinnamon held out to her for instructions, but she might have forgotten touching it in the shock of the aftermath. Beyond that, other activities—even smoking a cigarette—can leave traces of antimony.

It was not enough to outweigh a detailed confession. And Cinnamon had confessed to Fred McLean and Pam French. Indeed, there was even a *written* confession, her suicide note, quite literally tied up with a ribbon bow.

Orange County deputy district attorney Mike Maguire took over the prosecution of Cinnamon Brown—with Jay Newell assisting as his investigator. For Newell, this would be only one case among many; he would do his usual thorough job of investigation, then move on to the next homicide.

Cinnamon's trial was to be in Central Court—Orange County's courthouse in Santa Ana. Building 30 in the new complex on Flower and Civic Center Drive is a mini-skyscraper of a courthouse. Palm trees and a cascade of Pfitzer's juniper crowd close to the circular driveway off Civic Center Drive. Beyond that, those who have business in the courthouse approach the building along the shaded walkway leading to the main entrance. The shallow reflecting pool to the left of the walk, only inches deep, affords the illusion of coolness— even when the baking Santa Ana winds blow in.

Only those who know the Orange County Courthouse intimately are aware of the hidden little jungle that flourishes there. Outside the ground floor of the DA's office, wild rabbits skitter through the underbrush. Feral cats and their kittens exist there too. Although the former sometimes fall victim to the latter, most of the creatures do very nicely with handouts from soft-hearted courthouse employees and food tossed aside by litterers.

Cinnamon would be tried in Judge Robert Fitzgerald's Superior Courtroom—not as an adult, but as a juvenile. *The State of California v. Cinnamon Darlene Brown*, Case Number J-123914. She had no true sense of what was happening; she still expected to go home.

And perhaps she would. The prosecution's case against Cinnamon Brown received a seemingly fatal blow when Al Forgette's motion to have Cinnamon's confessions to police officers thrown out received a favorable ruling. Forgette argued that Cinnamon had been under the influence of painkillers and other medications when she talked so freely to Fred McLean in the Garden Grove Police Department, and later, to Officer Pam French in the ambulance. Since Cinnamon lapsed into near-unconsciousness before McLean's interrogation could be completed and had to be rushed to the hospital, Forgette thought her condition spoke for itself.

So there it was. The only real suspect in Linda Brown's murder had, in the eyes of the law, *made* no confession. There was no physical evidence linking Cinnamon irrevocably to the shooting, and no eyewitness. Cinnamon was very close to walking away free.

Jay Newell went over and over the case file, looking for some crack in the defense's armor. And yet even as he worked, he felt ambivalent. He suspected that their investigation had only scraped away the patina of the *real* case that existed beneath—impenetrable from every angle they had tried so far. Until he could find the key to the case within the case, he knew he had to move ahead with his support of the prosecution of the *visible* case. And that meant convicting Cinnamon. If Cinnamon Brown should be acquitted, she would undoubtedly go back into her father's home.

Jay Newell did not want that to happen. Something was wrong— but he could not put into words just what it was.

Newell hunched over the medical records from the Garden Grove Medical Center and then from the University of California Medical Center–Irvine: the classic doctors' scribbles, so consistently illegible that he figured it had to be a black art taught in med school—symbols, medications, times, dates, temperatures, fluids in and fluids out. His eyes blurred as he tried to make sense of it.

He could see that Cinnamon Brown had been one sick kid, and that she had been given more stuff to swallow and inhale that made her—at least initially—sicker. As he turned the pages of medical gobbledygook, he saw that she had improved steadily.

Newell set aside the Garden Grove Medical Center records and turned to those from UCI. As he read down the shiny copier paper, he suddenly came across sections that he could easily read. Precise notes in a careful hand. The notes reproduced almost word for word the confession Cinnamon Brown had given to Fred McLean. Odd. Newell wondered how part of a confidential police file could end up in medical records.

He turned the page curiously and saw the initials "K.H." at the bottom of the first entry detailing Cinnamon's statements. And Jay Newell realized to his growing fascination that *this* was not the actual confession Cinnamon had given to McLean—this was *original* with the writer. He looked further into the records, found more revelations from Cinnamon to "K.H.," and finally, the name Kimberly Hicks.

Kimberly Hicks, whoever she was, might just have pulled the State's case out of oblivion.

Newell went to the University of California Medical Center and asked to talk to Kimberly "Kim" Hicks. He found that she was a third-year medical student who had spent a good deal of time with Cinnamon Brown in the custodial ward of the facility. Kim Hicks was on call during the night shift when Cinnamon Brown was transferred in. Cinnamon Brown had needed to talk—and Kim had been there to listen.

When Newell talked to the med student, she explained that she tried to be careful in keeping up the medical history on her patients. If it was her turn to "present" to the attending physician, she wanted to be as accurate and thorough as she could. And part of her evaluation would be based on how well she kept up her charts. Then again, Cinnamon Brown's case was fascinating both as a medical management problem and as a psychological study.

Kim Hicks had listened as Cinnamon talked, but she had been cautious not to inject her own opinions. And then, along with notes on Cinnamon's medical progress, Kim *had written down Cinnamon's confession to murder*.

The prosecution had its case back.

Cinnamon had her fifteenth birthday in Juvenile Hall on July 3, 1985. Her trial for first-degree murder began on August 7.

Cinnamon had not been home for a long time, not since Fred McLean led her out of the doghouse in that March dawn five months before. She wasn't sure where her father and the baby were living now. She figured probably Patti had gone home to the Bailey family in Riverside.

Cinnamon knew nothing of all the changes that had taken place. She missed Krystal, and she was disappointed that she hadn't gotten to see the baby take her first steps. She missed going to the beach and watching the surfers. She missed listening to New Wave music. Only last July, the worst trouble she had gotten into was ditching summer school to run away to the beach.

She missed her mom and Krista Taber. She missed Linda, and then remembered they kept telling her that Linda was dead. That didn't seem real. She missed her dad, and she didn't understand why he couldn't come to see her more often.

Cinnamon didn't know that Patti was still with David and the baby, and that Linda's memory was steadily being erased—no, not erased, supplanted. Cinnamon didn't know that Patti had carefully taken all of Linda's pictures out of their frames . . . and replaced them with her own likeness.

Jay Newell hurried to Deputy DA Mike Maguire to let him know that they might have something up their legal sleeves. Even though Cinnamon's original confessions were now excluded, he had a witness for Maguire: Kim Hicks.

All California juvenile trials are held before a judge, without a jury. Judge Fitzgerald would decide if Cinnamon was guilty or innocent. If she should be deemed responsible for her stepmother's death, Al Forgette was prepared to argue that Cinnamon had not been mentally competent at the time of the "incident." Forgette, aware that Kim Hicks was waiting in the wings to repeat Cinnamon's confession, had little choice. Cinnamon faced Judge Fitzgerald with a plea of not guilty to a charge of murder by reason of insanity. She still insisted she had a complete loss of memory for that period in March when Linda had died.

Forgette requested a closed courtroom. Motion denied.

Neither Forgette nor Mike Maguire made an opening statement.

Maguire called his first witness against Cinnamon—Patti Bailey. Cinnamon seemed stunned, confused. This was the girl who had been her "sister."

Patti described Cinnamon as her niece—which, technically, she was. She identified Cinnamon as "the girl in the light blue shirt" sitting at the defense table and recounted the "misunderstandings" Cinny had had with Linda over chores. These, Patti testified, had progressed to "arguments. When there were arguments, I usually left the room because I didn't feel I had a right to be there."

Patti was soft-spoken, almost demure. She had difficulty understanding big words and often asked Maguire to rephrase his questions, saying, "I don't understand what that means."

So far, Patti wasn't a damning witness. She identified Cinnamon's printing, and her own, from letters and poems in evidence.

Maguire moved on to March 19, 1985. Patti Bailey said she remembered that day dimly. But as Maguire questioned her, she seemed to have most precise recall. Her recital of the events of the murder night was the same as she had told detectives. She spoke in a soft voice and trembled noticeably.

Patti could no longer remember when she had heard the first shot, but refreshed her memory by looking at the police report. Yes, now she recalled she had looked at her luminous clock and seen 2:23.

With further questioning, there began to be slight, ever-so-slight, changes in Patti Bailey's memory. She now recalled seeing David come home and head for the master bedroom, and that she had called, "David, something went wrong," instead of "something happened."

As far as his reaction, he said, she now remembered, "Calm down and sit down. I'll go call the police."

Mike Maguire had to help Patti remember that David had asked her to go look for Cinnamon. "I tried to find her, but I was too upset. . . . I looked at my bedroom, the bathrooms, the . . . and then the laundry room. . . . I just knocked on her trailer door, and there was no answer. And I figured either she was asleep or she wasn't in there."

Patti testified, crying as she did so, that Cinnamon had been "moody" and "depressed" in the weeks before the shooting. She recalled skirmishes over chores and school attendance between Linda and Cinnamon, but said she had never heard Cinny say she hated Linda. Rather, she could remember any number of times when Cinny and Linda had hugged each other.

Responding to Maguire's questions, Patti attempted to trace the family's makeup and the many moves they had made, the comings and goings of Cinnamon. Her answers were short, sometimes just a dull "Uh-huh." She said that she, as well as Cinnamon, had looked upon Linda as their mother—even though Linda was only twenty-three.

Could Linda be threatening, Maguire asked, extremely angry at Cinnamon?

"When Linda was in a bad mood, she got upset with everyone; but we all learned how to handle it."

Patti remembered that it was "agreed by both of them [Linda and Cinnamon] that Cinnamon would go out there [to the trailer]," but she would not say that this agreement had come at a time when Cinny had argued with Linda over chores.

Patti Bailey was not a particularly effective witness for the State, nor would she be for the defense. Al Forgette elicited a recounting of the night of the shooting from Patti, but she seemed less sure of every detail than she had been in March. The figure she had seen in her doorway—the figure she was so sure was Cinnamon who had fired at her—was now only a "silhouette." She had connected the "silhouette" with the sound of gunfire, but she was no longer nearly as sure that it had been Cinnamon.

Earlier, when she had showed Cinnamon how to fire the gun, she was positive she had not touched it. No, she told Forgette, she had not been concerned enough that Cinnamon was walking around with a gun to tell anyone, or warn anyone. She went to sleep easily, with no worries.

Yes, Cinnamon had been "upset, depressed, like something was bugging her or something." But then, Patti testified, Cinnamon had been getting moodier since maybe January or February.

Pressed for some specific example of Cinnamon's moodiness—even her possible drug use—Patti thought hard.

No—no drugs, ever. "Just depression and upset and like . . . and like the world was going to come to an end. You know, how people look when they're on drugs or something, they look like they don't have a care in the world."

"And that's the way she struck you?" Forgette asked.

Patti shook her head; she was sure Cinnamon had been very, very depressed, and *not* happy—as drug users appeared.

Patti Bailey had a certain flatness of expression, an inability to describe her *own* emotions. Yes, she had been frightened. Yes, she had been apprehensive. Yes, she had been agitated and crying. But the descriptive phrases came from Forgette and Patti only agreed.

Patti's recall now made David's actions on the murder night sound braver. He had been in charge, calling the police, calming her down. She had apparently forgotten his panic, his pleading call to his father.

And now, five months later, Maguire could not shake Patti by letting her read her earlier statements that she was sure the shooter was Cinnamon. "I wasn't sure it was Cinnamon. I didn't know who it was."

"Are you trying to protect Cinnamon now?"

"No."

Jay Newell sat in the back of the small courtroom, observing Patti Bailey as she testified, and the reaction of the spectators in the gallery. It almost seemed as if she were trying to smooth everything over. David Brown emerged sounding nearly courageous, and the shooter was no longer Cinnamon—only a vague, blurry silhouette. The witness Newell had tracked down himself—Kim Hicks—was coming through the door, prepared to testify against Cinnamon. He should feel good. Then why did he have such an emptiness in the gut? Why did he catch himself looking again and again at the small figure huddled at the defense table, her face a mask of pain and disbelief?

"Call Kim Hicks!"

The young, black soon-to-be doctor explained that she remembered well the three A.M. call she had received to report to the custodial ward on March 20, 1985.

Kim Hicks had found Cinnamon in bed—*shackled* to the bed—still nauseated, but alert and well oriented. Hicks said she had asked Cinnamon why she had taken the pills. "She explained first of all that she had shot—she had shot someone, okay? And it was said that it was her stepmother and that she shot her twice."

"Did she say what she did—if anything—after she shot her stepmother?" Maguire asked.

"After she did that, she said she went to her father's drawer and took some pills out. . . . She said she took one whole bottleful, and the other bottle. . . . They fell and she took some of those and somehow she had a glass of water and she took those; she took the pills that she had."

Maguire showed Kim Hicks her original records and she scanned them, nodding. "Right . . . okay. That's my writing. She stated she ingested about eighty pills from one bottle and an unknown number of pills from two other bottles."

Cinnamon had told the medical student that she shot her stepmother about three A.M. She had shot her once and then heard her crying out, "Help me! It hurts!" At that point, she had returned to Linda's room and shot her once more. This time, there had been no sound from Linda. Cinnamon told Hicks she had waited half an hour and then gone out to the doghouse.

In answer to Maguire, Hicks added, "She went out to the doghouse and she was—she slowly just became sick, you know, and she started vomiting. And she remembers urinating on herself, and just progressively got sicker, heard sirens. No one came and found her or anything like that. She heard the sirens leave and she was still there in the doghouse until later the police came back."

Over the next few days, Hicks had had occasion to spend quite a bit of time with Cinnamon.

"Did Cinnamon indicate to you during this 'small talk' any reason for shooting her stepmother?" Maguire asked.

"She did, and even on the night of admission she told us why she did it. . . . She said she didn't know what else to do. Her stepmother had threatened—had told her that she had to leave, that she can't stay there anymore, and they had been arguing that night and specifically that her father was home; he heard the argument. He left, said he couldn't take it anymore. Then he left and they stopped arguing. And that they just basically hadn't been getting along."

Most of the story was familiar. Hicks repeated Cinnamon's alleged fear that Linda wasn't taking care of Krystal, not paying attention to her when she cried. "She was more scared and concerned. Sorta she didn't seem real angry about it—more confused."

But this was, again, a little different version of the night of March 19. David had said he left *after* the girls and Linda were all in bed. But Cinnamon had told Kim Hicks that David had stomped out because he couldn't "take it anymore," all the arguing and bickering. If David Brown knew how explosive emotions were at home, why had he driven off into the night?

Al Forgette questioned Kim Hicks carefully. Why had she spent so much time listening and questioning Cinnamon about the murder?

"That's part of the social history."

Hicks explained that, at first, Cinnamon had seemed very frightened and murmured, "Gosh, what do you think's going to happen to me?" and "I shouldn't have done it," but she grew quieter and more introspective as the days passed. Hicks said she had tried to comfort her patient, saying, "I just told her it would be all right, you know and just—it was more supportive than that, more supportive."

Cinnamon sat at the defense table, her face a bleak study. It was impossible to tell if she remembered Kim Hicks or any of the statements the young medical student attributed to her.

Kim Hicks explained that Cinnamon had been both a person and a patient to her. Yes, she had gone in every morning at eight to take Cinnamon's vital signs, check her heart, blood pressure, and her general condition, but she had also tried to treat her like a human being. She was scared and alone. "Her mom or dad wasn't there."

On cross-examination from Al Forgette, Hicks denied that she was trying to elicit information that would be helpful to the police or the district attorney's office. She asked nothing, she said, after the first day. "The first day we all had to find out. We're admitting the patient. We need to know everything we can possibly know about that patient in order to treat that patient effectively."

This was the witness most dangerous to Cinnamon, and Forgette cross- and recross-examined her. He made it plain that Cinnamon had been in a separate part of the hospital, a part operated by the sheriff's department. Barred. Locked.

"The patient can't walk out of there," the defense attorney said.
"But you can walk out of there?"

"Yes."

"There's a deputy sheriff on duty to make sure they don't misbehave
and that they're shackled to the bed?"

"They do."

"All of these conversations took place in that area of the hospital?
Is that right?"

"They did," Hicks agreed.

Forgette tried to stem the damage Kim Hicks had done to Cinnamon's case. "A motion by the defense at this time. The motion would
be to exclude and strike all testimony of the previous witness, Kim
Hicks, as it relates to statements made by the minor while she was
in custody at the jail ward of UCI. My position is that even though
this lady is not an argued police officer, but rather personnel of the
hospital—or student—her actions . . . make her an agent of the authorities. The records show that this minor was . . . in custody,
shackled to her bed.

"My position is that absent an advisement of rights and waiver by
the defendant or minor of these rights, that statements elicited from
her under those conditions amounted to custodial interrogation."

Forgette, this kindly bear of a man, was fighting for his client.
Newell couldn't help but admire him. Cinnamon didn't seem to understand any of it.

Maguire argued that Kim Hicks had merely been taking a social
history. Indeed, although it was not argued, Kim Hicks had never
gone to the police. It took Jay Newell's careful page-by-page perusal
of Cinnamon's medical records to discover this third confession.

For a moment, the courtroom was quiet; Cinnamon Brown's future
was suspended on this one, vital motion.

And then Judge Fitzgerald said briskly, "Motion to strike by the
defense the testimony of Kim Hicks is denied. Next witness."

11

T H R O U G H O U T her trial, Cinnamon occasionally glanced quickly over the gallery. She did not understand that proposed witnesses were excluded and she wondered where her father was. She could not believe that he wasn't there supporting her, as he had always promised he would. She hoped maybe he was out in the hall. Her gaze swept over the tall man at the back of the courtroom. She had no idea who Jay Newell was, and neither had any idea how entwined their lives would become.

The witnesses moved through the double doors of the courtroom, approached the witness chair, testified, and were gone. Some of them were from Cinnamon's short life *before*, and some she had met after. She listened to her oldest friend in the world, Krista Taber—who seemed so nervous and sad—as she told how Cinnamon had been summoned home from Ted Hurath's house, how often she was on restriction.

Fred McLean testified. He identified pictures of the rooms of the house on Ocean Breeze Drive, pictures of the doghouse. He talked about arresting Cinnamon. McLean recalled how and where he had found Cinnamon.

She didn't remember him at all.

McLean identified the suicide note written on pink cardboard, and the purple ribbon wound around it to curl it into a scroll. In his deep Kansas voice, he read aloud, "Dear God, please forgive me. I didn't mean to hurt her."

It seemed a hundred years ago to her now.

Cinnamon could not follow the trial nor understand all the clipped, official police lingo and the medical testimony by forensic pathologist Dr. Richard Fukomoto. A homicide trial, the intricate details of forensic science, the sometimes gory explicitness of a pathologist, who has long since grown used to such matters, can be incomprehensible to the layman—a foreign language to a fifteen-year-old girl.

Hours and hours of testimony from experts on ballistics, on fingerprinting, on gunshot residue, on blood-typing. Blood. Cinnamon had never seen the blood; the house was so dark, and it was easy to think of the sound of the gun and the smell of gunpowder as only part of a nightmare. They were saying that Linda had had type B. That was on the pillowcases. Cinnamon had type O.

What difference did it make? Cinnamon closed her eyes and hunched her shoulders closer together, her mouth set.

All of it was really backup testimony. Cinnamon's future had shifted and twisted like a high bridge in an earthquake the moment Kim Hicks's testimony was allowed to remain on the record.

Court recessed Friday afternoon, August 9. Cinnamon could not understand where her father was. Patti had testified. Where was her dad?

David Brown's name was heard in the courtroom, but he was not there. He sent word to the district attorney's office that he was too ill to attend his daughter's trial. His testimony was offered by stipulation.

Mike Maguire explained that *if* Brown were called as a witness, he would testify to the events of March 18–19. Whether Cinnamon understood that her father, if he came to court, would have been *against* her—not *for* her—was unclear.

Maguire droned out the stipulations. "If David Arnold Brown were called as a witness, he would testify that he had kicked Cinnamon Brown out of the house three weeks prior to March 19, 1985, and that it was then agreed upon that Cinnamon Brown would live in the trailer in the backyard . . . David Brown would also testify that Cinnamon Brown and Linda Brown were not getting along in the weeks prior to March 19, 1985. . . . David Brown would also testify that Cinnamon Brown was told that either she lived in the trailer or she went back to live with her mother, Brenda Sands."

"Entered."

What did "stipulate" mean? Cinnamon still didn't understand what they were saying, that both sides had just stipulated that her father believed she was guilty.

On Monday morning, August 12, at nine-thirty, they began again. Only two witnesses before Judge Fitzgerald ruled on whether Mike Maguire had proved his case against Cinnamon beyond a reasonable doubt. Bill Morrissey and John Woods testified on their administration of GSR tests.

Cinnamon did not testify. Forgette had decided it would be better for her if she didn't. If she didn't remember anything—and she assured him she did not—what good would it do for her to go on the stand?

In final arguments, Maguire deemed Cinnamon's alleged crime as premeditated, "cold-blooded murder," committed by a depressed and angry girl. Cinnamon slumped lower in her chair, and all the curves and angles of her face seemed to pull downward as she listened to Mike Maguire. It sounded so ugly the way he said it, the way he described how Linda had been asleep in her bed when she—Cinnamon—crept beside her in the dark and shot her at close range. He was talking about "cold-blooded murder," and it seemed as if he were talking about someone else, as if his voice were coming from a long way away. *Cold-blooded murder*.

Forgette talked next, and he seemed to be far away from her too, even though she knew he was on her side. He said she had been insane, legally insane. Otherwise, she would never have shot Linda.

"Why in the world would a young lady who had a great deal of affection for her stepmother have a rational motive to kill her? Most troubling is the complete absence of a motive for this child to murder her stepmother."

Insane, legally insane. Was that the reason Cinnamon had shot Linda? Why indeed? It was a question that beggared an answer, but there was none.

Monday, August 12, 1985, was to be a long day utilizing all its minutes in court. If possible, Fitzgerald hoped to hear final arguments, give his verdict, and then, depending on that verdict, possibly move on to testimony in the second phase—the insanity phase—of Cinnamon's trial.

It seemed to Cinnamon that they were propelling her faster and faster toward . . . what?

After Crime Scene Investigator Bill Morrissey's and Sergeant Woods's testimony, Judge Fitzgerald called for a fifteen-minute recess. When he returned, he announced that he had reached a verdict.

"The Court finds as follows: I find beyond a reasonable doubt that the minor known as Cinnamon Brown, in fact, did kill the victim Linda Brown. She did so with premeditation and deliberation, with malice aforethought.

"Court further finds that this was in fact an intentional killing by this minor, specifically the minor intended to kill the victim, Linda Brown.

"The Court then does find the minor Cinnamon Brown to be guilty of murder of the first degree. . . . Her age at the time of the killing was apparently fourteen."

It had happened so swiftly. Al Forgette tried to explain to Cinnamon what it all meant. She had just been found guilty of first-degree murder. She shook her head ever so slightly and looked down at her lap.

Now Forgette had to prove to the judge that Cinnamon Brown had been totally unable to understand the nature and quality of her act of murder. He would call witnesses who would testify to the fragility of her sanity. It was the only way he could keep her from going to prison. The murder made no sense to Forgette, and he could not see how anyone else might view it otherwise.

He first called Brenda Sands, Cinnamon's mother, to bolster his contention that Cinnamon had been out of her mind that March night.

Brenda was a bit confused about *what* she should say. David had been so anxious for her to tell police that Cinny was weird, and she didn't trust David as far as she could throw him. But David could talk so well and make things seem the way he wanted her to believe. He had told her the police were just trying to railroad Cinny. Mr. Forgette too had said it was okay to reveal any emotional scenes. It would help Cinnamon. Brenda knew that Cinny was basically a good kid, and emotionally sound.

But she would do anything to save her child from prison, so she brought up all the blowups they had had. Mother-daughter arguments and yes, Brenda had sent Cinny to live with her father and stepmother. Cinny had been so snippy that Brenda had slapped her and Cinny had tried to hit her back.

"We got into a little mother-and-daughter, you know, argument, you know, fighting, you know, because she stayed out late, and it had something to do with her, you know, about obeying rules. . . . Just slapping. I struck her first and then she hit me, but I put my arm up to block her from hitting me."

"And it was thereafter that you sent her back to her father?" Forgette asked.

"Yes." Brenda hastened to explain that she and Cinnamon talked on the phone often and spent many weekends together.

And yes, she remembered that Cinny had called her about a week before Linda died. "She was feeling ill. She told me that her stomach hurt. She wasn't feeling too good. She said she felt like she was going crazy because everybody kept fighting there in the house.

"I just said, well, you know—you know, I didn't understand what was going on. And I told her I don't know what to tell you. I can't solve your dad's problems."

Cinnamon had not asked to move back with her mother. Whatever was troubling her remained bottled up inside.

Krista Taber testified that Cinnamon had not seemed as happy as she had before. But she struggled with specifics. The best Krista could do was to answer Al Forgette's question "Well, if you saw her five times, how many times was she unhappy in the five times?"

"Once." And that was the time Cinny had been ordered to leave the gathering of friends at Len Miller's house and come right home.

Krista had a vague recollection that Cinnamon had once told her she had taken fourteen aspirin. She didn't know why or when; Cinny had not even gotten sick. It wasn't a big deal.

Patti Bailey testified again, emphasizing how strange Cinnamon had acted the night of the shooting. Patti once more relived her terror as she tried to protect herself and Krystal from a berserk Cinnamon.

Patti stressed how moody and depressed Cinnamon had been, how much time she spent carrying on conversations with imaginary friends. "She'd be talking to them and say, 'What do you think, Maynard?' "

And then, of course, there were the sinister Oscar and Aunt Bertha, all invisible, all imaginary, but according to Patti, very real to Cinny.

Manuela Brown took the stand to testify as to her granddaughter's bizarre behavior. She had taken care of Cinny weekdays when her granddaughter was about four.

"Describe her demeanor when she was with you," Forgette urged, "if you will."

"Very quiet. She very seldom smiled, you know, not as happy as she was when the marriage was happy and everybody was—"

Forgette cut her off before she launched into a rehash of Brenda and David's divorce a decade earlier.

Asked about Cinnamon's state of mind when she lived on Ocean Breeze Drive, Manuela shook her head and sighed. "Sometimes she'd be happy and sometimes kind of moody, like she was depressed a lot of times."

Manuela too brought up the ubiquitous Maynard, the invisible friend. Members of the gallery stifled giggles as the stout lady explained how Cinnamon teased her.

"She asked me to come upstairs—she wanted me to meet her friend. And I thought maybe it was a hamster or something—kids usually have hamsters or guinea pigs or something. When I went upstairs, I was going to sit on the bed and she said, *"Don't!* Be sure you don't sit on Maynard."

Manuela saw no humor in that at all. "We were going to the Target Store in the van once, all of us, and she says, 'Grandma, be sure you don't sit on Maynard.' "

Cinnamon Brown had not slit her wrists nor run naked down Main Street nor babbled gibberish. She had done nothing that any normal teenager—with a well-developed sense of humor—might not do. Teenagers *are* moody and often depressed. As hard as Al Forgette fought to prove Cinnamon psychotic, he had so little to work with.

"Call Dr. Howell!"

Cinnamon Brown's relatives and friends had scoured their memories for remembrances of some significant aberration on her part. And had come up with virtually nothing. Dr. Thomas Patrick Howell, a clinical psychologist employed by the Orange County Department of Mental Health, would be the first professional to testify for the defense.

For almost three years, Dr. Howell had been assigned to do court-authorized psychological evaluations to diagnose disturbed adolescents and help in crisis intervention. In the month after Linda's murder, Howell had examined Cinnamon, and he had also talked to David Brown and to Juvenile Hall staff members. He had worked with only a brief summary of the case and had not accessed police records for more specific details.

"The interview with her biological father, Mr. David Brown, was for what purpose?" Forgette asked.

". . . To get some type of developmental history, family history, and understanding of what was occurring in the family, psychosocial stressors, any problems in the family configuration that the—"

"So you relied on Mr. Brown essentially for family history as much as you could?" Forgette cut in.

"Yes, I did."

What Dr. Howell had gotten from Cinnamon's father was akin to a miner striking a vein of pure gold—a profusion of mental pathology. Brown had arrived an hour late for his appointment, seemed frazzled, disheveled—but clean. He had explained his many ailments—hypertension, ulcerated colon, allergies, bronchitis, and he was obviously anxious.

Brown praised his father and damned his mother, blaming her for most of his own emotional problems. Although he could not reconstruct dates for Dr. Howell, he talked of his suicidal thoughts and three hospitalizations. He blamed Brenda as much as his mother.

As for his marriage to Linda, he described it as *"perfect*, a good marriage without any real problems."

Testifying now, the psychologist talked of that interview with Brown. "Mr. Brown provided me with an extensive history of patterns of physical abuse, sexual abuse, and violence and drug abuse contained within his own family and within himself."

"Well, are these things relevant to evaluating Cinnamon?" Forgette asked.

"Yeah, I think they're relevant because they had some impact upon her emotional makeup in terms of learning how aggression is to be handled and in learning how to deal with crisis situations. . . . One area that was specifically important was that he [Brown] had *three* psychiatric hospital admissions . . . he indicated that he had threatened to kill himself and to also kill Cinnamon's mother with a gun at one time during this period after their divorce. And that he had a propensity for using guns, and that on the request of friends and . . . his therapist, he decided to place those in the custody of the Orange Police Department.

"Additionally, in terms of history, he was raised in a very physically abusive home, a home that provided very poorly for his needs and forced him to leave his home at the age of fourteen, a very young age for someone to be out on his own. So poor parental discipline, how to function normally in society . . . As it applies to Cinnamon, parents learn how to deal with their children, how to discipline them, primarily from their experiences, from their own parents.

"He was probably a poor disciplinarian and was, in fact, probably physically abusive himself. I had to file a child abuse report on his statements to me that he had struck his daughter when she was twelve years old, pulling her pants down and spanking her with a belt so forcefully that he was trying to get her to cry and she steadfastly refused to do that.

"That experience shows once again a perpetuation of the poor parenting techniques that he had experienced, and in fact, that was found and documented also by Cinnamon's statements to me."

Dr. Howell's information on his family background, on Brenda's, and on the Bailey family, all came from David Brown. In one sense, Howell seemed to have believed all of it. In another, he found Brown's statements contradictory.

"I feel that the father felt that his daughter was incapable of committing such an act [murder], and his quote was 'Cinnamon is about as capable of hurting others as I am!' And in my opinion, he *is* capable. His past history documents that. So it was kind of a strange statement for him to make."

Dr. Howell did not think David Brown was dangerous, although his past history indicated a definite pattern of physical violence.

"Would Mr. Brown's mental state or mental status have any bearing, in your opinion, on Cinnamon or the way she would react to given situations?" Forgette asked.

Over a half dozen objections from Mike Maguire, and several rephrased questions from Forgette, Howell was allowed to answer. "Basically, you have an individual modeling different types of behavior. The child would notice her father. How does he handle conflict? How does he handle stress? How does he respond to the demands of the reality of living? And in fact, you might see the expression of inappropriate anger—you get angry and threaten to harm yourself. . . . I think that was part of his pattern that he was sharing with me, that he had come from a disturbed family."

Few would argue that Cinnamon's family life had not been exactly normal. Yet, no one yet knew to what degree it was dysfunctional or what effect it had *really* had on her.

Dr. Howell had administered a number of psychological tests to Cinnamon herself: the Shipley Institute of Living Scale, Wide Range Achievement Test, the Benton Visual Retention Test, the Hand Test, the Minnesota Multiphasic Personality Inventory, the Thematic Apperception Test, and the Kinetic Family Drawing Test. They were given first to determine if there might be a need for an EEG or CAT scan to check for a possible organic—physical—cause for her sudden eruption of violence.

Dr. Howell explained that he had found Cinnamon's behavior appropriate, and he detected no psychosis, no audiovisual hallucinations. Her intellectual functioning appeared to be within the average to above-average range.

But Cinnamon could not remember anything from the time she was watching television in the living room on Ocean Breeze Drive until she woke up seeing "doubles" and "triples" of everything. She denied to Howell that she had ever made a confession of murder to anyone.

She balked at the psychological tests Howell asked her to complete, and by the third one, she refused to continue, saying, "What are you going to do? Hit me?"

"She was able to regroup," Howell said, "contain her anger, and go on with the testing and complete it."

The test results convinced Howell and the chief psychiatrist, Dr. William Loomis, that Cinnamon was not suffering from any neurological damage and did not require the EEG or the CAT scan. To be on the safe side, she was given both.

And both were normal.

Dr. Howell stressed that he had never intended to make a diagnosis as to whether Cinnamon Brown had known the difference between right and wrong at the time of the murder—or even if he felt she had committed the murder of Linda Brown. He offered a tentative diagnosis—valid only if Cinnamon should be deemed truly guilty of the shooting of her stepmother: "isolated explosive disorder."

This aberration is described in the *Diagnostic and Statistical Manual of Mental Disorders*, the bible of the psychology world—the *DSM-III*. Isolated explosive disorder is discussed in a chapter that covers impulse control problems "not elsewhere classified."

"The essential feature is a single, discrete episode of failure to resist an impulse that led to a single, violent, externally directed act, which had a catastrophic impact on others and for which the available information does not justify the diagnosis of Schizophrenia, Antisocial Personality Disorder, or Conduct Disorder. An example would be an individual who for no apparent reason suddenly began shooting at total strangers in a fit of rage and then shot himself. In the past this disorder was referred to as 'catathymic crisis.' "

Dr. Howell stepped down. His tentative diagnosis was as good as anything anyone had come up with yet for a seemingly incomprehensible act of murderous violence.

Jay Newell, from his observation point in the courtroom, felt as if all of them were attempting to complete a crossword puzzle, unaware that their answers did not fit into the spaces provided.

Them? Who was he kidding? So was he.

The parade of psychologists and psychiatrists continued. Dr. David Sheffner, a forensic psychiatrist, testified that he had attempted to get through to Cinnamon.

"She wouldn't let me in. . . . I had the feeling that there is a tremendous amount of chronic emotional turmoil in this young woman, and with the assumption that she indeed did what she is accused of, in my opinion this represents severe interpersonal and emotional difficulties."

Sheffner was in as much of a quandary as Dr. Howell had been. Cinnamon's behavior and response, her memory loss, her refusal to be interviewed, the fact that she'd just been convicted of first-degree murder, suggested that she had suffered "very severe abuse," but he had found none—not to that extent—in her family. Sheffner could not form an opinion on Cinnamon's state of sanity at the time of the shooting. He recommended psychotherapy.

Dr. Kaushal Sharma, also a psychiatrist, had actually met with Cinnamon three times over the long summer following Linda's murder. On the first meeting on May 31, 1985, he had a number of earlier reports to go on, but virtually nothing from Cinnamon.

"She told me that she was not able to remember anything about the incident. . . . She told me basically what her life was the day prior to the incident. She told me background history, but she did not tell me anything about the circumstances or any factors which may have played any role in the commission of the crime."

"You met with her later, the fourteenth of June?" Forgette asked.

"She told me she believed her stepmother was not dead . . . because she told me she wanted to believe only good things about her stepmother and did not wish to even think about the possibility that she might be dead."

Even when Dr. Sharma showed Cinnamon copies of the police reports, she read them, tossed them aside, and said, "So what. That does not prove anything."

On July 2, the psychiatrist's visit was just as nonproductive. Cinnamon was alternately hostile and smiling. She did not want to talk. "She told me I was boring her. She told me that I had no business suggesting that her stepmother might be dead. She told me that she did not really wish to discuss anything because there was nothing to discuss."

Not surprisingly, Dr. Sharma could not come up with a diagnosis about Cinnamon's sanity, nor speculate if she had known right from wrong on the night of "the incident."

Either Cinnamon Brown was very, very clever and able to keep experienced doctors off-balance, or she was truly suffering from amnesia. There appeared to be no other explanation.

When court convened on Tuesday, August 13, for the penalty phase of Cinnamon Brown's trial, there was yet another stipulation offered regarding possible testimony from David Brown.

"I would advise the court," Al Forgette said, "that the reason for her father's absence is that he's quite ill and he was ordered by his physician to remain in bed and is not able to come to court. I have furnished the district attorney with a copy of the letter from his physician, Dr. Goldstein. He was actually, on the sixth of August, ordered to remain at home and in bed for a period of approximately two weeks."

Jay Newell was aware that David Brown complained of a number of ailments. But it seemed odd that he should be struck down by illness on the *exact* day his daughter's trial began.

"I've been in contact with Mr. Brown daily in hopes he could come to court so we could get the benefit of his testimony," Forgette said. "But as late as last night, he informed me he was not up to it. He felt it appropriate to obey the doctor's orders. So we have a stipulation to offer the court now.

"The Defense would offer to stipulate that David Brown, if called to testify as a witness, would testify that in the approximate two- to three-week period prior to the death of his wife, Linda, that the minor,. Cinnamon Brown, appeared very moody and talked of suicide during this period."

"So stipulated," Mike Maguire murmured.

"Stipulation entered," echoed Judge Fitzgerald.

"One additional stipulation, Your Honor," Forgette asked, "that relates to witness Patricia Bailey. We offer to stipulate that during this two- or three-week period, she heard the minor, Cinnamon Brown, talk of suicide by use of a firearm."

"So stipulated."

"Entered."

Jay Newell stopped breathing for a moment. If Patti Bailey had *known* that Cinnamon was thinking of committing suicide with a gun two weeks before the night of the murder, why had she so willingly showed Cinnamon how to use the .38 and then gone serenely to sleep? He made a note. He wasn't sure why he bothered keeping notes at this point. They had won the case already. They were practically across the finish line.

Al Forgette called his last witness, his big gun, psychiatrist Dr. Seawright Anderson. Anderson testified that he had evaluated Cinnamon Brown on March 20, the first day she was in the custody ward at UCI, as she lay shackled to the bed, an IV line in her arm.

On the first of two consultations, Cinnamon had been open with Dr. Anderson. She told him she was in the ninth grade and her grades were mostly Cs and Bs, but she had gotten two Fs in history and mathematics. She also told him she sometimes worked with her father, "a computer scientist," denied ever experiencing sex, denied drug use, and had never had an alcoholic drink—"except once or twice on New Year's Eve."

Cinnamon said she had suffered a head injury in a car accident two or three years ago, but hadn't gone into a coma. The only serious illness she had ever had was tonsillitis, when she had had a reaction to penicillin and had begun to shake uncontrollably.

Cinnamon gave her religion as Catholic, and her hobbies as going to the beach and collecting stamps. She said her mother was "nice" but had a "bad temper." Her mother, Brenda, currently worked in a vitamin factory. Cinnamon told Anderson that her father was also "nice."

Asked if she had ever suffered from hallucinations or ideas of persecution, Cinnamon had spontaneously begun talking about Linda's death. She told Dr. Anderson that Linda had suddenly "flipped out and said she would kill her if she was not out of the house. She said she didn't love her . . . and then the minor mentioned that her father was on the recliner and the minor was sitting on the love seat at that time, and then her father had left. And the victim was asleep . . . the minor ran in and got the gun and shot the gun in the aunt's room . . . and the minor said she didn't know what she was doing; she was really scared. She ran in and shot her, that is—the victim— twice, threw the gun down, began hitting herself, became nauseated, opened up the drawer, found three bottles, heard her stepmother cry, 'Help me! Help me!' and minor stated she took all the pills and began shaking, and she went into the doghouse and she wrote a note saying for God to forgive her and she did not mean to hurt her."

When Anderson asked her about her thoughts before the shooting occurred, Cinnamon had told him she could not recall her thoughts, that it was all like a bad dream.

Anderson said Cinnamon had told him she had tried suicide twice and was often depressed. She felt her stepmother wanted to kill her. "She denied compulsions and phobias. When I asked her about obsessions, she stated she had an obsession concerning dreaming about flying a lot like a bird without feathers. . . ."

"After reviewing the police reports and psychological evaluation by Dr. Howell," Forgette asked, "and in light of your direct examination of the minor, were you able to reach any diagnostic impressions?"

"Yes, sir, I was. . . . My impression at that time was that she was suffering from a major depression, recurrent type."

Dr. Anderson also felt that this major depression gripped Cinnamon at the time of the shooting, and that it "interfered with her ability to know the quality of her actions and also to know the difference between right and wrong."

The psychiatrist had interviewed—or *attempted* to interview Cinnamon once more—on July 28. "She did not recall having seen me before," he testified. "She did not recall telling me about the shooting of her stepmother. . . . She did, however, review with me her personal history materials . . . but she denied any suicide attempts. . . . My feeling was she had developed this psychogenic amnesia to protect herself from feeling more depressed or to protect her from going into a psychotic state."

Dr. Anderson modified—or rather *expanded*—his diagnosis of Cinnamon Brown after this second half-hour consultation. "I felt that she was suffering from a disassociative disorder, a psychogenic amnesia type with a history of major depression, recurrent."

Mike Maguire cross-examined Dr. Anderson for half the morning and into the afternoon. "Isn't it a fact, Doctor, that depression in and of itself doesn't cause people to lose sight of what is right and what is wrong?"

"That is correct."

"And in this case, because of what Cinnamon told you, you feel her depression caused her to lose sight of what was right and what was wrong?"

"On the basis of what she told me and the battery of reports indicating the severity of the depression, I would say it's of such severity to interfere with her ability to know right from wrong."

They worried the question, back and forth, and neither witness nor prosecutor would budge.

In the ensuing cross- and redirect examination of Seawright Anderson, many psychological terms were tossed around. Cinnamon was more confused than ever. She had already been adjudged a killer. Now, her own attorney said that, under the law, she was insane. The prosecutor said she was not. "Cinnamon is not now insane, nor was she insane March nineteenth when she pulled the trigger twice to shoot Linda Brown."

She didn't know what any of it meant.

What it meant, of course, was that if Judge Fitzgerald agreed with Forgette and found her mentally ill, Cinnamon would receive treatment. If he agreed with Mike Maguire, she would go to prison.

Judge Fitzgerald ruled against Forgette. In his estimation, Cinnamon Brown was quite sane. He said he would sentence her on September 13.

• • •

Cinnamon Brown appeared for sentencing on Friday, the thirteenth of September. She was very pale and trembled as she sat next to Al Forgette. Where she had seemed only immensely sad during both phases of her trial, she now appeared shaken. It was as if she had suddenly hit a wall—an unexpected wall. Mr. Forgette had told her all the things that might happen, but she had never thought it would be this.

Jay Newell glanced around the courtroom to see who might have had reason to sit in on this sentencing. It hadn't gotten more than a back-section story in the *Orange County Register*, and less in the *Los Angeles Times*.

Brenda Sands was there, looking as agonized as Cinnamon, and David's sister Susan Salcido. Cinnamon's grandfather, Arthur Brown, was there. And behind Brenda, *at long last*, Newell saw the elusive David Arnold Brown. He wondered what the real reason was that Brown had been "too sick" to come to Cinnamon's trial. Had he been afraid of testifying? Did he have information that would have made it look worse for his daughter? It didn't matter now; the trial was over.

As Newell covertly studied the squat, dark-haired man, he saw Brown's hand suddenly dart out and tug at his ex-wife's hair. Brenda lifted her hand and brushed him away like a pesky fly. No, he wasn't that. He was like a kid in school, Newell thought, as he saw that Brown was also kicking the back of Brenda's chair with his foot. He was like a naughty kid pulling the braids of a girl he had a crush on, even as his own daughter was being sentenced to prison for murder.

David Brown was smiling. A sly, happy smile.

Newell was mystified—and intrigued.

As Brown reached out again to tease Brenda, Judge Fitzgerald described the slaying of Linda Marie Brown as a heinous act that he deplored. Cinnamon looked at Fitzgerald. He was asking her if she understood the procedure for her sentencing. She shook her head slightly and her voice broke as she said, "I don't understand."

Why was she going to be sentenced? Why wasn't she going home?

Tears slipped from Cinnamon's eyes and rolled down her cheeks. She stood woodenly and waited.

"I sentence you to serve twenty-seven years to life. . . ."

Cinnamon swayed. Brenda gasped.

Neither one of them really heard the rest of what the judge had to say. It was enough that they had just heard that Cinnamon, fifteen years old, had been sentenced to be in prison at least until she was forty-two years old, maybe longer.

"My hope is that you progress," Judge Fitzgerald was saying. "And don't have to serve the maximum term." He recommended that Cinnamon be imprisoned at the California Youth Authority facility— Ventura School—where she could receive psychiatric treatment and be housed with girls her own age.

Brenda Sands left the courtroom in tears.

Mike Maguire explained to the press that the "target time" for youthful offenders in California was, historically, about six years. That meant that Cinnamon might be out when she was twenty or twenty-one. But it wasn't a given.

Cinnamon didn't hear that explanation nor did she understand that she probably wouldn't really be in prison for the rest of her life. It wouldn't have mattered. When you are fifteen, six years is a lifetime anyway.

She looked around for her father, but he was gone.

The case file in the Orange County DA's office filled one sturdy cardboard file box and half of another. The Brown case was adjudicated now; it would go down into the vault. There were always other cases to work, so many new cases they tumbled over each other. No time to look back on and ponder this strange story of Cinnamon Darlene Brown and her dead stepmother.

With Cinnamon's sentencing, Garden Grove Case 85-11342 was closed. There was no viable argument for reworking a case where both evidence and confession had convicted a killer. The fact that the killer was a sweet-faced fourteen-year-old girl was tragic, but justice ground on in Orange County, barely skipping a beat.

It was officially over.

Cinnamon Brown had been committed to the Ventura School in Camarillo, placed under the jurisdiction of the California Youth Authority. She would never again attend a public high school, nor would she grow up through her teen years with her friends. A chunk of her young life, a very important chunk, had been amputated. Instead, on October 17, 1985, she was taken from the Orange County Juvenile Hall and driven eighty miles north to the Ventura School in Camarillo. Cinnamon, who had always loved the beach, would be close enough to the Pacific Ocean to smell the salt spray when the wind changed in the afternoon, but she would not get to sunbathe on the beach.

Home would be so far away that it might as well have been ten thousand miles. But then, Cinnamon had not really had a home she could count on for a long time; she always felt like an appendage, a tagalong to whichever family she was living with, an interloper. Whichever home she was in, Brenda's or David's, she had always felt torn, disloyal to the absent parent.

At first, she was only surprised to find herself in prison. Her being there had to be a mistake. And then she was stunned, disbelieving. And so alone. She tried to convince herself that she would not be at the Ventura School for very long; her father had always promised her he would take care of her, and she trusted in his assurances.

She could have visitors on every other Saturday after she was settled into her cottage, into the routine of the Ventura School. She hoped her father would come up so she could talk to him and get a hug. She hoped he would bring Krystal. She hoped Brenda could borrow a car and come up with Penelope. She missed her baby sister. She missed both her baby sisters.

She had a new fear now, no matter how irrational it might seem. She was scared to death that everyone would just forget about her.

PART TWO

• • •

The Investigation

12

T H E R E was *one* man who had not forgotten Cinnamon. For some reason, Jay Newell could not get her out of his mind. He knew full well the Brown file was about to gather dust. That was the way it went, the inexorable progression from the investigation to the intensity of a trial to oblivion. But Newell simply could not let go of it. There was no use trying. He looked at his own working file and made up his mind. He put the well-worn binders, transcripts, tape recordings, and videotapes into his desk drawer, close by, where he could pull them out whenever he wanted. He was not satisfied that the whole truth had ever come to light.

Fred McLean felt the same way. He always had. Something was "hinky." It only reinforced both detectives' sense of an unfinished case when McLean had run into Susan Salcido, David Brown's thirty-four-year-old sister, in the parking lot after Cinnamon's sentencing. Brenda Sands was with her and introduced Susan to the detective.

"I almost didn't come today," Susan said. "I did it for Cinnamon. I haven't had much to do with David for a long time—he was really cruel to one of our brothers. David can be mean. "I was the one who apologized, finally," Salcido said, as Brenda Sands added, "David *never* apologizes to anyone."

"You know," Susan said, "the last time I talked to Linda was on the day after Valentine's Day—over at their house on Ocean Breeze. Alan Bailey was there too that day, and he was ticked off about something—I can't even remember what it was. Alan gets ticked off easy. Something David had done to him, or he thought David had done to him.

"I remember what Linda said, probably because that was the *last* time I ever saw her. Linda wasn't happy; she was miserable. She said she and David were fighting a lot, that they'd been having trouble for a long time, although it was better for a while after Krystal was born."

Susan said she asked if Cinnamon's living with the family was the main source of trouble, but Linda had assured Susan that she got along fine with Cinnamon.

Cinnamon wasn't the problem.

"The only reason Cinnamon was living in the trailer," Susan said, "was because Patti wanted her own room in the house and didn't want Cinnamon sharing. Patti always got her way with David."

Susan told McLean that Linda had actually seemed concerned that Patti might be dangerous. When Susan had demurred, surprised, Linda gave examples. "Linda told me that neither she nor David allowed Patti to take care of the baby. She was afraid Patti would hurt Krystal. Linda told me that Patti had somehow killed a puppy that belonged to Cinnamon. I'm not sure just how that happened, but she was very worried about Patti's behavior. She said Patti was acting strange, and she thought maybe she was anorexic. Linda thought Patti was going to commit suicide."

"Was that a surprise to you?" McLean asked, and Susan shook her head. "Patti is kind of strange."

She had noticed that Patti looked smug when Cinny got in trouble. She was competitive with Cinny. Now, Patti wouldn't have to share her home with either Linda or Cinnamon.

The three of them had stood in the parking lot across from the courthouse, the hot August sun beating down on them. Brenda looked dazed, not yet able to comprehend that her child had just been sentenced to life in prison. She nodded and agreed with her ex-sister-in-law's assessments of Patti Bailey.

"Since Linda died, Patti and David are inseparable," Susan Salcido confided. "They leave the baby with my parents and they're gone all day."

And then Susan Salcido reported that David also had rushed to warn her only hours after the murder—just as he had warned Brenda—that she was *not* to describe Cinnamon as normal when the police asked. If questioned, she was to say that Cinnamon was disturbed, possibly suicidal.

"*Why?*" McLean asked.

Salcido didn't know—whether it was because David hoped an insanity plea would save Cinny from going to prison, or for his own reasons. David *had* always liked to orchestrate events, molding them and changing them to suit him.

"All I really know is our whole family thinks it's peculiar that Patti still lives with David. They go everywhere together. It doesn't seem right, letting my mother have all the care of Krystal while they go off alone. Patti's seventeen. She should be home with her own family."

McLean and Newell had no official place to go with their misgivings about the Cinnamon Brown case. Because that was all they had—

hunches. *Feelings*. A sense that justice had not been served, or at best partially served. But the law demands facts, direct evidence, witnesses, confessions—a reasonable, orderly case built step by step. And Newell and McLean didn't have any of those. During the investigation and Cinnamon's trial, they felt they had come to know her a little, although they were a long way from understanding her. The person who eluded them completely was her father.

Who *was* David Arnold Brown?

He had told investigators only the most cursory details about his life and seemed disinclined to tell them anything more. They knew he was wealthy, that he owned Data Recovery and claimed to be a computer genius, that his health was fragile, and that he seemed to associate almost exclusively with his family.

There was nothing to link David Brown to the murder of Linda Brown. It had seemed a bit odd to McLean and Newell that a man so upset by an argument with his wife should have remembered his whereabouts so precisely. A skeptic—or a detective—might even deduce that Brown had intentionally established an alibi. But that was only a feeling, not solid evidence. Police investigations had checked out Brown's story; he was, indeed, where he said he was at the time Linda died. In the *official* eyes of the law, Brown was a law-abiding citizen. He had no criminal record—not with the California Bureau of Criminal Identification and Information, nor with the Federal Bureau of Investigation's National Crime Information Center. McLean had checked, and Newell had checked.

David Brown was clean.

McLean had to let it go, at least for the moment; he had other duties. Newell *could not* let it go, even though he wasn't even sure what he was looking for. Newell was a man born to ferret out things hidden, a low-key bulldog who refused to accept easy solutions. He worried a case, turning it over and over, kept coming back to it until *he* was satisfied that he had discerned every facet of the truth.

Jay Newell didn't grow up in a cop's family; his dad was a school custodian in La Habra, and Jay and his two sisters had come with their folks from Oklahoma to Norwalk, California. There, young Jay's hero was a Los Angeles County deputy who lived across the street and took the time to talk to neighborhood kids and listen to their problems.

When Newell got out of the army in 1971, he signed up with the Los Angeles County Sheriff's Office. The first assignment for rookies just out of the Academy was working in the jails, not the favorite duty for most cops. "If you want to get through the jail assignment quick," Newell explained, "you pick the toughest jail you can. That's what I did. I volunteered for the old HOJJ—the Hall of Justice Jail in downtown Los Angeles."

The HOJJ was full of difficult prisoners, including Charles Manson and his followers, who were housed there during their marathon trials. Newell was startled to see what a diminutive man Manson was, and how, even locked up, he had a mesmerizing effect on young prisoners. The man who should have been reviled was, instead, idolized. Studying Manson taught Newell a great deal about charismatic manipulators. "He had a whole block of cells to himself—to keep him isolated— but some of the other prisoners would pass by him when they were transferred in or out. They polished his shoes for him; they would take his jail clothes and put creases just right in them—anything to please him," Newell recalled, shaking his head. "He had a creepy kind of *power*."

In many ways, working the Hall of Justice Jail was far more dangerous for rookie deputies than being on the streets. Simply locking down the jail for the night could be risky. "All the cell doors slammed shut at once," Newell remembered. "We'd yell, 'Comin' closed!' to warn the prisoners to step away from the doors. But some of them would toss blankets in the doorway, and that made the handle the deputy was pulling fly back and smack into him hard. Luckily, I was in and out quickly, but I learned a lot in the process."

Next, Newell went to patrol. He was out on the road only three days when he was involved in a shoot-out. Two suspects were wounded, but Newell and his partner emerged unscathed.

He liked police work, the variety of details a street cop deals with, and yet it was the *continuing* investigation of crimes that truly fascinated him. As a patrolman, he only got to see the beginning of a case, and then he had to hand it reluctantly over to the detectives for followup. It left him wanting more. He saw only the surface, when everything in him wanted to dig deeper. In the hierarchy of the Los Angeles County Sheriff's Office, it can take a long time to move up into the detective unit, and Newell chafed at the wait. After eight years with the Sheriff's Office, he resigned and signed on with the Orange County District Attorney's Office as an *investigator*.

Newell's first assignments were hardly the stuff of mystery thrillers. He worked in the Family Support Division, then investigated welfare fraud for a year. By 1981, he had moved into the Juvenile Division where he worked juvenile-related homicide cases and tried to stem the damage from a growing problem: gangs. Orange County saw the unwelcome emergence of some of the first of the gangs that would soon plague the West Coast, and Newell had his baptism of fire. He investigated *forty-seven* gang-related homicides. He had wanted into the thick of criminal investigation, and he got his wish. Crips. Bloods. Skinheads. Newell played a key role in producing training films that taught cops how to deal with the skinheads and the ethnic gangs that were proliferating. He got along with the gangs—as much as any cop could.

Cinnamon Brown was no gang member. She *was* a convicted juvenile homicide offender. Why couldn't Newell just let go of her case? It was a question with no answer, only a gnawing gut instinct. Newell's curiosity about her father was an itch that demanded scratching.

After the murder of Linda Brown, David Arnold Brown told anyone who would listen that he was a man torn, caught between his grief over the loss of his wife, pity for his motherless baby, and concern for his firstborn child. Cinnamon was criminally responsible for making Krystal a half-orphan, he said forlornly, and that fact would fill him with wrenching ambivalence for the rest of his life. Seeing Cinnamon reminded Brown of the tragedy and of her participation. But he couldn't just walk away from his daughter. She needed him now more than she ever had. He vowed to visit her as often as his health permitted.

Brown had always called Cinnamon "Cinny" and stressed to police that there was an extremely strong bond between them, even during those times she was living with her mother. He bemoaned the fact that she had stubbornly resisted when he tried to get her into counseling. He blamed himself, he said, for not trying harder to get help for Cinnamon. But he accepted the fact that his fourteen-year-old daughter had murdered his beloved, perfect wife.

When he could take the time from other investigations, Jay Newell began to dig beneath the surface of David Brown's life, locating any number of people who were quite willing to fill in a chink here and a missing space in time there. He discovered that David Brown was something of a ladies' man. Linda had been his fifth wife. Newell also located a dozen or more women Brown had been involved with *between* marriages. He was neither tall nor handsome, but it hadn't seemed to hurt him with women. As one of Linda and Patti's relatives said graphically, "He always got the beauties. None of David's women were dog meat."

Newell found that David's existence had been marked by soaring peaks and desolate valleys. Still, all things considered, he had been quite successful—until Linda's murder. He bragged that he had a talent for survival, along with an innate intelligence and acquired skill. The numerous statues and sketches of birds in the Ocean Breeze Drive house were David's. Family members told Newell that David identified with the phoenix, the mythic bird rising from the ashes of disaster to soar again. He even wore a symbolic pendant. His personal jeweler had created the image of a phoenix just as Brown ordered it, with its wings down—not spread—as it rose with ease from "flames" formed of yellow and orange topaz. The custom piece cost $1,500.

David Brown liked to say that in the end, like the phoenix, he always won.

No one could argue that David was not a high achiever, a middle child who had struggled to break out of the pack of many children in a family with limited income. Perhaps that was why prestige and wealth mattered so much to him. And why he detested authority figures. Perhaps it was his mother's control over him when he was a child that made David so resistant to anyone's telling him what to do.

Well, he had weathered the latest storm. Cinny was safely behind bars where she could hurt no one. He would visit her, of course, but Brown had his business, his clients and his employees, along with the total care of Krystal. His parents were upset, naturally, and Linda's family was devastated. They looked to him for decisions.

Apparently everyone in both families had come to depend on David Brown for jobs, and in a pinch, for money. He had succeeded in the business world far beyond what any of them had accomplished. David liked to think of himself as the kind of guy who could walk in and do what needed to be done. It was true he could be self-important, and as one of Linda and Patti's brothers said, "a pain in the butt" about it. He was not averse to strutting a little bit, letting his wife's family know that he was in charge.

But success had cost David Arnold Brown. He was the first to admit that the stresses in his life had exacted a toll. At thirty-two, he was invariably taken for much older. In his computer data retrieval business that wasn't necessarily a bad thing; the corporations and government agencies he dealt with seemed more secure believing they were dealing with an older man.

Despite his accomplishments in the corporate world and with women, David's health was not good. He had been treated for high blood pressure, heart trouble, headaches, asthma, allergies, insomnia, stomach problems, ulcerative colitis, liver problems, kidney problems, depression, and "nerves." His roster of prescription medicines equaled that of most senior citizens. He worried aloud, voicing his belief he would die young, and his family worried with him.

Beyond his illnesses, David had been in a number of automobile accidents: seventeen, in fact. He was either an abysmal driver, or unlucky. Nevertheless, insurance claims had enabled him to replace—even upgrade—his damaged vehicles.

The effect on his already debilitated health was harder to assess. His calendar was blocked out with appointments with his physician and his chiropractor. Just to keep going, he explained, he had to have frequent spinal adjustments. His lifestyle didn't help; David smoked three or more packs of cigarettes a day, ate junk food almost exclusively, and his only exercise was the walk from his house to his car—unless his self-avowed rigorous sex life counted as exercise. Close-mouthed about many areas of his life, he spoke freely of his sexual prowess.

Digging even deeper, bit by bit Jay Newell began to piece together an intriguing biography of his inscrutable subject—without knowing where it would lead or what it might prove.

13

D A V I D Brown was born in Phoenix, Arizona, on November 16, 1952, near the end of the Korean War. He was the sixth of eight children. His father, Kansas-born Arthur Quentin Brown, thirty-two when David was born, was an auto mechanic who usually worked two jobs to support his family.

His mother, Manuela Estrada Brown, was born in El Paso, Texas, and married young. The babies came along soon, and with regularity. Manuela was only twenty-seven when she bore her sixth child— David. Arthur junior was first, then Bob, Shirley, Linda Sue, Susan, and David. After David, came Tom and the baby, Steven. Linda Sue died as an infant, and the Browns lost their firstborn, Arthur junior, in an automobile accident when he was eighteen.

At eight, David Arnold Brown was a winsome-looking child who resembled Beaver Cleaver—his hair, home crew-cut, his shirt wrinkled and missing a button. His eyes were large and clear, his front teeth too big for his mouth and slightly protruding. He was a little boy who looked as if he needed a hug.

David resembled his mother physically and grew to look even more like her as he matured. They were both brunettes (although Manuela hennaed her hair to a maroon shade.) Manuela's heritage was Hispanic, but as he matured, David played down his Hispanic roots, distancing himself from that culture. He often voiced prejudice against Hispanics, as well as most other minorities.

Bitter in-laws later described Manuela as so overweight that four chairs collapsed beneath her. She was not that heavy; she was only a compact, stocky woman. Both mother and son had the same amorphous body structure, short in stature, with chubby arms and small star-shaped hands.

As much as he looked like his mother, he pulled away from her early in his life. He seemed to feel far more affinity for his father, whom he found positive and caring. A slight man, tentative about his role in life, Arthur Brown always tried to do the right thing. But he had little power, and he had spent his life trying to appease those around him. How strange that David had chosen to call his father before he called the police the night Linda was murdered. His father seemed the last person to turn to for quick, decisive answers in a moment of crisis.

On the other hand, his mother was a vocal woman with definite opinions. He denied that he ever loved her and described her as selfish, controlling, greedy, and violent. When he was older, he teased and tormented her with sadistic jokes until she got angry or broke into tears. (His daughter Cinnamon, while fond of her grandpa, unwittingly spoke of Manuela in a deprecating manner, as if she were not quite bright—echoing her father.) Yet, Manuela visited often and sometimes *lived* in David's many adult homes. And David had taken Manuela's side in an argument with Linda only hours before his young wife died.

In truth, David Brown probably felt ambivalent about his mother. Even though he didn't like her, perhaps he always needed her to take up the slack in his often untidy personal life. In times of trouble, Manuela Brown was the decisive voice, while Arthur fluttered ineffectively, uncertain of what to do.

The Brown family remained in Phoenix until about 1960, then, when David was eight, moved to Needles, California. Needles, just at the eastern boundary of California, is often listed on weather charts as having the highest temperature in America, a town surrounded by desert. After that the family moved around, following jobs for Arthur, and lived over the next thirteen years in Bakersfield and various towns in Los Angeles County. Arthur eventually went to work for Arco. Manuela never worked outside the family home.

David told contradictory stories of his childhood. When talking to a counselor, he recalled that he enjoyed a "wonderful relationship" with each of his family members. But the childhood that he described to others was horrific. Bizarre, violent episodes burst forth unbidden from his memory. Beyond his alleged early hatred for his mother, David told of a number of traumatic assaults. He recalled being beaten up by a gang of Indian youths. He spoke of being sexually molested by an old man in a park. He witnessed a close relative's suicide attempt when he was only ten and was rendered immobile with terror as he watched the knife stabbing repeatedly into wrist arteries, and the cascade of blood that followed. Although the attempt was not successful, the moment stayed frozen in his mind.

As hard as Arthur worked, his combined salaries covered only the basic living expenses of his large family. David spoke with pride about his own resourcefulness. "If we wanted anything for school—binders, rulers, school supplies—we had to earn it. I pulled weeds, trimmed trees, mowed lawns, from the time I was eleven. I was washing dishes in a café after school too when I was eleven," David recalled. "When I was still only eleven or twelve, I ran a gas station all by myself— up to sixteen hours a day. I loved it. It was way out in Mettler, a little crossroads about twenty-five miles south of Bakersfield. I was pretty tired when school came around, but it was the only way I could have real nice clothes."

Arthur and David's older brothers worked in the café too, but David was the only one deemed competent enough to be in charge of the gas station.

The family moved on—to a yellow stucco house on M Street in Wilmington near Long Beach. And it was well nigh impossible to track accurately David's various recollections of his early teens. His memory was spotty, like a radio signal in stormy weather. His most consistent story was that he was physically punished at home to the point of abuse—and that his only recourse was to run away from home at the age of fourteen.

His formal schooling ended in Los Angeles's Banning High School where he completed the eighth grade. He was, according to his summing up of his life, on the road and on his own when most kids were still in junior high school. Given David's inventive, innovative mind and his talent for survival, it was not surprising that he maintained himself quite well, despite his age.

At fifteen, David had a steady girlfriend. He met Brenda Kurges through his sister Susan. "Brenda taught me about sex," he insisted. Brenda was also fifteen, a small attractive girl with chiseled features, olive skin, compelling brown eyes, and long, straight, almost black hair.

She was fathered by her mother's first husband, who left when she was small. She would look for him for most of her life before she located the stranger who was her father. No man could have lived up to her idealized picture, and of course, her real father did not. Brenda's life was bleak. Her half-siblings came along with regularity, and she was a little ashamed that most of them had different fathers. She had virtually no clothes and far too much responsibility for a fifteen-year-old.

She was desperately unhappy at home. "I was the oldest of eleven kids, and I was the 'mother.' I ran away twice. The first time I ran was with David's sister Susan, and we went to Lawndale and got caught. We got caught the next time too."

David was well aware of Brenda's home situation, and of her desperation to be free of it. He was attracted to the petite brunette, partially, he believed, because she too was living in an "abusive" home. "She was very lonely. . . . Her mother was worse than mine."

Ideally for his needs, David had found someone dependent, suggestible, and trapped in the cage of her life, her prettiness dulled by poverty. He recalled that Brenda dressed in "rags." He saw himself in the role of her rescuer.

Indeed, he was.

Brenda had a boyfriend, Andy, who was also a friend of David's. "Andy was just a nice boy. He wasn't mean or demanding. No sex or nothing like that," she remembered. "Andy took me to the first movie I ever saw. It was *The Yellow Submarine*." David asked Andy if he could take Brenda out—just once. "Andy said okay, and we went out," Brenda said. "That was just kind of it. From then on, I was with David. He said, 'You're going to stay with me.' So I did."

It was not so much David's physical appearance that appealed to Brenda, but rather the fact that he was the first person in her whole life who seemed to want to protect her. She had learned to expect nothing, and suddenly there was someone who cared for her. She was vulnerable, innocent, and artless. "He was kind of 'puffy' then too—not like later—but a little overweight," Brenda recalled, sounding puzzled that she was once married to David Brown. "He had acne—but it wasn't too bad, and then he started to pick at it, and it bled."

David lost weight when he started seeing Brenda—to the point that his jaw was lean and hard, and in some pictures taken during that time in the midsixties, he had a Presleyesque look. Many girls might have been drawn to *that* David. In fact, there was a profound sexual attraction between pretty little Brenda and the boy whose voice and words were so persuasive, although she could not—and cannot—explain it. He sent her original poems written just for her. His poetry was amateurish and cloying, but his thoughts and feelings seemed so loving.

Brenda saw David's deep depressions early on. One day, she went to the yellow house on M Street after school and found him on the patio. "He was just staring at his feet, and he was so down. He said, 'Nobody loves me. I have no friends. No one cares,' and I told him, 'I care about you.'"

David was jealously possessive of Brenda from the start. He even made her wait outside men's rest rooms while he was inside. "Like he thought someone was going to come along and pick me up!" Brenda said. "One time, the police picked us up in Redondo 'cause I was waiting by the men's bathroom and they didn't believe I was waiting for David."

Brenda was jealous of David, too. During the early years of their relationship, she loved him completely. "He told me he knew I was going to run away again, and that I couldn't take care of myself—so he was going to go with me and take care of me."

And so he did.

When he was barely sixteen, they ran away together—first to Brenda's grandfather, who lived in a hotel in Wilmington. "He tried to talk me out of it and told me I should go back to school, but I'd made up my mind to stay with David." They got a job at her grandfather's hotel—painting the stairways—to pay for their room, then moved on when that work ran out. They lived by their wits, finding work for a few days or a week.

David was adept at taking care of them. "We worked at odd jobs— waiting tables, doing yard work, or in service stations, fast-food places. We paid our own way," he remembered. And then they were hired by a place called Aunt Sally's Guesthouse* in Lawndale. Elderly people lived there in a cluster of cottages. Brenda cooked and served breakfast and ironed. David did maintenance work.

At first, their situation was idyllic. They had their own room, warm and private and hidden from the world. The work wasn't nearly as hard as Brenda's duties at home. She was wonderfully in love with David, and so grateful to him that he had rescued her. Sexually, *then*, they were perfectly matched, and their escape from home had brought them to floating, dreamy days, a honeymoon where only the two of them existed.

"The guy who ran Aunt Sally's was really generous," Brenda recalled. "He only had one hand, and he needed help—so he didn't even check our ages or anything. We didn't have to pay rent, and we had plenty to eat. I didn't get to eat like that at home! We could have ice cream or whatever we wanted! We had clothes and we had movie money. We were teenagers just having a good time."

Twenty years later, there was awe in Brenda Kurges Brown Sands's voice as she spoke of having enough of anything she wanted to eat. *And clothes . . . and movies . . .* And someone to love her and take care of her. David sang along to Neil Diamond songs, and because she loved him, Brenda thought he was romantic, "but really, he couldn't sing that well."

David was funny too. He would tease Brenda when she was trying

to discuss something seriously, saying, "Well, let's go ask Maynard."
"Maynard wasn't anybody but a joke David made up."

But even in that paradise of Aunt Sally's Guesthouse, there was a
rude awakening. David discovered an odd little switchboard behind
the bread box in the kitchen and soon deduced that anyone could
listen in to activity in the different rooms and cottages by flipping a
toggle switch. The system was designed to check on the welfare of
the elderly guests, but David explained to Brenda that they were
being spied on. *Someone* had been listening to them when they thought
they were alone. The tone of his voice, the fear he conveyed to her,
had a profound effect.

"We were scared," Brenda said, a shiver in her voice. "We began
to think that the place was evil, that people had been listening to us
and maybe *watching* us when we were in our room. One night, we
were holding hands and walking to the store to buy some Ripple wine,
and we could just feel hidden eyes looking at us."

David had always believed in evil forces and ghosts, and the more
the two teenagers talked about it, the more they were afraid. "Finally,
David just said, 'This place is evil,' and we called his parents and
they came and got us and took us back to their house on M Street."

Brenda envied David the yellow house and his parents. "David said
his mother beat him with the pipe of her vacuum cleaner, and that
he was the 'black sheep' of his family—but I didn't believe it. I got
along fine with his parents. They fed me, and they gave me a room
to sleep in. Manuela was good to me. But David would tease her and
call her stupid and say she didn't know nothing."

Even as a teenager, David was preoccupied with his health. He
either believed, or wanted others to believe, that he was dying of
cancer. He told Brenda that his colitis was just eating him up. She
wasn't sure what colitis was, but it sounded deadly. "He always had
the runs, and he was always sweaty and he got overheated so easy."

When David had his tonsils out—paid for by his parents' insurance—Brenda sat beside him, terrified that he would die in his sleep.
Suddenly, he started throwing up blood, torrents of it. Brenda believed that he was in his death throes, the bloody fate David had
always predicted. Panicked, Brenda ran for the nurses.

David had only coughed and ripped the stitches in his throat open.
They took him back into surgery and repaired the damage. But the
episode served to convince Brenda even more that David had only a
tenuous hold on life.

David's health problems did not affect his sexuality. "He wanted sex three times a day," his first wife recalled. At the same time, David wanted his wife to appear circumspect, almost prim. "He wouldn't let me wear makeup."

David, who had no high school diploma, found his job opportunities limited to "good old fast foods—El Taco, Der Wiener Schnitzel— whatever it took to keep me and her fed." Then in the fall of 1969, Brenda and David traveled to Salt Lake City and stayed with Brenda's grandmother. David worked for one of her relatives who was building a house, and they spent Thanksgiving and Christmas in Utah, enjoying the snow, but also realizing that their economic situation wasn't much better in the Mormon community than it had been in California.

"We came back home on the bus, and we applied for welfare," Brenda said. "It *bothered me*. My mom lived on welfare, and I never wanted to do that. David hated it too." But they had little choice. Brenda was pregnant, an unplanned event that strained their barebones budget. They moved into a tiny apartment in Wilmington. Unwieldy and clumsy as only very small women can be in late pregnancy, Brenda nevertheless helped paint the house next door to earn extra money.

David said he pleaded with his family and hers for their permission to marry Brenda. At length, the families relented and signed their consents. David and Brenda were married in Los Angeles on May 13, 1970, and they moved into apartment E at 1474 Magnolia Avenue in Long Beach. Brenda went into labor on the first of July and spent two days alone with hard contractions at the Harbor General Hospital in Torrance. David had a weak stomach and couldn't bear the sight of blood, or the sounds of pain.

Their baby girl was born on July 3, 1970. She weighed six pounds, fifteen ounces. Her parents were four months short of their eighteenth birthdays.

They named her Cinnamon Darlene.

"It was pretty and it was different, and we wanted her to be special," Brenda recalled. "In case she was ever famous, she would have that special name."

_D A V I D_ was very proud of Cinnamon Darlene, and Brenda took innumerable snapshots of him cradling his baby girl in his arms. A coming-home-from-the-hospital picture of father and daughter, with David holding Cinnamon in front of his parents' house on M Street, as he stared into the sun. David and Cinnamon in front of a Christmas tree. David and Cinnamon at Disneyland. In those early days, his hair was thick and slicked back into a pompadour, and he had long sideburns and the half sneer/half smile so like Elvis's.

Cinnamon was a chubby, beautiful baby with huge brown eyes and thick dark hair who laughed all the time. Her daddy held her in another photo in their apartment on Magnolia. David stood in front of drapes patterned with yellow and avocado daisies.

He quickly became the center of Cinnamon's world. He made a concentrated effort, it would seem, to capture and hold her absolute devotion. He was the _fun_ parent, the one who took her to Disneyland, who zoomed around the block with her on motorcycle rides as she squealed happily, who tickled her and teased her until she giggled.

Brenda did the "scut" work, the boring, tiresome part of parenting. She handled the discipline and she walked the floor with her sick baby. David was the parent with the fey sense of humor, the wit that Cinnamon would inherit. From the very beginning of her life, David programed Cinnamon to believe that her daddy was the most wonderful, funniest, most powerful man in the world.

She adored him.

David Arnold Brown's ambition accelerated. He and Brenda were still on food stamps and received a partial grant of $235 a month from Aid to Dependent Children, Los Angeles County Department of Public Social Services.

He wanted more. So much more.

David enrolled in the WIN, Work Incentive Program, through the welfare department, a government program designed to train—or retrain—welfare recipients for the job market. He rapidly achieved his high school degree by taking the GED (general equivalency diploma) tests. In April of 1971, he received his scores:

	Score	U.S. Percentile
Correctness of Effectiveness of Expression:	55	69
Interpretation of Reading Materials, Social Studies:	58	79
Interpretation of Reading Materials, Natural Sciences:	53	62
Interpretation of Literary Materials:	59	82
General Mathematical Ability:	53	62

David Brown, with only an eighth-grade education, scored well above seniors in a sample of 38,773 high schools in America. He was not a runaway genius, according to the GED tests, but he was smart. David wanted to be a computer technician and the WIN program agreed to send him to the Control Data Institute in Los Angeles. He had to wait almost a year before he actually began training at Control Data, and in the meantime, he applied for a number of jobs in the computer field. The rejection letters were all the same: "We do not have an opening commensurate with your background."

Despite insistence that he was in failing health, David was classified 1-A by the Selective Service, Local Board 127, in Long Beach in July 1971. He requested a hearing in August, and whatever he told them worked. He never served in the military.

Brenda, David, and Cinnamon moved from the little upstairs Magnolia Avenue apartment in Long Beach to a larger one at 2162 Canton Street. David worked part-time pumping gas in a Mohawk station and commuted to work on a motorcycle. Later, he bought an older yellow Ford Galaxy from Arthur for $75. On a WIN form, he listed his last three jobs as a "materials handler" for a foam company, a carpenter/mason for a Lawndale builder, and a nonpaid data processor for a computer company.

"We went to Gold Key and bought furniture for the apartment on Canton Street," Brenda remembered. "I was the one who ended up paying it off. I liked that apartment. Later, David's mother borrowed the bedroom set, and I haven't seen it since, except for one chest I needed later."

The marriage was relatively happy, although David seemed determined to keep Brenda dependent upon him. They were much happier when she trusted only in him. He didn't even want her to have a driver's license. "He thought I was a dummy," Brenda said. "I asked a neighbor to teach me how to drive, and David was mad when I surprised him and showed him my license."

David wasn't *physically* violent with Brenda—not for a long time, and then only once. While they were living on Canton Street in Long Beach, he did beat her. She called her father-in-law. "I told Art and Art came over and told David, 'You lay a hand on her again, and I'll beat *you* up!'"

Arthur Brown's wrath had a significant effect on David.

They moved yet again, this time to a two-bedroom apartment on Juno Avenue in Anaheim. Their marriage was destined to be short, however—an estimation of its actual length depended on whether Brenda or David related the story. She said they were married about three years and David recalled it was five, although he admitted to an abysmal memory for dates, times, anniversaries. Since David was married to someone else by 1974, Brenda's recall appeared more accurate.

Brenda characterized David as totally, constantly consumed with women—all women. "He was oversexed. That's the only way I can say it. He was always leaning out of the car or turning around to look at women. He knew it made me mad, but he was *obsessed*. It didn't matter if they were young or old, or whatever. . . . I just couldn't stand it." David, in turn, accused Brenda of infidelity and said she was violent and psychologically abused him.

Even though she and David had sex three times a day, she said he wasn't satisfied. "He still wanted more. He came to me and told me that he thought he'd gotten married too young and hadn't had enough sexual experience. He asked my permission to go out with a woman he'd met at work at Cal Comp in Anaheim. She was older and had two kids. I really tried to understand him, and his argument kind of made sense, so I said okay."

After that, there were trips overnight. David told his wife that he was going "deer hunting" with a male friend. She wasn't duped. "I knew it was a woman."

At the same time, David was still jealously possessive of Brenda. He forbade her to go to lunch with her coworkers and when she defied him, accused her of infidelity. Brenda recalled her shock one day in 1974 as she stood frozen at the entry to a local café. Her husband was sitting in a booth, his hands caressing another woman. It was the first time she had actually *seen* him with someone else, and it hurt her badly.

Her name was Lori. "She was a plain girl—slender," Brenda said.

"I asked him about it and he said he was working." She knew he was lying.

Soon after, when Brenda was working a Saturday shift in her office job and David was taking care of Cinnamon, he brought the child in and plopped her down, saying, "You take her—I'm busy." Brenda asked Cinnamon what they had been doing. "She told me she'd been riding on a motorcycle with 'Daddy and a girl.' I thought she meant one of her little friends, but she said, 'No a *big* girl—for Daddy.' It was Lori."

Shortly after that, David brought Lori home to the apartment he shared with Brenda. He had divorce papers in his hand. He gave them to Brenda and announced he wanted custody of Cinnamon. "He introduced Lori to me by saying, 'This is the woman I'm going to marry.' " Brenda refused to divorce David, thinking that he would tire of Lori.

David, of course, remembered a different scenario. He insisted that he met Lori Carpenter at work at Century Data. She was an assembler on the line, "just a friend" who comforted him when Brenda was unfaithful to him. "My *sister* caught her cheating on me. I just packed my clothes and took the car and left everything to her. That divorce really tore me up."

Whichever version was true, the brief marriage was clearly in its death throes, and at some point as their relationship unraveled, Brenda became eerily afraid of David. "I don't know why, but I had this terrible fear that he was going to smother me to death with a pillow while I was asleep. He never tried it as far as I remember, but I used to wake up unable to breathe, dreaming, maybe, that he had covered my face with a pillow." She lay awake, long after David seemed to be asleep, watching shadows slide down the wall, afraid to close her eyes.

Brenda finally got up the nerve to leave David, enlisting her boss's help to move her furniture out. When David came home that evening, he walked into a completely empty apartment. The landlady was there, checking it over. David told her that he must be in the wrong apartment. She assured him that he was in the correct apartment, but that his wife and child were gone. "They took everything when they left."

David was enraged.

"David came to where I worked and held a gun up against my head and said that if he couldn't have me, nobody could," Brenda remembered. "I just didn't care. I told him to go ahead and shoot me, because he'd never get away. The police would lock him up forever. I was just so tired of fighting him. He finally dropped the gun and walked away."

Brenda had moved to a smaller apartment, also on Juno Avenue. There was a brief—one week—reconciliation when she let David move in with her. She came home after work to find him calling Lori on her phone. "That was it. I heard him telling Lori he loved her. I chased him out."

A day or so later, he came back to get his rifle. Brenda was afraid to let him have it. That was when they struggled over the rifle and David hit Brenda with his car.

Brenda didn't dislike Lori and felt more relieved than anything when David left her. "No more colon cancer talk all the time. No more other women." But Brenda was terrified that David would win custody of Cinnamon, because Lori's father was an attorney. "I didn't have any idea how to get a lawyer, and I didn't have any money. I looked up some lawyer's name in the phone book, and I went to the California Building on Euclid and rode up on the elevator and walked right into his office. I told him, 'I need help and don't have any money.' He said we could work that out in time payments. I didn't want any alimony. I just wanted child support."

David was astounded. The fourteen-year-old girl he had protected was now twenty-one and able to take care of herself.

Brenda—the *young* Brenda—was the prototype, David's sexual ideal, and she always would be. His image of the ideal sex object did not mature as he aged. He would continue to fixate on teenage girls. After his first divorce, he was still in his early twenties and there was only a slight discrepancy in age between himself and pubescent girls. As he grew older, that discrepancy grew larger.

Girls in their teens gave David more respect and listened raptly to his stories of his accomplishments. They appreciated the gifts he gave them. Their skin was smooth and soft, their breasts and bellies unmarred by stretch marks, their legs long and coltish. They seldom drew back in shock when David told them his sexual preferences; they were still malleable and suggestible—unlike grown women.

Brenda and David's parting was most assuredly not a friendly divorce, but the bitter feelings eased after the decree was handed down. Brenda was given custody of Cinnamon and raised her with the help of sitters. David had weekend custody. Cinnamon was her daddy's girl, according to David. "She was the perfect child. Well mannered . . . polite. After the divorce, she flipped from that to a withdrawn child who didn't like to be held and was nervous, fidgety, and constantly drifting off."

David didn't do well after the divorce either. Young as he was when he began with Brenda, he had fallen easily into the pattern that would define all his relationships with women. He had to be in charge. Brenda had *belonged* to him, and she had looked up to him. Her defection took the spine out of his self-confidence. He remembered the first gun incident and described how he placed the rifle to Brenda's head with the firm intention of killing her and then himself. But she had proved stronger and gutsier than he. She had shown disdain— not fear—even with the immediate threat of the gun against her flesh.

After his divorce from Brenda, David's episodes of overwhelming depression exacerbated. His sexual appetites waxed and waned— either causing (or caused by) his depressions. At times, he felt tremendous sexual drive. Conversely, he periodically suffered from a complete loss of interest in anything sexual. Since his libido approached satyriasis, this diminution of desire left him a hollow man. Sexual performance and fulfillment were central to his existence; he was a man consumed by sex. It was during this ten-year period when his sexual performance and outlet were sporadically blunted that David was hospitalized three times for depression and suicidal thoughts.

But then, like the phoenix itself, he always pulled himself together and rebounded. He now had his technical degree from the Control Data Institute. However much he tended to embroider and pad his résumé, to boast of his accomplishments, one thing was immutable. David Brown proved remarkably adept in the burgeoning computer industry.

After working for Century Data in Anaheim, he moved steadily upward over the next five or six years, employed by a half dozen other computer companies. "I doubled my salary. In this business, they'll bid for you if you're good—and I am good."

He saw a way to become wealthy and respected.

15

M O R E   T H A N most people, David had lived his life in clearly
defined phases, the demarcation points generally determined by the
beginnings and endings of his marriages. He was thirty-two, and there
had been five of them, so many in such a relatively short time frame
that his confusion with dates might have been expected. Each wife
changed his life, but he had long since forgotten the dates of his many
weddings and divorces.

Records show that David married Lori Carpenter on October 4,
1974, in Yorba Linda, and then moved into a rental house on Randolph
Street in Riverside. It was a drab house and so was the street it sat
on. David could not recall how old he was or how old Lori was,
beyond his impression that she was "a couple of years younger than
I was." He was actually twenty-two and she was nineteen, a bit older
than he preferred. Lori loved four-year-old Cinnamon, and Cinny
visited them regularly on weekends.

"My dad was fun," Cinnamon remembered. "He played with me,
tickling me and acting silly, or he'd build things like a railroad track.
He included me in the things he did . . . or shared enough to please
me. That was when I'd visit him on the weekends after my parents
divorced. I got attention from him that my mom didn't—*couldn't* give
me because of work."

Brenda worried. One weekend, she had a nightmare that Cinnamon
was drowning. "It was so real that I called David and asked him to
check on Cinny. He just got mad and said I was stupid." Cinnamon,
however, remembered that she *had* almost drowned. "It was in a pool
by his and Lori's house. That day, my father was playing 'shark' with
me, and I remember being so frightened. . . . Sometimes my dad
would keep playing even after I was frightened already."

Although Lori had accepted Cinnamon eagerly, David's second
marriage foundered in four years. They separated on October 13,
1978. David cited "incompatibility." It was not surprising that they
were incompatible or that Lori left him. Her husband had long since
found someone else.

David encountered Linda Bailey for the first time while he still lived
with Lori. His attraction to her was immediate, much as it had been

when he was first drawn to Brenda. The fact that he had grown older mattered not at all.

Linda Bailey was only thirteen or fourteen when she caught the eye of the man who lived two houses down the street. She was pretty and blond and sweet. It was as if David had found Brenda again—the Brenda who thought he was God a long time ago and had laughingly come to call him "King David."

Like Brenda, Linda Bailey was one of eleven brothers and sisters in a home held together only tenuously by a single mother. From oldest to youngest, the Baileys were Sheri, Rick, Jeff, Tom, Pam, Linda, Alan, Randy, Larry, Ralph, and Patti. Ethel Bailey, born Ethel Anderson in Nebraska and trapped now in Riverside, California, was forty-two years old and overwhelmed by the emotional and financial responsibility for a near-dozen offspring. Like Brenda's family, Linda's family lived on welfare payments.

"There were seven little kids at home, living on noodles, rice, and Kool-Aid," David said. "No meat. Ethel spent her check on beer and cigarettes. I gave them a turkey and a large ham for Christmas." Nobody recalled exactly when David Brown began to visit the Bailey household in Riverside, but once he entered their lives, he became a familiar face, and he seemed at first like a godsend.

Ethel Bailey said that David came to her and explained that he was dying of colon cancer; he wondered if her teenage daughters might help out with cleaning his house—for a wage, of course. The doctors had told him that he probably wouldn't live more than six months. His marriage was disintegrating, his house was a mess, and he desperately needed help.

Ethel Bailey accepted David Brown at face value. A sick man who needed help—but who was also willing to help others. "How do you say no to a dying man? I had no reason to doubt him—then." Beyond that, David had the ability to stay cheerful, despite his grim prognosis. He had a great sense of humor and he was a pleasure to have around. It seemed rather brave of him to go off to work each day, with the death sentence hanging over his head.

Ethel Bailey didn't know that David Brown was playing Fagin to several of her daughters. He delighted in persuading them that it would be a "trip" to see if they could steal tools that careless owners had left lying around in the backs of pickup trucks. They grew quite adept at lifting things. David made it a game. He could make anything sound reasonable and doable. Later, he would urge Cinnamon to steal small items.

The months passed and David didn't die—nor did he seem to be getting worse. He couldn't explain his miraculous remission. He still complained of pain and rectal bleeding, but it looked as if he wasn't going to die soon, after all.

David first began to date Pam Bailey, a girl in her midteens, almost ten years younger than he was. He became a fixture at the Bailey house, his eye really fastened on thirteen-year-old Linda. If he dropped in and saw the young Baileys were eating corn flakes for supper, he simply headed down to McDonald's or to a pizza place and brought back food for everybody. Or he would pile two or three of the kids in the car and take them along. Because they were so dirt-poor that there seemed no way out, so *young* and poor that schoolmates' gibes about clothes cut to the heart, David Brown had an enormous impact on the Bailey children—particularly Linda, who soon supplanted her older sister as his special friend. David was Santa Claus and the Easter Bunny and their savior. With no father in the home, or even in contact, with a mother who blunted her misery with alcohol, the younger Baileys quickly learned to depend on David.

He was making good money working with computers, and he spent a good deal of it on the Baileys. "I bought those kids the first store-bought clothes they ever had. I bought them clothes, toys. . . . I took the whole stinkin' family to Disneyland and Magic Mountain. Yeah . . . I'm a *horrible* man," he later said sarcastically. "The older kids didn't care that the younger ones had no Christmas."

Linda Bailey was barely budding into puberty when David first saw her, and he was cautious in his infatuation with her. She was slender and fresh faced, so compliant and so impressed with everything David Brown said or did. She hung around him and gazed at him with adoring eyes. There was little doubt that she loved him, quite literally, until the day she died.

Linda was the seventh of Ethel Bailey's eleven children, a twin; one of the last half dozen fathered by one Clyde Dalrymple of Pennsylvania—a man long gone from her life. She told David she was miserable at home. He was a most sympathetic listener. Linda confided her problems and her fears to David, grateful that, at last, she could tell someone.

He was the first hope she had of getting out.

Still legally married, David finally began to date Linda. She was no more than fifteen at the time. A mature fifteen, but still a young teenager. He was twenty-four. Then David announced one day that a miracle had occurred; he had beaten the cancer. The doctors were cautious—but it looked as if he might be around a little longer than they had originally estimated.

Linda went to her brother Rick's wife, Mary, and explained that she wanted to be sexually active. She asked about birth control. Mary tried to dissuade her, but when she realized Linda was determined to sleep with David, she advised her to go down to the free clinic and get birth control pills. When Ethel Bailey heard about Linda's plans, she was furious. There was an argument, and neither mother nor daughter would back down.

Linda left home and moved in with Rick and Mary. "She was quite a basket case when she first came to us," Mary recalled. "She felt bad about splitting with her mom. She lived with us for about two years. Then she decided she was going to marry David."

Six months later, when Linda was seventeen, Ethel Bailey finally gave her consent, and Linda and David, accompanied by Ethel and Linda's twin brother, Alan, drove to Las Vegas where they were married on June 21, 1979.

David was working as "the youngest manager of a worldwide customer-service department" for Memorex and making good money. For the first time in her life, Linda Bailey Brown had the home she had longed for. The man so sexually attracted to her was her husband, and she welcomed his attentions. Even so, David's third marriage ended even sooner than the first two, despite his avowed infatuation with his young bride. Maybe Linda was too young for marriage. After living together only one month and twenty-four days, they separated on August 14, 1979. On September 18, David sued Linda for divorce.

"David kicked her out of his house and divorced her," Mary Bailey remembered. "She moved back in with us. She dated other guys, and I would have chosen any one of them over David."

Mary Bailey, a robust, take-charge woman, was relieved that Linda's marriage had ended. She didn't like David Brown, found him "weird," and thought that Linda should be dating boys closer to her own age—not living with some man who was nine years older than she was, had already had two wives, and always had an eye out for other women. Mary Bailey felt she had his number. "Linda had other boyfriends, lots of them," she said. "It wasn't as if David was the only one who wanted her. But he had some kind of hold over her—she just never really wanted anyone but David. Don't ask me why."

David insisted that the marriage foundered because of Linda's immaturity and her lifestyle. "We were married, for, I think it was like several months. And I found out that, uh, I'm not even positive if it was alcohol or drugs, but she knew that I was against both very strongly, and, uh, she couldn't break it, so we got a divorce and I immediately bounced to a girl that worked for me, while I was manager at Memorex. *Cindy.*"

David was married again, for the fourth time, almost immediately. He was twenty-seven, and in his own words, "on the rebound." But true to form, he could not recall his age or Cindy's age, or their wedding date or where they got married. The wedding date of record was May 24, 1980. They separated on Christmas Eve of the same year, and David sued Cindy for divorce on January 28, 1981.

David described Cindy as "a gorgeous one" and sounded slightly guilty at the way he had deceived his fourth wife. He had never truly let go of Linda. "I was cheating on Cindy—Linda and I kept seeing each other while I was married to Cindy." But David also complained that, although Cindy was absolutely beautiful, she had a "limited intellectual capacity," and while they had a steamy sexual relationship, they had had little in common beyond that. Cindy also had two children for whom David felt no affinity.

Despite his many intervening marriages, David asked his first wife, Brenda, to baby-sit for Cindy's kids often, and she usually acquiesced. "He told me he and Cindy could never go out because of the kids." Brenda also stayed on good terms with David's second wife, Lori. "Lori was good to Cinnamon. Even after David divorced her, she still came and got Cinnamon and bought her clothes."

Cindy, wife number four, had been impressed with David's job, but proved to be a little too acquisitive for her bridegroom's taste. "She wanted everything—monetarily—and I was unable to keep up with her demands." David was doing well at Memorex—$36,000 a year—but he had hinted to Cindy that he made more than that; it was one of his failings, that self-aggrandizement.

Whatever the true reason for his fourth divorce, David returned to his third wife, his teenage love. David said he had left Linda the first time because she took drugs or drank too much; he couldn't exactly remember which. No one else remembered that Linda had a problem with either drugs or alcohol during her first marriage to David. Years later, David's memory of Linda's fall from grace was more precise. He said that she had been using cocaine. It was a moot point. Linda was dead by then.

David's courtship of his third—and soon-to-be *fifth*—wife accelerated. He showered Linda with presents and overwhelmed her with promises that this time things would be different. He told her that he realized he loved her, and he always would. Their sex life had been a powerful part of their relationship, passionate and innovative. Both of them had missed that. David bragged to anyone who would listen that they made love at least once a day, and never the same way twice.

Around Christmas of 1980, Linda moved out of Mary and Rick Bailey's home—and back in with David, almost before the door had shut behind Cindy. She was older when she moved in with David again. This time, she believed they would make a go of their relationship.

It should have been a happy ending, two young people who loved each other so much they could not stay apart. Even so, Linda's return to David alienated her from her family. "We considered him a user," Mary Bailey said bluntly. "We didn't want her to go back. But she wouldn't listen to anyone. . . . David could make women feel important. Just the way he talked. His voice could convince you or persuade you. He could turn it on."

The estrangement didn't last long. Linda's family cared too much about her. Mary remembered Linda as one of the kindest people she ever met. "She couldn't stand to see anyone suffer. One time, she saw this guy in the winter without a coat, and she went and bought him a nice new leather jacket and gave it to him. I didn't have the heart to tell her he'd probably turn around and sell it. That's the way Linda was—she couldn't do enough to help you. She couldn't stand to see anyone cold or hungry or unhappy."

Of all the Bailey sisters, Linda was the one who was the warmest, most affectionate, and fun loving. What she felt for this man so full of pretense and braggadocio was a mystery to her family, but they loved her and wanted to stay close. They had mixed emotions when Linda and David announced plans to remarry. Mary Bailey, of course, disapproved. Frankly, she thought Linda could have done better. She had argued against David as a husband until she was blue in the face—but to no avail. Linda adored the man.

"I finally gave up and said nothing. I could see it wasn't doing any good, and it was driving a wedge between Linda and me. But even when we made up with Linda, we didn't see her often. David didn't like to have her spending time with her family, our visits weren't encouraged, and he was furious if she ever discussed any problems with us. He wanted her all to himself."

Others in the Bailey family were glad to have David back in the fold. He was such a go-getter that they believed him completely when he talked about all the businesses he was going to start. He was an egomaniac and a bullshitter, but David Brown might well be a way out for more of them besides Linda. He hinted that there would be jobs for many of them when he got his enterprises going.

Manuela and Arthur Brown, while a little surprised at their son's many marriages before the age of thirty and not particularly fond of Linda, were relieved that he finally seemed to have settled down. All those marriages and divorces couldn't be good for his health. The emotional strain of having one marriage after another disintegrate must surely have contributed to his ulcers and colitis and asthma, and all the other ailments he suffered from.

The mercurial state of his health was only one of the many paradoxes about David Brown. He talked of being constantly ill and of having little energy, and yet he exuded an aura of self-confidence and can-do. Nobody he interacted with ever seemed to doubt him—in either mode. David was not a well man and had to be coddled, but he was also a winner in the world of business.

Either deliberately or with some innate sense he possessed, David surrounded himself with people who viewed him as an infinitely superior man. He was smarter, savvier, better educated, and older than all his women. He really had no male friends—only employees. He had crafted his own world—where no one would question him or doubt him, or second-guess him. He was good to those he let into his life, free with his money, and he continually hinted at rewards yet to come.

He gave the women in his life jewelry and presents and promises and poems. He made jokes and kept his women laughing. He became, for three young females, as vital as the very air they breathed. Interestingly, they all used the same phrase to describe him: *their life support system*.

EXCERPTS FROM TWO ORIGINAL POEMS BY DAVID ARNOLD BROWN
(TO HIS WIFE)

That Inward Sun Is Our Hope & Faith For Tomorrow
One Good, Happy Tomorrow Can Wash Away A Lot of Ugly
Yesterdays.
I Am Here For You—Today, Tomorrow, Forever.

Life Will Be Wonderful
Love Will Be Too
Both Will Be Cherished
While I Share Them With You

16

R O M A N T I C that he was, David Brown did not let it interfere with his own ambitions. "The Process" was his breakthrough. It verified what he had always promised. The Process would bring him financial rewards far beyond what even he had visualized. And it would give him prestige and respect, which he craved even more. No one would ever remember the David Brown who had scraped by on welfare. He had already done well financially; he wanted to be a millionaire.

In a mushrooming computer age, there were inherent nightmares. Anyone who has ever relied on a computer lives in dread of losing the precious information stored on disks. Business files, customer lists, accounts payable, creative work, in the blink of an eye, all of it can disappear, swallowed up somewhere deep in the bowels of a previously user-friendly computer.

In the early 1980s, even more than today, computer data was vulnerable to siege. Fires, hurricanes, earthquakes, tornados, floods, power surges and outages, and human error can wreak computer disaster. "Disk error" was a message that sent a chill through the user. A "crashed" system could bring a company to its knees financially.

David Brown was not an "egghead"—computer-programer type; he was a specialist in a new kind of rescue service. His knowledge was deceptively simple—but there was a demand for it, and he always spoke of it in a hushed voice, enhancing the impression that he was onto something really big.

David started his own company, which he called Data Recovery, and he got a big leg up in 1981 when he went to work for Randomex Inc. in Signal Hill, California, as a subcontractor. Randomex had designed a system to repair damaged computer disks so that they could be read for backup and the vital information hidden there miraculously recovered.

Randomex profited from the fact that too many computer users neglected to keep backup disks stored outside their offices or had backup systems that had failed. The specialists at Randomex had refined their techniques to the point where they could recover data from fourteen-inch removable disk packs, and from hard drives and floppy disks. They were successful in retrieving 40 to 60 percent of the data lost by their frantic customers. That salvage could mean the difference between bankruptcy or survival for the small businessman.

David Brown studied the Randomex system as he worked for the company. He learned how to treat and clean the "media"—the disks—and make the heads fly back over the damaged area, bring the drives up to speed, and copy the *good* data onto another disk or tape. If he could improve on Randomex's percentage, David figured he would have himself a gold mine.

As indeed he did.

Randomex made all the contacts with potential customers, and David or Linda or some other family member on David's staff would pick up the damaged disks for treatment. When David came down himself, he never talked much. The executives at Randomex didn't like him, and they didn't dislike him. They never really knew him. He was simply "Data Recovery," a little subcontractor.

David added a few twists of his own and came up with what he call The Process. It was his, and his alone. He gave no credit to those who had taught him; his improvements were the real key. He soon was able to retrieve consistently a solid 70 percent of the data on the damaged disks given to him. David's special area of expertise was minidisks, the tiny hard disks that hold an unbelievable amount of data.

Cautious almost to the point of paranoia, David trained only those people he truly trusted, or over whom he wielded some power, in The Process. Even to detectives later, he could not bring himself to describe The Process in any detail. He called it "a hands-on project—what people out there call 'the magic of making it work' . . . I guess you call it the power of what we do—see, all this time, no one else can do this."

He always lapsed into inscrutable and deliberately vague phrases when asked to describe The Process. Linda was the first to have all the pieces of his formula. David trusted Linda because she adored him. "Well, I developed The Process," he explained. "I designed computers and disk drives and all kinds of stuff like that. I trained people like Sperry Univac. . . . I trained other engineers, so training Linda . . . I used training materials I used to teach other people to teach her, training materials I had written and developed."

Linda had no high school education, but The Process didn't require that. It required careful, tedious attention to the job at hand—but no special intelligence or talent. Actually, despite all the mystery surrounding David's process, and his determined efforts to remain obscure about the magic he wrought, his technique required little more than patience, Q-Tips, rubbing alcohol, and nonoily detergent. Sometimes he and Linda would have to run the damaged disks through The Process only once, and sometimes over and over, but they delivered what the customer wanted, and Randomex rewarded them with more and more jobs.

David Brown's 1099 income tax forms reflected his growing skill at data retrieval. In 1981, he was paid $11,255 by Randomex. In 1982, $98,143.85; 1983—$124,905.82; 1984—$171,141.79. His data retrieval income dropped in 1985 to $114,081.02, but that was understandable, given his shock and grief over the loss of his wife and business partner.

The Randomex income was gross—not net; David had to pay salaries and the required state taxes and withholdings out of that for his employees. His employees were all "family." Linda's twin brother, Alan, worked for them some, and sometimes David's father, Arthur, helped out. Once in a while, David gave some work to Linda's brother Larry, but he had slight confidence in Larry and was cautious with him. Larry was fired more than he was hired. Later, David taught Arthur some of The Process.

Still, nobody but Linda and David knew the whole process.

That was best. Even though it was not nearly as esoteric as David liked to suggest, it took exactly the right combination of ingredients. That belonged to David Arnold Brown and he was zealously protective of his technique.

Beyond David's Randomex income he had other interests—coin collecting, for one. No one who knew him doubted that David Brown, from one source or another, was well on his way to becoming a millionaire.

As the 1980s progressed, both David's second and fourth wives were long since relegated to dim history. He kept in touch with Brenda only because of Cinnamon. He enjoyed the fact that she still lived with all the old furniture she had cleared out of their apartment. "She's bitter because I'm a millionaire," he liked to tell people.

He and Linda were solid. His place in the Bailey family was established. He was the rich relative. Thus far, the changes he had wrought in their lives were mostly positive. Even those who didn't care for David's high-handedness acknowledged him as a member of the family. They maintained only a gritty, bare standard of living.

David Brown had the power to cast a warm, monetary glow over their existence.

Although he barely noticed her at first, there was another member of the Bailey family who gazed at David with eyes glazed with pure worship. She had been only a little girl of seven or eight when she sat shyly in the corner and listened to the man who brought them hamburgers. She found him quite wonderful and loved to listen to the rumble of his deep voice. He was a man and she was a child. Almost sixteen years yawned between them.

But Patti Bailey adored David Brown almost from the start. He was kind to her and to the rest of the family, and she had always wished she could curl up in his lap and feel safe forever. Patti was so young the first time David married her older sister, not old enough to feel real jealousy—only a kind of wistful longing. Linda got to move into David's nice house and be safe with David. And Patti had to stay behind.

"With Linda gone, Patti was the last young girl left in the Bailey household. She had no one left to run to." Patti was afraid so much of the time. She slept with one eye open, aware of soft male voices and the smell of sweat. Men's and boys' whispers in the dark, their quick hands. Patti thought that, if only she could live in David's house, she would be in heaven.

When Linda's first marriage to David ended, Patti wasn't sure what she felt. Sadness certainly that David wouldn't be part of their family any longer, and perhaps a certain smugness that Linda wasn't as smart as she thought she was. Patti held on to her little girl's dream that someday David would come and take her away and marry her. He was always so nice to her, and he winked at her as if they shared secrets together. She found him handsome with his shiny brown hair and his mustache.

When Linda and David started living together again, Patti was jealous and angry that Linda had had two chances, and she none. She was twelve and she would be a teenager soon. Why hadn't David waited for her? In a way, it was the plight of little sisters everywhere who suffer from hopeless crushes. But Patti Bailey had real, dark reasons to long for rescue. She was as vulnerable as a rabbit trembling in a clearing, and she viewed David Brown as all things kind and good and safe.

Linda knew how things were at home in Riverside, and she invited Patti to spend many weekends with her and David in Victorville where they were living then. David was buying a small house up there and the acre of land surrounding it. Victorville was about forty-five miles north of Riverside, up near Barstow and edging into the Mohave Desert. Patti loved it up there; it was another world. She dreaded going home when Sunday night came. Finally, Linda took Patti aside and told her that she didn't have to go back to Riverside anymore. Linda and David were going to get married again, and that meant Patti could stay.

Patti was ecstatic. When Christmas vacation started that year, she moved out of her family home and into David and Linda's. She would go to Yucca Valley school. Patti Bailey was delivered from despair into the fulfillment of most of her young aspirations. She would live in a clean house with new furniture. She would have all she wanted to eat. She would go to school wearing clothes bought at K Mart and J.C. Penney, new and fashionable. She would watch color television and be able to buy records.

Best of all, she would be near David.

David had rescued her, and Linda had said she could live with them. Her gratitude to both of them was boundless. But most of all, she loved David. He made her so happy. Years later, she would remember the exact date she moved in with David and Linda: "December 19, 1981. I was thirteen."

Once more, David and Linda drove to Las Vegas to be married. She was both his third and fifth wife. It would be the first time in years that David spent two consecutive Christmases with the same wife. And from that point forward, Patti was an integral part of David Brown's family. David and Linda and Patti. And sometimes Cinnamon.

Cinnamon was bounced back and forth between her parents; they often seemed to treat her more as a weapon against one another than a child to be loved and nurtured. If Cinny didn't mind Brenda, she called David and demanded he come and pick Cinnamon up. If David wearied of the day-to-day care of a small child, he packed her clothes and sent Cinnamon home.

Cinnamon was living with David and Linda in Victorville when Patti moved in. They soon moved to a house on West Street in Anaheim. Cinnamon was attending Patrick Henry Elementary School, and she lived with her father's family until July 1983. The girls got along, fighting occasionally as sisters will. They had known each other since Cinny was four or five. Cinnamon was two years younger than Patti, and they were very different. They were not really sisters, not even cousins—but friends. Even after she eventually went back to live with her mother, Cinnamon didn't seem to be jealous that her father let a girl close to her own age live in his home all the time when she only visited during weekends and vacations.

Cinnamon's trial time with her father and Linda and Patti didn't work out. Nobody could really explain why. But she didn't fit in, and her independent spirit was an irritant. Cinnamon was an extrovert where Patti was quiet. Cinnamon had a sense of humor, even then, and she was quick to see the humorous side of things. Patti was solemn and failed to get the puns and quips that Cinnamon tossed out. Cinny was slapdash and detested doing chores, the vacuuming and dishes that were required of the two girls. Patti was neat, maybe because she had lived so long with disorder and because she treasured her new possessions so much.

As dissimilar as the two girls were, Cinny was part of the family. This new family. Linda and Cinny got along fine for most of the year they shared a home, and Cinnamon apparently accepted her step-mother—even though Linda was only twenty. Her father recalled that Cinny was sent back to Brenda "because she wouldn't obey Linda."

Cinnamon was humiliated when David ordered her to stand in front of the whole family in her underwear while he spanked her with a leather belt. (The incident that caused Dr. Howell to report David to authorities for child abuse after Linda was murdered.) Despite the red welts David's belt raised, Cinny refused to cry. She only looked at him defiantly and said, "I hate you. . . . I can't live with you anymore. I hate you."

Cinny went back to Brenda in Anaheim, brokenhearted. She didn't really hate her father. She loved him beyond reason.

If Cinnamon was really incorrigible, it was not apparent to anyone but David. Everyone who knew them had always marveled at how well Linda and Cinnamon got along. Cinnamon would be tossed back and forth a lot over the next few years. At an age where she especially needed to know where she belonged and that she was a worthwhile person, she was tethered nowhere; she floated like a balloon without a string.

She was, however, a child with remarkable insight, who unlike most of her peers accepted the consequences of her own actions. She was frank about her flaws. "I totally hated everybody at the time," Cinnamon recalled. "I felt mad and I was a big snot." At other times, she said she was "a brat. I drove my mom nuts."

But *incorrigible?* No. Perhaps she seemed so to a mother who was only thirty herself and was trying to juggle a new marriage, a new baby, and problems of her own.

"Living with my mom was much different than living with my

dad," Cinnamon said. "Living with my mom, I felt more independent. I got to go with Krista and my friends. I learned to appreciate things more while living with my mom—I valued things more. But I didn't receive as much attention as I wanted. I understood that my mom worked very hard and tried her best. I tried to do things to please my mom. I always wanted better communication with my mom, but she would yell a lot. I'd ask for an explanation and be spanked. I was curious to know what I'd done wrong—so I would not do it again. But she'd be so stressed and impatient, she didn't take the time to communicate."

Still Cinnamon's thirteenth year was, comparatively, her best. Her *only* teenage year. "Krista and I were very happy and active teens. Always doing things like riding each other on my Beach Cruiser [bike] handlebars all over Orange County. . . . Going to the beach with Krista seemed like another life or chapter. We spent a lot of time together. I was active in running and bike riding. I rode my bike to and from school too, while I was living with my father."

Cinnamon still visited her father's home, and she lived by his rules when she stayed there. Everybody did. David wanted to know where they all were, and he expected them to be home on time. David was always in charge. People who didn't obey David's rules didn't stay around long.

"Eventually, I didn't receive as much attention from my dad," Cinnamon remembered of the visits. "Because of his marriage changes and divorces . . . I had to share him with Patti. I wasn't included in family affairs anymore—well not as *much* as before. I wasn't receiving any quality time with my dad. Of course, we still had some great memories. I appreciated my dad's sense of humor, but I also saw my father as selfish with everything . . . he wanted to be the center of attention. He was greedy with material things. Those are things I noticed as I grew up with him."

The doors of any house David Brown and his girls lived in were revolving. He was sporadically generous about letting Linda and Patti's family visit—if they toed his carefully defined marks. Ethel visited with them from time to time, and Linda's twin, Alan. Even Larry stayed over on occasion. But David discouraged more than surface relationships outside his immediate family. He much preferred his own household—not the extended Brown-Brown or Brown-Bailey families. He stressed the need for a closing-in, his modern circle of wagons against intruders.

From the time she was twelve, Patti Bailey believed in the family that David had created. His philosophies became ingrained in her mind, and she followed David as devoutly as any cult member. Anyone who observed his interaction with his teenage sister-in-law could see that Patti had a crush on David, but nobody teased her about it. Linda mentioned it to Mary Bailey, and they smiled and shook their heads. They knew Patti would outgrow her feelings for David when she started to date boys her own age. Linda still thought of Patti as her baby sister, a child.

Patti didn't know much about David's job at first, but she knew it had something to do with computers, and that it was very important. They moved often, so he could be closer to work, and sometimes because he and Linda wanted a nicer house. They always stayed close to Orange County, and they always stayed together so it didn't really matter to Patti that they moved so much. The family meant more than any friends she had at school.

She had to struggle to remember the different places they had lived. Most clearly, she recalled visiting her sister and brother-in-law first in Victorville. Then there was Anaheim, Yorba Linda, Brea, and finally Garden Grove, all within a space of three years. She wasn't concerned about graduating from high school. Linda hadn't graduated, and she had what Patti perceived to be the perfect life.

The family always had fun together. Often David's parents joined them for trips out to the desert or the mountains. They watched television, rented movies, and played board games. David was no athlete, but he was superb at organizing family get-togethers. "It's hard to believe now—but *I* was funny," David recalled much later. "I was always—whatta you call it—the life of the party."

When they lived in Victorville, the house David was buying had plenty of open space around it, and David and Linda and Patti—and whoever was living with them or visiting—would shoot at beer cans, laughing as the cans flew off stumps and somersaulted in the air. David kept several guns, both "big and little." That was the way Patti distinguished between rifles and handguns.

They often drove deep into the Mohave Desert beyond Barstow to the ghost town of Calico. David had a camper and they took iced chests of food and soda pop up into the Calico Mountain area. They would spend hours horsing around on the all-terrain vehicles that David bought them. David loved his "toys," and when he was feeling all right, he played with them just like a kid.

Patti and Linda soon learned that David grew bored quickly with his possessions; he always wanted the newest model. Larry Bailey was driving one of David's ATVs when he crashed into something and bent it up, but didn't do serious damage. David saw it as an opportunity, not a loss. "I don't know the damage," Patti said, "but I know it was minor. David discussed it with Linda and Larry that, well, hey—if we took it out to Calico and pushed it off a cliff, then it'd get really smashed up. Then the insurance company would pay for it."

Patti and Linda helped drag it back out of the gully where it lay crumpled after the "deliberate" accident and steadied it while Larry and David put it on the trailer. "David took it back and he filed a claim. That's when I got an Odyssey instead of an ATV," Patti remembered.

Although David Brown was almost doubling his income each year in his data recovery contracts, he frequently used insurance companies as a way to update his equipment. He collected on a number of automobile accidents. He sued a supermarket, claiming he had injured himself tripping over an extension cord. There was a shed, filled with old furniture and building materials, on the Victorville property. David no longer wanted any of it; he rented a bulldozer and tried to enlist Alan Bailey as the operator. He wanted Alan to crush the shed with the dozer so that he could collect insurance on both the outbuilding and its contents. Alan reneged. He didn't think they could convince anyone that he had *accidentally* run into a structure of that size, and that he would have kept on going until the contents were smashed.

And after they all moved to Garden Grove in 1984, a neighbor's driving mishap proved fortuitous for David. An elderly lady next door lost control of her car in her own driveway when she panicked and pressed down on the gas pedal instead of the brake. Her car leapt across the narrow space between the homes and hit below the window on the side of the Brown house—right at the middle bedroom. Although the damage was minimal, David saw a chance to replace the Commodore computer he was using. He wanted an IBM.

"He moved his desk and the old computer out of his office into the room where the house was hit, and then I guess the computer fell on the floor somehow," Patti recalled. "I wasn't there—I didn't see it happen. Anyway, he made it look worse outside, added dirt and stuff." The neighbor's insurance paid off, and David Brown replaced his computer with a state-of-the-art IBM. He explained to Linda and Patti that that was what insurance was designed to do—pay people for their losses.

All along, David was building up his collections. Rare coins. Gold and diamonds. His rings were all custom designed. The phoenix pendant. David also had business cards printed, with a stylized phoenix "guarding" computer banks. He liked the imagery. He retrieved and revived data that seemed to have been hopelessly lost in fires. He helped it to emerge almost unscathed.

David Arnold Brown saw himself in the phoenix. Mr. Magic.

David not only employed his in-laws, he drew his own family members into his business ventures. He boasted that he had taken a brother and a sister "out of ceramics and started them in data retrieval." The data retrieval business fit right in with David's view of family life. Much of it could be done at home.

David claimed to have fielded extremely important phone calls "from the government or some major corporation. The phones rang all day. It might be the Pentagon or Coca-Cola or whoever." He was quick to brag that he was instrumental in rescuing data from some vital projects and businesses. Data Recovery, he told everyone, had reconstructed most of the lost data in the "towering inferno" First Interstate Bank fire in Los Angeles. He loved to describe his role in rescuing dozens of people from almost certain death in the MGM Grand Hotel fire on November 21, 1980. Because the hotel computers were badly damaged in the conflagration, David said the hotel turned to him for help. Within two hours, he was able to reconstruct its files. This was vital, he pointed out, because the files were the only way to show which rooms had occupants and which were vacant. "I was instrumental in saving the lives of one hundred and twelve hotel guests by directing rescue efforts in Las Vegas—while I was in California. They went directly to the rooms with people in them and didn't waste time on the empty rooms." Despite David's alleged role in the rescue attempts, eighty people did perish in the MGM Grand fire.

When the San Diego blood bank was also hit by fire, David said he was able to restore its computer network so that blood bank employees could trace blood units desperately needed in southern California hospitals.

And then there was the Coca-Cola Company. "Linda and I weren't supposed to fly together," David explained. "The Coca-Cola Company wouldn't allow it. If we were both killed, they'd be in deep trouble. They even called us Mr. and Mrs. Coca-Cola! We were that vital to them. But we didn't care what they said. Neither Linda nor I thought we could go on without the other. If we went down, we wanted to go down together."

The boy who never got past the eighth grade was the man who

proudly boasted of being referred to in both *People* and *Time*. "I'm known as the 'Red Adair of the computer industry.' " It was he, and his particular skill and talent, David bragged, who unlocked the tragic puzzle of the explosion of the *Challenger* space shuttle on January 28, 1986. "I worked for two days with NASA and the Department of Defense to find the cause of the explosion," David explained in his deep baritone. "I was able to prove that the crew members were killed instantaneously—I could guarantee they didn't suffer."

This claim, at least, was an outright lie. But few people questioned David Brown and his skill; he had a convincing way about him and he talked computerese like an expert. He was making money and he was sought after in the data retrieval industry. Who could say how many of his stories were true and how many were gross exaggerations?

Whatever the truth, by 1984, business was booming. Patti and Linda folded and stuffed envelopes. They took turns typing. Phones in the house were all on speakers so David could talk to his many clients from every room without having to pick up the phone. That way everyone in the family could keep up with which orders were coming in. There were no secrets in the business, not among the three of them.

Or so it seemed.

Had Cinnamon Darlene Brown been a jealous child, she might have had good reason to feel she was odd child out in her parents' lives. She was always being shuttled back and forth, and she had no sense of permanency. If she was even a half hour late getting home, her mother would sometimes call her father and demand he come and get Cinnamon. She was a pawn used for threats and revenge.

Cinny loved both her parents, but her father had Linda and Patti; her mother was remarried—to Tracy Sands, a man a few years younger than she—and had given birth to a second daughter. Cinnamon's stepfather was a struggling musician, and much of the attention in Brenda's house in Anaheim was given either to Tracy's career ambitions, or to the new baby girl, Penelope.

Cinnamon, however, loved her half sister, just as she greeted the news that Linda was pregnant with happy excitement. Linda was due to deliver in July of 1984. There would be almost exactly fourteen years between children for David. Cinnamon had been born to poor teenage parents; David was now in a financial position to give this expected baby *everything*. The preparations for the birth rivaled those for a royal offspring. The family had settled into the rental house on Ocean Breeze Drive in Garden Grove by 1984, and there was room for everyone—the master bedroom for David and Linda, the large front bedroom for Patti, and the middle room as a nursery.

Room for everyone but Cinnamon.

Every minute that she wasn't working with David or cooking or cleaning, Linda spent fixing up the middle bedroom for a nursery. David let her buy anything she wanted for the baby. She got the nicest crib, the kind that could be turned into a youth bed later, and matching chests and a little chair swing that moved automatically and played music too. It made Linda happy to know that her baby would have all the things she had never had.

Still there were clouds over her bliss. Even though she was thrilled about her pregnancy, the final months were difficult for Linda Brown. She felt fat and awkward in the heat of a southern California summer. She wore smocks and shorts with elastic panels and her feet swelled. That same summer, her sister Patti, who had the perfect figure that only a well-endowed sixteen-year-old can have, looked exquisite in shorts and halter tops.

For the first time, Patti's obvious crush on David niggled at Linda. She wasn't a kid anymore, and Linda's patience was wearing thin. Patti was so transparent in the way she looked at David. He could do no wrong in her eyes, and Linda felt a shiver of fear as she watched Patti's adolescent attempts at being seductive. She had been there herself—with David—and not so long ago.

Linda was used to going everywhere with David, and he had always bragged, "I won't go to work without Linda." Now, there were days that David *did* go to work without Linda; sometimes, he even took Patti with him. He was training Alan in The Process too, since the baby would require so much of Linda's time. She couldn't feel bad about that; it was her idea. Even so, Linda felt her closeness with David evaporating.

Friends who spoke to Linda on the phone that July recall that she sounded depressed and unhappy. Her mother, Ethel, knew that Linda wanted Patti to move back home. Linda mentioned it to her several times, but David always refused to let Patti leave.

Linda and Patti seemed to be getting along better by the time Linda gave birth to Krystal Marie on July 20, 1984. Everybody loved that baby and took turns taking care of her. After Krystal's birth, Linda had a lovely baby shower. Even Brenda attended, and Linda seemed happy and thrilled about her baby.

David was just crazy about Krystal and didn't mind at all that he hadn't had a son. He played with the baby and rocked her and tickled her. He would brag later, "That little girl loves me. I had her laughing from the day she was born." He took pictures of Linda and their new baby and hung them in his office.

Linda put her jealousy over Patti down to plain old pregnancy blues. Now, as far as anyone could tell, everything was fine with the family. If problems remained, Linda never mentioned them. Only a few weeks before she died, she had stopped over in Riverside at Mary and Rick Bailey's house after visiting a friend. She had both Patti and Cinnamon with her, and Mary saw nothing but harmony.

Brenda Brown Sands, however, saw things that troubled her. "I wanted to have Cinnamon baptized and David said no. He said he'd drag her out of the church if I did that. I needed her birth certificate, and it was in David's safe. Linda said she'd look for it while David was gone. She said, 'I'm scared—but I'll do it.' Well, she had the safe open and I heard her gasp and say, 'Oh, my God, he's coming in the door!' Believe me, she was afraid of him!"

A few weeks later, Brenda saw Linda and Patti at the Department of Motor Vehicles and noticed how sad and tired Linda looked. "I wanted to just go over and tell her, '*Leave* him—things are not right.' "

When school started in September 1984, Cinnamon moved back into her father's house. Linda explained to Mary Bailey, "I took her aside before any decision was made. I told her, 'This will be the last time, Cinnamon. No more moving in and out. If you want to live with us, that's fine—but you'll have to go by our family's rules.' She took it just fine."

Cinnamon had no problem with that. She moved in with David and Linda in time to start school at Bolsa Grande High in Garden Grove. She and Patti both went there. And Patti shared her room with Cinnamon. Patti had the white iron daybed next to the wall, and Cinny slept on the trundle bed that pulled out.

Neither of the girls had many friends among their peers. Patti sometimes talked to a girl who lived across the street, and they both liked Betsy Stubbs, whose father, Al, was David's insurance agent. Betsy was plain and not the smartest girl in the world, but Cinnamon thought she was a riot because she coined original phrases that sent Cinny into gales of laughter. "Neat things like calling people 'Sheep Dip' or she'd yell, 'Oh, you rowdy poopster!' " Patti could never see the humor in it, but Betsy broke Cinnamon up. They saw Betsy quite a bit because David had a lot of insurance business, and the girls often rode along with him. David didn't care for most of their friends, but he liked Betsy.

Still, basically, David had only his family. Just David and four females: Linda, Patti, Cinnamon, and now, Krystal. Later, one of David Brown's detractors would liken his living situation to "his own little fiefdom." In a sense, the characterization was apt: "an estate in land held from a lord on condition of homage and service."

Everyone danced to David's tunes.

Even with all of them living so close together, sharing meals, sharing evenings in front of the television, sharing outings up to the Calico Mountains, and working in Data Recovery together, there were a number of secrets in the Brown household in Garden Grove. Cinnamon stumbled across one of them in late January 1985.

The family stopped at a K mart to make a purchase. David, Patti, and Cinnamon went in to shop, leaving Linda with Krystal in the van; Krystal needed a diaper change, and Linda told them to go on in to shop without her. She arranged a blanket on the tailgate so she could change the baby.

Cinny headed for the stereo tapes, vaguely aware of her father and Patti as they walked toward the clothing department. When she found the tape she wanted, she hurried to find them. Cinnamon turned the corner around a rack of dresses, then stopped, feeling icy shock wash over her. Here, back in a far corner of the sprawling store, her father was *kissing* Patti. Not a friendly kiss or a fatherly kiss, but an intimate, passionate kiss. Cinnamon watched, her feet frozen to the spot where she stood, unable to believe what she saw.

"I stared. . . . I couldn't breathe that well. I was in shock. . . . I was all—oh, no, something's wrong here! . . . They were holding each other . . . I thought I was going crazy or something.

"Then my father turned quickly, and he looked at me," Cinnamon remembered. "I ran across the store and he chased me. He goes, 'Cinny, Cinny! What's wrong? What's wrong?' And I said, 'I saw you!' And he goes, 'What did you see?' and I told him, 'I saw you kissing Patti.' And he goes, 'I'm sorry you had to see that. Kissing Patti was an accident.' "

Cinnamon's head buzzed. How could he have kissed Patti by accident? She darted a look at the parking lot and was relieved to see Linda was still standing out by the van. Stunned and confused, she began to cry. "Are you trying to drive me crazy?" she asked. "I don't understand." Her father was asking her to forgive him, but she didn't want to talk to him. She ran away and huddled, shaking, at a counter where he couldn't see her.

After a long time, Linda found her and was alarmed at how distraught Cinnamon looked. "What's *wrong* with you?" she asked.

"Nothing," Cinnamon lied, "I'll be all right."

Cinnamon was silent as they paid for their purchases. She couldn't tell Linda what she had seen. "At the time I was scared of my father. Otherwise I would have been assertive and told Linda."

It made her feel especially bad because Linda was so concerned about *her*. She moved back in the van to sit by Cinnamon and tried to find out why she was so upset. Linda seemed to think that Cinnamon had wanted to buy something and hadn't had money. Cinnamon turned her face to the window and shook her head. Linda had no idea how bad it really was.

"When we got home, my father stopped me by the front door and he goes, 'Don't tell anybody about what you saw in the store. It's very important to me.' "

She promised him she would say nothing.

"Okay, fine. I'll respect that," David said.

Cinnamon ran out to the little trailer in the backyard. She didn't want supper, and she certainly didn't want to talk to her father. "I didn't know how to deal with him." But David came out and pounded on the door until she let him in. He tried to explain to her that what she had seen wasn't anything special. "Sometimes, these things happen."

"I don't want to talk about it."

"It wasn't anything, Cinnamon."

"I don't want to talk about it."

But she *thought* about it. All night long. It made her sick to her stomach and she didn't want to eat, although Linda came and tapped on the trailer door and tried to coax her into the house for supper.

How could her daddy kiss someone almost as young as she was like that? How could he do that to Linda? She didn't care what he said. It wasn't supposed to be like that. And she didn't believe it was an accident. Thinking about it just made her more confused.

Cinnamon finally fell asleep in the trailer, but she had nightmares, seeing her father and Patti kissing over and over.

17

H A V I N G temporarily exhausted his list of relatives, ex-relatives, ex-wives, and acquaintances who had things to say about David Arnold Brown, Jay Newell took another tack. As any other private citizen could have done had he been curious, he began to keep track of Brown by checking public records. It wasn't easy. The usual paper trail left when people move—mail forwarding, disconnection of gas, electricity, and water—was no help.

After David Brown moved out of the rental on Breckenridge, Newell lost the scent. All refunds and mail had been directed to Arthur Brown's Carson address. But that house seemed shuttered and empty, as if David's parents were gone too. Newell was sure that Brown was still in the Orange County area—but where?

Because he had a relative in the real estate business, Newell was more savvy than most in checking property transfers. He found one item that fascinated him. Within three weeks of Cinnamon Brown's murder conviction, David Brown had purchased a new home. Real estate transaction records in the courthouse indicated that David Arnold Brown had purchased a home on August 30, 1985. He had received a grant deed—*paid in full*—on a house selling for $330,000.

Newell went looking for it and found it easily. And what a house it was—in a most exclusive area of Orange County: Anaheim Hills. Brown had purchased one of the most lavish houses in the new subdivision called Summit View. All the homes there are set along hilly, curving streets—most of them with names ending in *ridge*. The name was apt; at the top of Summitridge Lane, the view of the Santiago Canyon far below is breathtaking.

The street was so new in 1985 that all its trees were staked and spindly, but begonias, petunias, gerbera daisies, and the fragrant wild plum with its tiny five-petaled white-star flowerets had already taken hold in most yards. All utilities were discreetly underground. Ironically, four huge high-powered electrical towers perched almost malevolently at the very top of the hill. The surging power beneath the ground had to come from somewhere, and a dozen high tension wires hummed as they stretched from tower to tower along the hill's spine.

The house at 3823 Summitridge Lane was clearly that of a rich man, a 1980s version of what an "olde English country manor" might look like if it were relocated from Stratford-on-Avon to Orange County. Fieldstone and stucco with crossbeams, shake roof, leaded windows, a recessed entryway with massive double doors.

A dream house on a dream street.

Each house on Summitridge Lane was grander than the next; every lawn manicured and boasting a huge stone or brick planter that matched the house's facade. Housing codes obviously dictated that even the *mailboxes* were to be enclosed in stone or brick stanchions, and each also matched its house perfectly.

Of course the house on Summitridge Lane had a triple garage. The balconies in the rear of Brown's new house overlooked the azure swimming pool, and the attached hot tub. Twin hexagonal, two-story towers abutted the pool. There were *two* weathered-brick barbecues, and the fence surrounding the backyard was of the same brick and wrought iron.

Since the back door opened onto a stone patio that led directly to the unfenced pool, the layout of the new house seemed an unsafe choice for a man alone with a baby. Krystal Brown could crawl so easily toward the pool.

By visiting Summitridge Lane whenever he could, Jay Newell quickly saw the reason for the empty house in Carson. Brown had moved his parents in with him. There would be Manuela and Arthur to help keep an eye on Krystal. And then, Jay Newell saw Patti Bailey in the car with David Brown as they drove away. Patti had apparently made the move to Summitridge Lane too.

Newell could not know at the time, not from his solely exterior vantage point, but this was not a happy house. Manuela Brown complained to her husband about Patti's continuing place in the family. Why didn't the girl go home with her own family now? She had no business being with David any longer. Arthur agreed; he felt privately that Patti wasn't good for David, that she might even be a bad influence. But he was never a man who told his son what to do.

The house on Ocean Breeze Drive had been a nice, cozy run-of-the-mill bungalow. David had leapfrogged to the similar rental on Breckenridge, then to *this* house, this near-mansion that bespoke quiet elegance, understated wealth.

It was the sort of place where David had always pictured himself, even way back in the years when he and Brenda were living hand-to-mouth with minimum-wage jobs and welfare. Well, Brenda should have had more faith. He was well on his way to being a millionaire now, and Anaheim Hills suited him. He was sure Brenda was jealous, and that pleased him.

Despite the tension that never quite left him, David felt that, all in all, things were turning out well. Krystal rarely cried for her mother any longer; she had Manuela to rock her, and she had Patti to carry her around. The memory of her mother evaporated so rapidly from her baby mind. Linda had had only eight months with her baby girl.

For those who had known Linda, especially for those who had loved her, the sight of Patti wearing Linda's things was an icy jolt. Like seeing a ghost. They had looked so much alike, so *very* much alike. The only difference was that Patti was younger.

Sitting beside his pool on his patio, sipping a soft drink and smoking his fiftieth cigarette of the day, David Brown spent many evenings reflecting upon his life. He was in complete control of his world again and his sex life was great—if a little tricky with his parents living with him. He still managed to keep his private life untouched. As tragic as it was, Linda was gone. The past had buried the past, as it was meant to do. Life was for the living, and he was going to wring all the juice out of it he could.

David's business continued to boom with rising computer use. He no longer had Linda to help him. He taught bits and pieces of The Process to new employees—mostly family. Arthur helped out, and Patti.

Alan and David had apparently settled their differences because Linda's twin was back on the payroll. Larry Bailey, whom David had never trusted, was, nevertheless, brought into the business. Odd—since David had once suggested to Fred McLean that he suspected Larry might have crept into his home and shot Linda. Larry had been in jail just before her murder, and David told McLean that Larry was furious when Linda wouldn't bail him out. The police had checked that theory and found it without merit; it appeared to be only one more of Brown's attempts to divert suspicion from Cinnamon.

Arthur Brown didn't really understand how they retrieved data from the computer disks, and he didn't care to. His son was the brilliant one. Arthur often went down to Randomex in Long Beach and picked up damaged disks and brought them back to David to evaluate. If David spelled it out to him step by step, Arthur could follow his directions. But that was it. He couldn't begin to try it on his own. All the elder Brown really knew was that David worked for the government and for a lot of big, important corporations. His son had told him that.

One of David Brown's favorite claims about his burgeoning business enterprise was that he had to be available to his clients to reassure them that he would save their lost data. He could explain what had happened and why—and tell them just enough about how he would bring the damaged disks back to life again. He liked to tell his clients that they had been lucky enough to find the one man in America who could help them—that his expertise was highly technical and uniquely his own.

It wasn't a total scam. He *did* know his stuff. He might make his skill sound a bit more miraculous than it was—but hell, he was a businessman in a competitive field and a little razzle-dazzle helped.

Executives at Randomex would dispute Brown's claims that he had invented The Process, stating that the data retrieval techniques David used were actually refined by several experts at Randomex. And in the beginning, David rarely, if ever, talked to clients. However, as the years passed, David wasn't averse to making Randomex's clients *his* clients.

David was so adept at diagnosing the problem with a disk that he could quote a fee to retrieve data before he ever got into the disk. He usually required the money up front before he began. With bigger corporations, he could quote a bid for a major job that usually came in on a dime.

Linda's twin, Alan, was impressed with David and a good audience for a recitation of his ambitions. David assured him that one day he would build his own towering office building, own his own company jet. The way David's income had jumped year after year, Alan had little doubt that David would accomplish just what he said he would.

With all his new business success, with his pleasure in his luxurious new home, David Brown appeared to move through the period of mourning for his murdered wife with remarkable ease. And if he felt low, he was surrounded by people who cared about him, some to the point of adulation, some because they feared him.

It wasn't that David Brown was physically threatening; he was an admitted coward who ran from fights. It was because David always seemed to know secret things, to refer obliquely to some nameless danger that awaited anyone who crossed him. Among his handpicked associates, his devoted family, David *was* power.

He was in control and meant to keep it that way.

David Arnold Brown, of course, had trouble he was not yet aware of. When he walked, he did not walk alone. When he cruised the

streets and freeways of Orange County in one of his expensive new
cars, he had company. Jay Newell was often just behind him, his
tape recorder and notebook filling up with every change in David's
life, every move, every new acquisition. Newell didn't know himself
where all this information was going to lead—maybe nowhere.

Newell had checked every county in California by computer to
see what properties David Arnold Brown might have purchased. It
would have been easier if Brown's name had been rarer; Newell got
dozens of Browns back, but he also got some hits on the man he
wanted. Every time David Brown bought a lot or a house, Newell
knew about it.

It was the same with cars. Tedious computer checks spit out volumes on David's car purchases. The guy was spending money as if
he had found a lost gold mine. David had the Bronco and the Chevy
Monte Carlo when Linda was murdered. Almost immediately after
her funeral, he bought a Nissan 300ZX Turbo, 1985, a sleekly expensive sports car. He ordered vanity plates, reading "Data Rec."

Between August 1985 and the spring of 1988, Brown changed cars
almost as frequently as the seasons changed. He bought:

A Chevrolet Suburban station wagon, 1985
A Honda Accord LX, 1985
A Dodge D-50 1986 truck (with camper)
A 560 two-door convertible Mercedes, which bore the license plate
"Phoenix" (Estimated cost: $70,000)
A 190E Mercedes (Estimated cost: $25,000)
A Ford Bronco, 1986 or 1987
A Ford station wagon, 1986 or 1987
Two identical Nissan Sentras, 1987
A third Nissan Sentra, 1987 (orange)
A Ford Bronco, 1988
A completely equipped motor home, 1988 (Estimated cost: $60,000)
A Ford station wagon, 1988
A Ford Escort, 1988

Fifteen expensive vehicles in three years . . .

David had not had the Nissan sports car long when he and Patti
were driving on Katella Street in Orange on November 22, 1985—
shortly after ten P.M. on that Tuesday night. David, behind the wheel
of his new 300ZX, was stopped in the left turn lane when the car
was struck from behind by a small Renault Alliance. Patti screamed
and cried and grasped at her neck. She was soon hysterical. As her

sobs and screaming grew louder, David explained to the Orange Fire Department medics who worked over her that she had been through a great deal of tragedy recently. "Her sister was murdered only a few months ago—she was my wife. I don't know what this is going to do to her. How much are we expected to take?"

Not all that much, it would seem. The "accident" was scarcely more than a nudge. California highway patrolmen investigated the incident. The other driver admitted that it was his fault. "I was slowing down, maybe going ten miles an hour, when my foot slipped off the brake pedal and hit the accelerator." The impact had been enough to knock David's shiny black car forward. The CHPS investigator noticed the Renault driver was wearing cowboy boots—that could account for his foot's slipping.

There was no damage at all to the Renault and only a number of minor scratches to the rear bumper of David Brown's car. But neck injuries "whiplash"—are tricky, and virtually impossible to diagnose. They are the bane of the insurance industry. Patti Bailey was now complaining of increasingly severe neck pains and a terrible headache. She was treated at the scene and rushed to St. Joseph's Hospital by ambulance.

David and Patti had both been visiting a chiropractor frequently *before* the accident, including the afternoon before Linda died. With these new injuries, they saw the chiropractor even more often.

David had insurance with Allstate. He insisted that he had reported the accident to his insurance agent at once, but the first record the Garden Grove office had about the "rear-ender" was when David made a claim more than four months later, on April 3, 1986. Giving him the benefit of the doubt, that office brought up David's auto insurance policy on the computer, and it showed that David had more than adequate medical coverage on his policy—$100,000.

Six months later, David brought a stack of medical bills in for payment—almost $25,000 worth. This was a bit of a jolt to Allstate. The police accident reports depicted an essentially minor collision. Most of the claims were for "soft tissue injury." Patti asked for $1,000 for pain-clinic visits. On many occasions, the bills noted several chiropractic visits on the same day. Nevertheless, Allstate eventually paid David $12,500 and Patti $10,500. A check with Farmers Insurance, the insurer of the driver of the other car, showed that Farmers had also paid—under the liability provision—to the tune of $38,500.

Insurance investigators are a suspicious breed by nature, and they began to work back through David Brown's insurance history. To them, $61,500 seemed an inordinately large payoff for a low-speed, rear-end collision that resulted in a few scratches, most of which, probers found, had been there when David bought the Nissan. Moreover, Patti's neck showed no lingering symptoms of soft-tissue or cervical-spine damage.

Allstate had other policies with David Brown; the house on Summitridge Lane (and later, the house on Chantilly). He had also attempted to insure Linda's jewelry with Allstate, but it was so valuable, the company declined.

A check of David's driving record in Orange Country revealed several speeding tickets and showed accidents in 1970, 1972, 1978, two in 1980, and 1982.

After payment had been made on David's claims, Allstate's recheck of its computers for David Arnold Brown's car insurance brought a shocking revelation. Although agents swore that their initial computer check indicated that he had $100,000 medical coverage, it no longer showed on computer screens or printouts. Nor was it listed on any hard-copy documents on the auto policy.

Nor *could* it be there. Allstate *didn't* offer medical coverage on the kind of policy David had. But somehow—for a time—the computer printout had said David Brown was insured.

The only conclusion deductive reasoning could suggest was that someone had illegally accessed the company's computers, inserted the $100,000 coverage in David Brown's policy, and then, silently, erased it.

Further, one Allstate investigator checked in the central file that lists all claims against the company, and against other companies, for another claim she knew David had collected on. It had to be listed in the computer files.

But it was gone.

Such computer wizardry could be accomplished only by someone with extremely sophisticated knowledge and skill regarding operating systems, programing, and data entry and retrieval. Someone who knew that illegal computer access can be accomplished in three ways, known in colorful computer lingo as "data diddling," "Trojan horse," and "superzapping."

No charges were ever filed, but with the realization that it had paid David Brown and Patti Bailey's medical claims of $23,000 on a policy that had never *had* any medical coverage, Allstate quietly beefed up its computer security.

18

W I T H   A L L of David's new cars, it was difficult for Newell to keep track of him. It did little good to know what kind of car he drove; the next week, the next day, he might have a new one. He tired of the two Mercedes sedans quickly and sold them to invest in Fords.

Following another trail of his investigation, Newell tediously filled in all the gaps in David Brown's credit profile. He found out about federal tax liens on Brown's property in 1983 and saw they were paid off within a few months of filing. He even knew the credit cards Brown carried, and that they were paid to date. However, he detected a pattern of wobbly credit and money problems *before* Linda's murder, and emerging affluence and larger luxury purchases after.

"It was good to have that background, to know as much as I could about him," Newell would say later. "But the one thing I wanted most was to talk to David Arnold Brown."

It was galling to think that he had yet to meet the man's eyes, to exchange the most innocuous words. For Newell, a master at assessing nonverbal communication, a chance to observe Cinnamon's father close up might well answer the question that plagued him. Was David Brown really the childish, insensitive boob who had teasingly pulled his ex-wife's hair in the courtroom even as his daughter was being sentenced for murder? Or was he a brilliant manipulator who had somehow managed to pull off a murder and walk away with no particle of evidence clinging to him?

Where was all the money coming from? Was Brown's business truly as successful as he bragged it was? Investigators knew of one insurance policy payoff on Linda, but that would be long gone by now at the rate David spent money. Either there had been more policies, or Data Recovery *was* raking in the contracts from frantic corporations and government agencies. Perhaps both suppositions were true. All Newell needed was a face-to-face confrontation with Brown and he thought he could find out.

It shouldn't have been that difficult just to *talk* to a man. But David was like quicksilver. Although Newell called at the Brown household on Summitridge Lane at disparate times of the day and night, he was never able to penetrate the protective wall that surrounded David Brown.

Patti or Manuela or sometimes his father, Arthur, answered the door. They explained that David was at the doctor's or away on business, or in the bathroom or too ill to talk. They were polite, evasive, wary, and obviously well trained. Sometimes, they didn't even open the door, but talked *through* it; they told Newell that the alarm was activated, and they didn't know how to operate it. If they opened the door, the alarm would go off.

Newell knew that David Arnold Brown really *did* exist. He thought he knew the man as well as anyone could without ever talking to him. He had read the entire case file a couple of dozen times, reviewed the statements Brown had given, and seen him up close that one time at Cinnamon's sentencing, and even now, he frequently caught glimpses of David at a distance.

If Brown bothered Newell, the reverse was true—and double. Jay Newell had shocked Brown with the way he had managed to keep up with the family's moves. David didn't like people coming to his door, asking for him. If he had had any idea how many times Newell was only fifty feet away from him, he would have been outraged—and panicked.

But Newell had the advantage. David didn't know what Newell looked like. He knew his name all right; Newell had left enough cards to paper Brown's entry hall—but that was all. If he was truly concerned, he could have done some research and found a picture of Newell. But David never bothered.

Jay Newell had the definite impression that David Brown had no wish to see him or talk to him—ever. And there was no legal way to force such a conversation. Perhaps David's reluctance was born of some instinctual wariness. He knew he could routinely charm both clients and females with his voice and his repartee. He was good. He *had* to be good; the man had parlayed an eighth-grade education into a million-dollar business, and even though he was short, stout, and far from handsome, he never lacked for women. But a police detective was another matter. Here was a man who might cut through the bullshit and snare him.

If, indeed, there was any crime to snare him for.

And still, Newell kept up his quiet pursuit. He had to squeeze in time to spend monitoring David Brown; he was deep into myriad investigations of gang activity. And David Brown was officially old business.

"It sounds dull," Newell would say later. "I didn't do anything that dramatic. I just watched him and followed him and monitored public records. I'd see him leave the house, often with Patti Bailey, and I'd see him come home. I wanted to know *who* this man was—where he went and what he was doing. I was never far behind him, but I doubt if he realized that for months."

19

J A Y N E W E L L knew far more about David's whereabouts and lifestyle than David's own daughter did. Cinnamon had no address for her father, and she had no telephone number. She didn't know where he lived or who lived with him.

But he did come to see her occasionally on the every-other-Saturday visitors' day at Ventura School. He explained to Cinny that his deteriorating health made it hard for him to make the drive often. If the weather was hot, he wouldn't be able to stand the long drive. He might hemorrhage. He might pass out.

She believed everything he said.

Every time he left after a visit, Cinnamon worried that she might never see him again, that he might really die as he always hinted he would. Her feelings were so mixed up about her father. For so long, he was the only magical person in her life. Her mother worried about even normal, everyday things. Her father just wanted to have fun. When he made her laugh—ever since she was little—they had so much fun. Even when he was sick, he took care of her, and of so many other people. He was smart and he was rich and people respected him.

When he *did* come to see her, he was still funny and made her laugh, but the visits seemed to be over before they even came close to talking about the things that worried her. There were certain subjects that spooked him, and he either ignored her questions or told her, "I'm working on it. I'm contacting lawyers—investigators. You'll be out of here soon."

She believed him.

Although David didn't come to see Cinny often, he did keep her commissary fund supplied with money, and she was allowed to order items by mail and charge them to his business accounts.

Cinnamon's first psychological screening tests at Ventura took place in November 1985. The diagnosis was as vague as it could possibly be: "unspecified mental disorder—nonpsychotic." In layman's terms, the examiner thought that there was probably something wrong with Cinnamon Brown, but she wasn't crazy. He went on to say she was not a danger to others, but that she *might* be dangerous to herself; that was unpredictable. Psychotherapy was recommended.

As always, there was little information for any examiner to go on. Cinnamon's memory was apparently lost in some abyss in her own mind.

The psychiatrist found Cinnamon to be a cooperative, friendly young woman who was adjusting well to being incarcerated. She was adamant that she was not interested in psychiatric help.

"Although subject has no memory of the events [of the crime], she somehow feels she is not guilty—and will eventually be proven innocent."

One thing was obvious; Cinnamon didn't want any psychologist or psychiatrist poking around in her subconscious, trying to bring up memories. She seemed almost alarmed at the thought of it.

Each year, near Christmas, Cinnamon would go before the parole board. She didn't really expect to be paroled that first year; she had only just got there. It was a mere formality when she went before the board on December 12, 1985.

Parole denied. The "ward" would be retained in the CYA system for treatment and training; "recommend psychiatric and psychological examinations and reports at each annual review."

Her parole date was tentatively set as September 1992. Seven years away.

Cinnamon had told the examiners on the board that she had no involvement in her stepmother's murder. She also told them that she remembered nothing of the early morning of March 19 or the days following.

There was a question in the examiners' minds about the possibility of conspiracy involving "other family members." They found Cinnamon to be "not criminally sophisticated" and noted that "she appears emotionally immature."

She was fifteen. It seemed a given.

They recommended therapy for an extended period of time. They gave her no "good time" at all.

On January 6, 1986, Cinnamon appeared once again for review. As in her first review with the parole board, the examiners felt that she was not dealing with her offense, and that she needed extended psychiatric treatment. The problem was that Cinnamon still absolutely refused treatment. She had a blank spot in her memory, and she wanted it left that way.

Cinnamon was only one of 1,100 boys and girls locked up in

186 · ANN RULE

Ventura. The campus was green and dotted with trees. Cinnamon lived in a "cottage" called El Toyon. " 'E.T.,' " she explained. "It's for the younger girls, fourteen to eighteen. I had my own room at the end of the hall. Our cottage held fifty girls. I was trusted and placed at the end. . . . I had my bed with my old beach towel across it. I had a desk and shelf across from my bed, and also a tall, thin locker and a sink and toilet.

"I've always been very neat—clean, *picky*. I guess everything was organized. I had a color TV, Walkman, and bear pictures on my wall, and frames with pictures of my family. I had a lot of things. . . . I was very comfortable; I enjoyed my room. I had quality time alone. But the funny thing about my room—my things looked new because I took good care of them. I always had all the material things I needed. Staff would normally not allow such a thing, but because I was on good behavior, I was allowed to have the things I did and in the quantity I did.

"I also had pink curtains on my windows to cover up the bars. Eight bars down and three bars across: I could open a portion of the window myself. Our doors were always locked at night for security reasons. Mail was pushed through the door during the night."

Cinnamon did well in school, and in her cottage. During her first two years at Ventura, she was assigned to the kitchen and cooked and served food to the girls in E.T. cottage. Breakfast at seven, lunch at noon, and dinner at five. She could go to canteen every two weeks, and have visitors twice a month. "Security" escorted all her movements inside the school.

School officials noted that Cinnamon did not align herself with any of the gangs at Ventura. The Caucasian girls urged her to come into the "White Car," their slang for the white girls' gang. She declined. She was something of a loner, doing her time, and waiting. She seemed always to have that air of waiting about her, as if she truly believed that someone—or something—was coming for her soon.

Cinnamon remained sweet, somewhat naive in manner, and was easy for prison officials to deal with. But she could not—or *would* not—remember the murder night. Until she did, prison officials thought she would not get well or move toward freedom.

In one sense, it almost seemed that Cinnamon felt safer in prison than she had on the outside. At least, she was no longer being bounced back and forth between her mother and father. She had her room, her private space, albeit with a locked door and a window with eight bars down and three bars across.

20

O N   A P R I L 19, 1986, David Brown purchased a second piece of property, an investment. He bought a house at 1510 East Lincoln in Anaheim. He moved Alan Bailey in, with only a sleeping bag for furniture. Alan slept there to protect the property from vandals and break-ins. Jay Newell checked the place out from time to time, but David never moved in. The place was located in a commercially zoned area, and David had obviously seen the possibility of a quick turnover.

He was right. He sold the Lincoln property within months for a $15,000 profit.

In the summer of 1986, although she was completely unaware of it, Cinnamon Brown had a new stepmother, Patti Bailey.

"He asked me to marry him because he knew he was dying," Patti would recall. "Then Krystal would be all alone when he was gone. If she had a stepmother, he could die without worrying about her. As his legal wife, I would have no trouble getting custody of Krystal."

It was not the most romantic proposal in the annals of love—but it succeeded. Almost any proposal would have; David was the only man Patti Bailey had really ever known. She had loved him for her whole life, or so it seemed to her. She was delighted to become the sixth Mrs. David Arnold Brown.

When asked about his sixth marriage, David snorted at Patti's recall and insisted his sixth marriage was not legal, nor was it ever intended to be. His reasoning was either a prime example of David Brown's confabulation after the fact, or as he swore, the "honest-to-God" truth.

"Go look in the records," he said. "If you give false information on the application, then the license isn't valid and the marriage isn't valid. Patti and I both deliberately lied on the application. We only got married as a favor to a friend of Patti's who was pregnant. The gal— Dee Ann*—begged me to suggest to her boyfriend, Tony*, who was a friend of mine, that we all four go to Vegas and get married. She was upset, naturally, and kept coming over, and she just begged me to do it, so I pulled the guy aside and talked him into it. I *never* intended to marry Patti.

"Tony and I each paid three hundred dollars to get a prenuptial agreement from the same lawyer. Same form and all; we just filled in our own stuff."

If David never intended to marry Patti Bailey legally, he certainly went to great pains to separate their property. David's half of the prenuptial agreement, signed by Patti, stipulated that—should they ever divorce—David would get:

1. Real property at 3823 E. Summitridge Lane, Orange, California—with a current equity of approximately $480,000.
2. The business known as Data Recovery . . . and proceeds of employment of David A. Brown.
3. IRA accounts, savings account, checking account . . . with a current balance of over $150,000.
4. All furniture and furnishings . . .
5. 1986 model 560SL Mercedes-Benz.
6. 1986 Ford Bronco.
7. 1986 Honda Accord LX.
8. 1985 Honda 500 Shadow motorcycle.
9. Two 1985 Honda Odysseys with trailer.
10. Rare coin and paper money collection, currently valued at $350,000.
11. Dali *Women Rising* painting, valued at $12,000.
12. Rockwell *Old Man and the Sea* painting, valued at $12,000.
13. Variety of lithographs and original artworks, valued at over $10,000.
14. Oriental ivory and jade sculptures, carvings, and artwork, valued at over $30,000.
15. Russell bronze and marble sculpture entitled *It's Not Meat Until It's on the Table*, valued at over $500,000.
16. Future proceeds from personal injuries sustained in November 1985 automobile accident.

Patti's list of assets was shorter:

1. 1955 MG.
2. Future proceeds from personal injuries sustained in November 1985 automobile accident.
3. Future proceeds from personal injuries sustained in September 1983 automobile accident.

She didn't care. She signed the document eagerly on June 30, 1986.
It was not exactly a romantic madcap jaunt to Vegas. One bride was pregnant and queasy, and the other obeyed her groom like a

robot, almost scared to breathe for fear David would change his mind. They left for Nevada on July 1, 1986, Patti Bailey's long-awaited wedding day.

"So we went to Vegas," David continued to explain, "and Patti and I falsified whatever we could, everything that wasn't on our driver's license, so we wouldn't *really* be married. See, it couldn't be a common-law marriage either—because Patti was my *dependent*—not my wife. So, even if she'd lived with me all that time, it wasn't like she was a wife."

The two couples got into the long line—what David termed a "production line"—and were married in the We've Only Just Begun wedding chapel by the Reverend George M. Stover, ordained minister of the Abundant Life Christian Center. There was no reception, and no announcement to friends or even immediate family.

"Afterward we ate at Caesars Palace—or maybe the MGM—Dee Ann was one of these 'yuppics' who had to have Chinese food with sushi, and Patti got sick as a dog."

That made two brides who were feeling miserable.

And so they were married—"but not really," according to David, who smiled slightly as he related how Patti's "wedding day" was ruined by food poisoning.

Las Vegas was David Brown's preferred wedding locale, just as the Orange County Courthouse was where he got all his divorces.

"I knew we weren't married," David said. "Patti might have *thought* we were married." In point of fact, they were, indeed, legally married. The wedding certificate exists, as does the prenuptial agreement, all in perfectly legal order.

At the age of thirty-three, David Brown had married for the sixth time, a wedding so private that it defines the meaning of the word. No one beyond the bride, the groom, and the other half of their double wedding knew. Patti could not have a ring, or a honeymoon or a shower. Neither his family nor Patti's approved of his closeness with Patti. Besides that, people might look askance at a man who married his sister-in-law so soon after his wife's murder—although David considered a mourning period of fifteen months more than sufficient.

Back home on Summitridge Lane, the mixture continued as before. Despite Manuela and Arthur's resentment at having Patti live with them, she stayed. Patti begged David to let her tell his parents and her family that they were man and wife, but he was inflexible on that subject. People might jump to stupid conclusions—they might even say that they had something to do with Linda's murder— "like this was our intent all along."

They especially could not tell Cinnamon. David warned Patti that, if Cinnamon had been so bent out of shape about a kiss in K Mart, there was no telling what she might do if she knew they were actually married.

Patti remembered when Krystal was just a newborn and Linda was in that weepy, postpartum-blues stage. She had made her sister promise that, if anything ever happened to her, Patti would take care of Krystal. It made Patti frightened and sad to think about it.

And something *had* happened. Linda seemed to have known it would. Now, Patti lived in quiet dread that *David* would die and leave her all alone.

She loved him so.

During the few visits David made to the Ventura School, he brought his parents along. He did not mention Patti, who either stayed home or waited in the new camper out in the parking lot—far from Cinnammon's view. Grandpa Brown was the only one who ever told Cinny anything anyway. And he only muttered a few hints here and there about where and how they were living. Arthur Brown dearly loved Cinnamon, and it broke his heart to see her locked up for so long.

In September 1986, Cinnamon was again recommended for psychological counseling. She was a very confused, extremely frustrated— and frustrating—subject. While she knew that the parole board would not consider setting a release date for her until she "dealt with her offense," she could *not* deal with an offense she didn't even remember. And there were very, very important reasons why she must not remember.

She did not want to take any more of their silly tests. She resisted their test for academic ability, but she obediently completed the psychological tests, even though she said she saw no reason for them.

Cinnamon was given another Minnesota Multiphasic Personality Inventory test with its 566 true-false questions, and her results were normal, with the exception that she was attempting to deny and avoid the MMPI "honesty" questions, the deliberate lie questions that anyone would answer "true" to—if they were totally honest. Questions such as "At times I feel like swearing," "I get angry sometimes," "I like everyone I know," and "Once in a while, I think of things too bad to talk about."

She carefully printed "False" to all of them.

What was she trying to hide? Why did she try to appear impossibly perfect?

On the Thematic Apperception Test, the TAT, Cinnamon once again showed herself to be "markedly guarded," unwilling to let anyone inside her head. "Subject views the world as an untrusting and uncaring place that is cold and rejecting," her psychologist wrote.

Interestingly, her Kinetic Family Drawing test showed figures that demonstrated hostility toward the Linda figure from the Patti figure, and Cinnamon, in a corner, desperately seeking attention.

Overall, Cinnamon's tests showed a young woman who felt both rejected and dominated and who was suffering from a mild depression. The tentative diagnosis showed no psychosis, and only mild mood swings. It would fit any teenager. Everything was normal about Cinnamon Brown—*except* that she was a teenager in prison for murder.

In November, the official diagnosis resulting from her latest testing was "unspecified mental disorder, nonpsychotic: possible psychogenic amnesia." Her examiner had barely scratched the surface of her mind and gone away stymied.

Nothing had changed, and nothing new had been revealed.

The therapist felt that Cinnamon would never be able to move forward until she was willing to close the distance between herself and the night of the murder. She was holding the horror away, unwilling to deal with the memories. He did not know why; she was a sweet, pleasant child, but as closed off from him as a building shuttered against an approaching storm.

Again, psychotherapy was recommended. Again, Cinnamon refused to accept treatment.

Cinnamon had her second review with the parole board on December 18, 1986. She was given a six-month time cut for "positive adjustment to the program." Her behavior was excellent. She had been imprisoned for fourteen months, and she had caused no trouble at all. She was adjusting well, save for the fact that her memory was as blurry and gauzy as ever.

Cinnamon Brown did mention to her examiners, however, that she had had a visit from her grandfather, Arthur Brown, about four weeks before. He had explained to her that *he* knew who had killed Linda, and when the time was right, he was going to tell who really did the killing.

Because of the inconsistencies in Cinnamon's case file, her amnesia, and this new information, on January 5, 1987, O. J. Harkey, a parole agent with the California Youth Authority, asked the Orange County District Attorney's Office to interview Arthur Brown. There appeared to be more to her case than had been officially acknowledged.

This communication was, of course, no surprise to the District Attorney's Office. It only validated the doubts that McLean, Newell, and Fredrickson had had for almost two years. In a letter responding to Harkey, Deputy DA Dick Fredrickson succinctly summed up the position of his office to CYA authorities and offered all the help his office could provide:

"It is clear that Cinnamon either was the sole actor in the killing or was acting as part of a conspiracy. Under the current state of the evidence, however, Cinnamon's recollection is the key to any ultimate resolution of the possible involvement of the others. We do not, however, regard the case as closed, but are continuing with our investigation as time and manpower permit."

Cinnamon was the key. She always had been. But she had long ago closed up and closed in. Every time Jay Newell reread the incriminating statements she had made in the few days following the murder, he saw a pattern. The language was repetitive and stilted. It sounded as if she had memorized a script. And then, suddenly, she recalled nothing at all. What had happened to wipe out her memory like that? Who had talked to her? He looked at the list of visitors: her attorney; Kim Hicks, the young medical student; her mother; her father. . . .

The CYA parole board set the next review for Cinnamon in just ninety days, in the hope that Jay Newell might be able to learn more from Arthur Brown. If Arthur had gone so far as to visit Cinnamon and tell her that he *knew* who the real killer was, he might be waiting for someone to give him a chance to talk. The old man had always been skittish, afraid to talk with Newell before. David didn't like him talking to people.

On January 28, 1987, at the request of the CYA board, Newell went back to try again. He drove up the long, winding hill to Summitridge Lane. This time, he preferred *not* to encounter David Brown. He sensed that the old man would shut up like a clam if his son was listening.

The layout of Summitridge made it difficult for Newell to drive by the Brown house casually and see who might be home. The incline was steep, and the street was not a well-traveled thoroughfare. Strangers stood out. He parked down the street on the other side and strolled along, looking at the houses. In a pinch, he would become an instant real estate agent, a breed that swarmed over Orange County.

David's most recent car wasn't in the driveway. Still, Newell felt relieved when he spotted *Arthur* Brown in the yard. Wary, the old man agreed to talk—but only for a moment or two. He would not sit in Newell's car and kept edging away nervously.

Newell explained that Cinnamon was upset over something her grandfather had said to her, and that the counselors at CYA were concerned.

"I don't know what I could have said to her," Arthur Brown waffled as Newell began to question him. But he readily agreed to keep the conversation confidential. As frightened as he was, it was clear he cared for Cinnamon: "She's a very darling little girl."

"Do you have much time to talk to Cinnamon?" Newell asked. "You and she evidently have some rapport. Does she ever open up to you?"

"No—I'm always . . . with David, her dad."

Arthur Brown said that he and his wife had been unable to visit Cinnamon for some time because Manuela had lost her ID card and he hadn't wanted to go up without her, but "Cinny did call me and said she wanted to talk to me, so I just went on up there by myself— and let the wife sit in the car."

"What did she say?"

"Just how much we loved each other, and how she got six months off her sentence."

"You wouldn't say anything to her to give her false hope, would you?"

"I try not to."

The old man was nervous as a cat. "That's no place for her. I don't believe that she had anything to do with it. And I still don't. I never will."

"Well, what did you say to her?"

"I told her that I was sure I knew who planned the whole thing."

Carefully, Newell suggested that Cinnamon might not be carrying the whole burden of guilt, even though she had been convicted. He watched the old man's face and saw silent agreement there, but Arthur Brown was clearly scared to death of saying the wrong thing.

"I told Cinny that I felt like I knew who planned it, because I heard her say that she was going to do something to save David—"

"Heard *who* say?"

"Her . . ." Arthur Brown looked over his shoulder, as if expecting someone to come up behind him. "The little girl he's taking care of— Patti. . . . I was with them the night she made the statement that she heard Linda [on the phone with her twin, Alan] planning to do away with David—to take his business. And she said that [David's being hurt] wasn't gonna happen even if she had to do it herself . . . she'd get rid of her."

Jay Newell felt a surge of triumph. This was the first break-through—the first overt admission that Patti Bailey might have been part of a plot to kill Linda. Newell kept his face calm and let the old man ramble on.

"When she was killed, I just lost my goddamn mind."

Newell waited. "How long before Linda was killed did you hear this conversation?"

"Might have been two weeks—might of been two days—I was in the car with all of them. David and Linda and Patti and Cinnamon. Linda got out of the car and Patti started shootin' off her mouth like she always does."

"Where were you going in the car?"

"Looking for some place to have a picnic."

Manuela had stayed behind with Krystal. Grandpa Brown had sat in the back of the van, but he had heard a lot. "She's a foulmouthed bitch," he said, spitting on the ground to emphasize his disgust with Patti. "She was discussing it when Linda got out of the van to pee—Linda had kidney trouble. Patti's got a very vile, big mouth. Just to talk to her normally, you'd think, 'Damn—she's a doll,' but she's a bitch—pardon."

Patti had, Arthur Brown claimed, said she *would* get rid of Linda to save David.

"You feel," Newell asked, "that maybe that's what happened?"

"It took me five or six months to remember all this. I couldn't remember hardly my own goddamned name for a while. I haven't liked Patti since—and I never will. I have to live here with David and Patti because . . . it feels like he owes her his life."

And yet, Arthur Brown could not remember that he mentioned any of this to Cinnamon. Pressed, he admitted he might have told her. But what was the use? He didn't believe any of it would hold up in court.

"Even if someone can't be prosecuted," Newell offered, "we want all the details. It may or may not help Cinnamon. If Cinnamon isn't fully responsible for this, why should—"

"I'd bet my life on that," her grandfather cut in.

"You wouldn't make up a story just to get Patti in trouble because you don't like her, would you?" Newell asked.

"No way. No, sir. If it wasn't true, I wouldn't of said it . . . it's bad enough that it happened—no use of me adding any stories to it. · I was in hopes it might help Cinny because as far as I'm concerned, she's a doll."

The case had just taken a complete spin. If Arthur Brown was believable—which was the salient question—Patti Bailey, not Cinnamon, was a killer.

Newell heard a car engine lugging up the hill behind him and turned to see David Brown himself driving up. Arthur looked panicked.

Sotto voce, Newell said to the old man, "I'm a real estate man. If you want to maintain that, fine."

"Okay. If I stick my neck out too far, I'll lose my son, my granddaughter, plus another granddaughter."

"We don't want that to happen—but we are concerned with the truth," Newell stressed. "Here comes David. We can talk about it later," and then, in a louder voice, "Yeah, I've sold a couple of houses on this block."

Newell grinned, held out his hand, and introduced himself to David Brown as "Jerry Walker, Realtor."

"How ya doin'?" David Brown answered.

For a beat, Newell's breath caught, and then he knew that Brown had not recognized him. His eyes were drawn to a solid-gold pendant of some creature that David wore on a chain around his neck. It glittered in the sunlight—gold, and beneath that, orange and yellow stones. He knew what it was; he'd talked to the jeweler who had made it, but he wanted to hear David's explanation. "That's unusual," he said, "what is that—a dragon?"

"A phoenix." David offered nothing more.

Newell launched into a discussion of what a shame it was that a neighboring house, needing paint, was such an eyesore in such an expensive neighborhood. "I feel guilty showing houses up here because of that."

Newell slid his eyes toward the old man and saw that Arthur Brown's mouth was shut tight. He wasn't going to give him away.

It was odd. Finally talking to the man he had stalked for almost two years. David Brown was animated in the way of weak men who strive to appear influential and macho. He was most interested in making more money in real estate, he said, although he explained he'd already done very well indeed. He did not seem ill, although he was certainly out of shape, and he smoked like a chimney.

"This stuff is goin' up though," Newell continued, as smooth as if he had been selling real estate all his life. "Anything over three hundred thousand dollars is selling."

David brightened. He had been thinking about making a change.

"This new tax thing is forcing people to get something more expensive, and the write-offs are gone, and old Uncle Sam gets it," Newell said easily. "I have four condos myself, and I don't know if I'm gonna be able to keep them. But these bigger houses—they're selling. I've got friends interested in moving up here."

Newell tossed off some impossibly high figure he could get for David's house, and he could see David salivate.

Grandpa Brown, standing behind David, was getting nervous, sweat beading on his forehead. He would never make a poker player.

Newell slapped his breast pocket, murmured that he had run out of cards, but he would be back. He turned and strolled easily down the street to his car.

He had plenty of cards, but they all read "Jay Newell, Orange County District Attorney's Office, Senior Attorney's Investigator." At the moment, they didn't seem appropriate.

"Well, have a good day, you guys," he shouted.

Newell had been in any number of dicey spots, pretending to be someone he was not. Drug buys. Gang infiltration. But there was something about David Arnold Brown that chilled his blood. A certain flatness in his eyes, even when he was grinning. From a distance, he looked like a tubby cartoon figure. Up close, he looked like . . . what? *Evil.* Newell surprised himself with that one. Evil wasn't a concept he usually thought about.

He wondered if the old man could hold firm. He had gone on and on about *his* illnesses and ailments. Between Arthur and David, the Brown men seemed to suffer from every ailment mankind is prone to. Newell believed that Arthur Brown wanted to save Cinnamon, but he also knew the old guy was weak. He had been strong enough to finger Patti Bailey, to suggest that *she* was the shooter—not Cinnamon—but would he ever be strong enough to get up and say it in court, or even say it in front of his son? Grandpa Brown seemed to shrivel up when he was around David.

Newell had good reason to doubt Arthur Brown's fortitude. Even before that evening was over, he had confessed to his son that the man he had been talking to was not "Jerry Walker," but rather, Jay Newell of the Orange County District Attorney's Office.

David was both furious and alarmed. He called his father a fool, told him that he had endangered the whole family by even considering talking to the police. It was not Arthur's place to protect Cinnamon; that was David's job, and there were a lot of things that Arthur did not understand, could never understand.

Chastened and fearful, Arthur went to his room and stayed there.

David, enraged, confronted Patti. She didn't know what had happened, but she obeyed him as he told her to find their wedding certificate and the prenuptial agreement she had signed. Weeping, she did so. He tore them into small pieces, and then he marched her out to the backyard and pointed toward the brick barbecue.

"Burn them."

"*Why?*"

"Never mind why. Burn them and stay here until you're sure every single piece of them is ashes."

As she always had, Patti did as her husband said. But watching the flames, it seemed as if her marriage were going up in smoke too. She didn't know, and apparently David didn't think about it, but the original of the marriage certificate was on file and could be replaced. David's lawyer had a copy of the prenuptial agreement. That document, giving her only the old MG, had been to protect David—not Patti. But it could come back to haunt him.

Patti knew only that something had gone terribly wrong. It would be days before David stopped scowling. And Grandpa Brown tiptoed around the house as if he were going to jump right out of his skin.

Even though they were legally married, Patti and David had to sneak to be together. If they waited until the old couple were asleep, they could share physical intimacy. Even better, they had time alone when Arthur and Manuela went home on weekends to take care of their house in Carson, mow the grass, and trim the hedges.

David was jumpy. He no longer wanted Patti talking to her own family—about anything. "He was afraid my family would connect us to the crime 'cause we were still living together," Patti said, "and I hadn't gone back to live with them." But then David had never wanted the Bailey family to know about his business. That distrust was simply magnified.

It seemed to Patti that David was getting more paranoid all the time, that he didn't trust anyone—not even her. Ever since the night he made her burn her marriage papers, it had been getting worse. David became obsessed with knowing where she was *all* the time. He fitted her with a beeper so that he could always find her and check on what she was doing. She was never allowed to leave home without David, and when *he* left, he called her often on the beeper to be sure she was still at the house.

Throughout the winter and spring of 1987, David, Patti, Krystal, Manuela, and Arthur lived their uneasy existence in the palatial home in the Anaheim Hills. Arthur's fervent wish to have Patti out of the house went unheeded. If anything, she seemed more entrenched.

Arthur longed to live back in Carson, no matter how fancy David's new house was, but Manuela didn't trust Patti with the baby, and David wouldn't let the older couple take Krystal home to Carson with them.

"Patti's so goddamned, stinking jealous that she keeps Krystal away from Grandma," Arthur complained to anyone who would listen. Still, they didn't leave. With David being so sick, his parents hated to leave him alone. You could never tell when he might have an attack of some kind.

Things got a lot dicier for David in February 1987 when Patti told him she thought she was pregnant. Whatever his many physical ailments, they had apparently not compromised David Brown's sex life. He remained both potent and virile. But he was outraged at what he considered Patti's stupidity. A pregnancy for Patti could bring disaster. David insisted that she have an abortion. For once, Patti refused to obey him. No matter how vehemently he argued, she would not kill this baby.

She had played what she considered a loving trick on David. She had told him that her doctor said she would never be able to conceive a child. And he had believed her—and never concerned himself with birth control. Now, Patti allowed David to believe that her pregnancy was a strange aberration of fate—that she was as surprised as he was when she proved fertile after all. David was mad enough at her without her telling him the whole truth.

David insisted that, if their *marriage* had to be kept secret, her pregnancy would be doubly dangerous for them. The cops kept sniffing around, looking for some damn motive to show they had been involved in killing Linda. It didn't matter if they had or hadn't—the cops enjoyed trapping innocent people, just to make themselves look good. A baby was superfluous, anyway. They had Krystal to take care of. Wasn't that enough for Patti?

Patti balked at David's insistence that she get an abortion. She wanted her own baby. She had never had one thing in her life that was just hers to love. True, she had supplanted Linda in David's life and given him everything Linda had—*except* a baby. She was sure he would change his mind when it was born. He was so crazy about Krystal. He would love this baby just as much.

Time passed and Patti's swelling abdomen could not be ignored. Manuela looked at her sharply and whispered to Arthur. They had always considered themselves several rungs above the Bailey clan— although they had grudgingly come to accept Linda. Patti's obvious condition only verified what Manuela believed. The Baileys were trashy, and Patti was one of them. What could you expect?

When the pregnancy was no longer a secret, David denied that he was the father. He told his parents and anyone who expressed interest that Patti had "gotten herself pregnant" by some guy named Doug who lived near Betsy Stubbs and drove either a Camaro or a Trans-Am. "He's a Greek."

"Doug" was blatantly a mythic character, a man no one who knew either Patti or David had ever seen. Since Patti was always with David, and only a beeper away when she wasn't, it would have been all but impossible for her to sneak away for an intimate liaison with the swarthy "Doug." But relatives knew better than to question David. If he said Doug was the father, then Doug was the father. To beef up the Doug story, David ordered a large bouquet, enclosed a card signed "Doug," and had it delivered to Patti at the house.

Jay Newell noted Patti's condition as he continued to watch David and Patti together whenever he had the opportunity. Patti followed David obediently, as always. She didn't look happy, and David looked annoyed. Newell figured he knew who the father was.

On September 29, 1987, Patti Bailey gave birth to a baby girl, whom she would name Heather Nicole. David insisted that she pay her own hospital bill—out of her share of the 1985 accident settlement. In truth, David now had three daughters: Cinnamon, seventeen, Krystal, three, and Heather. While he embraced Krystal as the perfect baby and showered her with gifts and attention, it was not so with Heather. Heather was only a dangerous embarrassment to her father. He would never claim Heather as his.

It hurt Patti that David did not acknowledge Heather. She was far too unsophisticated to realize her main attraction for him had been her youth, and the fact that her body was unmarred by stretch marks. In her efforts to hold on to David, Patti had unwittingly done exactly the wrong thing.

David liked pubescent teenagers. Young mothers didn't turn him on. Patti had been his ideal when he married her—as had most of his wives. But the inexorable passage of time, maturity, and/or motherhood had diluted his passion for each of them.

Now, Patti was almost twenty—not old in most men's books, but *old* to David—and she was always fussing over Heather. She looked so much like Linda that, in a certain light, it was spooky. Her mouth was a trifle fuller, her breasts larger, but her features were almost identical. If his marriage to Linda *had* been as idyllic as David claimed, then having her image returned to him might have ensured that Patti's devotion would be rewarded.

But according to innumerable observers, the marriage to Linda had not been all that happy. And now, David had the *matured* Linda— or the closest thing to her—back again. And Patti fought with his mother a hell of a lot more than Linda ever had.

Patti Bailey Brown had become the very antithesis of what he wanted.

She must have known that. Periodically, she tried to destroy herself. Pathetic, ineffective suicide attempts that left thin white scars trailing along her arms. She had become David's childhood nightmare.

Despite David's disinterest in his new daughter, Heather, he did persuade Patti that it was foolhardy not to have insurance on the baby. He applied with a number of agents for several hundred thousand dollars' coverage on Heather. He was turned down everywhere he tried; not one of them could justify that much insurance on a newborn infant.

21

IN NOVEMBER 1987, Cinnamon was given another interview in an attempt to isolate her emotional problem—and find a way
to treat it. It was the first of two evaluations ordered by the parole board.

In December 1987, Cinnamon had another psychiatric examination.
She arrived late for her appointment and apologized for oversleeping.
She pointed out that she had already had an evaluation only a month
before. Told that *two* evaluations had been requested, she seemed
puzzled and a bit annoyed that so many doctors were trying to unlock
her subconscious. Almost a year ago, she had had hope—her grandfather had made her think that he might be able to help her.

But nothing had come of it. She was still locked up, and her father's
visits were less frequent than ever. If he had an investigator working
on her case, she sure didn't know anything about it, or a new lawyer
either. She wasn't bitter; she had just had to grow more philosophical
about everything.

As always, Cinnamon's response to the psychiatrist's questions was
very general, veering off from areas that got too close to the night of
the murder. She was not impolite; she was merely evasive. She said
she was busy with college courses, and the Christmas holidays. She
admitted there were "a lot of things that get me really upset," but she
did not want to explore them. She had "tons of homework" and that
came first.

Pressed, Cinnamon insisted she had not committed the crime for
which she was locked up, and that she still had no memory of Linda's
murder.

"How do you feel about the fact that your stepmother's killer might
presumably still be at large?"

She pondered the question for a moment, then answered inscrutably, "I have anger in me, but I'm not angry at that *person*—I don't
have the right. It was not her fault. She was not in control of the
situation."

Her fault. . . . It was not clear whom Cinnamon was talking about.

Cinnamon admitted freely that, yes, she was angry that she was
still in prison. But she was used to dealing with that. She was also
angry about the crime, but "did not hate the person who did it for
who they were."

Cinnamon's examiner looked at her perplexed, and she said she could not explain fully, and she did not expect anyone else to understand what she meant. "No one else has been through this."

This seventeen-year-old girl accepted what was—what had to be—in a sad, world-weary way. She said she suspected that the parole board also knew she was innocent, but that, without new information its members could do nothing to help her. "And I don't expect new information to show up," she said quietly. "This doesn't bother me."

"What if you should be confined *beyond* your parole date?"

"That's great," she said flatly. "I have nothing to do outside that I'm not doing here. I might like to take more college courses, but as for being outside—all I see on television is hate."

Beneath Cinnamon's brittle, listless veneer, there was fear. It showed only sporadically, but it was there. She made veiled references to the possibility that someone on the outside might harm her; inside, she was safe.

She had participated fully in every program, in every educational opportunity offered at the Ventura School—everything but group therapy. "It would be ridiculous for me to go," Cinnamon said softly. "With everyone talking about their offenses and dealing with them—and me saying I was innocent. There's no point. I'd be uncomfortable."

Cinnamon Brown missed her little sisters—Krystal and Brenda's younger daughter, Penelope. (She did not know that she had another little sister, Heather, two months old.) She wondered aloud about why she had been locked up for so long. Going on three years now from the time of her arrest. And yet she seemed resigned to staying incarcerated; her biggest concern was finding enough college courses to keep her busy.

Looking at the *girl*, it was difficult for even a trained psychiatrist to view her as a cold-blooded killer. Still, reading the details of Linda Brown's murder, there was no other way to describe the crime and the shooter.

But something was off-center. Something didn't mesh. Cinnamon's test results had always showed very low readings in the hostility index, and her other scores indicated she was a well-functioning, untroubled personality. Her reasoning and vocabulary were in the normal range.

Cinnamon had blossomed from the chubby fourteen-year-old Fred McLean had found vomiting in the doghouse. She had slimmed down, and she worked out with weights. She was a pretty girl, with long-lashed olive-brown eyes. She had started a part-time job as a reservations clerk with a major airline (albeit working at her computer well inside the reformatory's walls). She did cross-stitching and fancy needlework, and she went to school. Her days were full. She did whatever was asked of her; she was a credit to Ventura School.

But she was blocking her psychiatrist. Asked why she was incarcerated, she answered swiftly, "Why, to be rehabilitated."

"Rehabilitated for what?"

"Why, to have a better life."

Pinned down, she admitted the judge who convicted her had felt she was guilty of first-degree murder. She was sorry she had not had a jury trial, although that had never been an option in Juvenile Court. She denied committing the murder, and indeed, all wrongdoing . . . ever.

It was impossible to dislike Cinnamon Brown, and almost as hard to believe she was guilty of murder. Was she a multiple personality perhaps, a girl who truly did not know what her other self was doing? Was she a sociopath who could lie glibly? Was she hiding the truth because she was still terrified of something—or someone—outside the walls of her prison?

She was evasive, that was certain. She stalled, repeating nearly every question, rolling it around on her tongue while she formed an answer. When a question was too probing, she giggled to buy time. The giggle was a practiced device, a happy, light laugh, but one designed to ignore questions.

Cinnamon's psychological test scores warred with a diagnosis of multiple personality, sociopathy, or some other dark personality disorder. There *was* no convenient niche in which to fit her. The worst infraction she had committed at Ventura School was forgetting to tuck in her blankets when she made her bed.

Hardly the sign of a cold-blooded killer.

But her evasiveness troubled the interviewer. Confronted with the fact that she skirted around questions, delaying, Cinnamon answered that she wanted to be sure she got things right—so she had to take her time to answer.

"The subject is neither psychotic nor depressed."

It was a familiar diagnosis. It was indeed true that Cinnamon Brown was evasive, as if she was fighting to guard some terrible secret, afraid of what might happen if the truth should ever surface. Too many questions, too much probing—even too much sympathy—were threats she had to deflect.

But sometimes, she was so lonely. Sometimes, when lights out had been called, she thought of being home again, going to Disneyland or being on the beach watching the surfers or being free to go to college on the outside. She wondered about where her life was going. Or indeed, if it was ever going anywhere.

It was true that the world she saw only on television seemed ugly and dangerous. It was true that she was so far behind that world outside that she could probably never catch up. But sometimes, it didn't seem fair that she should spend her fifteenth birthday, her sixteenth birthday, her seventeenth birthday, and—soon—her eighteenth birthday behind bars.

Nothing her father promised her had come to pass. She had trusted totally, and as disloyal as she felt, she wondered sometimes if she had trusted too much.

22

W H I L E Cinnamon was undergoing her second psychiatric examination in as many months, her father was once again changing his residence. He needed bigger quarters. Actually, it wasn't even that. He required quarters that would allow him to separate the two main women in his life. Manuela and Patti continued to circle each other warily, and as grand as the house on Summitridge Lane appeared, the actual square footage wasn't that large. There wasn't room for both women to live there in harmony.

Something had to be done. David's nerves were frayed, and his health was worse than ever. He couldn't stand the bickering.

He looked around for property where there might be a mother-in-law apartment downstairs, or a detached cottage. Manuela and Arthur were a permanent part of his household, even though they still kept their place in Carson. But Manuela looked upon Patti and her baby as intruders, and Patti felt that Manuela was bossy and mean.

Finally, David found a place that looked as though it would solve all his problems: 1166 Chantilly Street had both a big house and room for a guesthouse. It wasn't as upper class as the Summitridge address, but it had more land, and it would afford more privacy. There was a pool, and it was close to transportation.

It was also less *exposed*. Sometimes, David felt as if somebody was staring at the back of his neck. But when he turned around, he saw nothing behind him—or no one he recognized. The house on Chantilly Street afforded him walls all around.

David borrowed $257,000 on the Summitridge house, and on December 29, 1987, he paid $177,300 cash for the Chantilly place. Then he immediately ordered remodeling that would cost another $100,000. As soon as he sold Summitridge, he would own a huge complex free and clear. They wouldn't be able to move in until late spring or early summer, but at least relief was in sight.

David was always scrupulous about keeping his insurance updated. When he purchased the home at 1166 Chantilly Street in December 1987, he immediately had it insured for $182,000. On June 23, 1988— after the extensive remodeling—he upgraded that insurance to $667,000 on the dwelling, and $500,250 on personal property, paying, of course, a hefty premium.

The personal property he listed was far more than the average Orange County family possessed. David included certified appraisals on some of his jewelry in his application. Among the jewelry described were: "A 14 Karat man's custom ring with a 5.25 carat pear-shaped diamond and 12 approximately 10 carat brilliant cut diamonds, all channel set, hand-engraved design—retail value, $36,450.00; a 14 Karat man's custom-designed emerald-cut diamond ring with eight approximate 10 carat brilliant diamonds channel set, diamond center approximately 4.92 carats, custom hand-engraving—retail value, $41,000; a 14 Karat lady's custom marquise diamond ring with approximately 2.10 carat in center, and 16 1.1 carat baguette diamonds, and 31 approximately .04 carat brilliant cut diamonds, all channel set—retail value, $28,950; A 14 Karat lady's ring with approximately 1.08 carat center stone diamond, and baguette channel set diamonds—retail value, $18,950."

Despite all his wealth, misadventure dogged David Arnold Brown. The 1986 Dodge pickup that he had purchased in September of 1986 and financed with forty-seven payments of $315.22 was stolen in the spring of 1988. David reported the theft to the Buena Park police, since he recalled parking the truck in the Buena Park Mall. Although he did not get around to making a formal report until April 26, David told the Buena Park police that the truck had vanished on April 23, 1988.

One of the odd aspects of the theft was the uncanny speed with which the truck was discovered. David reported it stolen to the Buena Park police at two P.M., and California Highway Patrol officers found the blackened hulk way up in the desert, many miles away, *forty-five minutes later*. The 1986 Dodge D-50 truck with the camper had been stripped, rolled, wrecked, and burned when it was discovered by California Highway Patrol officers in Deep Creek, south of Rock Springs—and only a hop, skip, and jump from Victorville where David had once lived. You couldn't even *drive* to Victorville from Buena Park in forty-five minutes—much less have time to cannibalize and incinerate a truck. (Later, Bailey family members admitted that David had told them to take the truck—he was tired of making payments—and that they could have anything they wanted off it, as long as they wrecked and burned it later. Before the "thief" could strip it, it was stolen by an acquaintance—who finished the job.)

Despite all of his run-ins with Allstate, the company nevertheless paid his claim for the truck—deemed a total loss—promptly. This time, the payment wasn't to David himself, but to the Chrysler Credit

Union. Allstate paid off the balance of his loan: $7,545.28 on May 27, 1988.

No one was ever charged in the truck theft. And once again, David Brown came out ahead. He no longer had to make the hefty monthly payments on the Dodge truck.

At that point, Data Recovery Incorporated was doing better than ever, and David expected to have a tax-reportable quarter-million-dollar year—or more—by the end of 1988. After three years of upheaval, it was beginning to look as if his life were going to settle down a little.

Cinnamon was almost eighteen, and she was still locked up, more cut off from home than ever. She didn't know about the new house—or the old house, for that matter. Certainly, she knew nothing of her father's Las Vegas marriage to Patti. Or of the new baby sister. Nobody told her when Heather was born; she had only heard rumors that Patti was pregnant, but Cinnamon's information came from Grandpa Brown, who muttered Patti had "gone out and gotten herself pregnant."

This puzzled Cinnamon. She could never remember Patti dating anyone, or even showing an interest in anyone. And Grandpa's latest rumor disturbed her more than anything she had heard yet. If it was true, then Cinnamon was afraid she knew with *whom* Patti had gotten herself pregnant.

It was a thought so ugly she shoved it away, so ugly that she asked no more questions about the subject. She didn't want to have her conclusions confirmed.

Cinnamon found herself farther and farther removed from the family. She spent a lot of time looking at old photographs, trying to picture herself back with all of them—but it was hard. She asked to have family albums sent, but David never quite got around to sending them.

It wasn't that Cinnamon lacked for anything. She still had her color TV in her room, and when the electricity was turned off at midnight, David had rigged up a self-charging battery pack to operate it. But institutional food had long since begun to pall. "The salad is O.K.," Cinnamon wrote in a letter, "but the rest I don't attempt. I eat the food I buy in canteen—soup, chips, pastries, cookies, peanut butter, jelly—*anything*."

There was always money in her canteen account; sometimes that was the only way she knew her father still remembered her. He hardly ever visited anymore.

"My father visited very regularly in the beginning," Cinnamon said later. "He asked a lot of questions, like 'How much pressure do they apply dealing with your commitment offenses?' and 'What will you tell them?' He told me not to say anything—just that I don't remember.

"He'd frighten me with thoughts that Linda might not be dead." Cinnamon shivered. "I had a few nightmares, but I knew she was gone.

"His visits got farther apart. He wrote cards and four or five actual letters. I saved two cards from him. His visits got to where I had to ask him to please come up because I missed him. He said he was sick or admitting himself to the hospital or he was dying. I was scared and worried. I called to see how he was, just checking to make sure all was well. But my grandparents would say, 'He's shopping' or 'At the movies.' Well, how could he be there if he was sick or in the hospital?

"This happened several times. Around this time, I realized that my father wasn't truthful with me. I'd ask my grandparents things and see if my father's story matched. Grandma said him and Patti shared a room. My father denied it, saying, 'Grandma's crazy.'

"New cars were bought, and my father denied it. New houses—and he denied that. Grandpa said he collected money for Linda's death. My father denied it. He lied to me a lot. The lies made me realize that I was alone. . . . I was still in Ventura. . . . I wasn't going anyplace for a long time.

"People never came to talk with me from my father [attorneys] about going home again. Daddy said home wasn't fun, and I wasn't missing out on anything. He said all they did was spend their days at home—which wasn't true."

Cinnamon's mother stuck by her, and once in a great while, she would hear from an old classmate from elementary school. Her first stepmother's—Lori's—parents kept in touch. Krista's life, naturally, changed, and Cinnamon's old friend had little in common with her any longer.

Cinnamon began to feel that she had been forgotten. Worse, she suspected that she had been lied to for a very long time. She didn't tell anyone. She certainly had no idea at all that a man named Jay Newell existed, or that he was working on the outside to verify the very doubts that haunted her days and nights.

23

J A Y   N E W E L L decided it was high time that someone wised Cinnamon up to what was going on at home. As far as he could tell, the only information she ever got was from her grandfather, and that came to her in obscure bits and pieces. But Newell could not go to her directly. Since Cinnamon was still a minor and would be one until her eighteenth birthday on July 3, 1988, he could not talk to her without her parents' permission.

Cinnamon's custodial parent at the time she was arrested was the very person Newell was investigating—David Arnold Brown. Everything he was coming up with made Newell that much more suspicious that Brown had played some role—however ephemeral it might have been—in the murder of his fifth wife. He was obviously still living with the suspect Grandpa Brown had fingered. Brown was a smart man; he had to be aware of the possibility that Patti was involved. Why would he stay with her?

David Brown was the last person Newell wanted to alert. He preferred to watch David and Patti without their knowledge. And he sure as heck didn't want to ask David Brown for permission to question Cinnamon. He couldn't imagine that Brown would acquiesce.

One thing that Jay Newell *could* do and remain strictly and ethically within the bounds of the law was to pass certain information to Cinnamon's parole officer. Newell couldn't talk to Cinnamon, but he could have a kind of secondhand input. It was akin to fishing in murky waters at midnight; he didn't know what would come up on his line.

Newell was convinced now that Cinnamon Brown was serving out a kind of penance, shouldering all the punishment for a crime she might not have committed. Something was keeping her from talking to the parole board or to her counselors. He didn't know if it was fear or misplaced loyalty, or part of some prearranged plot.

Newell would have liked to let Cinnamon know she had a friend working on the outside for her. Himself. But he didn't dare tell her. By the time he finished his investigation, he might even turn out to be an enemy instead of a friend. He didn't know the girl. He didn't know what drove her, and what it might take to get her to tell the complete truth.

If she even knew it anymore.

Jay Newell began by taking pictures of the lovely new homes where David and Patti lived—the sumptuous fieldstone mansion in the Anaheim Hills, and the sprawling six-bedroom complex on Chantilly. He took a picture of the pool at the new house. It was blue-green with statues of Grecian goddesses watching over it. Luxurious tables and lounge chairs were grouped around the sun-drenched patio. He took the photos with him when he drove up to the Ventura School in Camarillo. He moved through the high-security check-in building and asked to see Cinnamon's PO.

As he waited, Newell could not help but notice the tremendous contrast between David's living conditions and his oldest daughter's. David had it all—and Cinnamon had almost nothing.

The school itself, with its low red-brick buildings, swimming pool, grassy area, and round picnic tables with umbrellas, didn't *look* that forbidding. But it was an institution; all the windows were secured, announcements blared continually. The sound of flat keys in slotted locks was familiar—a sound Jay Newell had left behind long ago at the HOJJ. This was Cinnamon's world, and it had been for three years. Guards and body searches and passes and lockdowns.

Newell discussed with Carlos Rodriguez, Cinnamon's parole officer, the feasibility of letting her know what was going on at home. He gave the pictures of the homes where David and Patti had been living to Rodriguez.

Jay Newell felt Cinnamon deserved to know that her father and Patti were still together. That they drove expensive cars, traveled often to Las Vegas to gamble and see the shows, that they not only walked free, they were also living high and well. David, at least, walked free. Patti was constantly leashed in with her beeper.

"I didn't know at the time if she saw the pictures or not," Newell said. "I didn't want to know." But if Cinnamon did see those pictures, she could not help but be shocked by how well her father was living.

Maybe she already knew—but Newell doubted it.

The counselors at Ventura School told him that Cinnamon still had no way to get in touch with her father directly. She could call the answering service for the business, or she could write to the business address, a box number in Anaheim, but for all the information she had, her father might be living in Australia. One thing seemed to bother her, however, more than anything. She had been asking questions about Patti's baby.

Newell kept track of Cinnamon and of how she was doing at Ventura, although he never spoke to her directly. Occasionally, he caught sight of her across the quad, but she didn't see him. He had never spoken to Cinnamon. By the time he would normally have questioned her after her arrest in March 1985, she reportedly had no memory of what had happened.

Newell learned Cinnamon was a loner who didn't hang out with any particular group, not the Caucasian girls or the Hispanics or the blacks or the Asians. After three years, she still kept to herself, didn't cause trouble, and cooperated with the cottage parents and teachers. Her grades were nothing to brag about, but she wasn't flunking either. Except for the fact that "Ventura School" was a prison, Cinnamon's reports were probably exactly what they would have been if she were back in Anaheim going to Loara High School. But instead of heading for the beach on weekends and in the summer, Cinnamon went back to her cell after school.

Newell learned from her counselors that she hadn't become institutionalized, and she certainly hadn't become tough or hardened. She was a normal kid, save for the fact that she had been removed from real life for so long that she seemed almost afraid to go back out into a changed world. She had a "boyfriend"—not a real boyfriend, but a young man she saw and talked to when she went to work in the evening. She would lose him too; he was being paroled.

Newell had no idea what Cinnamon was really like now, nothing beyond what others told him. He doubted that he would be able to reach her—at least not emotionally. No one else had. If all the psychologists and all the counselors and her own attorney had been unable to break through her wall of forgetfulness, how on earth could he hope to? If Cinnamon *had* seen the photographs of the fancy houses her father now lived in, how had she reacted? She might have closed up even more. Her psychological tests had shown a young woman almost totally devoid of hostility. Newell wasn't a psychologist, but it seemed to him that that kind of personality might not come out fighting for her fair share of life. A girl with no hostility in her might simply turn her face to the wall and give up.

Cinnamon had now been locked up for three years, three of the most important years of a teenager's life—from fourteen to seventeen. Newell had seen the visitors' sign-in sheets and noted that David rarely visited his daughter any longer—although he kept her commissary account solvent. It was as if he had written his oldest child off, giving her *money* and *things* to assure himself that she wouldn't bother him. More incomprehensible, it was as if he had his new life and he had left Cinnamon, at least figuratively, to rot.

At some point, might not Cinnamon Darlene Brown get mad? Even for a girl with only a teaspoonful of hostility, couldn't there be a breaking point?

The case had become an obsession with Jay Newell. He took the case file out of his drawer often, reading it over, worrying it, approaching it from oblique angles. More than three years. A man with good sense would have given up long ago, he told himself.

But every time he opened up the dog-eared file, he found something else—some little fragment of information—that made him believe he was on the right track. He didn't know *who* had shot Linda Marie Brown as she slept, but he was absolutely convinced that the impetus that led to her murder had not originated in Cinnamon Brown's mind.

Somebody else had to be involved. And since Cinnamon was the only one locked up, that somebody or *those* somebodies were walking free. Maybe it *was* Patti, as Grandpa Brown insisted. Maybe it was David. Maybe it was even other members of the Bailey family as David had suggested. And even if it turned out that Cinnamon herself *had* pulled the trigger, Newell wanted to find a way into the void of her memory and learn *why*.

Newell contacted Brenda Sands, hoping that she might help him get Cinnamon to open up. Fred McLean had talked to Brenda several times with no problems. Newell barely survived his first encounter with Cinnamon's mother. With all his experience with the toughest gangs in southern California, with all the midnight drug busts, getting shot at on patrol, and staring Charles Manson straight in the eye, Newell had never met anyone like Brenda Sands.

Their meeting was akin to a hawk trying to peek into a mother wren's nest. David had convinced Brenda that Jay Newell was a major force threatening her daughter and one of the villains who had put Cinnamon in prison (which, in truth, he had to admit he was). Brenda chased him from her door, and the big detective ran for cover when the petite brunette took off after him. A friend waiting in the car for Newell saw him come bucketing out in total rout and said, laughing, "Are you sure you *like* this job? It sure doesn't look like much fun from here."

Brenda kept in touch with Cinnamon and visited her whenever she could, driving a funny old humpbacked station wagon that David had given her so she could make the trip up and back to Ventura. Fortunately, as time passed, Newell was able to convince Brenda that he was still trying to unearth the truth about her daughter's case. They met again and she told him everything she knew, but it was so very little. Yes, David had rushed to her and to Susan Salcido on the very day of Linda's murder, hurrying to warn them to be sure to portray Cinny as flaky and suicidal.

Brenda smelled a rat too, but she was in the same position as the rest of them. She had misgivings and doubts; she did not have proof. And she was still afraid of her first husband, terrified to cross him.

24

W H E N   T H E call came, Jay Newell was absolutely astounded. He had laid the groundwork, he had hoped that it would happen— but he had never really believed it would. Then, and in retrospect, it was the longest shot he had ever played.

But it worked.

It was July 19, 1988, and the caller on the line was Cinnamon's parole officer, Carlos Rodriguez, at the Ventura School.

"I have someone here who wants to talk to you. She wants to talk about her case."

It was Cinnamon.

Newell quickly called Deputy DA Dick Fredrickson to pick up an extension, and the two members of the Orange County DA's staff heard the small voice come across the phone line from the Ventura School. It was a wispy, half-frightened voice.

"Hello, Mr. Newell?"

"Cinnamon?" Newell identified himself, and at the same time re-assured himself that it was, indeed, Cinnamon Brown at long last.

Cinnamon Brown wanted—*needed*—to talk to someone. She did not balk at having Fredrickson listening, but her first question was startling—and telling: "Will I be protected, or will my father be listening?"

"Who?" Newell asked, surprised.

"My father."

Assured that David Brown was not listening, she burst forth, "He was in the wrong for what he did, and I was too young to realize it. I know now that it's time for him to take the responsibility for the crime that's taken place. . . . I was a little bit involved 'cause I knew what was going to happen—but I didn't actually do the murder."

Jay Newell's voice was as calm and steady as always. But there was an undercurrent of excitement and relief in his voice when he spoke to Cinnamon. She finally felt safe enough—or mad enough—to call. She was hesitant to go into details on the phone, but Newell needed to know more, to be assured that she was really ready to deal in specifics.

"It's possibly something you can work with," she told him. "He said that Linda was going to be killing him, for insurance or something for her and her twin brother, and he said *we* had to do something about it. I said, 'What is it that you want me to do?' and he said, 'We're going to have to think of a way to get rid of her or I'll have to leave town.' I said I didn't want him to leave town, and he said, 'You're going to have to help me then.' So we went for several drives while he and Patricia thought of ways to dispose of Linda."

Cinnamon recalled to Newell her memory of catching her father kissing Patti in the store. "Later things started getting worse. He'd take off with Patricia, and sometimes I'd go with them. To banks and stuff to cash checks. We'd be gone for hours. Well, him and Patricia started talking about ways to get rid of Linda—like we'd throw her out of the van when we were driving down the freeway . . . she suggested hitting her over the head to knock her out . . . different ways . . . I was listening . . . I wasn't involved."

Oh, my God . . .

The long-held secrets burst out like floodwaters knocking down a wall. After the crime, Cinnamon said her father had first told her to say she had done it, and then he had told her not to say anything, not to remember anything. "I didn't because I trusted him."

Newell questioned Cinnamon about the gun, and she said she knew it was Linda's, and she knew that Patti had wiped it off with a towel.

Cinnamon said she had not talked to her father for four weeks, and then only to ask for some supplies she needed. Asked if she had ever confronted him with her thoughts on Linda's murder, she said she had, but that her father always pushed the subject away and said, "Well, you'll be out soon."

"For some reason, he won't talk about it at all. He pretends not to hear."

Cinnamon said Patti never visited her, never talked on the phone, but sometimes listened in when Cinnamon called David.

"Do you know Patti had a baby?" Cinnamon asked suddenly.

"Yes," Newell answered.

"Do you know that baby is my father's baby?"

"I know all about that."

That was it. Cinnamon Brown had been betrayed in so many ways, Newell suspected, and in ways he didn't even know about yet. But the birth of Patti's baby, fathered by David Brown, had shattered her steadfast belief in her father. She finally realized she had simply been thrown away.

"Are you willing to give a formal statement about this . . . and open up the investigation?" Newell asked.

"I could probably help you . . . but I don't want to endanger myself with my father."

"Are you afraid of him?"

"Yeah, I'm afraid of him. To me, he seems very powerful."

Cinnamon's coming forth might help her in her hopes for freedom, but Newell was adamant that he could give no such assurances. "I don't know what you're going to lead us into."

Over and over again, Cinnamon asked that her call be kept confidential from her father. She asked for protection. Newell told her that, if it seemed necessary, she would be protected.

Dick Fredrickson came on the line. He had two questions to ask. "You said you heard your father drive away before you heard the shots?"

"Yes."

"Have you ever handled the gun?"

"I'm not sure. My father had so many guns. I'm not even sure which one it was."

"How do you know it wasn't Patti who drove away?" Newell asked.

"Because Patti didn't know how to drive."

Cinnamon thought she had heard the Ranchero leave, and that was David's car. It made a lot of noise. Or maybe his Prelude.

Newell told Cinnamon that he would have to come up to the Ventura School to talk to her in person. He asked her to jot down notes to herself, to help her remember. Nothing in his voice betrayed how he felt—whether or not he believed what she had just told him. He warned her to tell no one that she had called the DA's office—no one—not even her mother.

She promised she would not.

Newell and Fredrickson talked briefly to Carlos Rodriguez, and then this enthralling call was over.

Newell sat back in his chair in disbelief and stared at the lithograph on his wall without seeing it. It had finally happened, the first tiny crack in that vast wall of silence. Then he leapt to his feet and raised one fist triumphantly over his head, punching the air like a winning prizefighter. Dick Fredrickson raced into Newell's office and they clapped each other on the shoulder.

It was a moment of high emotion. The impossible had happened. Cinnamon Brown had talked.

But Cinnamon's rush of words puzzled Newell. For instance, he had not expected to hear that David Brown had left before the shots were fired. But then, Newell was not convinced he was hearing the whole truth. He was not convinced he was hearing *any* of the truth.

The most important thing was that Cinnamon had finally begun to talk. Three years and four months to the day after Linda Brown's murder, Cinnamon had broken her silence and had agreed to talk to Newell in person.

Would he come to Ventura?

You bet he would.

It was not as simple a process as it might have seemed. Newell had been working this case basically on a "request for more information" from the California Youth Authority. It was certainly not an official, full-fledged murder investigation. The murder of Linda Marie Bailey Brown had been *solved*, adjudicated, and the case closed long ago. Newell did not have the authority to take the giant plunge of reopening the case. It was one thing to keep track of David Brown and Patti Bailey. But it was a long jump from his surveillance to go to the California Youth Authority Prison and open up the can of worms he knew was waiting for him there.

Cinnamon's call left Newell both exhilarated and cautious. He had to find himself a deputy DA who had the time, enthusiasm, and temerity to reopen this case. Dick Fredrickson was behind him, but he had too many other responsibilities to see this thing through if it turned into something they could go back into court with.

An admitted killer, locked up in the joint for three years, who suddenly changes her mind, was not the ideal prosecution witness. She would be the prey of choice for a defense attorney. Most deputy DAs, given an alternative, would rapidly walk in the opposite direction if they encountered Jay Newell headed their way with such a case.

But Newell had somebody in mind.

Jeoff Robinson had no free time at all, but he was rumored to be ripe for impossible challenges and was gutsy as hell. A fighter such as Robinson was the kind of DDA it was going to take to reopen this long-dormant case.

Orange County deputy district attorneys worked their way up from misdemeanors to felonies—particularly homicides. Once they reached that rarefied position as a prosecutor of homicide cases, each worked a specific city in the county. In July of 1988, Jeoff Robinson was the DDA who handled all homicides in Garden Grove.

Robinson was something of a legend in Orange County. In many ways, he was exactly what central casting would have chosen to portray a crusading district attorney. In most others, he was a revelation.

Robinson, thirty-five, was a strikingly handsome man with dark hair and crystalline blue-green eyes. Six feet tall, 180 pounds, he had the physique of a star quarterback—which he was, at the University of the Pacific. "Well," he said with a laugh, "let's say at least in my own mind. To be honest, if I'd been six feet three and weighed two hundred and thirty, I would have wanted to play professional football. But I wasn't."

Six feet was big in the forties; in the seventies, it was the Goliaths who were the draft choices.

But it wasn't really that. It was the law itself calling to him. Jeoff Robinson had been weaned, reared, steeped, and tutored in the law from the time he was old enough to comprehend. Not criminal law. Civil law. It was assumed that Jeoff would come into the family practice. For a long time, he assumed he would too.

His father, Mark Robinson, Sr., was renowned for his landmark success in product liability suits. Jeoff's older brother, Mark junior, in partnership with their father, won a stunning victory over the Ford Motor Company in the incendiary-Pinto suits of the seventies, and they had since won many more multimillion-dollar judgments—both actual and punitive—for their clients.

"As a kid, I wasn't questioned," Jeoff Robinson remembered. "From the time I was five, I was cross-examined. I loved it. I loved watching my dad in court. I respect my dad more than any man I've ever known. He has an internal toughness that I've never seen in anyone else. My mother—well, my mother's a saint."

Mark Robinson, Sr., an Army Air Force pilot, was shot down over Yugoslavia in World War Two and was missing in action for several months before he was discovered to be a prisoner of war. His bride, Rita, nineteen, was pregnant when Mark vanished. His first son was born while he was missing in action and was named after him.

After the war, the family settled in Los Angeles's Hancock Park, on Irving Boulevard, and grew to eight children. "It was paradise for kids. I think we had seventy-five kids on our one block alone," Jeoff remembered. "Big older houses—when neighborhoods in Los Angeles were much different—a sort of Catholic ghetto."

Later, as his practice grew, Mark Robinson moved his family to Fremont Place where he had made a once-in-a-lifetime buy on a large house with a tennis court—and an elevator. But Jeoff was not raised a rich kid. His father's tremendous success peaked *after* most of his children were grown. The Irving Boulevard days had the most impact on the eight Robinson kids, rough-and-tumble, and in and out of neighbors' houses in a Los Angeles that no longer exists.

Like his siblings, Robinson was brought up to be unfailingly polite, devout, and to work like hell for what he believed in. There was a Kennedyesque energy among the Robinsons, and Jeoff inherited twice his share. Mark junior practiced law with his father, and brother Greg coached football for UCLA for nine years and would later join the coaching staff of the New York Jets.

Jeoff graduated from law school at Southwestern University in Los Angeles, and he would have been welcomed into the family firm. But he wanted to strike out on his own, to prove he could make it on his own merit, without being "one of the Robinsons." Once he had done that, he would probably join his father and brother—but not until then.

"I wanted to try cases too," he recalled. "About the only way a young lawyer got to try cases immediately was to go to work for the public defender's office or the district attorney. I preferred to *prosecute* crimes."

And prosecute crimes he did. Jeoff Robinson revved himself up for trial as if he were still playing football, stopping short of actually charging his office wall like a lineman attacking an opposing team. He worked through the night on arguments, acted out all roles, and prepared for any eventuality. He was also known for his willingness to get in there and dig for evidence—both figuratively and literally— with the investigators, and a forty-hour week meant nothing at all to him. He often worked sixty hours.

In trial, Robinson was utterly consumed by the case at hand. He was brilliant in voir dire and closing arguments. His direct- and cross-examination techniques were imaginative and maddening to the defense. He was emotional in the courtroom, but it was a sincere reaction, in no way contrived. He wore his feelings on the outside. When he was angry, the gallery knew it. When he was amused he had trouble hiding it.

Robinson could be a juggernaut. He was fiercely competitive. To almost everyone but defense attorneys, he was immensely likable. Intense and quick-thinking on his feet, he was also possessed of a comedic view of life that endeared him to juries—if not always to judges. One of his trials involved thirty motions for mistrial and so many bench conferences that Robinson quipped, "I could wear out my shoes this way, back and forth, back and forth." The judge frowned, and the defense attorney shouted for yet another mistrial.

At the same trial, the opposing attorney was given to references to his wife, and how he had discussed the case with his wife only the night before, giving the impression of his loving, stable home life. Robinson, a reluctant bachelor, looked at the jury with a mournful glance and said, "If I *had* a wife, I could ask her."

A juror in the back row, carried away with sympathy and the impulse to matchmake, cried out, "I don't have a daughter, but I have a granddaughter you'd love!"

Again, everyone—but the judge and the defense team—thought it was hilarious.

Jeoff Robinson had won fifty of his fifty-one felony cases. (He had one hung jury, but he went back and won that one too, second time around.) In short, he was a maverick. He respected the law, and he respected the truth and aimed for what was morally right. He might, however, seek out moral and legal truth in his own unique fashion.

This was the kind of DDA Newell needed. If he could persuade Jeoff Robinson to reopen the Brown case, they would have a triumvirate who were superb in their jobs, and who were all known to fight like tigers: Fred McLean, Jay Newell, and Jeoff Robinson. As different as three men could be from one another, but each of them obsessed with revealing a long-hidden truth. Newell liked the sound of it and headed from his office to the DA's Homicide Unit.

The Orange County District Attorney's Office was huge, both physically and in terms of personnel. The offices were spread out like rabbit warrens on both the first and second floor of the courthouse. Nobody beyond the district attorney's own staff, and the detectives who came there with cases to review, could find his way out—*if* he managed to get inside. The entrance to the District Attorney's Office was on the second floor, but once through the locked door behind the receptionists' desks, the uninitiated faced a bewildering network of hallways, offices, stairwells, and hidden doors. It was just as well; Orange County DAs had their share of threats. The maze they worked in allowed them to come and go at will, using elevators and exits that appeared to have nothing to do with the District Attorney's Office.

At full strength, there were 175 deputy district attorneys, and 140 district attorney's investigators. That much investigative assistance was a situation unheard of in most areas, but Orange County gave their deputy DAs exceptional support.

Homicide DAs occupied the first floor of the Orange County Courthouse; their offices were eight-by-ten cubbyholes tucked here and there, well off the beaten path. Jeoff Robinson's office was a mess. There was no way to cushion the description; his surroundings plainly did not reflect the precise organization of his thoughts. He was always on the verge of cleaning his office up, but he was also always in trial, preparing for trial, or waiting for a verdict, or—to ease the tension—running or playing basketball. Robinson *liked* to run, and sometimes Newell would run along with him, bored, because that was often the only time they had to discuss the fine points of a case.

Files and books and papers and who knows what covered every surface of Robinson's office. His phone-message spike still had calls from March 1988—which he insisted he had answered. A sign on the wall read "I hate USC!" and tickets to a Jimmy Buffett concert were taped to that. A gym bag stuffed with jogging clothes blocked easy access to his desk. Robinson's passions.

There was a photograph on one wall of Robinson digging for a missing body, caught unaware by some phantom lensman. Underneath, there were three dozen or so suggested captions, most of them obscene, from fellow deputy district attorneys. It was quite possible that there was, indeed, a law degree somewhere in the clutter. It was also possible there was a telephone somewhere on the DDA's desk.

It didn't really matter; Robinson was a man in constant motion who walked on the balls of his feet—like an Indian or like the athlete that he was—moving through the two floors of the Orange County District Attorney's Office. Receptionists usually paged him before they even tried to ring his office. They knew he wouldn't be there. And if he was, he took pride in having the most difficult office to locate in the whole maze of homicide prosecutors' cubicles.

His name was not on the door, but there was a page from a court transcript with a judge's oblique ruling: "Whether or not Mr. Robinson is a buffoon has no bearing on this case."

"I didn't put it there," Robinson said. "My door is known as a repository for the inane. I never know what's going to get tacked up there."

In 1981, Jeoff Robinson promised that he would stay with the Orange County DAs Office for at least two years. Seven years later, he was still there, happily entrenched.

His first homicide case was the nightmare that any prosecuting attorney dreads. He had to prosecute an elderly man who had shot his wife because she was dying of a terminal illness and in terrible pain. "How was I going to get that poor old man up there and cross-examine him?" Robinson asked. "I didn't want to. *I* felt sorry for him. And any jury with half a heart would too. Together with defense counsel, we came up with a way out—after many hours of collaboration. *The dead wife was the one who had actually pulled the trigger.* The defendant only helped the victim hold her finger on the gun's trigger. We were able to get the charge lowered to "aiding and abetting a suicide."

A convicted rapist who had served four years for his alleged crime had his conviction reversed when Robinson read the case and saw a number of flaws. "It appeared the man was innocent," Robinson recalled. "I went to his attorney—who happened to be Al Forgette—and asked if I could talk to the man, with the stipulation that his client's answers could never be used against him.

"It had been a very brutal gang rape of a couple on the beach. This man was the only one caught and convicted, and I believed there were others involved who were still free. It turned out this man had been dead drunk, dressed just like the actual rapists were, and the victims misidentified him. Unfortunately, he took the rap at trial. We were able to find and convict the half dozen *real* rapists—just six months before the statute of limitations ran out."

An innocent man was set free, but woe be unto the guilty defendant who came up against Robinson in court.

Jay Newell had never had occasion to work with Jeoff Robinson. But he wanted to. "The Cinnamon Brown case was so darned intriguing to anyone who started looking into it. I couldn't let go of it, Fred McLean couldn't let go of it, and I was counting on it hitting Jeoff the same way."

Robinson was semiprepared for a visit. Bryan Brown, the chief trial deputy in charge of the DA's Homicide Unit warned him that there might be an old case coming back—"a 1985 conviction." Brown mentioned no names.

"I was wary," Robinson admitted. "I wondered what this 'hummer' was that I was about to be taken in on." When Jay Newell came padding down the hallway with his request, Robinson had been waiting for the other shoe to drop. "He started laying out this Brown case for me, and I could see the work that would be involved, and I'm wondering why reopen something that's dead and buried. I was listening to Jay and thinking, 'This one's no slam dunk. This one could be trouble.' "

Robinson sat behind his desk and listened to Newell for fifteen minutes. Twenty minutes. "At about half an hour," he admitted, "I began to get excited. I thought I could smell miscarriage of justice. With that, he had me hooked."

As Gary Pohlson, a much-respected defense attorney and frequent opponent commented wryly, "Robinson will prosecute *anything*. Just toss him any case at all and he'll go for it. And he wins."

That was not quite true. Although he would be loath to admit it, Jeoff Robinson had a wide streak of "crusader" running through him. "I was getting fired up, listening to Newell. I'd rather take on a case that is morally offensive—yet tough—than a sure thing. As far as I'm concerned, I could lose the next ten cases, and I wouldn't care. Not because I like to lose, but because I guess I want to be part of doing the 'romantic' part of what's right. That's the great part of this job! This one cried out for the prosecution to ride in and save the innocent and punish the guilty."

Newell outlined his surveillances of David Brown and Patti Bailey, the phone conversation with Cinnamon. If what Newell believed was true, Robinson was a natural for this case. "I want to prosecute the worst kind of criminal," Robinson explained. "This may sound odd—but I have more respect for a bank robber who goes in and sticks a gun in a teller's face and asks for money, who is, in his own way, *truthful* and up-front about what he does, than I do for a white-collar criminal who pretends to be one thing and is something else. I am *offended* by moral crimes."

If Cinnamon Brown had taken the rap and long incarceration for someone else, this moldering 1985 case that Jay Newell was so obsessed with seemed to Robinson to be the most heinous of moral crimes. *Yes!* Yes, he would take it on. But he warned Newell that they had absolutely nothing at the moment. There was no way that he could reopen the case on Cinnamon's word alone. "I told him I was going to ask for more—and then more—and more and more."

Jay Newell knew he couldn't do all the legwork and all the investigating by himself. Fred McLean was no longer assigned to the Garden Grove detective unit, and Newell had to figure a way to get him back on the team. He went to McLean's old sergeant, who went to his new lieutenant. Would they cut McLean loose from his new detail for a while? Fortunately, they agreed. Nobody knew the 1985 case the way McLean and Newell did. In order to reconstruct it, it would take both of them.

Impatiently, the two of them—and Jeoff Robinson—had to wait for a go-ahead from the upper echelons of the Orange County District Attorney's Office. They could do no more until they had that. Newell could not even go up to the Ventura School and talk to Cinnamon.

It was the longest three weeks of Jay Newell's life. He got his permission to pursue the case. But even with all he and McLean had learned in the more than three years since Linda Brown's murder, neither they nor Robinson knew how complex the case would become.

25

J U S T   A F T E R sunrise on August 10, 1988, Jay Newell and Fred McLean were on their way to the Ventura School to talk to Cinnamon. Her phone call had provided them with enough information to get *this* far, on the road headed north. They had no idea what she was going to say, but they would be able to watch her face as she spoke, to evaluate her body language.

It was quite possible she only wanted to get out of prison—but neither McLean nor Newell truly believed that was Cinnamon's reason for calling. More likely, the secrets she had held on to so tightly had begun to burn. And she was probably angry. That was good; justifiable rage almost always brought forth the truth.

It was early when they drove through the gates at Ventura School, the August morning cool before the heat of the day to come. Cinnamon was still asleep when they arrived. Her work schedule on the TWA flight reservations line kept her up very late at night. They waited, and when she finally appeared, both Newell and McLean were stunned by the vast change in her appearance, her bearing. Cinnamon had dressed carefully, as if she were applying for a job and not meeting with detectives to discuss a long-ago murder. She had been short and a little chubby; now she was very slender. The pudgy cheeks were gone; the planes of her face were sculpted and enhanced with subtle, skillfully applied makeup.

McLean, especially, had difficulty equating this young woman with the scared, sick child he had pulled from the filthy doghouse three and a half years earlier. *That* Cinnamon had given him a confession he had never really believed, and then she had faded on him. All these years, he had been poised, waiting for the rest of the story; he had not realized how much so until this moment.

It was 11:37 on that Wednesday morning when Newell began the first tape. He had explained to Cinnamon that she needed no attorney. She had already been convicted of the homicide they would be discussing. She could not now be placed in double jeopardy. In other words, she could not be convicted *twice* for the same murder.

Again, Newell stressed that neither he nor McLean could promise her anything for the information she chose to give to them. No deals. No expectations of an earlier release from prison.

Cinnamon nodded. She understood that she would be flying without a net. It didn't matter.

Newell wanted to take Cinnamon back, figuratively through a tunnel of time, to elicit total recall of the events of early 1985, if that was possible. "First of all," he began softly, "put your mind back a couple of years ago when all this happened, to a point where you can even remember what the weather was like . . . it may be so insignificant that you don't think we even need to know . . . What were you wearing, whether or not the grass was mowed, how the air smelled . . . how old were you?"

"Fourteen. . . ."

Cinnamon had seen only the most rudimentary reports on her case, and that had been two years ago—the files kept on her at CYA. She had seen no newspaper accounts. She had not seen her attorney since her trial, and even then, she said, "Mr. Forgette didn't let me read anything pertaining to my case."

"You haven't refreshed your memory in any way then—other than by just thinking about it?"

She shook her head. "Just thinking about it. Trying to go back, because I've pitched it out of the way so far. Like I was told to—and I pitched it out so far that it got out of touch with me. I almost started believing it myself."

Newell laid down five proof sheets of photos of the exterior of the house and yard at Ocean Breeze Drive. Cinnamon identified the small frames easily, tapping them with one long, perfectly manicured fingernail. She pointed to the aqua and white travel trailer. "That's where I was told to stay."

She identified each picture, all correctly. The green house was caught in her memory, as much as she had tried to forget it.

"Why don't you just start anywhere," Newell suggested. "Tell us what you remember about the incident—leading up to it, that day, and from then on."

Cinnamon took a deep breath. "Well . . . I was in the living room one day with my father and Patricia. Patti had left to go to the kitchen—we had a dining room before you would reach the kitchen—and she stopped there by the door. . . . She goes, 'Shhh!' so I was quiet."

Patti had stood frozen for minutes. When she came back to the living room, she looked perplexed. "I just heard the strangest thing," she said. She told Cinnamon and David that she had overheard a phone conversation between Linda and her twin brother, Alan. She said it sounded as if they were planning to kill David.

Cinnamon had laughed, but Patti was adamant. "She goes, 'No, I'm *serious*. . . . Linda was talking to Alan about *killing* David!' My dad goes, 'What have you been smoking in the kitchen?' but she goes, 'I'm serious.' "

Cinnamon said David sighed and asked Patti what she had heard, but she had seemed very upset and said she couldn't discuss it in the house because Linda might overhear. "And I was saying, 'She's pulling your leg—she wants attention,' and after a while Linda came out and everything was okay. She told me to go get ready for dinner."

"Do you have a time frame?" Newell asked. "How long was this before Linda was killed?"

". . . At least seven months before."

The subject was dropped for the evening, but David had brought it up again the next day when he, Patti, and Cinnamon were going to the chiropractor. (They all had been in an earlier accident.)

"Patti said that Linda was going to kill my father to get him out of the way." Cinnamon said she could not believe it. She had looked at Linda later and thought, "Linda wouldn't say something like that. I was thinking, like, because she was so pretty. . . . No, Patti's hallucinating."

Cinnamon had tried to write it off as a practical joke. "Our family's a big bunch of practical jokers."

But the terror had begun. David said he *knew* Linda was going to try to kill him. "My father kept saying, 'Just believe me. I'm your father. I know she is trying to kill me.' "

From that point on, David had been in "almost a paranoid state," and he had come to Cinnamon often and said, "Linda's going to try to kill me."

Cinnamon didn't know how to respond. She was afraid to discuss her father's fears with her mother because she didn't want it to get back to David. She was frightened of David. He could get so angry.

It was during this period that Cinnamon had seen her father kissing Patti in the store. That made her even more confused. Linda was being so nice to her, so worried about Cinnamon's sadness. But Cinnamon certainly couldn't tell Linda about her father and Patti kissing. She couldn't tell anyone.

"The next thing I remember happening that concerns the case is me being out in the van with my father and Patti. My father just got back from Randomex, and we were going to cash his check. . . . I heard Patti talking to my father about *'we have to get rid of her.'* . . . My father was all—'I don't know how we're going to do it.' I sort of oozed into the next seat behind them, and my father looked back at me and he goes, 'What did you hear?' . . . and he said, 'You probably heard it already, so just sit there.' "

Newell darted a glance at McLean. The story was bizarre, but it had the ring of truth to it. Neither man had to say more than a word or two to keep it flowing. Cinnamon had held it in so long.

Patti reminded Cinnamon of the phone call she had overheard. "Well," Patti said, "I heard them again . . . and they said they were going to kill your father . . . this time, they're serious."

Cinnamon was hard to convince. She argued that Patti couldn't have heard what was on the other end of the line—not with the speakerphones turned off—but Patti said, "I just know, and we have to get rid of her before she kills your father. . . . You don't *know* Linda. I know Linda. She's my sister."

And then David himself kept telling his fourteen-year-old daughter that he believed Linda was plotting to kill him. "Either we could get rid of Linda—or I could leave."

Cinnamon was appalled. "Why would you leave us? What are you talking about? Why don't you just get a divorce?"

Cinnamon had had precious little stability in her young life, and her father seemed to her then very strong, very loving, the one constant she could cling to. He had groomed her to be that way. The thought that he might leave her seemed more real, more threatening, than Patti's story of murder plots. He had already been divorced four times, she argued. One more wouldn't matter.

"No," David said. "She'll still kill me if I divorce her. . . . I'll just leave you guys with everything and take off and start over again."

"I said, 'I don't want you to leave me, Daddy. I don't want you to leave me . . . and he goes, 'I have to. Either that or we have to get rid of Linda.' "

"So I said, 'How can I help? Can I talk to her for you?' But he said, 'No, don't ever talk to her about what we talked to you about.' "

"I said okay. And that's when I started listening to my father, and he started telling me things. And I was thinking that it was right—because I believed in my father."

The grotesque conversation continued as the van hurtled toward Garden Grove. David suggested that maybe they could just send Linda away, perhaps give her a lot of money and send her away.

"Patti said, 'No—that won't work. . . . We'd have to get rid of her. . . . We'd have to kill her,' " Cinnamon told Newell and McLean. "At that time, to me, that didn't seem like reality. It just seemed like Patti was talking. I said, 'How do you plan on killing her?' She goes, 'I've been thinking about that—maybe hitting her over the head.' And I go, 'With *what?*' She goes, 'With something hard,' and I said, 'Would that kill her?' She goes, 'I think so,' and my father butted in. He goes, 'Well, if she hits her hard enough in the right place, it would kill her.' "

Cinnamon still couldn't believe that they were talking about Linda, that Linda could possibly be a threat to anyone. It all seemed like a long-running sick joke. Her father was like that sometimes, thinking up weird practical jokes. She stared out the window.

"Patti goes, 'Do you have any suggestions?' "

"To kill somebody?" Cinnamon had asked, still thinking it was a game more than anything. "In the movies, I saw in the bathtub, you throw an electrical appliance in there, but I'm not sure how good that works."

Patti had laughed and said, "No, no, no. We'd have a hard time getting Linda in the tub . . . she's always *showering.*"

Cinnamon relaxed. It *was* a joke, after all. She moved back in the van and turned on her radio, ignoring her father and Patti.

Newell asked her if they had talked about the subject of killing Linda in the house. Cinnamon said no; they were afraid of being overheard. She wasn't even sure how long it was before David brought it up again. She remembered they were in the car, going to the chiropractor.

"Who was there then?" Newell asked.

"It was me, Patti, and my father.

"My father said, 'Cinny, it has to happen immediately.' He just popped out of the blue with 'it has to happen immediately.' [He said,] 'We have to get rid of Linda as soon as possible. I just know she's going to kill me soon. We can't delay it anymore. It has to happen, like, right away.'

"Patti said, 'Yeah, it has to happen.'

"I was all, 'Well, how do you guys plan on doing it?' and he goes, 'We need your help.' "

Cinnamon closed her eyes, reliving the drive with Patti and David, repeating what he had said to her.

"He goes, 'Do you love me, Cinnamon?'

" 'I love you. Don't be stupid!' I said, and I hit him on the back of the head.

" 'Do you love me?' and I said, 'Of course I love you.'

" 'How *much* do you love me?'

"I said, 'I love you a lot. I love you more than anything.'

"And he goes, 'Would you do anything for me?'

"I said, 'Yeah, I'd do anything for you. I *love* you.'

" 'I want to make sure that you love me enough that you'll do anything for me.'

" 'Of course. Don't be ridiculous.' "

"I'm being serious with you," David had said.

"And I said, 'I'm being serious with you too.' Then I started getting emotional. I was figuring, oh, no, he's going to leave me. I know he's going to leave me! He goes, 'Ummm, I'm thinking about leaving.'

" 'No, please don't leave,' and immediately, he goes, 'Well, then, how are you going to help me?' "

For an instant, Cinnamon remembered, she had felt as though she had just stepped through a door that had slammed shut behind her. And then she reassured herself that her father had always known what he was doing—that he was always in charge.

They rode along in silence for a long time, and she began to relax. It was the same sick joke again, some kind of test of her loyalty. Suddenly, her father spoke again. "I need you to help me. I need you to help me get rid of her."

"Do you want *me* to kill her?" Cinnamon had half-whispered.

"I want you to help, yes. And if you feel you have the stomach for it, I want you to do it."

It was still like moving underwater to Cinnamon. An alien environment. Her own voice echoed in her ears, and she heard her voice shake. "I like horror movies, but I *don't* have the stomach for that. You know me."

"I didn't think you would," David said. "I don't either."

Cinnamon said she had looked at Patti and said, "Does *she?*"

David explained that he and Patti had been discussing it.

"I don't even know what you guys are talking about," Cinnamon had cried. "I don't know what's going through you guys' heads!"

David's voice was very deep, very calm, and very determined. Cinnamon could see his eyes looking back at her from the rearview mirror.

"If you love me, you'll trust me. Just believe what I say. I'm your father. I know what's best."

26

F R E D   M C L E A N and Jay Newell listened with a kind of horrified fascination. They scarcely felt the heat that had crept into the room where they sat. If what Cinnamon Brown was saying was *true*, she was describing the most sadistic manipulation they had ever heard. A fourteen-year-old girl drawn into her own father's murderous plot.

To prove her love for him.

Without prompting from Newell, Cinnamon described the next time the subject had arisen. The entire family—including Arthur and Manuela Brown—had gone to Riverside to visit a relative who had just had a baby. Linda, Manuela, Patti, and David went into the hospital and left Cinnamon alone with Krystal and her grandfather. "The baby and I were too young and had to stay in the lobby, so Grandpa stayed with us," Cinnamon remembered, closing her eyes as if she could see that day.

Arthur had questioned Cinnamon about some plot between Alan and Linda to hurt David, asking her, "What do you know about it?"

"I said, 'I don't know. That's for my father to tell you.' "

When Patti and David came back to the hospital lobby, leaving Manuela and Linda to ooh and aah over the new baby, Grandpa Brown had brought the subject up again. "My dad said, 'Remember, Father, I told you briefly what was going on with Linda? Her threat she made over the phone?' "

Arthur wanted to know more, and Patti had piped up, "Well, we're thinking about taking care of it tonight."

David nodded. "Yeah, we're going to take care of it tonight on the freeway. . . . Don't mention it to Mother, because Mother has a big mouth," David said, referring to Manuela.

Cinnamon had listened with horror—was it more of "the game" or were they serious?

"We're going to be driving down the freeway," Patti was saying to Grandpa Brown. "David is going to go fast. Not real real fast to exceed the limit, but he's going to go pretty fast. And when Linda gets in the car, we're not going to shut the door all the way. We're going to take out the light there—so you can't see in the van when the door opens."

Just then, Linda and Manuela had walked into the hospital lobby.

Linda was smiling, and they started for home. Manuela seemed oblivious of the undercurrent of tension; she fussed over Krystal, adjusting the baby's car seat.

Cinnamon shuddered. "We were on the freeway and I was waiting for Patti to open the door and push her out like she said she was. And I didn't see anything, and I thought, 'Good. Good. . . . I love Linda and I'm not ready to deal with this. I need to spend more time with her.' "

But Patti had moved between the van seats—back to where Cinnamon sat. "You go do it," she said to Cinnamon.

"Are you crazy?"

"*You go do it,*" she whispered.

"No."

"Why not?"

"For one thing, I'm not strong enough," Cinnamon stalled. "No, I'm not going to do it." She said she saw her father look back at her in the mirror, his eyes trapping hers. "He looked at me, and I shook my head no."

"Was your grandfather doing anything?" Newell asked.

". . . I'm not sure, but he heard them talking about pushing Linda out of the van."

"He *did?*"

"Yeah, and he was telling my father, 'I don't think that's a good idea, David. You better not do it.' "

They had driven west along 91, stopping at a fast-food restaurant. According to Cinnamon, when she and Patti returned to the van, Patti moved back to where she was sitting and insisted that she carry out the plan. "You *need* to do it."

Cinnamon balked. "You don't know what I need to do."

"If you love your father, you'll do it."

"I love my father, but I'm not ready to do something like that!"

"You *don't* love your father—otherwise you wouldn't have any hesitation. You'd go do it."

The constant repetition of what she should do for love was beginning to get to Cinnamon. She began to feel guilty. Fortunately, her grandfather came out of the restaurant and sat by her.

"Your father's wrong," he whispered. "Whatever you do, it's wrong. He's a sick man. I'm telling you now he's a sick man."

Nothing bad happened. Despite all the intrigue and dark plotting on the freeway, they had arrived home in Garden Grove from what turned out to be an uneventful trip. Linda had no inkling how close she had been to instant, shattering death on the freeway. She carried her baby in and put Krystal down for a nap, completely oblivious to danger.

She had, perhaps, a month to live.

Cinnamon told Newell and McLean that the topic of killing Linda before Linda and Alan killed David was never really dropped again. Every time they were in the van or the car going someplace, either David or Patti would bring it up. And each time, there was more urgency in their voices. David told Cinnamon a hundred times or more that he would have to go away from her—in order to survive. If not that, Linda would have to die.

If this was true, McLean and Newell realized that Cinnamon must gradually have become inured to the inhumanity of the plot. What had seemed incomprehensible would have become almost common-place—when it was drilled into her mind continually, and when the manipulator was the man she trusted most in the world, it would have happened more quickly.

Had she been brainwashed? If she had, it was obvious that Cinnamon herself was not aware of it.

"The next time you discussed this—" Newell began, the question scarcely out of his mouth before Cinnamon responded. She had been gagged for so long that her words and thoughts burst forth in freshets of sound.

". . . The next incident I remember is we were planning a trip. Most of it took place in the van. My father had said we were going up shooting and also that there was some money he had hidden up there a long time ago."

"Up where?" Newell asked.

"Somewhere up in the mountains up in Riverside. . . . I think he was planning to take us on a long trip . . . so he said we needed to load up the first-aid kit, and the guns, some food, soda, the ice chest. The van had a refrigerator so I filled it with food and stuff. . . . Linda wasn't too thrilled about this trip. She said, 'I don't want to take the baby up there,' and my father was saying, 'We'll drop you off at your mother's house so you can visit your relatives.' "

Cinnamon recalled working most of the day before the planned trip, mowing the front and back yard, helping clean the house, loading all the heavy gear into the van. David asked her to load a very heavy box from under his bed. He also said, "Take the guns out there."

"There was a lot of guns," Cinnamon said. "There was some rifle guns, some smaller guns . . . I can't remember if we took the bow and arrows."

"A crossbow?" McLean asked; he had not seen any bows or arrows when he worked the crime scene—nor had Morrissey listed any. "The kind with cams on it?"

"I would think it had arrows," Cinnamon said.

"Yeah, but I mean cams for reducing the draw pull on your shoulder—but it increases the force of the bow. It's got wheels on both ends," McLean explained.

Cinnamon shook her head, baffled. She couldn't remember if she had loaded a crossbow into the van—her father had so many weapons—but she did remember David had reminded her to be sure the BB guns were in for herself and Patti.

They headed for the mountains, but David never stopped for BBs. Nor did he stop to leave Linda at her mother's house. When Cinnamon asked why they hadn't stopped, her father had told her to sit down and be quiet.

The tape clicked to a stop. Newell held up his hand to silence Cinnamon for a moment. He looked at his watch. It read 12:21.

A new tape started rolling, and Cinnamon began again. "At this time, we were way up there in the mountains somewhere. I reminded my father about the BBs again. He goes, 'You're on my last nerve. Go sit your butt down.' . . . My grandpa said . . . 'Don't worry about it. Just sit down.' "

"So your grandpa and grandma went too? Everybody went?"

"I can't remember if Grandma went. Grandma sort of blended into the carpet when she was in the van, and I can't remember if she was there or not."

Newell and McLean exchanged an amused glance. Despite the grim subject at hand, Cinnamon had a flair with words. Her recounting of the perambulations of the van packed full of Browns sounded like a day trip with The Family From Hell.

It was full dark before David would interrupt the trip to eat, and very, very late. They stopped finally at a Del Taco for food.

David had been nervous as a cat, his daughter remembered. When Cinnamon jumped out of the van, shouting, "I'm hungry!" he had told her to shut up. "I said, 'I've been back there really quiet for the past couple of hours and you're going to start yelling at me?' "

Linda had stood up for Cinnamon and told David to leave her alone. The tension between David and Linda had been almost palpable, but then David had backed off meekly.

Patti said nothing, watching them.

And then the oddest thing happened. They ordered their burritos and got right back in the van. They had been on the road for almost six hours. Cinnamon was "still vibrating" from riding so long and begged to at least stay in the restaurant long enough to sit down and eat. David flatly refused.

Linda was nervous too. "I think we should turn back. I think we should go back home. It's late."

David said, "Why don't we just stay here overnight?"

"I want to go home *now*," Linda insisted.

"Are you sure?" David asked. "We came this far."

But Linda was almost shouting. "I want to go home *now!*" She seemed frightened, no, *petrified*—of camping out in the dark March night in the lowering mountains.

And so David had turned the van around and they went back down the mountain, bouncing and bucketing over the road. "So we got in the van; we were eating and I was smashing the burrito in my face from all the bumps and stuff, and I was getting mad," Cinnamon told the two detectives. "A totally wasted trip."

Cinnamon had not understood the purpose of that abortive trip, the need to pack all the guns, bullets, arrows, and supplies—simply to drive up in the mountains, buy burritos, and turn right around to go home. McLean and Newell thought they did. With all the plots to get rid of Linda, perhaps she was not meant to return from that camping trip. Had David lost his nerve? What had thrown him off?

"The next day, my father told me to go get the stuff in the van and put it all back in the house," Cinnamon continued. "I said, 'Why don't you have Patti do it? I put it in there—you have her take it out,' but he just told me not to argue."

Cinnamon had obeyed that Sunday, March 17—St. Patrick's Day. It seemed dumb to her to unpack everything. They were supposed to go on a picnic to the desert the next day. Why not leave everything in the camper?

But then, it rained the next day.

And during that night, Linda was murdered.

• • •

Cinnamon seemed to be growing more nervous. She was supposed to go to work, she explained. Would she get in trouble with the staff at Ventura if she was late? Newell assured her that she would not. But he could sense that they had come to a place in a long, long recitation that would soon cast a chill over the hot room. All the earlier details had been, if not easy for Cinnamon, endurable.

Now, they had come to the day of Linda's death.

Newell had learned enough about Cinnamon Brown in these two hours to note that the more frightened she was, the more animated and humorous she became. She was smiling now, but he knew she was scared to death.

Cinnamon described Monday, March 18. Her mother and her aunt and great-grandmother from Utah had dropped by the Ocean Breeze house to visit. They had taken pictures, and she had shown them her new puppy. Her father had grudgingly agreed to come outside to greet his ex-in-laws. "He put on a good show for them because he'd been snapping at me a lot and the rest of the family."

Cinnamon visited with her relatives for a little while. "I went inside a little later. He goes, 'You didn't tell them anything, right?' I said, 'No, I didn't tell them anything. Stop getting paranoid.' He goes, 'Good.' And that night is the night Linda was killed."

"That night your grandparents came to visit from Utah?" Newell asked.

She nodded. "My *great*-grandmother and my aunt."

Cinnamon said that her father had called Manuela and Arthur at about six and invited them over for dinner and to play Uno. "Linda was cooking dinner. I can't remember what we had, but it was one of the bigger meals that took a long time to make. I was in and out of there grating the cheese and stuff. My grandma was just sort of helping her. Linda didn't like Grandma in the kitchen too much because she would, like, take over."

Newell and McLean let Cinnamon tell it at her own pace.

"And we were playing Uno cards. My grandpa was cussing me out. I kept on laughing at him in the game, giving him a whole bunch of cards which he didn't need. So he was yelling at me . . . and I was laughing. Well, then, Grandpa goes, 'I don't want to sit by *her* any-more,' and he was yelling. He was *serious*. 'Get her away from me.' And I sort of took it to heart, you know, because usually he'd just cuss me out and I enjoyed that."

It was such a cheerful recitation of a happy family evening—or would have been had Newell and McLean not known what was coming.

Cinnamon said she had run between the kitchen and the game, with people calling her from every direction. "I ended up getting kicked out of the game, right?"

"Oh, *literally?*" Newell asked.

"Literally. I mean I lost, okay? . . . They had really got me good."

Cinnamon had to do the dishes, her second night in a row. When she balked, Linda had said, "Just do the dishes. Don't make a scene with Grandma and Grandpa here."

There *had* been a slight argument between Linda and Manuela over whether or not to rock Krystal to sleep. Manuela had stalked off and turned on MTV music videos, her favorite. Finally, Linda handed Krystal to Manuela and said she was going to take a shower. Manuela got Krystal to sleep by rocking her and singing to her. Then the elder Browns had left.

Cinnamon drew a deep, shuddering breath.

"It was just me, Patti, and my father left in the living room. . . . My father was all, 'We have to do it— we have to do it. *It has to be done!*' "

Cinnamon had known what he meant. They had to kill Linda. She had asked, "Well, who do you expect to do it?" and he goes, *'You. If you love me, you'll do it. If you really love me, you'll do it.'* "

Cinnamon whispered, "How bad is it?"

"It's really bad. Any day now, she can kill me."

"Is it *really* urgent?" she asked desperately.

"Yes, Cinny. She's going to kill me. Do you want her to kill me? Would you kill her?"

"Yes," I said, "but I don't think I have enough strength to."

"Not even for me?" her father had asked.

Cinnamon started to sob, "I don't know. I don't know."

"Patti looked at me, and she goes, 'You're always crying.' She got mad. She yelled at me. Then she said, 'Well, we'll discuss it later. I have a few things in mind.' "

Linda was in the shower and heard nothing of the conversation. About ten minutes later, she walked through David's office to the kitchen to get some apple juice. "She was standing in the hallway when she said, 'Cinnamon, go to bed. It's late.' And I said, 'I'm going to bed right now,' and she goes, 'Okay. I trust you.' "

Linda and David disappeared into the master bedroom together. Things must be all right, after all, Cinnamon had thought, praying that was true.

Patti dozed on the floor, and Cinnamon sat on the couch in the living room. She too dozed off, serene in her belief that people who were planning a murder that very night wouldn't be able just casually to fall asleep.

She jerked awake when she heard a song on MTV that she liked. She woke Patti up then and suggested they go to bed. Both girls had fallen asleep in Patti's room.

"My father woke me up. He opens the door and goes, 'Girls, girls, wake up! Get up, get up! We have to do it now!' "

Patti had jumped up, as if she expected that command, Cinnamon said.

A few days before that, Cinnamon continued, her father had told her "to write a note that said something to the effect like 'I didn't mean to do what I did,' so I ended up writing, 'Dear God, please forgive me. I didn't mean to hurt her.' "

"Uh-huh," Newell grunted. Cinnamon's words were gushing out so fast, and the story was incredible. And yet he and McLean both knew that it all fit. So far, it all fit.

She described the note further. "I put my own personal touch. . . . I put a little ribbon around it . . . he told me to hide it inside the trailer."

Patti had been bossy and obnoxious that night, Cinnamon recalled. "I don't care for her at all." After he woke them up, "my father told me, 'Come with me,' so I went with them and I was standing at his master bedroom door. Linda was asleep, and I could hear . . . the Fisher-Price baby thing—she can hear the baby in her room. . . . She had it on full blast. I could hear the baby breathing—that's how high she had it up."

Cinnamon asked Patti why Linda had turned the monitor up on high, and Patti explained that Krystal had a cold, and that Linda wanted to make sure the baby didn't choke.

"My father had brought out bottles of pills . . . two or three bottles, and I go, 'What are these for?' and he said, 'Come with me.' So I followed him into the kitchen, and he told me to get a glass of water."

"Take these," her father had ordered.

"Why?"

"Because I want to make it look like you tried to kill yourself, in case it doesn't go through tonight."

"And if it *doesn't* go through tonight," Cinnamon said, "it's going to look like *I* tried to commit suicide."

"It'll go through. It'll go through. Don't worry about it. I have a feeling Patti's going to do it tonight."

"Will this hurt?"

Cinnamon was afraid. She had the feeling that all those pills would really make her sick. There were so many, and some of them looked like "horse pills" to her. But she obeyed her father, swallowed all the pills, and set the empty glass on the dryer.

Her father had turned the alarm off. He instructed her to go outside and get into the doghouse, assuring her that she could fit into the big one. She headed outside, but her father called her back and told her to get the suicide note. "So I went inside the trailer. I got the note. . . . He goes, 'Now did you write any notes previous to that— like trying to make it perfect or maybe you messed up or something?' I said, 'Yes . . . they're in my trash,' and he goes, 'Go get them and burn them.'

"Why?"

"Just do it."

"So I went and burned them."

"Where at?" Newell asked.

"In my trailer. It was in this little trash can. I started the flames; it was like a lot for little pieces of paper, because it sparked up, and I turned the trash can over onto the driveway. . . . I waited for it to cool down, and I tried to put it in a plastic bag in the trash can area."

Her father had seemed satisfied then and told her to go where he had told her, and to take the suicide note with her.

David Brown had said no good-byes to his daughter, only, "Now don't you go get crazy on me."

Cinnamon said that she had gone to the dog pen, and that the dogs ran around her and made her dizzy. She felt nauseous. She said she didn't want to know what was going to happen "because I loved Linda a lot."

She heard the car door open and close, and she peeked out and saw her father's car driving away. "And I'm thinking, did they do something and leave me here? . . . I heard something like—I wasn't sure it was a gunshot at first. . . . I wasn't sure if it was from the house or from around the neighborhood . . . so I went inside the doghouse where he told me to, and I curled up. I was in there shaking and I heard two more. Two more of the same sounds. They were like right after each other. Two of them. And I was shaking and then I started getting sick and I was vomiting really bad, and then I didn't hear anything after that."

Newell held out pictures of the backyard of the Ocean Breeze house to have Cinnamon point out where she had been standing when she heard the first shot. She pointed to a spot near the garage. She remembered nothing more, until, a long time later, she heard her father's voice someplace nearby saying, "It's done. It's over with."

"Previous to that, he told me if anything was to happen, that I would say that I did it . . . because I was younger and I'd get less time. . . . He said that I probably wouldn't get any time at all, that they'd probably just send me to a psychiatrist about twice a week or something. Because they'd think I was crazy. That's what my father told me that they would do if I ever did the murder."

She didn't know if it had been three minutes after the shots—or two hours—when she thought her father had come out in the backyard. "He was saying, 'If they ask you, say you did it, okay? Remember what I told you before. You're not going to get in trouble. If they ask you, you did it. *You* did it!"

He told her that Patti had shot Linda, Cinnamon said, and she was to say she did it—"because they [David or Patti] would really get a long time. And he goes, 'If you love me, you'll do this.' I said, 'I love you. I love you. I'll do it. I'll do it.' I remember I was talking real slow . . . and then I guess he was gone, because I didn't hear his voice. . . . The next thing I remember is some men coming to get me, but I can't remember what they looked like, who they were. I can't remember the questions they asked me either. Because I was gone."

Cinnamon remembered finally coming to in the hospital. Her mother came to see her first. Then her father came and told her that she was to say she had done it. "Don't make it complex; you'll confuse yourself," he had said.

"I had plotted out in my head . . . to tell them I did it. I had already planned that out in my head."

"For what reason?" Newell asked.

"For the protection of whoever did it. My father and Patti."

"What were you going to tell the police as to *why* you did it, or had you thought about that?"

"I hadn't really thought about that. What I told the police isn't too clear to me. . . . I remember hearing it on the tape in court—but I can't remember the actual talking to them. I must have been really gone."

Cinnamon did not seem aware that Fred McLean—who sat nearby—was the man who had rescued her from the doghouse, nor that she had spoken to him on the tape. He sat silently, giving no clue that they had met before.

"At one point, you said you didn't remember what happened," Newell said. "What made you change your mind?"

"My father was confusing me. . . . And Mr. Forgette had come to help. I had told him that I did it, and I guess my father talked to law-yers. . . . My father came in and said, 'Never mind. Tell them you don't remember *anything*. Tell them you don't remember anything at all."

Newell questioned Cinnamon carefully to see whose idea it was that she should fake amnesia.

"My father said that Mr. Forgette said it's not a good idea [to remember]."

"Okay," Newell said easily, knowing that that was not Forgette's style.

"My father said, 'Tell them you forgot. That'll work because of the medication. Just tell them you don't remember anything at all, because you'll end up saying something that will get all of us in trouble.' I said okay. And he told me this in Juvenile Hall too. . . .

"During the trial, Mr. Forgette came back to chambers and he said, 'If your father did it, or if Patti's involved, you tell me. You tell me right now. Because this is it.'

"And I was thinking what my father said, 'Don't ever tell anybody'; I was afraid of my father. He [Forgette] goes, 'If you're afraid of your father, we'll protect you.' I was thinking, no, I can't do this. And I said, 'No. No. Not that I know of—they don't have anything to do with it,' and he goes, 'You don't remember *anything?*' and I said, 'No,' and he said okay and so we went in and we had the last part of the trial."

And with that refusal to betray her father or Patti Bailey, Cinnamon had effectively tied her attorney's hands. If she was telling Newell and McLean the truth now, her story was truly tragic.

"Okay then," Newell said. "Here at the Ventura School, have you been to any psychiatric workshops or anything to discuss it?"

Cinnamon shook her head. She had kept up her stance of forget-fulness even at the workshops.

But she was *here*. Something had made her change her mind about telling the truth.

"What was it?" Newell asked. "What made you change your mind?"

"Well, within the past year, my grandparents have been telling me what's been going on with the house. There's been a lot of neglect going on with the baby—Linda's child. There hasn't been much atten-tion paid to Krystal. My father didn't tell me, but Patti was pregnant."

Cinnamon said she didn't know much about Patti's baby, not even how old she was. "All I know is her child's name is Heather."

"How did you find out the name?"

"Oh, my father told me. But he told me she got pregnant by a boy down the street. My father was very possessive, and there's no way that he would even let her out of the house to go down the street . . . even to *talk* to a boy. So . . ."

David had denied Cinnamon's outright accusation that he had fathered Patti's baby, but her grandfather said it was true. "He told me, 'Don't let him tell you any different. You know he doesn't let that girl out of his sight. . . . Don't listen to anything your father says. He lies to you all the time.' "

Cinnamon no longer believed her father was so ill that he never left his house. He was never home when she called. Arthur Brown had told her he and Patti were out together. "I don't have his address. . . . I send [letters] to his P.O. box. He won't tell me his address because he doesn't want the district attorneys to know."

Cinnamon said she had told her father that she thought the DAs already knew where he was, and David was anxious after hearing that. "Do you think they're watching us?" he had asked.

"I don't know," Cinnamon had told her father. "If I were you, I'd be careful."

"He's been acting really weird," Cinnamon said. "He doesn't come up—it's getting less and less visits from him, so now I hardly ever see him."

"So you're saying that the reason that you are now telling what you remember is—is *why?* Because he and Patti had a baby?"

Cinnamon looked down and shook her head, then lifted her eyes to Newell's. "No. I feel I was manipulated when I was younger, and I started dealing with it within myself. I had kept a journal here . . . about the incident, about what happened. And I feel like I was manipulated by my father by the whole thing—because he would say, 'If you *love* me, you would do this.' And inside, I knew that it was wrong. Now I *know* it's wrong, and I don't think I should take all the responsibility for what happened."

There were so many components of the crime that Cinnamon had known nothing about. She said "Board" had told her that there was a million-dollar insurance policy involved in Linda's death, and she'd been shocked. "I asked my father about that, and he said that he hadn't collected anything on insurance, because it did not pay off because Linda was murdered. . . . I just found out a month ago that he really *did* collect money."

Cinnamon acknowledged that she hoped to get out of prison, but she knew that just talking to Jay Newell and Fred McLean would not help her with the parole board. In order to be free, she would have to have a new trial, and she had little hope of that.

She was doing well at Ventura. She had graduated from high school—sooner than she would have on the outside. She was in college—at least taking college courses. She was working in the TWA program, four hours for pay, and four hours after as a volunteer.

But she was not free. She was eighteen years old, and everything that she had ever believed in had slowly but methodically disintegrated. She did not seem angry. She seemed, rather, to be very, very weary of carrying a tremendous burden for so long all by herself.

Fred McLean and Jay Newell said good-bye to Cinnamon after almost three hours of listening to her steady stream of words. They were noncommittal with her. They said they would be in touch. They would have to talk to the DA to see if there was any legal precedent for reopening her case.

They said nothing to each other until they turned onto the southbound on-ramp to the freeway, heading back toward Orange County. In a sense, they were both poleaxed by Cinnamon's story.

"What do you think?" McLean finally asked.

"I don't know. It's wild. If she's telling the truth . . ."

"You think she isn't?"

"Part of it. Maybe all of it. At least enough of it so the things she's telling us dovetail almost perfectly with what we know. I'm still not sure who the shooter was. She's got the sequence of shots exactly right. Could she have heard that from outside?"

McLean shrugged, remembering that shadowy backyard, the little girl in the doghouse. "Maybe. Maybe not."

"She still says he left before the shooting. She could still be protecting him and putting the blame on Patti. She doesn't like Patti."

"No."

"Funny," Newell mused. "I have this picture in my mind of Cinnamon all zonked out on the pills, of Patti actually propping her up and taking her in there and practically pulling the trigger for her. I still don't know if Cinnamon was inside or outside."

They rode along, each man caught up in his own thoughts, remembering all the things Cinnamon had said. She was so close to what they had thought was the truth all along. But was she right on the mark?

The details were correct, and hard to take, even for detectives used to dealing with violent death. They thought of Linda, sleeping peacefully, with her baby's monitor close to her ear. They pictured

David Brown forcing Cinnamon to swallow enough pills to kill her many times over. And all the while, he had said, "Trust me—I'm your father."

And over and over again, the ultimate manipulation, *"If you really love me, you'll do it.*

"If you love me, you'll help me.

"How much do you love me?"

As they pulled off the freeway in Santa Ana, Newell said, "We'll run it by Robinson and see where we go next—or *if* we're going anywhere at all."

The next morning, Newell and McLean met with Jeoff Robinson in his office. Both detectives felt they had finally gotten the first glimpse into the *real* story behind Linda Brown's murder.

Robinson agreed and shared their excitement. "But it's not enough to hear it from Cinnamon," he cautioned. "We all know she'd be easy to impeach in court—if we ever got that far. We have to hear it from David Arnold Brown. In his words, his voice."

Brown was never going to admit any culpability in the murder of his fifth wife; he wouldn't even talk to them. The only way to get verification for Cinnamon's claims from her father's own lips was to wire Cinnamon.

If they could obtain a court order to attach a recording wire to Cinnamon, was she strong enough to carry it off? She had grown up believing her father was perfect. Now she feared him. "She's unsophisticated," Newell mused. "She's smart and she's quick—but I don't know if she's got the guts to try to get him to tell the truth, knowing all the while it's being recorded."

"Let's try it," Robinson said. "Let's see if we can pull it off."

Sylvester Carraway, the superintendent of the Ventura School, and Cinnamon's parole officer, Carlos Rodriguez, were willing to cooperate. If Cinnamon agreed to wear a transmitter during a visit from her father, they would do everything they could to support her, and to facilitate the DA's men who would monitor the wire.

Cinnamon said yes.

She was afraid, but she would wear the wire. The trick would be to get David up for a visit. Sometimes, it was months between visits from her father. Her next official visiting day was only two days away: Saturday, August 13.

Newell instructed Cinnamon to call David and tell him that she needed to talk to him about something important and needed to talk to him right away. She had something to tell him. Newell suspected that Brown was running scared, expecting trouble. The man claimed, among his myriad ailments, a susceptibility to panic attacks.

Well, *all right!* Let Cinnamon's call panic him a little.

David was cautious when Cinnamon called him and was annoyed because she refused to discuss whatever was bothering her on the phone. He could not wheedle anything out of her, and that was worrisome. Cinny was usually so transparent. David promised he would be up to see her on Saturday—with his usual proviso about the mercurial state of his health.

On Friday, August 12, Jeoff Robinson went up to assure himself that the staff at Ventura was prepared for every eventuality. Everything was to be carefully choreographed to prevent slipups.

Superintendent Carraway would provide a room facing out into the outdoor visitors' area so that Newell and Robinson could monitor the conversation between Cinnamon and her father, be sure it was recording audibly, and also take photos of the meeting. With luck, they would be only about eight yards away—*if* Cinnamon could steer David over to the shady lawn beneath the trees.

Cinnamon would be taken to an office just before visiting hours to have the transmitter and wires attached. Armondo Favila, assistant chief of security of CYA, would be on hand, and he could take messages to Cinnamon if Newell needed to instruct her during her father's visit. Neither of the Orange County DA's men could chance being seen.

Jeoff Robinson was very high profile in Orange County; David might recognize him from media coverage on other cases. And there was little doubt that Jay Newell, aka Realtor "Jerry Walker," was burned into Brown's mind. Newell had had his one shot at being incognito.

"I was also the 'technician,' " Robinson remembered. "My sole assignment was to supply the correct batteries for the transmitter. And I managed to mess that up—brought the wrong size. The ones I brought were half an inch too short. We had a last-minute panic ourselves until our sound man, Greg Gulen, back at the DA's Office, told me to peel the foil off gum wrappers and wad it up to make the batteries fit. It worked."

Newell gave Cinnamon simple instructions. "Keep your voice up. Discuss the night of the murder, and keep telling your father that you have to know the truth. We'll be listening. If the transmitter stops working, we'll send Armondo over to tell you we're done for today. Okay?"

She nodded. She was pale, but she was resolute.

They were ready.

27

ON SATURDAY afternoon, August 13, 1988, Cinnamon wore blue jeans and an oversize light-blue sweatshirt. There was no visible sign that she was wired for sound as she hurried into the visitors' area—so intent on her mission that she had to be called back by a guard to show her pass. And then called back again to explain the Coca-Cola she carried. No one ran at Ventura; no "ward" moved from one area to another without a pass or a good explanation.

She spotted her father. He wore jeans, a gray sports shirt with red and black stripes, with the familiar pack of cigarettes bulging in the pocket.

She pasted on a smile and went to meet him.

"Hello."

"No 'I love you'?" That was her dad, playing word games and trying to throw her off-balance from the first moment.

"I love you," she said dutifully.

They made small talk as Cinnamon led her father toward a shady area. That was the easy part—he hated the sun. They had not yet reached the spot beneath the tree before David asked, "What do you have to tell me?"

"It's something concerning me being . . . confused. I have a lot of emotion lately and I needed to talk to you about it. 'Cause I feel like I'm lost."

David said nothing, but then he murmured something that made Cinnamon's heart stop, and Jay Newell's do the same in his hidden vantage point. "See," David said, "they don't know that I'm wired."

How could he know? Was he taunting her?

Cinnamon fought to keep her voice calm. "What are you wired for?"

"For my back. I've got things all over me."

Of course. He had those little electrical things the doctor gave him. Transcutaneous something—to cover up his pain. Relieved, Cinnamon laughed. "Me too. I'm wired for sound." Her father grinned; he thought she was kidding.

He didn't know.

She began again. "For the past couple of months I've been thinking . . . but I've been keeping it to myself. What am I going to do in here, Daddy? I'm so confused. It's been hurting me a lot. Partly because Ronny went home. [Her 'boyfriend' from work had been paroled.] Partly because I've been in here for so long."

David eased his considerable bulk carefully down onto the grass. He nodded sagely. "I figured that was what was bothering you. I know what it feels like to love somebody and not be able to be near them. You're proof."

"I'm very confused."

"What are you thinking about?" David asked. The sound was coming through loud and clear to Newell's and Robinson's hidden vantage point.

"I'm thinking about the things that keep going through my head at Board. . . . They keep on telling me the same thing over and over again."

"What's that?"

"We're going to keep you here to '92 to '95. They just keep putting more time on me, Daddy."

"I can't see why. You're working hard, graduated from school. I know that you're not a pain in the ass. What's their problem?"

"The *crime*."

It was as if he had completely forgotten why she was there.

"Why did you tell me that I would only be here for a little bit, and then they'd let me go home?"

" 'Cause that's what I understood the law was. Apparently I didn't—"

"I feel like you lied to me."

"No, I didn't lie to you. I swear to God that is exactly what I had understood. If you remember right, Cinny, I asked you not to—I told you I'd rather die because I'm in too much pain anyway. My whole body's falling apart, my nerves are gone. I can't think anymore. I can't do business."

Cinnamon would not be deterred. She had heard her father feign critical illness all her life; he had become like the boy who cried "Wolf!" Finally, she had come to the point where she didn't believe him any longer.

Her voice, as always, sounded like a little girl's, high and sweet. "What was the *purpose* of it all?" she asked.

He said nothing.

Cinnamon tried again. "It confuses the hell out of me. Because I'm always lying and I'm lying so much I forget what the lie before that was. . . . And then I tell them another lie, and they say, 'That's another lie.' "

"That's how they work on you," David warned. "The only thing I know is Patti . . . said that the whole idea was that Alan—okay, apparently you know that Linda was into drugs—"

"What kind of drugs?"

"Cocaine, and something else. But she was heavy into it."

David explained that Linda's twin, Alan, was still stalking him. "I even got a new place and I'm supposed to be moving, but I'm not healthy enough to move yet. And he already knows where it is."

"*Where* are you guys living now?" Cinnamon asked.

"In Orange—moving to Anaheim . . . but anyways, from what Patti said, Linda and Alan were apparently tied to some group that Alan dealt drugs with. . . . I don't know if Linda owed money or what. But they wanted Data Recovery. They wanted it bad. Real bad. Okay? They had Larry [Larry Bailey] locked up for two weeks in a house, tied to a chair. That's what the San Bernardino police told us. They found unlimited tons in the basement. Cocaine, PCP, and all kinds of drugs . . . and they found them on and in Linda. She was apparently a heavy user and I had no idea."

Newell and Robinson exchanged incredulous glances. David was lying "big time."

"No, I never knew she used drugs," Cinnamon murmured.

"It's in the autopsy report. That she was heavy into it, and very recently." (In fact, toxicologists had detected a minute amount of cocaine in Linda Brown's system after autopsy, a minuscule metabolite of the drug. There were many ways it could have been introduced into her system.)

"Anyways," David continued conspiratorially, "they were instructed to off me so that Linda would inherit the business entirely, and her and Alan could run it by themselves under whoever this mob group thing is. . . . The mob is still trying to get Larry or Alan to off me. They want Data Recovery. As long as I'm alive, the government and everyone else comes to me. I mean, I've done the Pentagon. I'm the one that found out what killed the shuttle *Challenger* crew. All that kind of stuff. The Stealth bomber—that's critical to the United States. I've saved all that shit since you've been in here. The Mafia wants to run it. They want The Process."

Newell listened, slightly shaking his head. It was easy to imagine that a man who wove such grandiose stories might influence his fourteen-year-old daughter. But now that daughter was eighteen, and no longer a child.

David Brown's deep, confident baritone rumbled on. "They [the Mafia] promised her money and all kinds of shit, for her and Alan to find a way to get rid of me. They wanted me dead. As long as I'm alive, no one else will be able to get Data Recovery. See, I don't charge a million dollars a job, like I could. I've done several lately that I could have charged a million dollars—like for the First Interstate Building fire. There's over a thousand computers in there. Okay, I got maybe five thousand dollars out of it. I do it honestly. I don't rip people off because it just isn't worth it. I charge a fair price for my service. . . . Anyway, Alan has apologized since then . . . but I can't trust him. He's still tied to the Mafia. Larry's even been caught with a gun on his way to shoot me again—"

"But," Cinnamon cut in, "what was the *real* purpose behind it all? What was the real reason?"

"That was the honest, real reason." And David was off again, describing Linda and Alan's plot to kill him, and Patti's decision that she would save him. But he would not say the words *to kill Linda*.

"But what should I tell the Board?"

In the twinkling of an eye, David reversed himself. "Why don't you tell them the truth was—*remember?* Linda wanted you out of the house and I didn't."

"Linda didn't *want* me out of the house—there wasn't enough room in the house."

Patiently, her father explained the scenario he wanted Cinnamon to repeat. "She wanted you to move out. And you ended up moving to the trailer. And then she wanted you out of the trailer and back with your mom. And your mom didn't want you. I told her [Linda] I waited too many years for you to be with me—we'd had too much fun. Linda wanted you out of the house. You and Patti both. She wanted you guys out—"

"Linda never told me she wanted me out of the house."

"I'd swear she did. But she made sure I knew. I thought she told you. I thought that's why you got in a fight with her once and moved out to the trailer."

Cinnamon shook her head and told him she had moved out because she didn't want to share a room with Patti.

And now, incredibly, David changed tactics again.

"Well, Patti said if worse comes to worse, *she'll* confess to it, but you guys are going to have to get your story straight. She'll take your place."

"Why can't you just tell the truth?" Cinnamon cried.

"I'll tell you why." He paused to think. "You can tell them the truth if you don't tell the *whole truth* . . . okay? Because if there was knowledge—if me, Grandma, Grandpa, Patti—everyone had knowledge in advance of what was going to happen, then we'd *all* go to jail. Everyone. That doesn't make any sense, because we weren't the ones who did anything wrong. As far as I'm concerned, *you* didn't do anything wrong—"

"As far as I'm concerned, I didn't do anything wrong either," Cinnamon agreed bitterly.

For Newell and Robinson monitoring this bizarre conversation, it appeared that every possible suspect in the murder of Linda Brown had just been neatly eliminated. Save Alan Bailey. Save Larry Bailey. And neither had ever been a serious consideration.

"I asked you not to do it," David was saying obscurely. "Because I wasn't taught about the repercussions—"

"Well, how did Patti feel about this? Doesn't she have any remorse? Doesn't she feel bad?"

"It's tearing her up."

"I don't hear from her," Cinnamon said softly.

David swore Patti had written often. And once again, he offered Patti up as a trade for Cinnamon. He explained that Patti had moved out of his house. "She can take the blame for it, and you just stick to your thing that you never knew anything about it. 'Cause she doesn't have anybody. All she's got is Heather."

My God, Newell and Robinson wondered. *Who was this man? Patti was expendable. All she had in the world was her child. David Brown's reasoning was, thus far, totally self-serving.*

Patti had moved out, he assured Cinnamon, but she had come on the trip—she was out in the camper right now—because he needed someone to accompany him to handle his medications. "She's not as dingie as she was anymore," he explained about Patti. "She's grown up a lot. She's in pain, Cinny. She hates what happened. Not because of Linda. Because of you."

"*Now* she hates what happened."

"No—she's hated it since it happened. She knows I wouldn't stay here a week. I would find some way to kill myself. She knows that you've got to be feeling something like that."

"I feel *stupid*," Cinnamon said with feeling. " 'Cause I'was so young. And I loved you so much. And I was gullible enough to do it."

Newell sat up straight. What did *that* mean? Do *what?* They couldn't tell. The words coming over the wire tumbled out in a non sequitur fashion. The only solid theme that never varied was that David had to be left in the clear. No one must ever, ever implicate David Brown.

"Grandpa was going to do it if you didn't," David was saying forcefully.

Cinnamon was shaking her head. "Grandpa loved Linda. Grandpa wouldn't do something like that."

"You don't know Grandpa as well as you think you do."

"I don't know anybody as well as I thought I did."

"Patti is willing to prove it to you by taking your place."

"She won't be able to take my place."

"If she confessed to it. There have been no confessions—the only confession was when you were under drugs in the hospital."

David's mind was clearly racing; the DA's men watching could see him lean toward Cinnamon, gesturing. He was explaining to her that there was nothing solid against her, that it would be easy to get her out and put Patti in. It was Cinnamon he really loved, the baby girl he had been proud of "since the day you were born." Patti didn't matter. Patti was moving out anyway.

"I thought you said she already moved out," Cinnamon shot back.

"She's here today to help," David repeated easily. He already had two housekeepers to look after Krystal.

"What about the baby?" Cinnamon asked suddenly.

"What baby?"

"Heather."

"What about her?"

"What's happening with the baby? I never hear you talk about Patti's baby."

Newell and Robinson knew this was the sticking point, the final betrayal that had brought Cinnamon to them. They smiled grimly as they heard David squirm trying to avoid the subject of Heather.

"Who's the father of the baby?" Cinnamon asked point-blank.

"Honestly?" David took a long pull on his cigarette, his whistling breath loud over the transmitter wire. "Patti went through a spell there when she didn't know. She thinks it's a guy named Doug. He's the one claiming responsibility for it. And Patti says he's a creep.

He's Greek. He's mean—he's hit her. She wants nothing to do with him and she's not giving him any visitation rights."

"You're not the father?"

"Hell no! I'm not the father. Are you kidding? I haven't been with a woman in so long I don't even know if I prefer men now. Sometimes I think about it. You think I'm joking? I'm serious. I don't think I could ever trust a woman again."

Newell and Robinson frowned. There was something offbeat, something grotesque, about the way David Brown spoke to Cinnamon, a vulgar intimacy about matters most fathers did not discuss with their daughters.

Cinnamon seemed used to such conversation. She ignored it. She would not be sidetracked. She had an agenda to meet, and she homed in on another question that had tormented her for years. The insurance payoff. She had never heard of it until they told her at Board. "They said there's a million-dollar life insurance involved. . . . They asked me, 'Did your father get it?' I don't know what to tell these people."

David's voice betrayed just a veneer of fear. He went into a long, convoluted explanation. He himself was uninsurable—ever since they found his "car had been shot up. . . . When Linda died, they canceled all our policies. I'm totally uninsurable," he said almost proudly.

"I am too." Cinnamon shrugged.

The girl had a wry sense of humor. She was quicker than her father, far wittier than any of the family Newell had yet spoken to. It wasn't mean comedy; she simply picked up instantly on plays on words. Three and a half years in this place hadn't knocked it out of her. Sometimes she was so quick that her humor went right over David's head.

Cinnamon wanted to talk about *the truth*. David clearly did not. He grew impatient with his daughter. Why wouldn't she just accept his offer of Patti as the guilty party and stop asking for the damn truth? David believed in Patti. She would sacrifice herself.

Or, if Cinny didn't like that scenario, he had a detective out there right now, trying to tie Larry into the murder. "Somebody broke into the house while we were all gone—the one in Garden Grove. The police were out there; they shut up the house . . . okay. What I've told everyone is that there is *no way* that you—any more than me— were capable of shooting somebody. Okay? So I am still paying a detective to investigate it."

Or wait—he had another option for her. "They say the only way you would ever get a reduced sentence is if you told them something convincing that did not indicate it was preplanned. That it was an act on the spur of the moment. Like a fight."

Suddenly, a shadow fell over David and Cinnamon, and Lieutenant Favila motioned Cinnamon over, saying gruffly, "Have you got your pass?" Under his breath, he whispered, "Make sure you say, 'Dad, I have to tell them the truth.' Got that?"

She nodded and showed the security chief her pass.

"What did *he* want?" David asked suspiciously.

"Something about I didn't check out in Unit, and they didn't know where I was."

He nodded, unconcerned. "Anyways, if you could think of something to tell them that would satisfy them—"

"How about the truth?"

"Okay. Do me a favor. Okay? Tell *me* the truth. Okay?"

"I didn't do it," Cinnamon answered flatly.

"That's the truth? . . . The honest-to-God truth? Did Patti do it or did you do it? . . . You remember clearly?"

"I remember."

"Well, you said you forgot a lot of things."

"*You* asked me to say that, remember?" Cinnamon almost sobbed. "I want to make sure you remember what you asked me to say. Because you said, if I loved you . . . Don't make me feel like I'm crazy!"

He backed off. He was a master at this. However repugnant Brown was, Newell had to give the guy points for controlling a conversation. "I'm not trying to make you feel like you're crazy. . . . I honestly do not know to this day if Patti did it."

"Well, I didn't do it. I didn't see her do it."

"Okay. Now, I understand your conclusion. I wish you had told me a long time ago."

"*You* do!" Cinnamon exploded.

"I told you, 'Don't do it.' You said you had to because 'I love you, and I'm not going to let Linda and Alan hurt you.' "

Cinnamon burst out. "*You said if I loved you* . . . and I would get less time for it. That they wouldn't even send me to jail. . . . I just want to make sure you remember what you told me because I am about to lose it in here."

Now, it was David's term to be alarmed. Obviously, the last thing in the world he wanted was for Cinnamon to flip out.

"Don't! Don't lose it. *Patti* did it," David said. "No wonder I've been afraid. Every night she stayed in that house . . . I never thought Patti was so capable of being so kind as to say that she would take your place for it. I couldn't understand. You didn't even see it then. . . . If I had known she had done it, I would have made her confess to it a long time ago. You didn't tell me. . . ."

"You told me what to say. You didn't ask me."

". . . Let Patti take the blame for it. You don't know anything. Okay?"

"They're not going to let me go. I've already been convicted."

David explained that he could arrange to have Patti convicted. Patti was the one with the gunpowder on her. "All this time I thought *you* did it because you love me," he breathed. "This is not what I wanted. I would have much rather had you home all the time."

"I would have liked to have been at home."

". . . Don't be angry at me for something I didn't know, Cinny. . . . All the books and stuff I read. I thought I knew a lot about everything."

And with it all, David Brown was still tap-dancing in, out, and around his interchangeable plots. He never once suggested that *he* had any guilty knowledge. Newell saw another zinger telegraphed every time he heard David say "honestly" and "honest to God."

David appeared to be thinking hard. The best thing, still, was for Cinnamon to pretend she remembered nothing—just as she always had. Yes, that was still the safest plan. He instructed her carefully. "Then your truth is that you don't know anything. *You don't remember anything.* 'Cause if they come to me, that's what I'm going to tell them. I don't know anything. And I don't remember anything. Because if *I* go to jail, I can't survive jail. Especially with my heart and my liver and my kidney problem. I can't. . . . I would kill myself before I would let myself die a slow and painful death in a cell. It's a lot worse, you know, for grown-up men in prison."

Lieutenant Favila checked Cinnamon's pass again as she and her father moved inside to join Manuela and Krystal and Arthur. He whispered to her, "They want you to tell them to bring Patti in so you can bury the hatchet. You want to hear from Patti that everything is done and over. You want to kind of make peace with Patti. See if you can get a confession."

But visiting hours were almost over, and Cinnamon was exhausted; her shirt soaked with sweat. There was no time. She knew Patti, and she knew Patti wouldn't tell the truth in fifteen minutes. It would have to be next time.

Cinnamon hugged her father good-bye, and Grandma and Grandpa, and Krystal. And then she hurried into the hidden room to have the wires and transmitter taken off.

"How do you feel?" a male voice asked on the tape.

"Nauseous."

"You can go in there and untape that stuff and get that off of you."

Drained, Cinnamon peeled the apparatus from her breasts. She had done it; she had defied her own father. She was still afraid of him, and suddenly, her legs began to tremble. She wanted very much to believe that Jay Newell and Jeoff Robinson could really keep her safe. Her father was going to be enraged when he found out what she had done to him.

28

S O M E H O W, in some combination, or separately, there had clearly been *three* main "players" in the sudden death of Linda Marie Brown.

Cinnamon.

David.

Patti.

Jay Newell and Jeoff Robinson had heard David—alternately stuttering, blustering, ordering, and cajoling—on their hidden transmitter, but it had been a long time since anyone had heard from Patti Bailey. With David blithely offering to exchange Patti's freedom for Cinnamon's, as much as admitting Patti's culpability, the dead woman's sister was next on the list for the investigators.

Cinnamon had urged David to bring Patti up for a visit, and he was apparently nervous enough about his daughter's unexpected assertiveness and sticky questions that he, indeed, brought Patti along on the next possible visit.

It was two o'clock in the afternoon on August 27, 1988, when Cinnamon whispered, "Jay . . . can you hear me? I hope so 'cause I don't really want to go and mess up the tape. . . . Hello. Thank you."

Newell could hear her well, but he could not see her. He was in the same room where he had set up his equipment before, and Cinnamon, Patti, and David would be across the quad, behind the guard tower, out of his sight completely. Walt Robbins, deputy security chief at the CYA, was in the guard tower, less than twenty feet away from where Cinnamon and her visitors would be. He would be taking pictures.

Cinnamon was not quite as nervous this time. She had managed to get through the worst part, the first time taping her father. Now she would face Patti Bailey, the girl—now woman—who had been a childhood friend, a teenage irritant, perhaps a co-conspirator in murder—and who she suspected was probably her father's mistress and the mother of his latest baby.

Cinnamon hadn't seen Patti for a long, long time.

Now she saw Patti and David headed toward her, holding Krystal by the hand. Patti looked older, a little heavier. She wore blue jeans and a pink blouse, and her thick blond hair was pulled back into a curly ponytail. Her father wore a pink T-shirt, stretched tight across his massive midsection, and gray slacks.

Cinnamon remembered his "gotcha" from the last time, and Newell grinned as he heard David say only, "Hi," and Cinnamon quickly respond, "I love you too!"

Cinnamon knelt to Krystal's height and said, "Hi! Are you my friend?"

Listening to this family visit inside the reformatory was strange. And a little sad. Children in the background laughed and cried. Krystal wanted a doughnut, then promptly dropped it. It sounded so normal, and yet it was anything but normal.

Cinnamon and her two visitors moved over to a round table, shielded from the sun by a large white umbrella. Twenty feet away, Walt Robbins snapped pictures. David drank Perrier while the girls sipped Cokes.

Much of their transmitted conversation was about mundane things, as if Cinnamon, Patti, and David were hesitant to speak of the real reasons they had finally found themselves all together again. At one point, David looked toward the young women playing on the field nearby.

"Great," Cinnamon teased. "You want to stare at the people on the field, don't you?"

"My daughter knows me," David said with a laugh. "And I like the dark meat myself."

"You like the *what?*" Cinnamon asked.

"The *dark* meat." He was referring to the black girls playing ball and vulgarly pointing out their physical attributes.

"You're disgusting," Cinnamon said.

"Yeah," Patti echoed.

There was that same inappropriate behavior. He was the adult, almost thirty-six, and yet Newell realized David interacted with both his daughter and Patti as if they were all the same age. The girls seemed more mature, however, and David only a case of ugly, prejudiced, arrested development. He complained bitterly about the freeway jam-up on the way up.

"They got the freeway up here—five lanes—and you get on this part, you know—"

"No, I don't know," Cinnamon said softly.

"Well, you get out of L.A., you come to five lanes—"

"I guess I miss out on a lot of things."

He was oblivious to her meaning. He rattled on, about traffic, about bills for Cinnamon's stationery. Suddenly, he asked, "Why did they hassle you so much the last time I was here?"

Why was he so wary? Newell wondered. There was no way he could have known that Cinnamon was wired. Not two weeks ago. Not today. She wore the same bulky blue shirt. Not a wire or a bulge showed.

Cinnamon fielded the question smoothly. " 'Cause my pass—the staff didn't know I was off the cottage."

"How did you get a pass if they didn't know you were off the cottage?"

Newell held his breath.

"They have shift trade at two o'clock. . . . And when I was up here in between the last—somehow they lost me."

"It was so irritating," David complained to Patti. "We were just sitting there on the grass. That stupid asshole kept coming over and scaring the shit out of us. [Mimicking] 'Are you *Cinnamon Brown?*' I need to see your pass. This pass is no good.' "

Cinnamon laughed. He wasn't suspicious. He just hated authority figures.

Both David and Patti explained that they *had* sent Cinnamon their new phone numbers—*David's* new phone numbers. The letters must have been lost. Newell waited for something he could sink his teeth into, but Cinnamon couldn't seem to steer them away from trivia. And this time, David didn't ask what she was worried about.

Patti explained that she had hired Betsy Stubbs to baby-sit Heather in the van. It had cost her $20.

"How old is Heather now?" Cinnamon asked suddenly.

". . . She'll be a year next month," Patti answered, biting her lip.

David quickly changed the subject. "Where did you find the doughnuts? Were they under the bed for the last thousand years?"

"*Hundred*," Patti said.

"Get your digits right—or don't get them at all," Cinnamon said.

"My digit's fine," he said. "Want to see it?"

Newell shook his head. The guy was always thinking about sex; he was steeped in it, and he censored nothing for his daughter.

Cinnamon was persistent. "I wanted to ask you some questions about the baby," she said to Patti. "I never get to talk to you."

Patti said nothing.

"I don't even know what the kid looks like."

"Like a turd," Patti answered.

"Doesn't she look like the father?"

"She doesn't look like anybody; she looks like a baby. All babies look the same."

"Who's the father?" Cinnamon asked.

"She told me she was dating Doug on—" David cut in.

Patti said nothing and stared down at the table.

Again, David changed the subject, back to Betsy Stubbs, who "said she was pregnant, but then she said she had a miscarriage. She said she threw up the baby. I told her if that was true, you got a major physical problem. . . . She's that stupid. . . ."

Patti brightened. "Honest to God, I'm beginning to think she's a lesbian!"

"She does," David said. "She follows Patti into the bathroom."

"I'm really scared to undress in front of her—"

"Well, you undressed in front of somebody," Cinnamon shot out. "And I'm curious. This is driving me crazy. Who is the father, Patti?"

Patti refused to discuss Heather's parentage. It was "too upsetting."

David started to chime in with his guess, but Patti stopped him. "Be careful. I don't want you to tell her."

Patti turned away and bent her head near Krystal's as David talked. "He's still living at home with his momma and daddy and he drives a Trans-Am or Firebird," David continued. "I've seen him once and he's about as intelligent as a grapefruit. He's got real, real curly hair, not like anybody I see here. Greek kind of looking."

Heather's hair was red, David said. "And you and her," he said, pointing to Krystal, "you guys have, you know, my color of skin, and this kid you can see almost through to the bone—just like her [indicating Patti]."

Cinnamon knew who the baby's father was. They all knew.

This time, Cinnamon allowed David to change the subject. For the next twenty minutes, they talked aimlessly. Newell waited impatiently. Why was she holding back? He didn't care about records or watches or Betsy Stubbs's latest peccadillo or why David preferred Perrier. David was offering Cinnamon more and more presents. Both he and Patti were being most gracious and generous.

They laughed, and Newell could hear David and Patti relaxing, assured that Cinnamon wasn't going to push this thing after all.

Abruptly, Cinnamon turned to Patti. "So—did Daddy discuss with you what we talked about last visiting?"

Patti stopped in mid-laugh and answered slowly, "And I told him and he told you."

"He did not tell me anything."

"That I'd trade?"

"I want to know what you think about it," Cinnamon said.

Patti was apathetic. "If that's what you want to do."

"We could walk on the Twilight Zone or something," Cinnamon said sharply. The idea was ridiculous, yet both Patti and her father seemed to think you could just shuffle prisoners around willy-nilly.

"The only thing," David pointed out, "you would have to still do what you've always done. You don't remember anything and she'll come forth with her story and clear you."

"But will she tell the *truth?*"

"She'll tell them whatever she wants to tell them."

"Are you going tell them the truth?" Cinnamon asked.

"What's the truth? I'm, I'm—"

David ignored Patti's question and drilled Cinnamon. "The thing is you don't know the truth. You don't know what happened. Stay the way you did from the day you got here. You don't remember—"

"So you're going to tell them the truth?"

David explained that Cinnamon was not to remember, because Patti was the one who knew everything. "She did it. That's how come you don't know."

Patti saw a flaw. "Then they'll ask *me* why did *she* take the pills."

"You gave them to her," David instructed.

"She didn't give them to me," Cinnamon argued.

"However you want to do it, I'll do it," Patti offered.

"Just tell them the truth," Cinnamon repeated for the tenth time.

What was David up to? Newell tried to follow the conversational volleys. David was reconstructing history. And Patti was allowing him to serve her up on a plate. *Why?*

And then the whole plan changed.

"There's nothing to tell them," Patti said.

"None of us remember a whole lot," David agreed.

Cinnamon was incredulous. You could hear it in her voice. *"You don't remember a whole lot of what happened that night? Even Grandpa knows."*

Cinnamon began to pepper her father and Patti with questions.

How many gunshots?

Who shot the gun?

You had me write that note. Why?

Both David and Patti were suddenly seized by a hazy kind of amnesia. They were stonewalling Cinnamon. David thought maybe Larry or Alan had broken in. Patti could not remember the tiger tapestry in her room. "I can't think of tapestry—I'm thinking Tupperware. I don't know. . . . Believe me, if I was to remember, I'd come here and talk to you."

Cinnamon stared at her visitors with incomprehension. They had come up to Ventura with their stupid plot to play switcheroo, and now, suddenly, their minds had gone blank. Neither remembered more than their own names.

"You don't remember anything said at the house or when we were in the van or *anything?*"

"The van?" Patti asked vacantly.

"Oh, now you're going to say, '*What* van?' Right?"

It must have seemed so ridiculous to Cinnamon that Newell heard her laugh. It must have seemed like a bad joke to her.

"No, I don't remember," Patti said. "All I remember is stuff that I read in the paper."

". . . You know I'm trying to make sure I'm not crazy," Cinnamon said. "That's what I'm trying to do—review some of this with you so that I—I'm trying to find myself—"

"I understand," David said with a trace of smugness. "And I don't have any problem."

"All the lies and stuff, it makes me go delirious."

"Delirious," Patti agreed. "I hallucinate the way you wouldn't believe."

Cinnamon asked her father if he remembered telling her to get rid of all the rejected suicide notes.

"Probably . . . I don't know. I don't remember."

"Are you *related* to me?" Cinnamon laughed. "Are you clones of the people that I knew out there?"

"Cinny, when my liver went bad," David whined, "it fucked up my whole body. I don't remember a lot about Data Recovery."

"I've been here," Cinnamon answered. "It's fucked up my life."

Newell listened to the mazes of David Brown's reasoning, once again marveling at his fancy conversational footwork. He was suddenly going the sympathy route, trying to convince Cinnamon that she had it a lot better in prison than he did on the outside.

"I know, I know," David said in a tired voice. "I have to rely on Dad—"

"If I can be strong," his daughter argued, "you also can be strong."

"I'm trying. I'm fighting the best I can, but that happened to my body. I've got nothing to do with it. Nobody asked you to care for the dying."

Cinnamon turned to Patti, determined to try again. "I asked Daddy last time why it was that we went through with this, and he told me his opinion. . . . What is your reason why you went through with it?"

"Because they were both after him and you didn't want him to be gone," Patti blurted.

"We're talking about Linda?" Cinnamon asked.

And suddenly Patti backed off. No, she recalled no phone conversation between Linda and Alan, had heard no plots against David. Maybe David had heard about a plot. She remembered nothing about it. "One of us overheard her on the phone. . . ." Patti trailed off.

"Well, eeney, meeney, miney, mo," Cinnamon said sarcastically.

Every time Patti's memory let in the slightest beam of sunlight, David cut her off. He reminded Cinnamon of a "memory" he wanted her to keep firmly in her mind. "I've been shot at before. If someone was going to kill me, let him try. Maybe they'll wound me. Maybe they'll miss, and they'll end up in jail. Let them try. I remember telling you guys that, and that's the last thing I remember telling you when I left the house—'Don't worry about it. I'm going to clear my head. I'm going to the beach. Just leave everything. You guys go to bed. Just . . . forget everything. If it happens, it happens.' You guys said something. I *remember* this. You guys said that 'Alan might be outside waiting for you. He knows that you go to the beach a lot.' And you guys said, 'Don't go.' "

Cinnamon shook her head, mystified. "I don't remember that. . . . I remember you talking to me and Patti. In the living room, saying, 'It has to be done tonight,' and that you were going to leave."

"I don't remember that either," David said earnestly.

Cinnamon laughed. She was hanging in there. Her life depended on this, and yet she seemed to find her father's spotty memory almost comic. Either Cinnamon had made up the story she told Newell and Robinson from whole cloth, or David and Patti were systematically lying to her, deliberately confusing her, keeping her at bay and most of all, away from the authorities.

"Why do you guys make it seem like I was alone in this—you guys had—" she pleaded. "You put all the responsibility on me! *I'm* the one that's in here." Cinnamon seemed to have forgotten the wire. She was speaking from what sounded like her very gut. "*Does it really matter who pulled the trigger?*" she asked.

Newell sat up straight. What was she saying now?

"I remember you," Cinnamon said, turning to David, "saying you wouldn't be able—you don't have the stomach or something to stay in the house."

"And I said I didn't have the stomach for anything that happened. . . . When I came home, Cinny, I was in shock." David's memory had shrunk, he said, sometimes to five minutes.

Disgusted, Cinnamon turned again to Patti. "How do you think I feel when I think that the father of your baby is my father—because of what I saw you and my dad doing inside the store that last time?"

"How do I think you feel? Hurt. Upset. Angry. PO'd . . . not understanding."

"Can you explain that to me?"

"I don't know."

"Why did you do it?" Cinnamon asked her father.

"Like in the store? Probably because I felt insecure. I was upset about everything that I've been seeing, experiencing with Linda. I had no idea she was into drugs. . . . I just felt like there was something wrong between me and Linda. . . . There are things in a marriage and all that and you need security. Now, you need somebody that'll hold you and all that when you feel like the whole world's going to shit on you any minute now . . . whatever it was that we [he and Patti] were feeling before . . . was very much not real."

"Then why was she still living with you?"

"Because we're all the family we have left. Who's going to help watch her?" He nodded his head toward Krystal, who, at four, was happily running after the birds who hovered nearby to peck at doughnut crumbs. Grandma and Grandpa couldn't care for Krystal, David said.

"Besides," Patti said swiftly, as if she could hold it in no longer. "I still care about him. . . . I care and I still love him. I'm not going to leave unless he tells me I have to leave. I want to be there for him the way he's been there for me."

It was a whoops. David had assured Cinnamon that Patti had left his home long before.

Patti watched David's annoyance and gradually changed her story. Yes, she had left—to go up to Oregon and find herself.

Cinnamon still wanted to know about Heather, but they would not answer her.

No, David had no interest—that way—in Patti. "I have seen a lot of women." He listed them, and Patti's face showed raw pain.

"I still love him, and I always will," she said with surprising fervor.

"And I don't like it. 'Cause I know that everyone else is just out for whatever he's got, and I honestly love him for what he is—not for what he can give me. I love him for what he is, but see—back then, I mean, I was still an immature little brat like I always was, and I didn't think twice before I did something. . . . It hurts, but I mean like—just because that's the way I feel doesn't mean that's the way he feels."

There it was, hidden in among the lies. Newell had little question that Patti Bailey Brown was telling the truth. For whatever unfathomable reason, she truly loved David Brown.

"My love for her," David told Cinnamon about Patti, "is no different than my love for you and my love for Krystal. There's nothing physical there."

"You mean, then, that would be considered as incest then—what I saw you and her do?" Cinnamon asked.

"Kiss?" David asked.

"Right."

"What's incest?" Patti asked.

"It's *not* incest." David spoke patiently. "A lots of parents kiss their kids on the mouth—"

"Not like that," Cinnamon tossed back.

"Maybe not like that, but it didn't feel right then and it's never felt right since."

"So you must've felt more for her than just a daughter?"

"I think I tried to because of an insecurity at the time. I might have tried to . . . fathers do it with their daughters, I mean, you know. That's not . . . that unusual. As a matter of fact, it's very common. They have sex with their daughters. It doesn't make any difference to them . . . whoever's handy."

Jay Newell turned away. He wasn't surprised at David Brown's philosophy on incest. That didn't keep him from being disgusted.

The kid was doing great. She was asking all the right questions, but the answers were coming back from left field.

Cinnamon asked about the insurance payoff on Linda. This time there was a new answer. "Krystal's got the insurance money," David said. "I don't need the insurance money. You know how much I've earned—since August first? One hundred and seventy-five thousand dollars. Why do I need insurance money? Cinny, my Data Recovery business account has—I don't even know how much money is in it. My personal account has always been like around seventy thousand dollars. . . . Cinny, I can make a hundred, two hundred thousand dollars a job. I could make three million dollars on one job we just did for the bank."

Cinnamon barely listened, but Newell made a note to recheck all insurance policies on Linda Brown. That one question had shaken David up more than almost all the rest. He didn't want to be connected with insurance payoffs.

Cinnamon asked Patti and David to go over the night of March 18, three years earlier, for her.

Patti quickly recalled everything to the point when she had gone to her room to sleep. David interrupted as she started to drift into the dangerous time just afterward. "I want to ask you a question," he said. "Do you guys wear state shoes right now? Do you have to wear state shoes during visiting?"

It was off the wall. It reminded Newell of the time he watched David pull Brenda's hair during Cinnamon's sentencing. Was it that he didn't care at all—or was he distracting Patti?

From murder to shoes in an instant.

But Cinnamon dragged him back to murder.

David was sure now that Larry Bailey had probably killed Linda, thinking he was killing David. "Linda was laying on my side of the bed. The cops told me. They got pictures of it and everything. . . . She was on my side of the bed, on the left. They said the room was dark, and I think whoever did it thought they were getting me."

In truth, Linda Brown was found exactly where she always slept, on the right side of the bed.

"You think whoever did it thought they were shooting you?" Cinnamon asked incredulously.

"Yes." David warmed to the story. "Too many weird things have happened since this all happened. I know somebody is out to get me. There's a good possibility that my liver was poisoned. Somebody's tried to poison me since this happened."

Patti nodded. "It happened [David's alleged liver failure] less than two months afterwards and they say that it takes a while for it to get there [to the liver]."

"But anyway, yeah—Linda may have poisoned me," David said almost cheerfully. "That's one of the other things they told me. She might have poisoned me. Alan might have poisoned me. But you ask about why she's still there. [He gestured toward Patti.] I am scared shitless. Every day, I'm scared somebody or something is going to kill me—every day because of Alan . . . Alan has maintained his threats. Larry is still—now he came back from Missouri and I've been trembling like a leaf and I wish Betsy was on your visiting list. She'd come in here and she'd tell you that sometimes I even sit there and cry."

David explained that he had seen three psychiatrists since the murder. The only reason he dated women was because he was terrified all the time. He was depressed. "Because I'm worried about you in here. I want you home."

The stories rattled on for another half an hour. Solutions came to David's mind and spun off like drops of water from a Frisbee. But "honest to God," David had no idea who had killed Linda. His memory was gone. He was not strong enough for prison, but he would be glad to let Patti confess.

When Patti and Krystal headed off for the rest rooms, David's tone with his daughter became confidential. "I know what it's like for you," he told Cinnamon.

"No . . . ," she said slowly. "You can probably imagine what it's like for me, but you don't know what it's really like."

"Cinnamon, you know what I mean. I've always loved you so much. I never wanted anything bad to happen to you. . . . Cinny, if you *did* do it, you did it because you love me just as much as I love you."

"But I didn't do it."

"I believe you. . . . You were always too lovable, you know. You were always too funny and cute . . . like me."

"Don't push it."

"You were. You were always funny. You like cracking jokes and doing things like I do. You didn't have a bone in your body that would allow you to hurt anyone. That's why I've always been convinced that it had to have been somebody thinking it was me.

"I want your honest opinion. From talking to her [Patti] just now, could she have done it?

"You've had me sitting on hot charcoals since you told me that over there on the grass," David said. "You've had me scared to death. I told Mother and Dad what you and I talked about and they've been scared to death. They've been trying to stay over at the new house as much as they can because they're afraid she's going to try to do *me* now. They think she's capable of it. Both of them do."

It made her dizzy. Her father going round and round with the same old lines. The same old suspects. The same old alibis. But then he always contradicted himself.

He trusted Patti. No, he was "scared to death" that Patti was trying to kill him.

It was Larry—or Alan. No, he wasn't sure.

He remembered nothing. He remembered exactly what he had told them.

His father was capable of killing. No, his father and mother were scared to death of Patti.

All Cinnamon wanted from him was the truth. If he told the truth, and if Patti told the truth, then she could tell the truth. But her father made jokes when the truth came too close, and he wasn't going to change. He thought he could just keep giving her *things* and never really think about her; he didn't care if she was locked up forever.

Cinnamon walked with him and Patti and Krystal out to see Grandma Brown. She smiled faintly at Manuela's gift of a teddy bear. And when they said good-bye, she winced as her father hugged her tightly—so tightly that she wondered if he felt the wire. Cinnamon had seen a camera pointed at them, just a flicker, just once. She knew Walt Robbins was in there in the guard tower. Had her father seen him? If he had, he said nothing. But he was so full of bullshit anyway, who could tell?

She hoped that Jay Newell had gotten enough information. There had been so many words. Maybe too many. Would it all come out like garbage?

Patti had said she would come in here. She said she felt like the song said: "I'll do anything for you, anything for you . . ."

But she wouldn't. It was all part of her father's game playing, and Patti would say whatever he wanted her to say. Just like always, Patti would do whatever he wanted her to do.

And her father was ready to betray Patti in the blink of an eye.

When she went back to the room where Jay Newell was monitoring the tapes, she saw him smiling at her. "Did you hear me trying to get him over here? Did you?"

"Yeah. You did a good job. They tried to get their story together pretty good."

He wouldn't know if he had enough until he got back to Santa Ana and listened to the tapes with Robinson.

But he had a good feeling.

29

T O   B U I L D —or in this instance, to *re*build—a murder case,
prosecutors and detectives seek to prove motive, means, and MO
(modus operandi), the three vital *M*s of murder. And then they need
both circumstantial and direct evidence to substantiate their case.
Cinnamon had been convicted principally upon her own confession
to the medical student Kim Hicks.

Now Jeoff Robinson and Jay Newell would have to come back
double strength to open a long-dead case. Their chief witness would
be a co-conspirator, not the witness of choice. It was legally tricky to
use the testimony of a co-conspirator in a court of law. In order to
allow Cinnamon's testimony—which would be essential to convict
David Brown and/or Patti Bailey—there had to be *independent* cor-
roboration of what she said. It could be physical evidence—a fingerprint, a DNA match—but not in this case. Since the three people
allegedly involved had all lived in the same house, the usual physical
evidence was worthless.

However, statements from the two suspects still walking free could
be corroborative too. If the long, long tapes recorded surreptitiously
during visitors' hours at Ventura School had enough in them to match
what Cinnamon had told Jay Newell, Jeoff Robinson could hope to
reopen the case and ask for arrest warrants.

Over and over, Robinson and Newell listened to the tapes. Each
playing brought forth another nuance. Robinson's grin grew broader.
There was no going back now. All unaware, Patti and David had
corroborated Cinnamon's story—even as they struggled to cover up
their involvement.

But Robinson would not rush this case. He and Newell brain-
stormed until they were sick of the sound of each other's voice.

"How could we make it better?" Newell recalled. "We kept asking
each other that. What could we add to our case to make it stronger?
There was no point in doing any more tapes at Ventura. We felt we
had as much as we were going to get from David and Patti.

"It finally came down to the only thing that could happen to improve
it would be to have either David or Patti point a finger at the other,
and that wasn't likely to happen until we could arrest them and separate them."

Motive for David and Patti was much stronger than it had been for Cinnamon. Lust. David had wanted Patti's youth, and her taped statements certainly showed she had coveted him for a long time. There was little doubt they had had a baby together.

Since David was by far the more pragmatic of the two suspects, and to put it bluntly, the greediest, a second and more pressing motive attached to him. Financial gain. He had always said that insurance was meant to be used, and he *had* used it. Payoffs on cars, on all-terrain vehicles, on computers, on medical and emotional damage, had all enhanced his fortune. No one would ever really know just how many claims he had collected on, given the peculiar glitches that appeared in his files in insurance company computers.

Lust and greed.

Two motives are always better than one.

Fred McLean worked the insurance angle, tracking down the agents who had sold David and Linda the life insurance that had paid off so handsomely after Linda's murder.

He found that there had been no less than *four* policies insuring Linda Brown's life at the time of her death! Why four? McLean learned that Linda Marie Brown, in her early twenties, a housewife without even a high school education, would not have been accepted by any one company for say, a million dollars' worth of insurance. Underwriters check policy applications carefully and advise acceptance and refusal of applications based on many factors and statistical averaging. To insure an applicant such as Linda Brown for a million dollars would be ridiculous. She would be considered "overinsured."

Excess insurance sends up a red flag to insurance companies. One way to circumvent that would be to obtain smaller insurance policies from a number of companies. The insurance industry had a safeguard here too. Applications have questions like "Is this to replace another similar policy?" and "Do you have life insurance with another company?" Moreover, there are central clearinghouses where underwriters can check to see if applicants are currently insured elsewhere. Even so, nothing is foolproof.

McLean's investigation turned up numerous applications for life insurance by both Linda and David Brown. Linda had been in perfect health; David had been meticulous about listing all of his many ailments. Not surprisingly, Linda had been accepted for coverage (all her applications said that she had no other coverage), and David was accepted only if he was "rated." If an applicant is in poor health or older, he may obtain insurance—but at a higher cost. Many customers decline policies that are offered only at "rated" higher premiums.

Which was exactly what David Brown had done. At first glance, he and Linda would have appeared to be a young couple seeking security. Looking closer, a suspicious detective might deduce that David wanted Linda's life to be heavily insured, but never intended to have policies on himself. Why else would he practically guarantee he would be turned down or "rated" by playing up his health problems? However, dual applications would have eased a wary wife's mind.

McLean found that David Brown had worn a path into insurance offices, applying many, many times. And yet, he himself was not currently insured. He was the chief wage-earner, the avowed head of the household. Wouldn't he have been the one to be insured? Apparently he was not as concerned about coverage as he appeared.

However at the time of her murder Linda Marie Brown had been insured with:

American General Life and Accident:	$100,000 and $100,000
Issued 2/24/84	(accidental death)
New York Life:	$100,000 and $100,000
Issued 3/12/84	(accidental death)
Capital Life:	$200,000 and $150,000
Issued 1/21/85	(accidental death)
Liberty Life:	$200,000 and $200,000
Application 2/21/85	(accidental death)

The last policy was never actually approved, but an application and a first premium were received on February 21, 1985, twenty-six days before Linda was murdered.

Within the thirteen months preceding her death, Linda Marie Brown's life had been insured four times, all double indemnity, all listing David Brown as sole beneficiary. Brown, McLean found, had collected rapidly. Shortly after the funeral, American General received a handwritten letter from Brown demanding payment, and he received a check for $208,043.60.

Capital Life paid Brown $361,833.08 on August 8.

New York Life paid him $200,000 on September 9.

The last policy had been in the underwriting process when Linda died. Liberty Life had not issued its policy, but had accepted the first premium that accompanied the application.

McLean contacted Dillard Veal of Rainbow, South Carolina, an agent with Liberty Life for thirty-three years, always in the home office, and a virtual walking encyclopedia of knowledge about the business.

Dillard Veal remembered David Arnold Brown well. His application had been turned down for health reasons. Linda's was pending when she died. "Because the premium was paid, we made a compromise settlement. Mr. Brown made a claim in April of 1985, and we negotiated with him that June in Orange County."

Veal said he and Brown had tentatively agreed on a $50,000 settlement, but the next time Veal returned to Orange County, that was not enough. "Mr. Brown referred me to his attorney. I negotiated with his attorney, and we settled for a payment of $73,750."

Actually, David Brown had done rather well. His first, and only, premium on Linda's policy had been $133.34.

Veal mentioned that Brown had made application for five members of his family—not only for himself and Linda, but for $100,000 double indemnity policies on Patti, Cinnamon, and Krystal. Cinnamon's had been postponed for a year, Patti's withdrawn, and Krystal's lapsed in November 1985.

In all, although he had denied it to Cinnamon on tape, David Brown had collected $843,626.68 within six months of Linda's death. If a few more months had elapsed before Linda's murder, if Cinnamon had died of an overdose, *and* if Dillard Veal had not found out that Linda was overinsured, David Brown's total payoff would have been $1,239,876.86.

McLean studied the signatures on Linda's applications; they looked dissimilar to him, but he was, admittedly, no handwriting expert. He contacted the agent who had sold the New York Life policy, Stanley Gudmundsen. McLean explained the case that had been reopened and asked him if he remembered his contact with the Browns.

He did. He had had no prior contact with either of them when they walked into his office to obtain life insurance for Linda on March 12, 1984.

"Can you describe them?" McLean asked.

"Let's see," Gudmundsen said. "I was working in the Bank of America Building at the City Mall in Orange when they came in. The woman—Linda Brown—was a slight, small person, with light hair, maybe long, worn down. David Brown was larger, and he had a—a 'chunky' face. I saw them just that once. After that, I had contact only by phone and letter with David Brown and his attorney."

McLean glanced over the application form with the insurance agent, and Gudmundsen pointed out two questions that were noteworthy.

Those questions asked if there were any other policies extant on Linda Marie Brown, or if this policy was meant to replace any other policy. Both questions were answered no.

McLean asked if David Brown had applied for life insurance on himself. Gudmundsen checked his records and phoned the detective. He had found a similar policy issued on the life of David Brown, but it was marked "Declined." "It was declined because of poor health," Gudmundsen said, "and adequate insurance already in effect. It possibly was a rated policy."

McLean wondered if Linda Brown had ever applied for insurance at all. Since she and Patti looked more like twins than sisters, it would have been a fairly easy thing to substitute Patti during the application interview. He made up a "lay-down" of photographs of young blond women, including pictures of both Linda and Patti, and asked Gudmundsen to point to the woman who had accompanied David Brown to his office.

Gudmundsen eliminated all but #4 and #5 and finally settled on #4. "This is closest."

It was Linda.

But McLean still wondered. Gudmundsen had not mentioned that "Mrs. Brown" was pregnant when she came to his office. On March 12, 1984, Linda had been five months pregnant. She was a small woman and her condition would have been apparent, *especially* apparent to an insurance agent who was insuring her life.

Newell checked with Linda's obstetrician on the off chance that she might have been in his office on March 12. No luck.

McLean took the signatures on Linda's applications to an expert. The word that came back was a little disappointing. "They're all signed by Linda Brown—they all match the exemplar of her handwriting. The changes only indicate different moods, whether she was in a hurry, tired—that sort of thing."

So there it was. Linda Brown had accompanied her husband to apply for insurance at least four times in the year before she was murdered. She had grown up so desperately poor; she wanted her baby to be taken care of. Did she ever know that David refused his insurance or made sure he was turned down? Perhaps not.

With McLean's persistence, Robinson and Newell had made the case against David Arnold Brown very much better. Over $800,000 sweetened the pot. But Robinson asked for more, more, and still more.

David Brown, age twenty-nine. "The Process," his invention to clean computer disks, had earned him a small fortune and fame in computer circles.

Linda Brown, age twenty. She adored her husband, David, and happily played "Mom" to both her younger sister, Patti, and David's daughter, Cinnamon.

Patti Bailey, age thirteen or fourteen. Unhappy at home, she was thrilled to be invited to live with her big sister, Linda, and brother-in-law, David.

Cinnamon Brown, age fourteen, a bubbly, quick-witted teengager, often shuttled back and forth between her mother, Brenda, and her father, David.

The green stucco house on Ocean Breeze Drive where Linda Brown was shot to death on March 19, 1985. When investigators arrived at the scene, Cinnamon was missing.

Linda died in the ornate iron bed she shared with David. The murder weapon was dropped on the floor of their bedroom.

David's dresser in the early morning after Linda was shot. He owned expensive jewelry, took many prescription drugs for his myriad ailments, and prided himself on being a wonderful father.

On the morning after the murder, Garden Grove Detective Fred McLean finally found Cinnamon shivering and sick in a doghouse in the backyard of the Ocean Breeze Drive home.

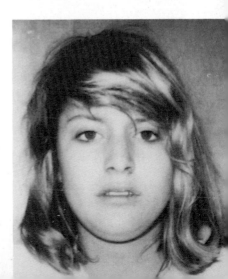

Cinnamon was taken to Garden Grove police head-quarters to answer questions that might identify Linda's killer. Suffering from a massive drug overdose, she collapsed shortly after this picture was taken and was rushed to a hospital. Later a confession was extracted from her, but that was not the end of the story.

A police surveillance picture of a visit David Brown made to the California Youth Authority school in Ventura. As Cinnamon, back to camera, talked with her father, their conversation was taped surreptitiously.

David Brown, age thirty-five, at the time of his questioning about the murder of his wife Linda.

Patti Bailey, age twenty, was also taken into custody and interrogated. Police suspected that both she and David were somehow implicated in the crime.

Leslie Rule

Left to right: Detective Fred McLean of the Garden Grove police, Orange County Deputy District Attorney Jeoffrey Robinson, and Orange County District Attorney's Senior Investigator Jay Newell. These three men worked overtime to unravel the baffling mystery of Linda Brown's murder.

Leslie Rule

Cinnamon Brown, now twenty, on the witness stand.

Leslie

At a tense moment in her testimony, Cinnamon broke down as she answered questions about Linda Brown's murder. Sandra Wingerd, court reporter, is in the foreground.

Leslie Rule

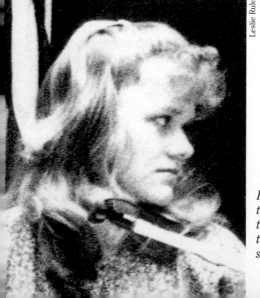

Patti Bailey, now twenty-two, gave nervous and at times almost inaudible testimony on the witness stand.

David Brown, in the court-room, turned to look at media cameras. He did not testify.

Leslie Rule

Richard Steinhart, aka "Liberty", former Hessian motorcycle gang member and one-time hired hit man, was a surprising witness at the trial.

Don Lasseter

Cinnamon Brown, twenty, as she waited for an end to her long ordeal.

Enough. The usually laid-back Newell looked at the prosecutor and said, "Damn, Jeoff. I'm giving you this on a silver platter. Now you want David Brown's name engraved on it!"

Robinson held up his hands in defeat. "Okay. Let's go!"

The charge would be murder. California P.C.-187.

And beyond that, the complaint would list "overt acts." Robinson and Newell discussed which overt acts they could include, and indeed, how many. It had been a long time coming, this moment when charges were filed. They worked over the document.

"What can we put in?"

"What else?"

Once the complaint was the way they wanted, Jay Newell would walk it through all the steps needed until he was handed two arrrest warrants. "If we waited for the usual slow progression from desk to desk and department to department," Newell said, "it could take awhile—and we had waited long enough. I walked it to the municipal court clerk, who sent me up to the judge's chambers. I briefed him, and he signed the warrants. I kept those copies in my hand right to the end."

And there they were, the most beautiful pieces of paper Jay Newell had ever seen:

THE PEOPLE OF THE STATE OF CALIFORNIA,)
)   FELONY COMPLAINT
                  Plaintiff,)
)   NO.
                    vs.   )

DAVID ARNOLD BROWN, DOB: 11-16-52)

                Defendant(s))

Personally appearing before me on September 21, 1988, J. NEWELL, O.C.D.A., who, being first duly sworn, deposes and says: That at and within the above County and State, the defendant(s) hereinbefore named violated the law as follows:

COUNT I: That on or about March 19, 1985, at and within Orange County, California, the crime of FELONY, to-wit: Violation of Section 187 of the Penal Code of the State of California, was committed by DAVID ARNOLD BROWN, who at the time and place last aforesaid, did then and there willfully, unlawfully and feloniously, and with malice aforethought, kill Linda Brown, a human being.

COUNT II: That between March 19, 1984 and March 19, 1985, at and within Orange County, California, the crime of FELONY, to-wit: Violation of Section 182.1 of the Penal Code of the State of California, was committed by DAVID ARNOLD BROWN and Patti Bailey, who at the time and place last aforesaid, did then and there willfully, unlawfully and feloniously conspire together and with another person and persons whose identify is unknown to commit the crime of murder in violation of Section 187 of the Penal Code, a felony; that pursuant to and for the purpose of carrying out the objects and purposes of the aforesaid conspiracy, the said defendants committed the following overt act and acts at and in the County of Orange:

OVERT ACT NO. 1

Defendant DAVID ARNOLD BROWN and Patti Bailey have initial discussions regarding the murder of Linda Brown.

OVERT ACT NO. 2

Defendant DAVID ARNOLD BROWN recruits Cinnamon Brown to assist in murder, stating that Linda Brown is planning to kill him.

OVERT ACT NO. 3

After Cinnamon Brown observes defendant DAVID ARNOLD BROWN and Patti Bailey embracing, defendant DAVID ARNOLD BROWN instructs Cinnamon Brown not to tell anyone of his relationship with Patti Bailey.

OVERT ACT NO. 4

While riding in van enroute to Long Beach, both defendant DAVID ARNOLD BROWN and Patti Bailey discuss murder. They both agree that they must "get rid of" Linda Brown.

OVERT ACT NO. 5

On another occasion in the van, with Arthur Brown present, Patti Bailey discusses specific methods of killing Linda Brown, with defendant DAVID ARNOLD BROWN. Patti Bailey suggests to defendant DAVID ARNOLD BROWN that they could throw Linda Brown from van.

OVERT ACT NO. 6

Defendant DAVID ARNOLD BROWN obtains two additional life insurance policies on the life of Linda Brown.

OVERT ACT NO. 7

Within one week of the murder, defendant DAVID ARNOLD BROWN tells Cinnamon Brown to take the blame for contemplated murder. He further tells Cinnamon that because of her age, that she will spend little or no time in jail.

OVERT ACT NO. 8

Defendant DAVID ARNOLD BROWN instructs Cinnamon to practice writing suicide notes; he further states that this will make the homicide look like a murder-suicide.

OVERT ACT NO. 9

Defendant DAVID ARNOLD BROWN prepares and instructs Cinnamon to ingest a mixture of drugs just before the killing of Linda Brown in a further effort to demonstrate a suicide attempt.

OVERT ACT NO. 10

Just prior to the murder, defendant DAVID ARNOLD BROWN wakes up Patti Bailey and Cinnamon Brown, gives final directions; then leaves premises per the original plan.

OVERT ACT NO. 11

On March 19, 1985, Linda Brown, while sleeping, is killed with a .38 cal. handgun.

It is further alleged that the murder of Linda Brown was intentional and was carried out by the defendant DAVID ARNOLD BROWN for financial gain, within the meaning of Penal Code Section 190.2(a)(1).

Wherefore, and based upon the declaration and reports attached, and incorporated by reference herewith, said complainant prays that a warrant may be issued for the arrest of the defendant(s) herein named, and that said defendant(s) be dealt with according to law.

Subscribed and sworn to before me,

On: September 21, 1988   _____ Complainant
    J. Robinson/al

MICHAEL R. CAPIZZI, DISTRICT ATTORNEY   _____ Judge
ORANGE COUNTY, STATE OF CALIFORNIA

By _____   _____ Clerk
       Deputy   of the Municipal Court County
                                        of Orange,
                                        State of California

Bail Recommendation - $ NO BAIL   _____ Deputy

PART THREE

• • •

The Arrest and the Death List

A T 6:39 A.M., on Thursday, September 22, 1988, Jay Newell and Fred McLean met at the 7-Eleven on Ball Road and Sunkist with a male "uniform" and a female "uniform" from the Anaheim Police Department for backup. At seven A.M., Newell and McLean would knock on the door of the big blue house on Chantilly Street, and they wanted every eventuality covered. They had come this far; they wanted no minuscule mistake now.

"I put tape into the recorder in the squad car," Newell recalled. "The female uniform would drive, and we planned to put David and Patti together in the backseat. If they said anything, I wanted to know what it was."

"At seven A.M., the blue house was quiet, but the nearby Orange Freeway was buzzing with commuter traffic. Newell knocked at the door, and he and McLean stepped back a bit and waited.

Nothing.

Newell knocked again.

An intercom near the door startled them as David Brown's voice sounded, "Yeah?"

"Mr. Brown," Newell said. "Can you come down here? There's a problem we need to take care of."

There was another wait, and then the door opened and David Brown stood there, muttering that he had been asleep. He had had to get dressed. He wore white slacks and a white T-shirt. His mood was anything but welcoming, but the moment he stepped back, the two detectives and the male police officer stepped in.

"You are under arrest, Mr. Brown, for the murder of Linda Marie Brown," Newell said quietly.

He searched Brown's face for some trace of emotion and found none. David didn't seem surprised, or shocked. He simply stared back at Newell with his inscrutable blank eyes.

This house was so much more expensive than the little avocado-colored stucco rambler on Ocean Breeze Drive. But it was a mess inside. Cartons of business papers and work to be done were every-where. The furniture was the same—at least it looked just like the stuff that Newell and McLean had seen on the day of the murder.

...hat house had looked as if a woman had taken care of it lovingly.
...is place looked unlived in, messy.

Newell headed up the staircase to the second floor. He looked into the first bedroom at the top of the stairs. Patti, wearing a nightgown, was in bed there, with Krystal. The four-year-old sat up in bed and stared at him.

"You are under arrest for the murder of Linda Marie Brown," he said to Patti.

She looked at him without expression. There were no tears in her eyes, and she seemed no more surprised than David was.

"This your room?" Newell asked, knowing that it wasn't.

"No, I sleep down the hall with Heather," Patti said, pointing in that direction.

Newell looked in the room and saw Heather in a baby crib. There was a bed, but it was completely covered with neatly folded and ironed clothes. Patti had not slept there. He doubted that she had ever slept there.

David asked to go to the bathroom, and Newell nodded, but advised him he would have to go along. The master bath was in David's bedroom, a huge room obviously recently remodeled. It had a large television set and an expensive stereo system.

The bed was rumpled.

Behind the bed, the carpeted floor rose to another level, and the area appeared to be an office. There was a refrigerator. Newell opened it idly; the shelves were packed with dozens and dozens of bottles of Perrier.

There was no argument about shutting the bathroom door; there *was* no bathroom door—the room was still in the last stages of remodeling. It was large and luxurious, with a bay window and a large circular tub with whirlpool jets.

"Can I take a Xanax?" David asked, pointing to a bottle of the heavy-duty tranquilizers.

Newell opened the container, handed one to David, and left the bottle where it was. He wanted to talk to David and he wanted him alert. He handcuffed his prisoner and walked him down the stairs.

Once in the squad car, David Brown began to call piteously, "Help me. Someone help me. I'm going to be sick. I'm claustrophobic."

Patti Bailey dressed quickly in white slacks, a pale-blue hooded sweatshirt, and white sneakers. Neither Patti nor David wore any jewelry. Newell discovered later that David had instructed her to give him her rings, and he had removed his own, secreting close to a hundred thousand dollars' worth of diamonds on top of his medicine chest before he answered the door.

Patti held her hands out silently as she was cuffed.

"Your children, Patti—" Newell began. This was the difficult part. The babies hadn't done anything to anyone. They were victims too. He fought to keep emotion out of his voice. "Your children can be taken to the Albert Sitton Home in Orange, or if you have someone you can call who could care for them?"

"Grandpa Brown," she murmured. "Call Grandpa Brown."

The Anaheim police officer waited with Heather and Krystal until Manuela and Arthur hurried over to take charge of them.

David recovered quickly from his panic attack. By the time the Anaheim police car headed down Chantilly, he seemed in control. When he saw the driver was headed for the freeway, he pointed out that they had taken the wrong route.

"He said the freeway would take forever that time of day," Newell recalled, "and he was right. But he directed us along this circuitous route that got us right to the Orange County Courthouse in no time. I don't know if it occurred to him that his route just got him to jail quicker."

Patti and David said little. The tape on the recorder in the police car, retrieved later, added almost nothing to the investigation. "Except for one thing," Newell remembered later. "David kept asking Patti about Heather. He kept saying, 'Now, who *is* Heather's father really?' He was doing it for our benefit. Well, why not? We believed he'd thrown away one daughter already to get what he wanted. Why not throw away Heather? She was only a mistake to him."

In denying Heather, the child who had come to mean more than life itself to Patti Bailey Brown, David may well have made the biggest mistake of his life. Patti would have done anything for David until Heather was born. When he failed to love their child, the tiniest seed of rebellion took root in Patti.

Was it possible that David was not her savior, her ultimate lover, the most wonderful man who had ever lived?

31

I N T E R V I E W room A-224 in the Orange County District Attorney's Office wasn't a very large room. Perhaps deliberately so. The subjects interrogated in that room and their questioners were close enough so that their eyes were forced to meet, so that sudden intakes of breath echoed loudly.

A-224's decor smacked of the sixties. There was a rectangular table, made of melamine in a dark wood pattern, scratched and marred, six faded orange-and-yellow-zigzag-upholstered chairs, and yellow walls with framed prints. A frenetic Jackson Pollock. An Henri Rousseau. Saint Francis. A Museum of Modern Art poster dated "April 5–June 4, 1967," which definitely established the era the room was last decorated. A mirrored clock ticked away on one wall.

The chairs were slightly sprung from years of suspects shifting, turning, some of them *squirming*, as questions grew invasive and close to the bone. Many of the interrogations were both audiotaped and videotaped.

Now, just before eight-thirty on the morning of September 22, 1988, David Arnold Brown sat heavily in one of those orange and yellow chairs, Jay Newell sat obliquely across from him, and Fred McLean took a chair at the near end of the table. David had requested Perrier, and he sipped from a plastic cup, then lit the first of many, many cigarettes.

He seemed quite calm, even confident—but faintly annoyed.

Newell's interviewing techniques were so low-key that the most tautly strung suspect tended to relax. Newell could say, "Now, you're under arrest for PC-187—ahhh, that's murder," so casually that it somehow didn't sound so bad, after all.

It may have been the remnants of a barely detectable Oklahoma drawl. More likely, Newell's approach to interrogation was the result of years of refining, practicing, utilizing. He was *good*. When he said, "You'll have to repeat that for me. I'm not that quick; could you run it by me again?" he was ultimately believable. Indeed he insisted that he really *wasn't* that speedy in grasping facts. But neither his peers nor the suspects he helped to convict believed that. Newell missed nothing; he only pretended that he had.

David Brown, however, was so concerned with impressing Newell and McLean with his importance and with the precarious state of his health that he misjudged Jay Newell.

Possibly a fatal miscalculation.

One day, a jury might watch this interrogation. The way *they* perceived it could be the linchpin of a trial. But for now, David listened to his Miranda rights, and he nodded agreeably. Of course he would talk to the two detectives. "I have nothing to hide."

He was shocked, of course, to be sitting where he was. He was ill, he explained, and suffered from a "bleeding problem" that would probably necessitate frequent trips to the rest room, and he apologized in advance.

"No problem," Newell murmured.

David explained that he suffered from a kind of "immunological disorder" that was "not AIDS—but a variation of it." It affected his heart, kidneys, liver. There was a chemical imbalance in his body that caused him to regurgitate, and he explained that he had almost suffocated from it several times.

If Newell believed his shopping list of miseries, it seemed a miracle that David Brown could get out of bed in the morning. He wondered if the man had an organ left that functioned. Well, at least one, Newell thought grimly; the existence of Heather proved that.

Asked about the night Linda died, David strained to remember the date and then commented that he remembered hardly anything. "I know that a lot of my health problems now are a result of my loss *of* her . . . because I never had and never will love a woman like the way I loved that woman."

Four weeks earlier, Newell had listened while David castigated Linda to Cinnamon, calling her a drug addict greedy enough to kill him to have his business, a woman who had poisoned him, a woman who had allowed her own brother to be tied up and tortured for two weeks. But Newell betrayed nothing of what he knew. He listened with his most concerned, interested—even sympathetic—manner while David rambled on.

"Tell me in your own words what you remember of that night, if you would," Newell asked.

David did not remember the day of the murder. "I was probably fielding calls anywhere from the Pentagon down to the local computer companies. That's what I usually did."

At the end of every responsive answer, David veered off into a discussion of his own emotional pain. "I've been to three psychiatrists because I just can't seem to deal with her death. I want to die. I'm suicide prone—"

"Do you remember that night though?" Newell cut him off with the same question each time David wandered.

Despite his protestations that he had no independent memory of "that night," Newell urged David to search the "computer banks" of his mind.

"We made love," David said.

"You had sex?"

"We made love, yes."

". . . When you say you made love, you mean you had sexual intercourse?"

"I don't remember *specifically* that night. Linda—that's one of the things I loved about her—she had quirks, you know, things she loved to do. One of her things was, whenever possible, was to drive me crazy, get me crawling and screaming is what I'm talking about. Ah, it's kind of hard to be specific."

"Well, we're all adults," Newell said dryly.

"Yeah, well . . . she loved to kiss me and touch me you know—foreplay—whatever you call it. Sometimes, she didn't mind having intercourse when she was having her period. I didn't particularly get excited about it."

"Do you remember that night?" Newell pressed again.

". . . I don't remember. I know she drove me crazy. I know we did something. One of the things she liked to do was . . . she used her hands to at least satisfy me."

"Did you get a climax that night?"

"Oh . . . *every night*. We'd known each other and been in love for too long. She knew what I liked and how to take care of me, and I took care of her . . . we tried very often not to do the same thing every night. We liked to keep the fire and excitement going."

"Was everyone still there playing cards?"

"I don't honestly know. It didn't matter to her, and she had this way of getting me going so it didn't matter to me. I don't know if anyone was still there or not."

How odd. How *extremely* odd that a man would begin an interview about the murder of his beloved wife by describing the most intimate details of their sex life. But if Newell and McLean even blinked, it was internally.

David talked and he talked and he talked. He smoked until the air in the little yellow room was blue. And still he talked. That was how he had always won. Just keep talking and people will come around. Throughout his interrogation, the damn cops had hardly gotten a word in edgewise, and David felt he had been in control of the conversation.

When Robinson and Newell watched the three-hour tape, they were gleeful. They had him. "Up to then," Robinson admits, "we had a skeleton case. We were going to go with it, no matter what. But in this long tape, David Brown *talked*. At first, it wasn't so much what came out, it was the fact that the man actually opened his mouth and *talked*. . . . Jay and I couldn't predict how a jury might view that tape."

For the moment, David Brown's biggest problem was that he would have accommodations far less plush than he had become used to. He was worried about what would happen if he needed medical help in a hurry. Jailers assured him that he would be taken care of; they would have someone review his medications. He was strip-searched and given a large pair of orange coveralls. David Arnold Brown, computer genius, millionaire, was now Orange County prisoner #1058076.

Lodged in the IRC—the Intake and Release Center—in the Orange County Jail, David thought about his sudden change of fortune, and he looked for ways to survive until his father bailed him out. He wasn't sure what they thought they had on him. That Newell was a closemouthed S.O.B.

He touched his neck, fumbling automatically for his phoenix pendant—but it wasn't there. It was safe with his other jewelry, back in the house where his dad could find it. It had to be that way. Damn cops would steal anything they got their hands on. He knew he could count on his father to take care of things.

Still, his throat felt naked without the phoenix. It was his security, his good-luck talisman, the symbol of who he was.

At 12:44 P.M., Patti sat in the same chair in the interview room that David had, and while David had barely changed position, Patti twisted and turned, tucked one leg beneath her and then turned and tucked the other foot beneath a slender flank.

Patti Bailey didn't talk. Not really. She *spoke* with Jay Newell in her husky, flat voice, but she *said* so little.

She remembered nothing. She had "blanked it out." A psychiatrist had helped her block it out. She couldn't remember how long ago it had been since Linda died. "She [the psychiatrist] got me to deal with it realistically. See, I always thought that Linda had just gone on vacation, and she got me to see that she wasn't just on vacation, and she wasn't coming back. But I don't remember the details. Everything's just a total fog. . . . I guess I don't want it to come back."

Patti said she was still having terrible memory problems. She could barely remember what happened last week. She never discussed it with Cinnamon. She had seen her a month ago, and not for a year and a half before that. "I remember the drive up [to Ventura School], but I don't remember a whole lot of what was said."

"What made you go after so long?" Newell asked.

"She's my sister—well, not really, but like a sister. . . . I had to see if she was still there—if she was okay."

"What did you talk about?"

"About Krystal."

"Did you talk about Linda's death . . . ?"

"No."

"What if I told you Cinnamon remembers discussing it with you?"

"I don't remember."

"What is the relationship between you and David."

". . . He's not my blood father—but he is my dad."

"What is your *feeling* for David?"

"Just the same as I would feel for a father."

"Do you love him?"

"No . . . as the aspect of 'Dad,' yes—but not as the aspect of any other way."

"There's nothing sexual between the two of you?"

"No."

"Has there ever been anything sexual?"

"No."

Newell asked about the long-ago kiss between David and Patti in the store. Patti said she couldn't remember.

Patti could barely remember what happened yesterday. She was dry-eyed, emotionless, and would not be swayed from her position of almost total forgetfulness. "Sometimes I feel I'm in a daze. I don't want to remember, or whatever."

Newell asked her about the time she had overheard a plot between Linda and Alan about killing David. She merely looked blank. Patti apologized for being so dense. She could not help her loss of memory.

"Do you ever dream about Linda's death?" Newell asked.

"I dream about picking her up at airports and stuff, but that's all."

Newell told Patti that he was going to have to dig deep into the mystery of Linda's murder, that he had a tape to play for her, and Patti suddenly began to choke up.

She begged Jay Newell to "go slow—'cause it really hurts. I just now woke up and realized she's really gone; she's not going to come back. 'Cause I'd find myself driving down the street trying to find her. So go slow. Go slow and deep if you have to, but it's going to hurt."

Newell left the room to find Patti some Kleenex, and she bent her head and sobbed. She did not know she was on camera; the tears were real, whether for herself, for her baby, or for her dead sister, whom she described as "more a mother to me than a sister."

Patti expected to hear a tape from the night of the murder, and she was afraid to hear it. No, Newell explained, he was going to play her a tape of David discussing her involvement—a *recent* tape.

Patti stared at Newell, uncomprehending. She insisted she and David never discussed anything about Linda's murder. They discussed only details of the house, buying clothes for Krystal. "He knows I don't understand what happened in the past."

Patti said she and David didn't get along.

"Why are you living there?"

"Because I take care of Krystal the best I can. That's the only key I have left to Linda. I don't want to lose it. Until I feel more stable about myself, or until there's someone to take care of Krystal, I'll stay. . . . I wouldn't leave unless he told me to get the hell out of his house."

Patti denied the slightest connection to David Brown in any way beyond father-daughter.

She did not—or would not—recall any conversation with Cinnamon at Ventura, nothing beyond talking about Krystal. Even when Newell played snatches of David's voice on the tape, implicating Patti in the murder, she balked. She did not remember. She would not connect David . . . or Cinnamon . . . or herself to Linda's death.

"Everybody's pointing at you?" Newell asked. "Why?"

"I don't know."

Patti's affect was flat. She scarcely reacted when Newell played the portion of the tape where David told Cinnamon he was "scared to death" that Patti was going to "do him" next.

"Maybe I don't want to remember. . . ."

". . . It's about time to start remembering. . . . David's pointing fingers at you, saying you did it."

"He can point all he wants. I didn't do it."

"What involvement do you have in Linda's death?"

"None."

"David is saying, 'Patti did it.' "

"I wouldn't be able to live with myself if I hurt someone—I can't tell Krystal no, or spank her. I can't yell at my mother without calling her to apologize," Patti argued.

Nudged to remember something, anything, about the night of May 18–19, 1985, Patti now recalled that David had summoned her and Cinnamon into the living room, but she had no idea why. She had no more memory of that night. "I go on and off. I really don't—that's the truth."

She would not talk. Even with the sound of David's voice on the tape from Ventura School, with the sound of her own voice on the tape—confirming that she had some part in a conspiracy to kill her own sister—Patti still clung to her position that she did not remember.

She was as white as paper; she looked scared, and the hidden camera recorded her sighs and her despair when Newell left the room from time to time. And still she protected David.

"Okay, Patti," Newell said, "we've got to start jogging your memory more . . . we're going to play this entire tape for the jury. They're going to hear that you got up in the middle of the night and discussed whether or not to go through with killing Linda. . . . You better start jogging your memory right now, Patti, because this is first-degree murder. Are you going to ride this out all by yourself?"

"If I have to."

Newell discussed the medication given to Cinnamon, suggesting that Patti had given the pills to her.

"I wouldn't even give her Tylenol without her father's permission."

"Ah, bullshit!" Newell shouted—this man who rarely raised his voice. "You tried to kill her that night!"

"*I did not,*" Patti hissed, the first show of hostility.

"And we're going to prove that!"

The moment Jay Newell raised his voice, Patti said between clenched teeth, "I want an attorney if you're going to be nasty."

The interview was over.

Patti Bailey, Orange County prisoner #1058088, was booked into the women's jail. She wore a gray jail sweatshirt with yellow numbers on it as she gazed stolidly into the mug camera.

Her baby, the only thing she had ever had that was her own to love, was in the care of Manuela Brown, a woman who detested Patti. David, the man she had loved for a dozen years, had betrayed her to save his own skin. Linda was dead. Linda was ashes now.

It was all ashes.

Arthur Brown, looking tired and worn, entered the little inteview room at two-thirty that long Thursday. Jay Newell had heard that Grandpa Brown was present during the trip to the mountains the night before Linda's murder.

"Was Cinnamon there too?"

"Yeah."

"Did Cinnamon get in that conversation?"

"No . . ." Art struggled to recall. "But that may be what I told her [at Ventura] that upset her so much."

"Did David get in the conversation?"

"He never said a half dozen words the whole evening when we were heading up the mountain."

"Just Patti's—"

"It was mostly Patti—running off at the mouth. I thought that's all it was—just static—and then this come up."

Arthur Brown could remember only that it was close to a weekend, and they had been planning a barbecue which was canceled by a "real bad storm."

That was the only conversation about getting rid of Linda that Grandpa Brown recalled hearing. He had told Patti there were a whole lot better ways to handle the situation. "But it don't do no good. She's like that—in one ear and out the other. I've tried to correct her, but it doesn't do any good 'cause David always takes her side."

It was clear that Art cared little for Patti Bailey. He felt all the lavish remodeling on Chantilly Street was David's attempt to please Patti. He was almost glad they had been arrested. "It's the best thing that ever happened to David," he said, wondering if now his son would "turn around and straighten out."

A familiar and pathetic blindness, the inability of parents to see flaws in their young, but Jay Newell said nothing, waiting. It was clear that Grandpa Brown viewed Patti as the killer, the only one involved. If that should be true, he could have his son and his favorite granddaughter back, and a semblance of a happy ending.

"I was in hopes it might help Cinny, 'cause as far as I'm concerned, she's a doll."

"Well, the truth can't hurt her—that's for sure. It's been so many years that nobody's known the truth," Newell agreed. "She went through a lot."

"That's the trouble with these two guys right now. They tell one goddamned lie and then they have to turn around and tell another one to cover it up. . . . David didn't used to be that way at all. If he told you the truth, that was his word."

Newell tried to keep Art on track—to be sure the old man was not fantasizing. Or engaging in wishful thinking.

The elder Brown said he worked with David in his business, although he was privy to few secrets. David was still working for Randomex, his father said, and then looked around nervously. "I'm not supposed to discuss it."

"Because it's government work, or because it's David's business?"

"No, it's David's idea, and his work. Nobody in the world knows it but him."

Arthur Brown explained that Alan Bailey had once again fallen into disrepute and was no longer connected to David's business. Alan had only known how to do *part* of The Process anyway; it had been Linda who knew it all. Linda could have run the business all by herself.

Newell could see that the old man was thoroughly awed by his son's genius. Even intimidated by it.

Brown said that David seldom went into the Randomex plant in Long Beach. "He used to—but since he's been so sick, he gets out in the heat and it just tires him up. A year—a year and a half now, maybe. He goes in occasionally, but not on a hot day."

Brown wasn't exactly sure what was wrong with David. Lately, it had been his gallbladder, but the doctors had never been able to put their fingers on a precise diagnosis. He didn't drink, never had, even though dozens of grateful customers sent him liquor at Christmas, especially brandy.

"Who drinks all the brandy?"

"Nobody, unless it's Patti. It's sitting right there next to the bed."

"Whose bed?"

"David's bed."

Newell didn't change expression. He was convinced that Patti and David slept together, but he wasn't sure that Art Brown knew it. Or rather, that he was ready to acknowledge that his son might be sleeping with the girl he had just called a killer.

The old man clearly considered Patti Bailey an interloper. She seemed to wield so much power, to act as if she were mistress of the house. "I don't want her *dead* or anything. I just want her out of the house."

Jeoff Robinson stepped in to talk with Brown. "Wasn't David along and talking with Patti about killing Linda?" he asked.

"No . . . he didn't say half a dozen words."

"But you were in the motor home on the way back from Ventura— they were obviously upset the last two visits?" Robinson pressed.

"The way that motor home is, you have to get your head right down between the seats to hear anything." Art Brown shook his head.

All fingers pointed at Patti Bailey. and it seemed she had not one friend left in the world. David had his parents staunchly behind him, defending him as a fine young man, led astray by the wicked Patti. Cinnamon had the support of *her* mother, and of Newell, McLean, and Robinson, who believed she had been treated badly by the law.

Patti had no one. Except Heather. David had thrown her to the wolves the first chance he got. If if turned out that Patti had killed her own sister over her passion for Linda's husband, would her own family desert her? Probably. She had left them behind long ago to go to David.

All the pieces were beginning to fit.

But still . . . Newell and Robinson felt hinky; what was missing?

Jay Newell put in a call to the Ventura School. He wanted to let Cinnamon know that her father and Patti had been arrested before she heard it on the radio or saw it on television. He got a counselor on the phone and told him to warn Cinnamon that the arrest story would be all over the media.

And it was.

From the *Los Angeles Times* and the *Orange County Register* to the *Weekly World News* and the voracious tabloid television shows, the David Brown family murder was headline material nationwide.

"Man Charged with Murder, Making Daughter Confess" (*Orange County Register*). "Businessman Arrested for Murder for Which His Daughter Is in Prison" (*L.A. Times*). "Teen Took Murder Rap for Her Greedy Father, Say Cops" (*Weekly World News*). The Associated Press wire story was headlined a bit less sensationally "Teen Recants Her Murder Confession."

Orange County residents were mildly surprised. Most of them vaguely remembered the girl with the unusual name—Cinnamon—who had been tried for her stepmother's murder a few years back. They hadn't given her a thought for years. There were always new murders, new scandals, to erase yesterday's news from memory. The father? He had never been mentioned much. The fact that the sister of the murder victim had been arrested too made the case kind of titillating.

Not for everyone. David *Ira* Brown, a computer expert who lived in Farmington Hills, Michigan, present of Data Recovery Inc., was less than enthusiastic with the headlines about the man with a name so similar to his own, *and* with a business name almost identical. His office fielded calls from people who wanted to know, "What in God's name happened to Dave Brown? Why would he do this?"

The nonarrested David Brown had incorporated under the Data Recovery Inc. name in Michigan in 1981. David Arnold Brown first registered his company name in Anaheim in 1988, after using a similar name in 1982.

David *Arnold* Brown was ordered held without bail. So was Patti Bailey. They waited in their separate cellblocks for the next step in their confrontation with the law, the preliminary hearing, set to begin the week before Christmas, 1988.

David hired Joel Baruch, a well-known—if somewhat flamboyant—Orange County defense attorney to represent him. Joel Baruch and Jeoff Robinson were an incendiary combination; if the case had not already promised sensational courtroom revelations, the combination of these two attorneys in one courtroom would have. Robinson had beaten Baruch twice in jury trials, and Baruch was not about to let it happen again.

Patti Bailey was represented by Donald Rubright, a tall, handsome defense attorney, also well-known in Orange County. David paid for both attorneys, just as he had paid for Cinnamon's defense in 1985.

David was arraigned on Monday, September 26, 1988, before West Orange County Municipal Court judge Dennis S. Choate. He pleaded innocent and was ordered held without bail. Patti awaited a hearing to see if she would be tried as an adult or as a juvenile.

For a very short time, there was a spate of rest, a chance for Jay Newell and Jeoff Robinson to catch their breaths, before they plunged into preparing for the trial that lay ahead.

Newell only rarely talked to the press. Robinson would say only—somewhat inscrutably—"Who pulled the trigger is really not important in the totality of the circumstances. We believe that we have all the parties arrested."

Jay Newell kept in touch with Cinnamon infrequently. During the week before Halloween, 1988, Robinson and Newell voiced some doubts that had been niggling at them. There were areas in the tapes of Cinnamon's conversations with police in 1985 that didn't mesh with what she was saying now. There were good reasons that she might forget, but one lie now would give Baruch and Rubright a chance to tear Cinnamon apart on the stand.

They could not risk that.

On October 27, Newell drove up to the Ventura School and talked with Cinnamon. The preliminary hearing was coming up in December. The decision about whether or not to hold David and Patti over for trial would be made then. There had never been a time when it was more vital that Cinnamon tell the absolute truth. If her testimony should be shaken, there would be no going back.

Ever.

Cinnamon had never testified in court before; she had not been allowed to in her own trial, and she needed to be fully aware of the consequences of evading the truth on the stand. Newell gave Cinnamon a "layman's" explanation of perjury. It was possible that she could get another charge if she lied on the witness stand. If she had held back anything from him, she had to tell him before they got into court.

Newell supplied copies of Cinnamon's earlier tapes to her, and transcripts of the hidden-wire tapes with her father and Patti, and asked *her* to listen to them, to read the transcripts. "Don't answer now. Listen to the tapes. Think about it. I'll leave my number with your counselor. He'll always be able to get in touch with me. If anything you've told me isn't true, let me know?"

She nodded.

The next day was a busy one for Jay Newell, and he had no chance to return a call left on his answering machine. The call was from Cinnamon's counselor at Ventura.

Weekends in the Newell household were devoted to kids or dogs—or both. On October 29, Jay Newell was getting ready to take his children to a Halloween parade. He nodded yes or no to last-minute decisions on costume additions, dodged big yellow dogs galloping through the recreation room, and reached for the phone.

It took a while to summon Cinnamon to the phone in her counselor's office. Newell had no idea what she had to tell him. He wasn't really apprehensive.

Her voice came through, that small, childlike voice. She might have been ten years old from the sound of her.

"Jay?"

"Yeah. What's up?"

"You said to call. What are you doing?"

"Getting ready to go to my kids' parade. What are you doing?"

"I have something to tell you."

". . . Yeah?"

"I was ashamed before—to tell you the whole truth. I just couldn't say it," she said softly.

"What?"

"Jay . . . I did it. I was the one who actually pulled the trigger. . . . I lied to you. I'm sorry."

Newell hung up the phone. How did he feel? He wasn't sure at first, and then he felt a surge of relief. Deep within his bones, he knew he had just heard the final truth, the terrible secret Cinnamon had kept submerged for years. They would no longer have to worry about the tiny tears in the fabric of Cinnamon's story. Jay Newell had been fairly certain that David himself hadn't pulled the trigger; the man was a coward.

Patti's part of it all was still a question mark.

He remembered Cinnamon saying plaintively, "Daddy, does it *really* matter who pulled the trigger?" Under the law, it really didn't.

When Jeoff Robinson heard that Cinnamon had admitted the shooting, he remembered being "totally relieved." Both Robinson and Newell were still convinced that David had set the whole murder scheme in motion, orchestrated it, pulled all the strings, and let someone else do the unpleasant part.

That still made him guilty as hell in the eyes of the law. It is a tenet in California law (and in almost every other state): "vicarious liability." Principals who aid and abet a crime are equally guilty. Anyone who aids, abets, instigates, promotes, or encourages murder is guilty of that murder, just as guilty—if not more so in some cases— as the actual killer.

32

I T   W A S Halloween when Newell headed north to see Cinnamon once again, this time to hear it all. The air grew crisp. It smelled like Halloween, and he thought of how excited his own kids were. His oldest daughter was now the same age Cinnamon had been on the night Linda died. Fourteen. He remembered now the Ocean Breeze neighbor girl's scorn as she laughed at Patti and Cinnamon for dressing up on Halloween. They had had such precious little time to be children; that night in 1984 had to have been one of their last attempts.

Patti, at least, must already have been playing David's "killing" game.

Even though, as a detective, Newell was eager to hear what Cinnamon had to say, this day would be rough. She looked pale and frightened when she came over from her "cottage." Newell took his time. They had lunch and talked about easy things, until he could sense that Cinnamon was relaxing.

Cinnamon nodded as he said, "You have told me that it was not true what you told me about being outside. Okay, everything else that we talked about that day—when Detective McLean and I came up here and talked to you on August 10—was *that* true?"

"Up until the time of her death—yes."

There was a symmetry in the way all of them—Cinnamon, Patti, David, Art Brown—had reconstructed the day of the murder, right down to the menu and the games they had played. That was the easy part. But now Cinnamon had to continue on with a chillingly true version of what happened next.

"Linda was already in the room taking a shower. . . . Me and Patti were left in the living room. My father was in there for a little bit, talking to us. He had left the living room and went in there with Linda. Me and Patti were in the game room; we were watching TV."

It was quite late—she wasn't sure of the time, but they had been watching music videos. "Patti fell asleep on the floor; I told her to get up, go sit on the couch. . . and we ended up going in Patti's room to go to sleep. . . . Later on that night—I'm not sure how long it was, but I know I was asleep—he came in and woke us up."

"Okay. Who came in?"

"My father. . . . He came in, and he woke us up, and he said, 'It has to be done tonight.' And he was to the effect saying that, if I loved him, then I would do it for him."

Newell had to help Cinnamon so much more in this interview. Her words and thoughts did not emerge easily, but caught themselves up and held on tight. It was too ugly to think about. Too ugly to say out loud.

"The same thing that he had talked about before then? Right?"

"Right. He was saying basically the same thing . . . and he said it had to be done tonight. And I was asking him *why?* And he just said, you know, 'Otherwise, I won't be here anymore. Linda's going to kill me.' "

"Did you guys stay in the room, all three of you, or what?"

No, Cinnamon remembered that David and Patti had talked softly between themselves, and then her father had instructed her to go with him. He led her to the door of his bedroom and told her to be quiet. "He went in and got some bottles and brought them out."

She didn't know what they were, just some prescription bottles. Then her father had led her to the kitchen and told her to get a glass of water.

"I took them. . . ."

"Took what?"

"The pills he told me to."

She had no idea how many pills there were. "He told me to take them. I took them. I was having a hard time swallowing them. He just said, 'Do what you can do.' I told him I felt like it was going to come back up again."

But she had kept swallowing pills, handfuls of orangey pills, and some other kinds of pills from a new vial her father opened. When she was done, he led her back to Patti's room. David was inflexible. "My father was talking about 'it has to be done tonight. It *has* to be done *tonight*. . . . And one of you is going to have to shoot her. That's the only way I can think of. That's the only way it's going to work.'

"He was telling me I had to shoot myself to look like I tried—like I was sorry."

Newell's surprise showed in his voice. "Shoot *yourself?* What do you mean, shoot yourself?"

"He told me that after Linda was shot—to shoot myself in the head with the gun."

"Well . . . Okay. How were you supposed to do that? What did you say to that?"

"I told him I was too scared."

"How were you supposed to shoot yourself in the head, Cinnamon, and not get hurt? I don't understand."

"He said that if I shot myself—just to where it would nick my head and make it look like I tried to kill myself. But I told him no, I was too afraid. And he said, 'Well, then, if you don't want to do that, then we'll just go with the medication.' "

There had been no gun in sight at this point, and Cinnamon didn't even know if there was one—beyond the big guns in the locked gun case. David explained to her that he was going to leave the house, "and when he came back, you know, if it wasn't *done*, then he was going to leave . . . leave me. Or he was going to kill himself. Or do *something*. Or Linda was going to kill him. He kept on saying that. And he said, 'You girls—' He was telling us in a way, 'You girls take care of business while I'm gone.' "

And then David had handed Cinnamon a brown-upholstered pillow from the back of his recliner. "And he told me to hold it over the gun. And I was going to ask him, *'What gun?'* 'Cause I didn't have the gun."

Cinnamon had no idea what the pillow was for. "I assume it was either to stop the noise or to stop powder or something from flying."

David had gone back once more to confer with Patti about something, and then he had left the house. "Patti went back to her room, though I was, like, blown away. . . . I went in the room and Patti was already sitting down, and she was moving the towel and started wiping off the gun."

David had given *Patti* the gun. And the towel. Newell asked where the towel had come from. Cinnamon didn't know; it was just a folded bath towel, with a gun between the folds. "I know she was wiping off the gun, but I'm not sure if she wiped off the bullets or not."

And then Patti had handed the gun to Cinnamon and asked, "Daddy told you what to do with the pillow?"

"She handed me the gun," Cinnamon said almost whispering. "I'm not sure if I pulled it—the thing—back or if she did it. . . . She was—she was telling me all I had to do was pull the trigger. . . . She told me to go in, go in. Daddy told me to. And fire the gun."

This was obviously so exquisitely painful for Cinnamon. Until this moment, as her words fell into the October air and became solid, living entities, none of it had been real. She could take that night and turn it around in her mind and cover it with veils so that the terrible part was deep inside.

Tears ran down her face.

"Okay," Newell said quietly. "So tell me what you did."

"Otherwise, Daddy would, you know, be hurt. So I . . . I went. I was holding the pillow the whole time—with the gun. I went in Linda's room. I don't know where I was standing in the room, 'cause I was too scared. I just fired the gun."

She could not remember if she was close to Linda or close to the bed. Yes, she knew where Linda was supposed to be in the dark room. She knew which side of the bed Linda slept on.

"I was just walking in the door. And I fired the gun. . . . I just fired it in that direction. And the pillow got stuck in the gun when I fired it. And I didn't know if I had broken it . . . so I ran back to Patti's room."

Patti had Krystal in her arms, as David had told her to do, so that she would be safe. The two teenagers, with the baby between them, had struggled with the pillow to pull it from where it was caught against the hammer. The trigger wouldn't work, and Cinnamon was sure she had broken the gun.

And then there was a roar that deafened both of them for moments. "And somehow I pulled the trigger. . . . I was afraid that I hit Krystal 'cause Krystal was right there near the end of the gun. . . . I was panicking."

Newell shuddered to think of how close it must have been. With Patti and Cinnamon hysterically tugging at the pillow and the gun, and the baby between them. It was a miracle they hadn't shot the baby.

"The baby looked like she was scared from the noise too. . . . Patti mumbled something about 'that's an accident.' . . . The gun wasn't supposed to go off in her room. She was pretty upset about that."

When their ears stopped ringing, they heard another sound, a whining, animal-like sound.

It was Linda. Linda wasn't dead. It was an eventuality that no one had thought of.

She wasn't really saying words, but she was half-crying, half-moaning. It didn't sound like Linda, but there was no one else in the house except the three of them and the baby.

Cinnamon was holding Krystal, trying to calm her after the loud boom in her ear, and Patti held the gun. Cinnamon watched Patti pull the hammer back. "She handed it back to me, and I handed her Krystal. And she told me to go—go in there. And it—when I entered the room, I didn't hear Linda. I didn't hear anything."

"She wasn't saying anything, moaning or anything?" Newell asked.

"No, I didn't hear anything. And I just did what I was told to. And I fired it again. And I was . . . the noise again . . . my ears were ringing. And I couldn't concentrate. And I was scared and I dropped the gun."

It was quiet in the master bedroom now. Cinnamon couldn't see anything. She had seen nothing this night in the dark room. She had just fired the cocked gun Patti gave her.

Twice.

Like an automaton, Cinnamon followed the rest of the plan. She took the "suicide note" from her trailer and went out to the doghouse.

Sitting with Jay Newell, Cinnamon sobbed as she let herself, finally, go all the way back to March 19, 1985.

"Did your father or anyone ever come out to that doghouse while you were out there?"

"No."

"Okay, Cinnamon, now I need to ask you . . . when you told me and McLean that you were outside when you heard the shots, after hearing your dad drive away in a car—why did you tell me that lie?"

"Because I'm ashamed that I loved my father enough to shoot Linda. I'm *ashamed* of it. And I didn't want to admit it. Or accept it."

Cinnamon had called her mom and told Brenda the truth before she had called Jay Newell. And Brenda had told her it was all right— that it was time for her to tell the complete truth.

Cinnamon was drained now, shivering from the shock of it.

"You know how many of those pills you got down?" Newell asked.

"No . . . He was just telling me to take as much as I could swallow."

"Did your dad ever show you how to hold the gun to your head . . . and shoot yourself?"

"Not that night, but he did before. When he was talking about me writing the note. He was talking about how I'd have to make it look like I tried to kill myself."

". . . You knew that it would be pretty damaging to put a gun to your head and shoot, didn't you? I mean, your own head?"

"Yeah . . . and I was wondering why he wanted me to do it."

Newell knew it would be well nigh impossible to "just nick yourself" when pointing a gun to your own head, short of shooting an ear off. Her father had told her to take what might have been a lethal dose of pills *and* shoot herself. She still believed he had wanted it to "look like" she had tried to commit suicide. Clearly, her death was an integral part of his plan. And yet, while Cinnamon could now shoulder the blame for what she had done, she seemed unable to face the possibility that her father had intended for her to die. It would be a long time before she could face that.

She did not remember talking to anyone at the hospital. She did not remember talking to Fred McLean. She only remembered being sicker than she had ever been in her life, and waking up, a long time later, in the hospital. From that moment on, Cinnamon Brown had been locked up, both physically and in a blurry cage of her own making.

In a sense, she was free now.

33

ON THAT last Saturday in October when Cinnamon talked to Jay Newell, David Brown wrote a letter to Patti Bailey. It was not a particularly unusual letter; indeed, his correspondence repeated the same themes continually. This was only one of dozens, sometimes two or three a day, that David sent from the men's jail to the women's section. Syrupy, seductive, manipulative letters and cards, along with articles on marital fidelity—reproduced from the *Catholic Digest*—all designed to quiet Patti's anger at his betrayal, and to melt her heart.

If David Brown faced further peril now—and he did—it would be from Patti. Cinnamon could be written off as "evil" and a "flake," but if Patti should defect from his kingdom, David's version of his fifth wife's murder would vaporize.

David *knew* Patti—what she felt, what she thought, what she hoped for, what she feared, what she dreamed of. He himself had programed many of those dreams into her mind. He played on that in his laboriously written letters.

> Hello, Patti,
> I hope you are doing well. I really wish I could see you and talk to you face to face. I could tell for myself that you are O.K.

David urged Patti to read the Bible, especially 1 Corinthians, Chapter 13, verses 1–13. *Particularly* verse 13. He even told her what page to look on in the jail Bible. Verse 13: "And now abideth faith, hope, charity, these three; but the greatest of these is charity."

She was not sure what he was asking for. His letter was very kind, very friendly, very cautious.

> I have been reading a lot of religious materials. I am relearning things I learned as a kid. Yes—I was a kid once. I truly hope you liked the cards and poems. A friend told me you weren't sure where a couple of things came from. Well, they came from my heart and my mind. Pretty sad—huh?

David concluded the letter by telling Patti she should let him know if his letters were irritating her, in which case he would stop writing.

A humble David was alien to his young wife. David was many things—but *never* apologetic and never humble. Patti wanted to believe that he had changed. But "charity"? Did that mean he wanted her to give him what he wanted most now—freedom?

Patti received two kinds of letters from David—as if he were really two entities, a split personality living in his jail cell: "David" and "Doug."

"Doug" was the lover. A different Doug from the one David had fabricated as Heather's father. This Doug was kind and loving. "David" was just David, working hard to convince Patti that he was on her side and that they must stick together. He underlined the word *family*. Patti had longed to be part of a real family her whole life.

Aware of Patti's distrust of him after she had heard his taped voice blaming her for the murder, David backpedaled smoothly. In another letter he wrote:

> No one wanted to hurt you at all. There was no way to know that anyone but Cinnamon would hear those conversations. But you should know better than anyone that Cinny never liked you and that we have always told her what she wanted to hear. She had confessed to killing Linda at least a half dozen times with you there at visiting, so I didn't mean anything when I said those things. I was just trying to play along with whatever game she was playing this time.

David continued in the same vein, stressing his belief that Cinnamon was a thief. He was, once again, "programming" Patti with the information he wanted her to remember. He reminded her that Cinnamon had grown "violent" when he had told her he trusted Patti more than her. Cunningly, he tried to reel Patti back to him. She was the only one who mattered. "You were trusted as much as anyone else I ever knew—probably more." Referring to the tape where he blamed Patti for the murder, David assured Patti that he was lying to Cinnamon so she would not be angry with Patti.

David was a man with interchangeable masks. Whomever he was talking to or writing to at any given moment was the one he trusted, the one he loved. All others were traitors. He was cunningly persuasive both in person and on paper. David stressed to Patti that the Family—Krystal, Heather and David—could not bear to be separated from her. Cinny, however, was expendable.

Patti, we all love you—don't let them win! Don't you see that this is what they and Cinny both want? To separate us and make us hurt each other and drive us apart? . . . I will come to your trial and explain in front of God and the world how I feel about you and why I lied to Cinny. I don't care if it hurts Cinny, my family, and your family. The only family that matters is ours.

Patti longed and needed desperately to believe the letters that came to her in the intra-jail mail. No one knew she and David were man and wife. He would not claim Heather as his own. Locked up, completely alone, Patti read David's words and "Doug" 's words and tried to believe.

Doug still wants to know about you too. He loves you, Patti, more than life itself. No past. Only future. Let your marriage grow. We can still be family. You are the only thing that makes losing Cinnamon seem not so bad. My parents know that you are a lot more of an honest loving person than Cinny ever could be. She is evil.

David encouraged Patti to think good thoughts, reminding her of good times ahead with the kids at the park to help her "through this baloney." And David held out more promises. His incarceration had forced him to have "control of my body." His colitis had been his excuse to stay home and refuse outings that Patti begged for. Now, he wrote, he could control both his bowels and his panic attacks. If she would only come back to him, he would take her and the little girls to the San Diego Zoo and to Sea World and to the park.

"Doug," the romantic persona, sent flowery cards with lovers walking into the sunset hand in hand.

> Love is forgetting
> and forgiving,
> Love's a delight
> the reason for living,
> Love can exist in a smile
> or a sigh,
> *Love is simple—you and I!*
>
> Love from,
> Doug
> by David

It was November 3, 1988, and David was getting antsy, despite his assurance that he had his panic attacks under control. Patti's short letters told him little about her state of mind; he looked for affirmation in them and found only suspicion.

His letters focused heavily on Krystal and Heather, on how much they *needed* Patti. Above all, David repeated that he would never testify against her—no matter what the authorities tried to do to him. He hinted that *he* was being offered "a deal" if he would testify against Patti.

"I swear to you, before GOD, I will do everything in my power to clear you and me. I pray you believe me. I swear Patti, I mean it. I'll do anything you want or need to help you!"

As his wife, Patti could not be forced to testify against him and could not reveal private marital discussions. That was good. However, if he *acknowledged* their marriage—and Heather—that might give Jay Newell and Jeoff Robinson more ammunition. Patti was still voicing her hurt at the interrogation tapes, and she would not tell him what he wanted to hear—that she would never testify against *him*.

"Are you willing to testify for me?" he wrote finally. "You should know that neither one of us has bad things to say about the other—only good. At least, that's all I've got. . . . Oh yeah, we can have our trials together, if you want! Do you? I might feel a lot better if you would. I'll ask my attorney. You ask yours."

David promised a new beginning, far from the ghosts of their past. They would move. Maybe to Oregon. Maybe Arizona. "A new life sounds great—to see new country—a little farm—animals—the kids playing. Happy."

"We fight together and win or lose together."

David pulled out all the stops—or rather, "Doug" did:

[Doug] knows that having to sneak around in order to be loving is what hurt your relationship together. But not any-more. . . . Doug says that since the attorneys will know, he will tell his family about you and him being married—O.K.? . . . Doug said, 'All I care about is our future to-gether.' . . . Personally I can see in you the same things Doug does. Boy, does he ever think all the time about you, that's why I know how much he *loves you and means it!* You are: Loving, Caring, Thoughtful, Sharing, Warm, Mature, Sweet, Innocent, Pure and Beautiful. I can see also why he's so proud to have you as his wife. . . . I think he's one of the Luckiest Guys on Earth.

And now finally, obscurely, David (as Doug) even accepted Heather. "Don't ever take her away from her father. She needs both parents, you know that yourself. Doug really Loves You and Heather more than *anything*."

"Doug" ended with a poem part of which read:

> Our Love is Not in the Past
> It Is In The Future
> Our Life Together is Not in the Past
> It Too Is In The Future
>
> With Love to Patti
> From Doug

David began to sweat in earnest when Patti did not respond to *that* letter. Someone was messing with her mind; he was sure of it. And one morning in early November, David's worst imaginings were confirmed. That may have been the first time he fixed on Jeoff Robinson and Jay Newell as his most treacherous enemies.

That morning, there was to be an appearance in "West Court" (in Westminster, California) prior to the preliminary hearing. David was annoyed anyway because the buses pulled out of the Orange County jail for West Court at six in the morning, and he had to wait in a holding cell for more than three hours.

On that morning, David saw his wife for the first time since their arrest, and to his horror, Patti was talking to Jeoff Robinson and Jay Newell. He would have much preferred to see her chatting with the devil himself. He was afraid she would give away their marriage, which no one had yet discovered. No, it was more than that; without him to censor her, Patti had a tendency to say too much about everything.

For David Brown, who had not even wanted Patti influenced by school authorities, the thought that she was talking to the man who arrested him and the man who might one day prosecute him was maddening. The memory of the three of them talking ate away at his confidence in his hold over Patti—no matter that he could not hear what was said. They might undo everything he had accomplished in his letters.

Even so, David still believed he could bring Patti back with his words. He wrote to her on November 9, 1988, resorting to leverage that had never failed him—his imminent death.

Dear Patti,

I sure hope everything is OK. I hope you are getting my mail. I'm sending 1 or 2 letters a day and not getting anything back. If you don't want me to write—let me know.

David assured Patti that he was "going crazy" waiting to hear from her, wasting away from the misery of being in jail. He was losing a lot of weight, and he expected that he would probably die soon.

"The pain is unbearable," he told Patti. He said he prayed to God daily, hoping to be saved before his condition deteriorated further. "To tell the truth, I am proud and surprised I lasted this long. . . ."

David was as transparent as cellophane. He hinted that he had found a guy in jail who would help him commit suicide.

That will be pretty soon now. Wish me luck! . . . Maybe I'll be watching you guys grow from up there—I hope. Take care. God Bless,

David.

It was clearly a suicide threat, designed to twist the screws even deeper into Patti's conscience. But she did not respond. An astounded David was still alive and well three days later, bombarding Patti with letters.

He did not know that it was already far too late.

On November 7, 1988, at eleven in the morning, Patti Bailey, accompanied by her attorney, Don Rubright, had—at long last—begun to do exactly what David had repeatedly told her to do—"Take care of yourself."

Cinnamon's Halloween confession to Jay Newell was detailed and believable. If Patti's recall correlated with Cinnamon's, the prosecution case would gain credibility exponentially. Patti did not *have* to talk to the Orange County DA's team, and they had offered her nothing. But she was a woman on fire, betrayed beyond betrayal. She was ready to peel another layer off the cocoon that still shrouded the complete truth.

Jay Newell asked Patti to go back to 1985. "How old were you at that time?"

"I'd just turned seventeen."

"Sometimes it may hurt to say things—if it does," Newell said, "tell me it's hurting, but you have to say it anyway. Okay?"

"Okay."

Newell asked Patti to do the telling, to choose her own words. She was not a particularly verbal young woman, and the words came haltingly at first.

"David said that he needed help working in Randomex, and he recommended that I quit school and stay home with him and Linda and have me and Linda both finish our high school degree at home."

Patti had been living with David and Linda for five years by then. The situation in the home seemed like a "normal . . . pretty happy family." But David had begun to suggest to Patti that Linda was "changing," that she wouldn't go horsing around with them on ATVs anymore, and she wasn't much fun. "So it was always me, David, and Cinnamon.

". . . And then he said he was scared that something was going to happen to him. I don't know how he led up to it, but he once suggested to me . . . when we were out in Calico . . . I had the gun on my lap in the backseat of the four-wheel drive—that if it accidentally went off . . . Linda would die and I'd be able to take care of everything."

David had said similar things before, but Patti had always thought he was joking. "I mean like when my mom used to always make jokes like 'I'm going to kill you, you brat!' "

They had been up by Yucca Valley when David made the "joke" about the gun going off. "We were on the freeway coming back from Calico . . . he didn't turn around and say it. I think Linda went in . . . to get a drink and he . . . just made a joke of it. But . . . I *did* have the gun on my lap. . . . Umm, that was the gun that, I think, Linda was killed with."

"Did he make the suggestion about accidentally shooting Linda or making it look like an accident more than once, or was it—"

"Yes."

"Okay," Newell said quietly. "Where were you when these other suggestions were made?"

"All over. We'd be in the car . . . the most recent one was before she died, that day she died. We were supposed to pull over, um—shooting, back out at Calico, and he used to make suggestions like if she fell off the cliff. I mean nobody'd ever suspect anything, um, if one of us took a running charge . . . that she'd die that way."

"Took a running charge?"

"No. If you're sitting on a cliff and she's looking out at the cliff, I mean, if one of us came by and ran and she fell."

Patti was talking about Monday, March 18, hours before Linda died, the day they had all planned to go out to Calico, but stayed home instead because it rained.

"Was he talking to you? Or you and Cinnamon?"

"I don't remember if Cinnamon was even around. I mean, there was always times that he'd let her in and then he wouldn't. Because he'd say, 'Well, she's too young . . . she'll go off and say something.' . . . Sometimes he'd talk to me all day about it, and then the next day Cinnamon would be part of it, and he'd make me tell her what he discussed with me so she understood."

As long as Newell had been working on this case—three and a half years now—there were still times that it seemed almost surrealistic to him. What he was hearing wasn't unexpected; he had somehow known it. But the subtle brutality of David Brown's killing plans, spoken out loud, chilled his blood.

Patti brought up the trip home from the hospital months before Linda died. "We went out to see my brother's new baby. He [David] made suggestions that, if we threw her out of the van, it'd look like her door flew open. . . . So I don't know if one of us came up with the idea or if he came up with it . . . and neither me or Cinnamon could because we were in the back. . . . After we got home, he said, 'Well, good thing we didn't 'cause the light would of went on and they would of caught on to that—"

"What light went on?"

"You know when you open up your car door, the light goes on. He said the people from behind could have seen what was going on."

". . . And he made it sound like it had to be done that day?" Newell asked.

"He *always* made it sound like it had to be done that day. He was always scared that someone was going to kill him or whatever."

As Newell questioned her for dates and times, Patti recalled that there had been long periods when David dropped the murder planning. He talked a lot about killing Linda when they lived in Yucca Valley, but then went for six or seven months without mentioning it when they lived in Brea. The real campaign to do away with Linda had taken shape in Garden Grove after they'd moved to the house on Ocean Breeze Drive in 1983.

David had once again begun to be afraid Linda would hurt him.

"He would discuss with you that Linda was trying to hurt him?" Newell asked.

"Linda or Alan."

"Okay. What would he say about that?"

" 'They're getting weird. Linda's not being the same person she used to be.' He was afraid that this family was going to be separated. There was a big tree in the back and ivy. . . . I think his dad would be on the lookout to see where Linda was when she came home. We'd be in the backyard talking, and he'd say, 'Well, someone could always shoot her and . . . hide the gun in the ivy.' "

Patti was quite sure that Arthur Brown had overheard David's plans that day. She estimated this plan was about a week before Linda died. "It wasn't very often that he'd let it go too long. I guess he wanted to keep the idea that the family had to stay together fresh."

Newell explained that Cinnamon had talked about suggestions that *she* had made about how to kill Linda. Had Patti ever come up with ideas?

She was quiet for a few moments thinking. Not one of the three men listening could easily place this sad young woman in the role of a conniving murderess—any more than Newell and Robinson could envision Cinnamon in that sense. They were pawns. But why? Cinnamon loved her daddy.

Patti? Patti was still something of a mystery. *Why* should she have been so slavishly devoted to the man the other jail inmates had nicknamed Hunchy?

"Ummm. Suggestions?" Patti mused, remembering. ". . . You know how they had that cyanide thing? When the Tylenol thing was going on?"

"Oh," Newell said, nodding. "I see, yeah."

"The accidents—or the people that did that in the pills . . ." She trailed off for a moment.

"The cyanide . . . who brought the suggestion up?" Newell asked.

"I think it was on the news and I think we both—or all of us— just looked at each other and thought, 'Why not?' . . . I mean, he got a lot of ideas from watching the news."

"And what about you? Do you remember any specific ideas you had yourself?" Newell asked. His deep voice was still easy, conversational.

"Umm, there was the time that David asked me. Well, I was *told*, however you want to put this, that if she was suffocated, that'd be an easy, painless death.

"But no. He usually woke me up at night talking to me. One night, I was told that if I just went in the bedroom, stuck a pillow right there while her back was turned . . . and just shot her, then nobody'd hear anything, and it'd be done and over with. . . . I couldn't do it—so I left."

So *Patti* had been David's original choice to kill Linda.

Jeoff Robinson had a few questions, but he and Newell assured Patti they weren't ganging up on her. "Patti, for a period of time, when David was suggesting these things, you say that you weren't taking him seriously?"

"No . . . I wasn't taking him seriously."

"All right," Robinson continued, "but there definitely was a time—up to the murder—when that changed, when you *did* take him seriously?"

She looked into Robinson's eyes and answered slowly, "When I *did* take him seriously? When he [really] did have me go in the bedroom with the gun. I mean, I had the gun in my hand and everything—and I just couldn't do it . . . *that's* when I started taking him seriously."

"Right. And what did he have you do—physically?"

"*Physically?* Patti suddenly looked alarmed, and then she understood what Newell was asking and relaxed.

"He just said okay, you can go in there. You can hold the pillow, hold the gun with the other hand, and you can shoot her and not very many people will hear it. And then you can just claim somebody came in and robbed us."

Robinson wondered just how it was that Patti had apparently agreed to participate in the killing.

"I never agreed. It's just the fact that he hands you the gun and I did take him ɜerious then, but I never actually agreed. . . . I felt *obligated*."

"Patti," Robinson said, "let me ask you a question. Yes or no. Okay?" She nodded.

"Whether you did it out of obligation—you told us that one of the things he has done continually is lay this business on you about keeping the family together, the guilt, he would be gone and so forth?"

She nodded again.

"Is that true?"

"Yes."

"All right. After he laid all that guilt on you about keeping the family together, *did you*—along with Cinnamon and David—agree and participate in the planning to kill Linda?"

She stared back at him. This was the question of questions. This was no-going-back time.

Robinson and Newell stopped breathing.

"Yes."

Once that single word was out, Patti Bailey Brown wanted it back. For minutes, she crept back to the safety of maybe believing that David Brown had only been joking.

But they all knew.

And gradually, with her own attorney listening, offering her a glass of water from time to time, Patti verified Cinnamon's confession. There were very slight variations; some details were agonizing for Patti to discuss. When she was asked what happened to the brown pillow David had given Cinnamon to use as a silencer, she looked blank for a moment. And then she said, "Oh—that was from David's recliner. He used it to support his bad neck. He just put it back on the chair, until it wore out."

Patti understood, as she answered Newell's and Robinson's questions, that one day she would have to tell this awful accumulation of truths in a courtroom.

Robinson leaned toward Patti and said quietly, "Patti . . . why did you want Linda dead at that time? What were your reasons? Was there something . . . for your own . . . reason, or was it because David had—"

"David had us believe that the family was the most important thing, and she was going to disrupt the family and we'd never be able to be a family once again. . . . And then he said, 'Well, see, *your* family was never'—*my* family was never a family. And this was our true chance of being a family and having everything that a family was supposed to have. And she was going to interrupt that if he had to leave, or they were going to get a divorce. Then we'd never be a family again. . . . I guess I needed the fact that there *was* a family. . . . He said Cinnamon wouldn't serve that much time. We'd all be happy, the four of us, forever, from that day forward. No matter what."

It was almost like a cult. A little family cult.

Where there was no room for Linda any longer.

Patti knew little about insurance or finances. She was aware of one insurance policy on Linda's life.

"Did you ever go into a joint [bank] account with David?" Newell asked.

"Yes. Not by choice—but yes."

"You know how much money was ever in that account?"

"It varied. When I turned eighteen, I had a trust account from the Bank of America that had twelve thousand dollars in it. David said his name had to be put on it because I couldn't handle money. . . . It was my way of paying him back, so I had to pay bills. After that money was gone, my account was closed."

But there had been other accounts. David put money down on a car for her, but she had to make the payments. "I had to make the payments by doing housework. . . . There was another time when I had seventeen thousand dollars from a car accident—that opened up another joint account. To pay bills, to buy furniture, to buy the stove, the refrigerator. There was a time I received social security for my dad, five thousand dollars, and that had to go into David's checking account."

David had held all the money strings in the family. Always. No one but David knew how much money he really had.

". . . Patti," Donald Rubright spoke up, "do you realize now that—ah, you feel like you were duped?"

"Hell, yes. . . . I knew someone was going to die, but I didn't realize that it was going to hit so close to home."

"You didn't realize what it was going to feel like afterwards?"

"Yeah. I didn't realize what it was going to be like. . . . I honestly believed that the four of us would maintain a decent family and nothing was ever going to tear us apart."

". . . *After Linda was killed?*" Newell asked incredulously.

"Yeah, like a little fairy tale."

"And, in summing up," Rubright said, "I mean—just so we can clarify—what you did—you *realize* was wrong."

"Yes."

"All right," Rubright continued. "In retrospect, you feel that you did it for reasons that you thought at the time were right, but now you know you were wrong."

"Yes."

"Do you feel remorse or sorrow for taking part or participating in the killing of your sister?" Rubright persisted.

"Yes. After she died, I felt so bad, so upset. . . . And I did try to kill myself because I couldn't live with the fact—knowing that—I had something to do with it. . . . And I couldn't live with it. I mean,

I lived with it, obviously, but there are several occasions that I did try to kill myself."

Unconsciously, Patti rubbed the white scars circling her wrists as she spoke.

Had she told the truth? Yes. Most of it. There had been no opportunities for at least eighteen months for Cinnamon and Patti to speak together alone. Each had now talked to Jay Newell, Fred McLean, and Jeoff Robinson from their own independent recall. And each remembered that ugly night and the pathological schemes leading up to it in almost exactly the same detail.

Neither had anything to gain by talking. Cinnamon had already lost, and Patti had much more still to lose.

And still, when Robinson and Newell listened to one replay—and then a second and a third of the interview with Patty Bailey Brown—they detected pauses in odd spots in the conversation, and a certain sense of holding back and holding in.

Patti had not told it all. Why?

David Brown had no idea how much Jeoff Robinson and Jay Newell now knew about him. He recognized them as enemies, certainly. And he hated them for what they had done to his life. With every setback, the bitterness he felt toward the deputy DA and the DA's investigator grew and festered.

Patti was the key to his freedom. He knew that, and he still believed that Patti could never be turned against him. Patti would protect him to her dying breath. He wasn't sure why she wasn't answering his letters and cards, but he knew she would come around.

He wrote his wife an original poem and sent it through the jail mail system. He could picture her with tears in her eyes as she read it. Patti was a sentimental fool. An excerpt began:

> MY LOVE IS A PROFOUND HEARTACHE
> AND THE FIRE OF MY SOLE [sic] LOST
> WHENEVER WE ARE APART
> THE VERY FIBRE OF MY BEING
> BECOMES LIKE DUST.

Patti read the poem, and then she turned it over to the DA's office, along with all the other letters from David.

And now, she told them part of what she had held back. "He's not just like a father to me. We got married two years ago."

Fred McLean called a friend on the Las Vegas police force, who checked vital records and called back. It was true all right. David Arnold Brown and Patricia Ann Bailey were legally married and had been since July 1, 1986.

Even so, Patti was still hiding something. All alone in jail, without the beeper summoning her, without David constantly reinforcing what she was to believe, she began to wonder if she should tell it all.

34

B Y   T H E time the Orange County Jail was serving a Thanksgiving turkey dinner, David Brown at last sensed that he was not going to win Patti back with his poems, love letters, and suicide threats. Something had changed, and someone had turned her against him. Patti was the loose cannon who could link him irrevocably to Linda's murder. In all the years he had known her, Patti had never had any power at all, except that which she drew from him. Now she did. The reality was that she would go down *with* him if she talked too much, but David figured she was too dumb to realize that.

There was no telling how much damage Patti could do before she was effectively muzzled.

David Arnold Brown was always a man easy to underestimate. His face and build were not prepossessing. He was not a snappy dresser. His grammar was flawed. But none of that seemed to matter. A look at what he had accomplished in a decade illustrated clearly that Brown always got what he went after. Those who fell out—or were forced out—along the way mattered little to him.

Now, David wanted to be free. That certainly did not set him apart from his fellow prisoners. But there were few men among them who would go to the lengths David would go to achieve his goal.

He had visitors, he could call outside—if he called collect—and he was rapidly making "friends" on the inside. He had found his footing, and he was advancing, albeit in increments small enough that his enemies had, at first, no warning of his dangerousness.

Patti Bailey knew all too well how David could work people. Some of the women she was living with in Module G-4 were giving her the creeps too. They came back from visiting and said that David's attorney was asking about her—that he wanted to know why Patti was testifying against David. They seemed to take delight in her fear. Everybody in the Orange County Jail apparently knew her business and kept track of what she was going to do. She knew David used money to get people to do what he wanted. And she had learned that money would buy you anything you wanted in jail.

Jay Newell talked to one woman who had been approached by an attorney on David's defense team. She confirmed that he was seeking information on Patti Bailey, that he wanted to know what Patti was going to say in the preliminary hearing. "But I told him he was there to talk about my case—*not* Patti Bailey's—and that was that."

Nevertheless, Patti was moved into protective custody on November 17, 1988. Frightened as she was, Patti had not changed her mind about testifying.

On Monday, November 28, his first day back from the Thanksgiving Day holiday, Newell spoke to Patti once more. Don Rubright, her attorney, was present as he talked with Patti about some of the myriad secrets David had ordered her to keep, including the identity of "Doug," who kept appearing in David's letters to her.

Patti half-smiled as she traced the existence of Doug. "In June of 1986, David asked me if I wanted to become Krystal's mother," she explained. She had agreed readily and signed the prenuptial agreement without even glancing at it.

There had never been a real Doug, a revelation that scarcely surprised Newell. "David was very upset after some investigator from the DA's office talked to Grandpa Brown. [Patti had no idea that Newell was that investigator.] He tore up our wedding license and the agreement. When I told him I thought I was pregnant a month later, he wanted me to have an abortion. I wouldn't—and that's when he made up 'Doug.' He told me to stick to that story."

Patti admitted that she already had "a physical relationship" with David at the time Linda was murdered. Newell could see this was an area of questioning that threatened her, and he pulled back—for the moment.

Patti was more comfortable talking about David's panic after Cinnamon had summoned him to Ventura. She described him as "very scared" by Cinny's questions. Up to that time, David had told Patti that they had to do whatever it took to "keep Cinny in a good mood—so she wouldn't tell the police or anyone."

In the forty-four months since the murder, David had continually repeated to Patti a litany that went: "You know Alan and Larry are really the ones that killed Linda" and "You know, I didn't want it to happen." Patti said, "He kept trying to put those thoughts into my head—even though I knew they weren't true."

But once Cinnamon demanded answers, David panicked. Patti herself had been ordered to tell Cinny she would take her place. "He told me to go to the authorities and make up a story that didn't involve him."

"Is there anything else about the night Linda was killed?" Newell asked. "Anything that you can remember now?"

"Just that David told me if the police asked about the pills, to say that they were taken from his top drawer."

"Did you see those pills or the bottles?"

She shook her head. "No."

There was something else that concerned Patti. She had been receiving visits from a man named Wallace DuPree*, an old friend of David's. These were "official visits." (At the Orange County Jail, an "official visitor" does not have to adhere to visiting hours and can talk as long as he or she wants. Attorneys and ministers enjoy that status.)

Patti remembered Wallace DuPree as a man who had visited David when they lived on Summitridge—when she was pregnant with Heather. She was under the impression that he sold used cars and was somehow connected to the computer business, but she wasn't sure; David had always made her leave the room when DuPree arrived for a business consultation.

Now, she was surprised to find that Wallace DuPree was a Mormon lay minister, and that he had come to visit her—as he told her he visited David—in the capacity of a preacher who was there to help both of them. DuPree, however, appeared to Patti to be acting as an emissary from David.

DuPree had penetrating blue eyes, stood well over six feet tall, and weighed 235 pounds. He talked to Patti persuasively, his face full of concern and sorrow. "He keeps telling me that David will probably get the electric chair if he's convicted, and that David would never testify against me, so how could I even think of testifying against him?"

Brother Wallace Elmore DuPree was a master of slathering on guilt with one side of his mouth, and promising wondrous rewards out of the other. He showed Patti a thick roll of bills and told her that David would buy a car for Mary Bailey (who was supportive of Patti at a time when she had almost no family backup.)

"He told me he was authorized by David to put money on my books [in her jail account] if I needed any." DuPree also told Patti that David trusted him so much that he had given him power of attorney to take care of David's business.

Newell was intrigued by the sudden appearance of the Reverend Mr. DuPree. As far as he knew, David was Catholic and had no interest in the Mormon religion. He ran a computer check on DuPree, and found that, although he had no status as a minister, he did have a rap sheet with the California Bureau of Criminal Identification that trailed back to 1958.

The fifty-year-old "preacher" who spoke about what a pity it would be for David to die in the electric chair (although California administers the death penalty by cyanide gas) had many sins of his own to do penance for. DuPree had been arrested for burglary, grand theft, illegal pricing, failure to appear, assault and battery, resisting arrest, battery on a police officer, receiving stolen property, fraud, fraudulent tax returns, and three counts of child molestation.

Newell wondered what business David Brown and Wallace DuPree had discussed after Patti was banished from the living room on Summitridge. It was clear now, at any rate, that David was employing whatever means he could to pressure Patti to come around to his side.

Patti, who was already nervous in jail, believed that if David wanted to get to her to do her harm, he would find a way. The preliminary hearing was only three weeks away. Patti planned to testify against her husband, but she had told no one in the jail. No matter. It seemed to her that David knew everything that was going on, that he could even see into her mind.

Brother DuPree brought up facts about Linda's death that only she and David knew. Now, DuPree was trying to get her to go along with an intricate call-forwarding plan that would eventually allow David to talk to her on the phone.

She didn't want that. David could spin her around with his words. She didn't want to hear his voice anymore.

DuPree, aware that the police were checking out his religious affiliations, suddenly stopped visiting Patti.

But David Brown was unconcerned. There were other ways to go.

35

THE CHRISTMAS season of 1988 was to be a bleak holiday for Patti and Cinnamon, and unsettling for David. Jeoff Robinson for the Orange County DA's Office and Joel Baruch representing David Arnold Brown squared off in the preliminary hearing in Superior Court judge Floyd Schenk's courtroom on December 19. This hearing would determine whether David would go free or would be bound over for trial.

Robinson had beaten Baruch twice before, and Baruch wanted this win badly. He was up and confident; he had just come off a successful defense case where the jurors agreed with his arguments so wholeheartedly that they had not only found his client not guilty, they had also joined Baruch *and* the client for a celebration after the trial. (The defendant was tried for murder; he had killed the man who beat and raped his fiancée. The jury agreed with Baruch that his violence was justifiable.)

Robinson, on the other hand, hadn't lost a felony case in years. No matter, he wanted this win more than any other. In January 1989, when it was over, Schenk's courtroom would still echo with the arguments, accusations, and insults that had caromed off its walls.

Returned to Santa Ana to testify, Cinnamon Brown had her first glimpse of the outside world in almost four years. There were so many changes. She clung to Fred McLean and Jay Newell like a child would on the first day in a new school.

It was Monday, December 19, when Cinnamon told her story in court. She admitted she had lied four times about the night Linda Brown died, first to protect her father and Patti, and then because she was ashamed. But there was no artifice now. Cinnamon dabbed at her eyes as tears streaked her cheeks.

David Brown, in a neat black suit and tie, sat impassively at the defense table, handcuffed to his chair. He stared hard at Cinnamon, but she would not meet his eyes.

Cinnamon told the whole story, just as she had told Newell and Robinson, but she was interrupted repeatedly by Baruch, who complained she was speaking too softly, and that Robinson was "leading" the witness.

Robinson fought back, accusing Baruch of trying to disrupt Cinnamon's testimony, and of playing to the television cameras and reporters who were packed into the front row.

"Mr. Robinson is a buffoon!" Baruch fired back.

Judge Schenk admonished Baruch and threatened to fine him $250.

The exchanges in the courtroom were pale compared to those outside in the hallway.

"You're going to get your petard handed to you," Baruch snarled at Robinson, mangling the cliché.

Robinson seethed, "You're the dirtiest, most unethical attorney I've ever seen."

The *Los Angeles Times* dutifully reported the state of siege between Robinson and Baruch. Indeed, it seemed for a time that the Brown murder case had fewer inherent fireworks than the attorneys' recriminations.

Cinnamon's first time on the witness stand was daunting enough. On the second day of the preliminary hearing, she faced cross-examination by Baruch, who attacked her mental stability. He recalled Cinnamon's imaginary friends of long ago—Oscar, Maynard, and Aunt Bertha.

Robinson objected, and Judge Schenk sustained the objection.

"Would you let me explain! *Would you let me explain?*" Baruch shouted at the judge, who was not pleased.

Instructed to control himself by the Court, Baruch cried, "Put me in jail!"

They wrangled, the deputy DA and the defense attorney. Baruch complained that he wasn't being given a fair chance to put on his defense, and Robinson accused Baruch of trying to intimidate Judge Schenk. "This is the way Mr. Baruch tries to get ruling in his favor."

Joel Baruch went too far as Robinson walked by him to make an objection. He turned and shouted at the prosecutor, "Sit down, Robinson!"

Judge Schenk rose up from behind the bench in a froth of black robes and fixed his eyes on Baruch. He held the defense lawyer in contempt of court. "I'll guarantee you one thing: you are not running the courtroom whether you think you are or not. I've had it with you!"

David Brown paled. Perhaps he had chosen the wrong defense attorney after all. He was paying enough for his legal defense—an estimated $250,000. That should have bought him a lawyer who wouldn't make the judge so angry.

Baruch's defense plan implicated Cinnamon and Patti as the sole participants in a wicked plot to kill Linda, and he presented his client as a man who had warned the teenagers that "nothing is supposed to happen" as he left for his drive to the beach. David Brown, he argued, was the innocent dupe, a man who had been desperately trying to hold his family together.

Cinnamon was not shaken by Baruch's concentrated attempts to trap her. When his questions were obscure, she simply answered, "I don't know." She admitted that she was "nervous in the courtroom," but she blamed her unease—not on Joel Baruch—but on her father. "I feel intimidated with him staring at me."

This was to be a long, intermittent preliminary hearing. It was obvious that Baruch wanted to start all over with another judge. He made a motion for recusal against Jeoff Robinson. (A recusal motion or hearing is designed to remove and replace the prosecuting team.) Baruch complained that Robinson was "overzealous and intimidating to me," making it impossible for him to defend his client.

And so the preliminary hearing was interrupted again—this time by a recusal hearing. Robinson, represented by attorney Tom Goethals, responded to Baruch's twelve allegations against him. Patiently, Robinson answered. Had he, indeed, called Baruch "the dirtiest, most unethical" lawyer he'd ever seen?

"Yes, I did," he responded calmly.

"Truth was my defense," he said later. "I meant it when I said it the first time."

The recusal was denied and they began again. With time out for Christmas, it was January 6, 1989 before Patti Bailey took the witness stand. She had nothing to gain by testifying, and much to lose. There were no "deals"; Patti had been offered neither a chance to "walk" nor "short time." She too was facing murder charges.

There was every chance that she would never get to raise her baby daughter.

What would Patti say? David tried to catch his wife's eye, but she would not glance his way. He was a little anxious, but not overly so. He had expected Cinny to burn him on the stand. That was no big deal. He figured that Robinson and Newell had really gotten to her, and besides, she would do anything to get out of prison.

But Patti. Patti was another story. Patti loved him. She *adored* him.

Sure, she hadn't answered his letters, nor had she opened up to DuPree, but when it came down to it, Patti wouldn't leave him. What would she do without him? Where would she go?

The most noticeable thing about Patti as she moved to the witness stand was her thick butterscotch hair, with heavy bangs and masses of long curls pulled back from her face with a clip. She was a pretty woman with a strong jaw, wearing a sweater of variegated colors. She trembled continually, as if her nervous system had been pushed beyond a point she could deal with.

David bade her with his mind to look at him, but she would not. He frowned slightly. That was not a good sign. As Patti answered Robinson's questions, David flushed. The bastards had gotten to her, all right. Each answer was worse, more damning than the one before. David stared harder at his wife, willing her to just shut up.

"We were always talking about ways to kill Linda," Patti testified, her voice quivering. "We were both discussing it."

Mary Bailey, Patti and Linda's sister-in-law—the woman with whom Linda had lived for years—sat in the gallery, her face a study of grief and horror. Her eyes flooded with tears and she dabbed at them absently.

Patti continued to avert her eyes from her husband as she related how David had instigated the murder plot and enlisted her, and then Cinnamon, to carry it out. "He said it would be best if we killed her first—before she killed him. . . . He didn't have the stomach to do it himself."

Patti said that she hadn't wanted to kill her sister. She had suggested to David that they might rig an accident so that Linda would be "crushed under a car" but would survive, paralyzed. "That way, she would always have to stay in bed," Patti testified softly. "She wouldn't be able to get up and around, but we'd be able to stay together."

And then, suddenly, Patti began to open up a secret door she had kept locked for half her life. She finally explained why she had become emotionally enmeshed with David Brown. No one—beyond herself and David—had had any idea until this moment of the methods he had used to trap and hold her.

Yes, Patti had loved her brother-in-law—"like a father"—until she was eleven, but those feelings soon became more complex. Patti's flat voice held the courtroom mesmerized, her words shocking and tragic. She recalled how David complained that Linda had changed and become "so moody and scary." Patti hadn't noticed anything unusual, but David was convincing. And then he captured the little-girl-Patti who had never been able to count on anything or anyone. He promised Patti that he would marry *her* someday, and they would always be together, no matter what.

"When was this?" Robinson asked.

"It started when I was eleven, and it continued until the day we were married."

David's manipulation of Patti was far more than promises of marriage one day. Patti shut her eyes as she revealed that David had sexually molested her—almost from the day she had fled to his home to escape the molestation she had suffered in her mother's house. Nothing had really changed. But David was gentler, and Patti began to think that maybe that was just the way things were. David had assured her that it was; most grown men helped young girls to grow up by teaching them about love.

Patti testified that David first encouraged her to perform oral sodomy upon him; he had assured her that that was the way she would develop into a woman. He also fondled her flat chest, offering to do so to help her to develop breasts. When Patti's breasts *did* bud and blossom, when her menstrual periods started, she testified that was simply more proof that David had been telling the truth.

When Patti was fifteen, she began to have sexual intercourse with her sister's husband. By this time, she was a willing participant. They grasped at every chance to be alone. "Anytime Linda left, there was usually some kind of physical contact. When she went shopping or took a shower," Patti testified.

Cinnamon had not been mistaken when she related the incident when she stumbled upon her father and Patti in the store, kissing passionately. She had seen one of a thousand stolen moments.

"I loved my sister, but I loved David even more."

David Brown stared at his wife, his mouth slightly open, his eyes unblinking, and shook his head slightly. He appeared dumbfounded by Patti's testimony.

On her second day of testimony, Patti discussed the final preparations leading up to Linda's murder. "We decided that Cinnamon should do it because she was young and wouldn't have to serve much time. We both assumed she'd be sent to a psychiatrist and sent back home. . . . [David] said he'd have to go out so that when he came home the car would be warm and he'd have an alibi for not being there."

Patti's testimony corroborated Cinnamon's. Both of the girls had now testified that David could never have been the shooter "because he said he didn't have the stomach for it."

Patti showed no emotion as she testified, even as she spoke of hearing Linda moan in pain after she had been shot. But when Robinson asked Patti about Heather, tears filled her eyes. She looked defiantly at David as she declared that he was Heather's father. She had not been with another man.

Patti described her husband as a man totally domineering, a man who controlled her life to the point that he would not let her visit her family or have friends. "I wore a beeper all the time, so he could page me. I wore it for when David needed me." If she didn't check in with him every fifteen minutes, David would be angry.

In his cross-examination, Joel Baruch suggested to Patti that she was lying about David because she was angry. Had not the DA's men told her that David had pointed at her as the killer? He suggested that Patti had been intimidated into testifying by the police and the prosecutors. Wasn't she saying what they wanted her to say because she wanted to get out of jail and be back with Heather before her baby forgot her?

No, that was not true. Patti stared back at Baruch. She was quite prepared to go to prison for her role in Linda's death. "At least I can go with a clean conscience," she said quietly.

Patti Bailey Brown had been David Brown's little homegrown sex object since she was in the sixth grade. Her participation in the plot to kill her own sister, the sister who was really a mother figure to her, was reprehensible. And yet, Patti had long since lost free will.

Patti had not seen her own father since she was a year old. As a little girl, she had felt so depressed that she tried to suffocate herself with a pillow. David had convinced Patti that her mother "sold" her to him, for $10,000—the "business loss" Ethel Bailey would sustain if she could not put Patti out for prostitution. There was no indication—other than David Brown's word—that this was true. Patti believed it.

From the moment David took her into his home, she felt no longer "like a black sheep," but "I felt like I had a family."

In an interview with *L.A. Times* reporter Eric Lichtblau, Patti tried to explain the hold David had over her. "He'd let me sit on his lap and give me attention and tell me I'm a good kid and go out and buy me clothes and make me feel real good about myself."

This was an eleven-year-old child, the very last of eleven children born to poverty. "He's a hell of a talker," Patti told Lichtblau. "If he told me the sky was purple, I'd have believed it. . . . David was everything to me. He was my family. If I thought he was going to be taken away, that'd be like pulling the plug."

With the threat of the loss of David, Patti had indeed participated in plans to kill Linda. She had yet to reveal the plethora of murder scenarios. Patti recalled later in jail that David had suggested running Linda down with an ATV in the desert; that Patti and Cinnamon ride their bikes to a shopping mall and shoot Linda as she shopped; releasing jacks holding up a car so that it would fall on her; running her over with a car; and creeping up on Linda from behind with a crowbar.

Patti had never allowed herself to think about what Linda's death would mean; she had blocked it off in a faraway place in her mind. But she had been so depressed. David had not allowed her to see a counselor unless he was in the room. Even after she tried to commit suicide by taking three boxes of No Doz pills and tranquilizers, when she slit her wrists, David would not allow her to be hospitalized. He was always afraid she would tell. And so, she could never confide her grief and terror to anyone.

Patti Bailey had belonged to David Brown, body and mind and soul, for a decade. He was the only male she had ever really known. He was practically the only *person* she had contact with. Was it surprising that she would have done almost anything to keep David safe? To please David?

On January 19, 1989, Judge Schenk ordered David Brown held over for trial for murder and conspiracy. Judge Schenk also decided that there was enough evidence to support a special allegation that Brown had plotted his wife's death for financial gain. This special finding meant that David Brown might face the death penalty.

On February 2, Superior Court judge Myron S. Brown set David Arnold Brown's trial date for March 29, 1989. Patti Bailey would face charges in juvenile court first, because she was only seventeen when Linda Brown was murdered. Jeoff Robinson said he would ask, however, that she be tried as an adult. Her age at the time of the murder ruled out the death penalty for the victim's sister.

36

B Y   T H E time David Brown had a trial date, he had already begun to construct other plans. As he was fond of saying, "I *always* know what I'm doing." David, in this new milieu, had new friends. Like a chameleon, he adapted quickly to any environment. The past did not haunt him.

Christmas in jail is, at best, a bleak holiday. Richard Steinhart, "Yahtahey" on the street, thirty-five, had found himself in any number of unusual spots on Christmases past—many of them plush and pricey, a good number of them dangerous. He hadn't spent a Christmas Eve "at home" in years. On December 24, 1988, Steinhart was arrested for probation violation and lodged in the Orange County Jail. In truth, he was picked up because he was a most important material witness in an upcoming murder trial (unconnected to the David Brown trial). The trial involved bikers and counterfeiting, and the accused were powerful men.

Orange County deputy DA Rick King needed Steinhart. He was a percipient witness; he had voluntarily told investigators of events in 1982 that strengthened the State's current case. The defendants had every reason to want Steinhart out of the way, and Steinhart had every reason to want to be swallowed up on the streets of some large city in southern California, to become anonymous. But Steinhart was in the Orange County Jail, Rick King would be able to find him when he needed him, and Steinhart would have to testify against some heavy hitters.

Actually, Richard Steinhart was a heavy hitter himself. He had been in jail before, and he knew the protocol better than a duchess going to tea with the queen. It was not his favorite place to be, but for the moment, it was probably safer than the streets of Orange County.

Steinhart was a long way from home, or where home had been once. Born on December 13, 1953, in Somerville, New Jersey, Steinhart never knew who his birth father was. His mother was an organist in the St. Luke's Methodist Church in Somerville. She played the massive pipe organ, dressed Richard in a "little Lord Fauntleroy suit," and did her best to raise her young son in the church, but he was such a wild one that sometimes she despaired. "My mom really did care about us when we were young," Steinhart recalled. "She worked two jobs—and it was really hard on her."

They moved from New Jersey, and Richard grew up with his mother and stepfather in Buena Park, California. He was a smart kid who did "very well in school" without really trying. He was a rebel, a hyperactive teenager who gravitated toward trouble.

Steinhart became a superb athlete. He was six feet tall, but he gave the appearance of being six three; his shoulders were massive and his chest was deep. He had black hair, long and combed straight back, a "cookie-duster" mustache, and a goatee. He was heavily tattooed and usually wore a black leather vest and Harley-Davidson T-shirt. When he was silent, he was unapproachable. When he talked, he talked ninety miles a minute. There was an electric quality about Steinhart, pure energy unfettered by restraints. He was always charismatic; he was often witty, and on occasion his intensity could intimidate.

If one thing only might be said of Richard Steinhart, it was that for most of his life, he had never been exactly what he appeared to be.

Steinhart attended Fullerton Community College where he played guard and tackle for a team that never lost a game all season. His interest in college dwindled as he began to make more and more money in other pursuits.

It was in martial arts where Steinhart soared. His stepfather had many master's belts, and Richard became the youngest certified grand master of the martial arts in the United States, a two-time national karate champion, and world champion of the UKKA, the Universal Kenpo Kung Fu Association. He had black belts in third degree—or higher—in six martial arts. He once had his own studio where he instructed his students in the techniques of laying a man out with quick blows from the hands and feet, graceful killing movements too fast for the eye to follow.

Not surprisingly, Steinhart was working as a nightclub bouncer by the time he was seventeen. He would become, in his own words, "a modern-day ninja. I worked for serious people in the 'professional' area; I was sought after as a bodyguard. I was an arm-breaker and a leg-breaker—if I had to be. . . . I had no feelings about what I did—not for the target; I was a professional." Steinhart would also become, at various stages of his life, "internal affairs officer" for the Hessian motorcycle gang, a bodyguard for comedian Jerry Lewis, a gunrunner, a drug runner, a drug *addict*, and a contracted hit man.

Steinhart worked, he recalled, for whoever had the money to pay him—the government, celebrities, the mob, the drug lords. Many of his contacts had the clout to keep him out of jail, and he often walked away when he knew he should have been booked. All it took was a nod and a word from the right agency or organization. But in the end, even Steinhart's high-placed government "friends" were telling him to clean up his act; they couldn't help him any longer, no matter how valuable his services were.

"I sold drugs for two years before I tried them," he recalled somewhat ruefully. "I wouldn't touch the stuff. Some of the clientele I worked for ran a half ton to a ton of cocaine. Everybody was trying to get me to sample it—but I held out. And then I tried it. Since 1978, I've put a half million dollars of cocaine in my own nose."

He also bought his mother a new upper plate and a house in Huntington Beach. "Those dentures made her the happiest I've ever seen her."

Steinhart's name was familiar to southern-California cops, and not because they admired him. Arresting Steinhart was a dicey proposition. He was almost impossible to subdue if he didn't care to go quietly. "I remember I got arrested once," he said. "They had me on my hands and knees, and this one cop came up and said, 'Mr. Steinhart, we know who you are—and if you move, I'm going to put a bullet in your head.' And I said, 'That's what I would do if I were you, 'cause *I know me!*' "

Steinhart could take on six or more opponents and "destroy" them. He had the respect of the Hessians; he taught them how to use martial arts, and he rode along with them on his big hog of a bike, his long hair streaming behind him. He always had a woman, or two or three.

But things started turning sour on Steinhart toward the end of 1987. "I was getting arrested for stupid drug beefs. I had no wife, no kid— I'd lost them. I had no place to live. I was burned-out. I always had girls who were willing to pay my way, but . . ."

Steinhart wanted to do "one big thing to pay for my kid," but he had somehow lost his timing, or maybe only his taste for the game.

On Christmas Eve, 1988, the newly arrested Richard Steinhart recalled that he just wanted to "mind my own business. I got my stuff and I went right to my cell that first night in there. I came out in the morning. See, there's a pecking system in the IRC. So I sat at the lowest table, kept my head down; I didn't want to mess with nobody." Steinhart had been booked into David Brown's module. By this time, David had been in the Orange County Jail for three months and had long since bribed and bragged his way to the head table.

Jail and prison culture spawns nicknames. Steinhart answered to "Goldie" when he was in jail. Other inmates were called Mouse and Cockroach and Shadow. It guaranteed a kind of anonymity. Outside this raucous boys club they lived in another world with other names.

The IRC prisoners called Brown "Dave" to his face; behind his back, they called him Hunchy for the awkward, hunchbacked stance he took when playing handball, his omnipresent cigarette clenched between his lips, or "Thurston Howell III" for the rich castaway—played by Jim Backus—in the television series "Gilligan's Island." David hated being called Thurston. But he had been quick to let his jail mates know that he was a tremendously wealthy man. They deferred to him, even as they scorned him.

"I remember the first time I talked to Dave," Steinhart recalled. "I'd been sitting there keeping quiet, but these guys were talking, pretending they knew karate and martial arts and everything. I was trying to keep my mouth shut, but it got my professional goat. Finally, I stood up and said, 'This is how you do it,' and went ka-ba-boom! The guy went, 'Arrghh,' and went down, of course, and Brown looks up and whistles and says, 'Hey, this is *my* kind of guy'—and invites me over to the head table."

Christmas Day dinner in the Orange County Jail.

Steinhart's "victim" got up from the floor holding his neck and muttering. The guards politely asked Steinhart not to demonstrate martial arts. "You move so fast, Richard; we don't know if you're just fooling around or . . ."

He nodded. They had a point, and he wasn't about to make the guards nervous.

Steinhart peeled his tangerine and observed the squat, pale man who had been so impressed with his physical prowess. This guy was no athlete. Steinhart saw at once that Brown was naive in the ways of the con, how he longed to be one of the boys.

"I watched him and studied him and saw that David Brown did not have a real friend in the world—probably never had. He was the abused little rag doll—the one with one eye—that the little girl gets mad at and socks a little bit, and then she goes and hugs the *pretty* dolls. David appeared to be that kind of person. Very vulnerable as far as being streetwise—but a ruthless, *ruthless*, person. Serious obsession. There was a very ruthless person inside."

Steinhart, operating then as the con man's con, *knew*.

Steinhart was looking for a chicken ripe for plucking, and the word in the module was that Brown was loaded. He was putting money on the books of many of the prisoners—for favors. Some bought him extra candy bars and cigarettes. (David went through his ration in no time.) Some hinted they might be able to help him win his case. For whatever reason, men with no money on their books suddenly had $10 to $50 deposited to their accounts by Arthur Brown (who used a number of transparent aliases). David convinced his family that his life was in danger, and that it was necessary to buy "protection" from other prisoners. Not until the advent of Richard Steinhart, however, had David found a man in whom he placed his full trust.

"David really opened up to me," Steinhart recalled. "And me just being me—from a professional side. See, you have to rise or lower yourself to the occasion and be what you have to be to any man to get what you can get out of it—whatever role-playing it calls for. It keeps you *alive*."

Another prisoner, Irv Cully*, who wore the "jacket" of a snitch, hovered obsequiously by David Brown's side. Cully had sat with David at the head table on Christmas Day because he had "seniority"; he had been there longer than anyone. When Steinhart joined their exclusive little group, he sensed he was in the presence of jailhouse power. "They had some little plan going—I didn't pay too much attention," Steinhart remembered. "Something with Cully and his girl, Doreena*."

Steinhart "worked" David Brown, listened with pretended fascination to his stories about his business successes, his great wealth, his women. He responded in just the way he knew would please Brown. He perceived that David longed to be a real man, macho, respected in jail. David, in turn, admired Steinhart, who came complete with *his* own set of war stories.

By the time Patti Bailey testified in January, virtually blowing David out of the water with her bleak confidences, David was ready to employ desperate measures. For the first time, perhaps, he realized that he might *not* be acquitted. His own attorney had warned him how good Jeoff Robinson was, filling him in on Robinson's track record.

It was unthinkable that David should go to prison. He had always told Cinnamon and Patti, "Keep me out of this." He had meant to be only the puppeteer, not a participant. He hadn't the stomach for up-close violence, and his health was far too fragile for him actually to serve time.

David didn't want to go to trial and have Jeoff Robinson cross-examine him. Nor did he want Jay Newell sniffing around anymore. Newell had found out things about his very private life that David thought he had covered over years ago.

Not to worry. David had a new best buddy who was going to take care of his problems. Richard Steinhart. Steinhart had convinced him that he could do *anything*—for a price—and what he couldn't do, he had the connections to have done. David and Steinhart planned how to raise money, escape, wreak revenge, *and* find a new life far away on another continent. "There was no emotion involved," Steinhart explained. "I wasn't his 'friend.' You might say I was an acquaintance. But he was talking big, big, *serious* money. Was I going to do what he wanted me to? Hell, yes. For three hundred thousand dollars, I was going to do it."

With Cully eavesdropping like some misplaced Dickensian toady, David approached Steinhart with plans. Steinhart hinted that he might be released at any moment, and David needed a good man on the outside. "David started talking about arson—to begin with," Steinhart recalled. "He wanted me to torch his motor home and the house. I was going to do that first."

Seeing Steinhart's apparent assent, David pushed a bit further. "Then he started with, 'What about an escape plan for getting out?' I just threw some stuff at him—just to keep him shut up," Steinhart said. "But *then* he started talking about escaping while he was at his dentist's office. Now, *I'm* serious, 'cause that *can* be done. I told him fifty thousand dollars, 'cause my buddies have enough loyalty to me— I'd planned on that—that they'd do it for me for free."

Each time Steinhart agreed to one of David's devious scenarios, the plans escalated. Soon, David had a four-phase program: he wanted his motor home and the Chantilly Street property burned for the insurance money—so that he could pay Steinhart; he wanted an escape plan in place when he visited his dentist; and he wanted three, perhaps five, people dead execution style. Any law enforcement officers who got in the way, would be, of course, expendable.

Once all this was accomplished, David would dispatch Steinhart to the desert where he said he had $3 million buried, and the two of them would head for Australia. David said he owned twenty-five acres of land there; they would ride into the outback, two on a motorcycle, free at last. They would eat all the pizza they wanted and drink all the beer they could hold.

The escape plan was doable. But if it should somehow fall through, and David *did* have to go to trial, the next phase would become operative. The two men and one woman David Brown hated and feared most in the world would be dead. Jeoff Robinson and Jay Newell would be first to die in David's plan. Then he wanted Patti, his treacherous wife, dead. He had no use for her; she was an anchor dragging him down.

David held fourth and fifth and even *sixth* possible victims in abeyance. One of the two hits on hold was Brenda Brown Sands and her second husband. David had warned Brenda he would never forgive her for having a baby with another man. It didn't matter that *he* had had five wives since Brenda, two babies, and countless sexual contacts. Victim five (and possibly six) was to be at least one of the Bailey brothers—Larry and/or Alan—whom David had come to detest.

"I was going to do it," Steinhart recalled. "It was no job for amateurs. I used to hate amateurs. . . . See, a professional will do it any way you want it to look. You can make a hit look like a gang did it— you do a drive-by. You can make it look black or Aryan Brotherhood or like some weirdo flake did it."

Richard Steinhart was prepared to do what he had to do—including arson, murder, and aiding and abetting escape—to get his hands first on the $300,000 David promised for the job, and *then* to go with David into the desert and find the boulder hiding $3 million. With his share of that, he could travel far, leaving behind the life that was rapidly closing in on him.

But Richard Steinhart had a stubborn, annoying streak of decency running through him, no matter how hard he tried to eradicate it. It surprised him, but he found it difficult to remain detached from David Brown. The guy was slime.

"I picked up a newspaper one day—I read about what David had done, the sexual molestation and stuff, and it just struck me in the heart—that piece of kaka. It really disturbed my spirit." Steinhart grimaced. "I had the full intention of when we got him out for the escape—getting him over in Australia, have the plane set, the monies transferred for cash reserves and all—of *taking* him to the outback, and he'd have been 'out back' with Crocodile Dundee somewhere being gator bait, 'cause I'd have took that three million dollars and buried him there and came back to the United States. With enough money, you don't need passports or IDs or anything, and I wasn't really that concerned about coming back."

The more Steinhart read and heard about David Brown, the more revulsion he felt. He was admittedly no angel, but he—like all cons—had his own ethical limits.

And David Brown had crossed far beyond them.

But then their bizarre plans took an unexpected turn. "I was in the yard," Steinhart remembered, "and I was telling Irv Cully how I really felt about Thurston, and he says, 'I'm glad you feel that way about it, 'cause I gave you up.' "

"*You what?*" Steinhart breathed. Cully, that fat little creep, had snitched him off? "I walked halfway around the yard, trying to absorb what Cully had just told me. My first impulse was to choke him, and I walked back. Then I said, 'You want to tell me that again?' "

Irv Cully had, indeed, gone to the authorities. He was a snitch—everyone who had spent any time with him in the Orange County Jail knew that. It was almost preordained that he would tell someone about David Brown's outrageous plans.

A snitch is a snitch.

Cully had palmed a note to a jailer, asking that he be "called out" for a dental appointment. Once out of the module, he announced that he had information that he was sure would be of urgent interest to the DA's office. Jay Newell talked to Cully on Friday, January 13, 1989.

Allowing for Cully's tendency to embroider facts a bit, the story that emerged was electrifying—and chilling. "David told me he has large quantities of cash buried in the desert, undeclared income from government and other business deals. He says the government has a 2.1-billion 'petty cash' slush fund that paid him. See, they paid him less than his ten percent fee but they paid him in *cash*."

Cully had no doubt that David Brown had enough money stashed to buy anything he wanted. He told Jay Newell that David had offered his girl, Doreena Pietro, a job. He had promised that she could live in the Summitridge house if she had herself arrested *first* so that she could be placed in Patti Bailey's jail module for a few days. "Then Doreena would be a witness for David and make Patti look bad, you know—like say stuff that Patti had said about doing the killing and all."

David had also had the Chicago data recovery firm that was handling his contracts while he was in jail wire Doreena Pietro six hundred dollars. If she wasn't willing to arrange to get booked in with Patti, she had promised to find another woman who would be—for a price, of course. "I told him that it would be five hundred more up front," Irv Cully explained to Newell. "Five thousand dollars total if the gal testified. I told him Doreena had found a girl and her name was 'Smiley.'"

David had instructed his brother Tom—who ran errands without asking questions—to put $500 in an envelope addressed simply to "The Girl" and deliver it to Pietro. It was to go either to Doreena Pietro or to Smiley—whichever woman broke probation and arranged to be housed with Patti Bailey. Tom insisted on a receipt, and Doreena signed the back of an envelope. She kept the money. Jay Newell didn't care about the money; he only wanted the physical proof that the envelope would give him. He didn't have it yet, but he knew it existed.

There was, of course, no Smiley—not yet. Cully and Doreena had made her up to get money out of David.

No problem, Newell thought. He would supply Smiley. He had to have David's voice corroborating the plot that Irv Cully had told him about. Although jailhouse snitches are often helpful in investigations, their value as witnesses in court was negligible. Now, all Jay Newell had to do was to find a woman who *was* willing to visit David Brown and pretend to be the mythical Smiley. She would, of course, be wired.

As Newell walked away from the interview, Cully took a deep breath and called him back. There was something more he should know. David had also come up with an extended surefire solution to the problem of Patti. "I think David's offered Richard Steinhart fifty thousand dollars to kill Patti when she gets out on bail . . . and if all else fails, David's going to give Steinhart all the money he has buried in the desert, to help him escape.

"He'll get another court order to visit the dentist. When he visits the dentist—that's when Richard would get him out—kill the deputies and all and help David escape."

Newell was aware that Irv Cully was a snitch, just as he knew that Richard Steinhart was not. Steinhart was not a game player. If he was involved with David Brown and making plans, that could mean real danger. When Cully revealed the magnitude of Brown's plotting, Newell knew that, if David had his way, a lot of people were going to die so he could go free.

• • •

When Cully broke the news to Steinhart that the DA's office knew about the plans to murder Patti and/or break David out, Steinhart regretted that he had ever met David Brown. "I was about to be called in to testify as a material witness in a big case, and I didn't want to do that. I was getting ready to call some of my government friends and have them get me out. But the way things were going, I knew I might end up in the witness protection plan in Akron, Ohio, or Walla Walla, Washington, and I didn't want to go to either of those places. David was ruining all my plans. I wasn't stupid. I knew that my next visitors were going to be from the DA's office. . . . I'm stuck. Cully's a self-confessed rat, anyway—but I kind of got a kick out of the guy. I was glad I hadn't choked him blue in the yard."

On January 18, while he was searching for just the right policewoman to play Smiley, Newell received rather startling—but intriguing—news. Richard Steinhart himself wanted to talk to him.

Steinhart admitted he was hoping for an immediate release—if the Brown case was "big enough." But he was realistic; he was more likely to be stashed away as a witness now to *two* major cases than he was to walk.

The next day, Newell met with Steinhart, who told him the details of David's escape plans. David was sure he could get a court order that would allow him to go to his dentist's office on Seventeenth Street and Tustin Avenue. He had asked if Steinhart had contacts that would help him escape. "He said he'd get me a car, and a place to stay when I got out—his house up on Summitridge in Orange was empty. He began to call me his 'protector' in here. He put money on my book. It was going to be fifty thousand dollars if I got him out of jail. Then he starts asking me how Patti could be killed—while she was locked up—'cause she's the only one whose testimony would really do him harm. He wanted to know what the cost of that would be."

David's other obsessive fear was about what the district attorney was doing to him. "He started talking about killing Patti Bailey . . . and *you*." Steinhart nodded at Newell, who kept his face expressionless as he absorbed this information.

"And then Jeoff Robinson too."

"What was he going to pay you for killing us?" Newell asked.

"Gold jewelry and maybe five hundred thousand dollars that he has buried in the ground. Plus he's got some one-of-a-kind coin collection and stamp collection."

The escape plan climaxed with Steinhart and David running off to Australia.

As Newell walked with Steinhart from the interview room, he turned to the big man beside him and asked, "Did you consider following through with the plan to kill Patti and me—and Robinson—at any time?"

There was a long pause, and then Steinhart nodded. "I wouldn't have done you *personally*, but I would have arranged it. By the time Cully told me he'd given me up, the plan was already in motion. Brown had arranged to leave some cash and a car to start things moving."

Early in January, David had instructed his family to take his Ford Escort up to Summitridge and leave the keys behind the house. They were to place an envelope containing $600 in the glove compartment of the car. David told his family not to ask questions. However, when Tom and Arthur went up to the house two weeks later to do some work on the pool gate, they found the car had been moved. The keys were in the ignition, and the Escort had a flat tire; the money was gone.

They didn't know who moved the car or took the $600. There was no way Steinhart could have done it; he was still in jail. Possibly, some joyrider had found the keys *and* the money.

(It was important legally that these preparations had taken place—*before* the DA's office learned of the murder-for-hire scheme. The $600 was pin money to David, and yet that $600 left in the Ford Escort was the single *overt* act that could prove David guilty of conspiracy. Later, when Jay Newell questioned Tom Brown about the money, he verified that David had told him to leave it in the car. And this first payment was weeks before Irv Cully went to the DA's office.)

It was a curious thing to hear your own murder plotted. Of all the precarious situations Jay Newell had found himself in, in sixteen years of law enforcement, this was, perhaps, the most surrealistic. Steinhart was so matter-of-fact that it was hard to disbelieve him or oddly, to dislike him. The man with the deep-set black eyes and goatee *was* a professional. Jay Newell, Jeoff Robinson, and Patti Bailey had been only "assignments" to him. And yet Newell sensed a kind of relief in this tough guy, almost as if he was glad he had been snitched off.

However, that left Newell with a problem. If Steinhart should back off from David Brown now, Newell might not know who the next "professional"—or the one after that—would be. He had begun to see how insidious the mind of David Arnold Brown was.

There was no one who was not expendable.

For the moment, the best plan would be to let David go on thinking that Steinhart was his man. As long as David believed he was covered, that the "hits" were in motion, he wouldn't look around for more assistance.

Newell told Steinhart that he would get back to him as soon as possible. Three days later, Jay Newell, Deputy District Attorney Tom Borris, Deputy Sheriff Dan Vazquez, and Richard Steinhart's defense attorney, Andy Gale, visited Steinhart again. Tom Borris would handle the alleged murder plot against his fellow staff members of the DA's office, while Jeoff Robinson moved ahead on the Linda Brown murder case. Borris *knew* Richard Steinhart; they had gone to school together, and then their lives had veered off in opposite directions. Fifteen years later, they recognized each other in the Orange County Jail.

Just as Cinnamon Brown's accusations had needed to be corroborated from David Brown's own mouth—Borris explained that Steinhart would have to be willing to wear a wire and have a conversation with David. "They told me this was it—I had to go with it," Steinhart remembered. "It was the only game in town. If I was in, I was in one hundred percent. I figured the worse that could happen was I'd end up in prison—as a snitch. I could take care of myself, and I was arrogant—so arrogant."

Steinhart agreed to cooperate and wear a wire. Borris told him that it had to be David who initiated the subject of contract murders and escape. Only then could a criminal case be filed for "solicitation to commit murder," and only then would Steinhart's testimony be accepted.

Things were getting heavier, Steinhart told the group. "Dave's now willing to pay one hundred thousand dollars up front to have Patti Bailey killed—while she's in custody. At the very least, he wants her to know that he can get to her anytime he wants." If Patti wasn't physically vulnerable, David wanted her mother and her brothers hurt—just to let her know he was out there.

Things, indeed, were getting heavy. It was time to move.

The wire for Steinhart had to be approved by either the Orange County Sheriff's Office, which supervised the jail, or the Orange County Marshal's Office, which is in charge of all prisoners while they are in the courthouse. The Sheriff's Office declined to become involved. Fortunately, the Marshal's Office agreed to help. Orange County Marshal Michael Carona assigned Capt. Don Spears to place Steinhart and David together, and to wire Steinhart.

With a lot of help from others, Newell and Borris arranged for Steinhart to be released from the Orange County Jail. But he wouldn't really be free; he would simply be transferred to another jail. Chief Grover Payne of Huntington Beach agreed to house Steinhart for a week or two. Judge David Carter, in Department 47, signed the order of transfer.

David Brown considered Richard Steinhart the closest friend he had ever had. No other man of such intelligence and strength had given him the time of day, but Steinhart was going all out for him. When David learned that Steinhart was being released on February 2, 1989, he knew he would miss the hell out of the guy. All the war stories, all the bullshitting.

But they would be together again, roaring around Australia, soon enough. Two adventurers . . .

David thought it was only benign coincidence when he found himself locked in the "Birdcage" holding cell in the basement of the Orange County Courthouse at noon on the very Thursday Steinhart was getting out. David actually had a hearing that day and was in the tiny lockup over the noon hour. Steinhart, of course, had been deliberately placed where he could talk to David—on tape.

The Birdcage was a bisected cell constructed of steel mesh. It had been painted so many times over the years that the layers of color could probably stand alone. Presently, it was a chipped, dull yellow. Each half of the Birdcage had its own bolted-down bench. Prisoners could not pass anything through the mesh, but there was a narrow space at the bottom of the divider, where they sometimes exchanged cigarettes, matches, notes. Men brought over from the jail waited in the Birdcage to go up to court, or to be transported back to jail. Outside, a ramp led to the glassed-in guards' station eight feet away, and in the other direction, stairs rose to the barred door to the sally port.

It was a noisy place, and the taped conversation between David and Steinhart was counterpointed with jail sounds—men shouting, doors clanging, laughter, profanity. Steinhart explained that he was getting out, but that David could call him at "Jackie's" house. Jackie was "Animal's" mother. Richard planned to use "Animal" for "the job." But for now David needed to know that their plans were set. They spoke in a kind of code, as men do who are locked up. Steinhart knew Newell and Borris would be listening to the wire tape, but he spoke obscurely because that was what David expected. ("The girl upstairs" was Patti Bailey; Jeoff Robinson and Jay Newell were referred to as "state attorneys," "the two cops," "my buddies," and "the local district guys.")

David was positive. He was ready. He wanted everything done as he had outlined. The only one he had not made up his mind about was the "one on Juno."

". . . Brenda?"

"Yeah . . . that's the only one there's any doubt about."

"So Bailey . . . ?"

"Yes, everyone else."

"Okay," Steinhart said, ". . . The two cops."

"Yeah."

"If upstairs [Patti Bailey] is done . . . how am I going to get the monies and stuff?"

"I'm working on it. I already have a check for seventeen [seventeen hundred dollars] with my attorney."

David explained that Joel Baruch was to get the money to either Arthur, Manuela, or to Tom Brown. "That's all I told him."

Steinhart said, ". . . I think we'll go with the dentist's office . . . we'll go with yours first."

David smiled. Steinhart would help him escape first, when the deputies who transported him to his dentist were caught unawares.

"The two cops . . . ," Steinhart continued.

"The girl?" David suggested. Patti's death was vital.

"The girl, yeah," Steinhart agreed. ". . . Anything else you want me to do for you?"

No, that would do for the moment. David wanted a telephone number for Jackie's house, and an idea of when he might be there.

"You know I won't be there," Steinhart said with a laugh. "Leave a message." He said he would pick his messages up at Jackie's until he got a phone. David seemed to savor every stupid little detail of this intrigue. Richard played along. "Okay, so you have seventeen hundred dollars for me. . . . You're working on that ten grand?" he said.

"I'm working on that."

"Now, do you still want me to go out and torch the motor home and your guesthouse? Doesn't that take thirty to ninety days for the insurance?"

"Not if it's totaled, no."

"All right so . . . you want Bailey first?" Steinhart switched the order of the plans.

"I would think so." David deferred to Steinhart always; he was, after all, the professional.

"Okay, but then I have to run my homework on some people to find out where I can get a sleeper in there to off her," Steinhart pointed out. "That's going to cost some bread. What about the maps? You going to give it to me right now for all the monies?"

The "monies" were, according to David, buried under a boulder in the desert. David's wariness seeped into his voice. If Steinhart had the maps and found "the monies," he could dig them up and be long gone.

David had never truly trusted anyone all the way.

Steinhart changed the subject. He wanted to know whom *he* could trust. David assured him he could trust Tom. Tom believed that Steinhart was only a bodyguard being paid to protect David and Krystal—from the dreaded Patti Bailey. Arthur and Manuela had been told the same story.

Steinhart could stay in the plush home on Summitridge—no problem. His cover story would be that he was there to protect the property. Not for long though. David was anxious to get going on the murders and the escape, but Steinhart cautioned him again that there was "homework" to do. He assured David he was trying to keep costs down. Calling in favors, he said, from old friends.

David wanted to speak again about the hits on "his buddies." Where would be a good place for Steinhart and his men to ambush them? The word was that Robinson and Newell were always coming and going from the courthouse, walking, jogging. There were lonely, shrubbery-shrouded passages where a hit would not be seen. "There's no problem, right?" David asked eagerly.

"There's no problem with me taking them out. . . . I'll kill them."

"Leave me out," David warned, suddenly nervous.

The payoff would come from the insurance after the fire. David figured $300,000 right away. (He didn't tell Steinhart it would really be $700,000—that he had upped his insurance by $400,000.)

"That's number one," David said, ticking off on his stubby fingers. The fire. ". . . Ah, I would say that the two cops and the girl should either coincide or be very close to each other."

Okay, say they saved the escape until after the murders. With Robinson and Newell dead, David would face a green team from the Orange County District Attorney's Office—a new prosecutor and a new investigator who would have to play catch-up in a hurry. That would put them at a great disadvantage in trial.

Unless they got to Patti before she was killed. . . . So Patti must not outlive Jeoff Robinson and Jay Newell by more than a few hours. "Whoever replaces them may want to go to talk to her," David reasoned hurriedly. "Yeah, it's got to be pretty close because if it happens to the girl first, it might make them aware."

David relished the thought that his tormentors would all be dead, and that he, the man still totally in charge, had a force such as Richard Steinhart to do his bidding. He dragged out the conversation, discussing victim combinations and times and who would die first.

And then the escape. It did not seem to occur to David that he might not be allowed a dental visit in the wake of the sudden violent deaths of the prime witness against him, the arresting investigator, and the prosecutor who had charged him with murder.

He had blind spots. He wasn't stupid. But he had blind spots.

He suggested that Steinhart use gas to set the fires on Chantilly Street, the reasoning of a rank amateur. Fires started by accelerants are the easiest for arson investigators to spot. Gasoline leaves behind a distinct tracing where it has been splashed.

While Steinhart expressed concern about who might be in the big house, David was not at all worried. The pool would keep the flames from leaping across. His parents and Krystal would have plenty of time to get out.

"See, I don't want to kill anybody I don't have to."

"No," David reassured him. "I'm getting them out of there as soon as I can. It doesn't have to be a total wipeout." But he warned Steinhart, "I do have various sophisticated alarm systems, so as soon as the smoke can be detected, it's reported directly to the fire department."

"Okay . . . I'll gas the whole house. I'll gas a good part of it." Steinhart knew better, but he was playing along.

David explained the way out for Steinhart. There was a wall in back, but he thought Steinhart could jump. No, maybe he should take a short wooden ladder with him. No, maybe a collapsible ladder.

"Well, how tall is this fence—six feet?" Steinhart asked.

"Ah . . . yeah."

"Ah, that's a piece of cake," Steinhart said. "Easy for me. I can still get over."

Inside, Richard Steinhart was laughing, but he repeated dutifully David's ponderous instructions. "Number one, the motor home and the house. . . . Number two, ah, depending on the order. It doesn't matter—the girl in G-4?"

"That's something you'll have to judge," David said.

". . . Brenda I can put on the back burner for now?"

"Yeah."

Steinhart needed money for throwaway pistols.

"And pizza," David put in, laughing.

"And pan pizza." Steinhart chortled in agreement. "Yeah, definitely put money in for pizza. Well, and I need that money for personal use."

A jailer approached the Birdcage, offering the two men a bathroom visit. As David was led out of his side of the Birdcage, the jailer whispered to Steinhart, "We need to know about the dentist's office and whether he wants them hurt or he wants them killed."

David returned. The man was a pigeon, Steinhart thought. It was fitting he was sitting in the Birdcage. David was locked up now because he had been trapped by the wire on Cinnamon, but Steinhart saw no suspicion at all in his eyes. Hell, David thought Steinhart was Superman, Bruce Lee, and the Hessians all rolled up together. Good old Thurston loved this too much to suspect his loyal bodyguard/hit man. His Goldie.

David hadn't missed a trick on his first visit to his dentist. He had memorized the whole damn place. He described the exact layout of the "miniplaza" where his dentist's office was. The front entrance on Tustin, the computer store, the doctor's office, the emergency treatment center, the walkways, the parking area. The walkway was hidden from the street; no one could see when the shooting started.

David had it all figured out. The deputies usually radioed the dispatcher when they turned into the driveway of the miniplaza to let him know they were arriving. "You know—whatever their language is—'Everything's okay and we're here.' . . . Both deputies sat in front and I sat in the back of the patrol car. . . . They walked me to the office . . . but first the driver got out. He walked up to the front parking lot, walked around, came back, and told him okay."

"So he does use a lookout first?"

"Correct."

David had noted that the deputies had checked all the areas around the dentist's entrance on his last visit. Then one walked ahead of him and one behind. "They both walked me in through the lobby. The dentist and her husband take me back without the deputies watching."

"What's that tell you?" Steinhart breathed with just the right touch of triumph.

"Man," David said, grinning, "that's why I'm telling you."

The deputies had locked David in the lobby and checked all the rooms. "When the dentist called me back to the chair, the deputy said they could just watch the door."

"Okay. So you don't have no problems," Steinhart said grimly. "I may have to kill a cop or two, and I just wanted to let you know."

"I realize that . . . I realized it all along. Better them than me."

They worried over the plan, the lookout points, the layout of the dentist's office. David gloated over each detail.

"All right, good deal," Steinhart said. "Well that makes it okay. I'm going to ask you something—professionally—and you got to—I just have to ask you this. See where your head's at. The two cops—the DA's—you want them dead . . . or hurt?"

David smiled at the ridiculous question.

"Dead."

David was concerned about other, more important, questions. For instance, he had not gotten his lunch. And he wanted to be sure that Steinhart understood that the real reason he had to escape from jail was for "my little girl, and I didn't see any hope."

"Right on," Steinhart said. "I'll get you out."

"Promise?"

"I promise. I will get you out of this."

"Guaranteed?"

"Guaranteed . . . as long as you can live with yourself after I kill the cops. As long as you can live with yourself—"

David laughed. "They won't—but *I* will."

"All right, you smart ass." Steinhart chuckled. "I think you like this."

"No, I don't," David argued. "But when it comes down to survival . . . Okay, I'm not egotistical at all. I think you know that. *But I think I'm worth more than they are.*"

And then two box lunches were delivered to the Birdcage. David was delighted to discover he had been given *four* packages of cookies. He and his very best friend discussed Australia and going to Disneyland, and pizza and Pee-wee Herman and guns.

37

D A V I D Brown almost choked up as he bade farewell to Richard Steinhart. Whether he was playing Steinhart as he had played everyone in his life—or whether he truly loved him—was an interesting question. In all their further conversations, which were also taped, David expressed affection for the big biker. He spoke to Steinhart as he might have spoken to a women he was enthralled with.

If David was depressed when "Goldie" Steinhart left, at least he reassured himself that Steinhart was out there working for him, orchestrating his escape and the destruction of his enemies. In reality, of course, Richard was locked up too—in the Huntington Beach Jail. The phone he talked to David on was wired to record. And Jay Newell would monitor every call.

"We had a cold phone connected in the Huntington Beach Police Department," Newell recalled. "That's a phone that absolutely cannot be traced. When David thought he was calling collect from the Orange County Jail to his good buddy on the outside, he was really calling the Huntington Beach police."

And so it began. Newell was about to become an information conduit between the man who had agreed to kill him and the man who wanted him dead. Although Steinhart wouldn't be free, he would have to report facts and details to David that made it sound as if he were out there circling Orange County, setting up the arson and murders that David had ordered. Steinhart also had to make David believe that the escape plan was in the works.

Since all Steinhart would "see" would have to come through the eyes of the DA's Investigator Jay Newell, Newell would, in essence, be helping to set up his own sudden "death." Sure, it was all playacting, but it cut close to the bone. The thought of what might have been if Irv Cully hadn't tattled never quite went away.

In every sense, this scheme was going to be a double reverse-twist, end around, gotcha.

Jay Newell was a big man, but he seemed somehow larger than he actually was, his stride as long and true as any rancher's back in the Oklahoma of his youth. He moved effortlessly, deliberately unhurried, silent. It was long-ingrained habit. He doubted that anyone would spot him as he strode across the Orange County Water Department land in the dark winter night. Employees had long since left the little service building at the end of the dirt road a hundred yards north of him. He had no company beyond an occasional wild creature startled into flight by his footfall. If anyone should approach him and question him, he carried ID that would satisfy the questioner.

Even so, on this mission he preferred to be invisible and anonymous. He was at his best on nights such as this. Newell was essentially a watcher, a listener, a quiet man by nature and by avocation. Silence had always served him well. He had reached this drab oasis in Anaheim by driving west along Ball Road, across the bridge that traversed the Santa Ana River, past factories and car lots, beyond the cement plant with its silos and chutes, and then suddenly turning right off the main drag onto a dirt road few knew about. He had parked his dark car on the hardscrabble sand and gravel of county property. Another eight seconds and he would have eased onto the ramp that led to the 57 North Freeway, the "Orange."

Now, he scarcely heard the steady hum of Ball Road as it merged with the roar of the Orange Freeway, a throbbing sound that never ceased. Every so often, there was a mufflerless engine as noisy as a helicopter or a scream of brakes that set his teeth on edge and his heart running double. With that background cacophony, there was no reason for him to walk quietly, nothing more than instinct.

Where Newell walked now, the night air smelled of almost-spring, car exhaust, fresh water from the reservoir beside him, orange blossoms, and burning rubber. Even though the homes ahead of him cost hundreds of thousands of dollars, they were continually dusted with the black powder of disintegrating tires, patio furniture and hibiscus alike sprinkled with rubber grit.

He could taste rubber, bitter on his tongue. Newell was not afraid. He avoided nasty surprises by being one step ahead of his adversaries. To the best of his knowledge, he was still ahead. He had scouted these acres in the daytime, but not as close up, and the dark made them alien. The slope toward the water was gentle, but half of its circumference was covered with broken rock and concrete, a quick way to break an ankle. He knew he would have to clamber up an eight- to ten-foot berm of earth just before he got to the backyard of *the house*.

His eyes adjusted to the dark as Newell drew nearer to his destination. The place loomed ahead like a fortress, a compound protected as if an assault were expected. Well, the assault had come and gone on the morning of September 22. And he had been part of the first enemy onslaught.

Chantilly Street South. A nice, upper-scale family street. He had gazed at 1166 Chantilly from the front and it looked only like a big pale-blue barn. Inside, it had been the same—square and dull. Now, Newell had to view David Brown's latest home as if Richard Steinhart's eyes stared through his own. Steinhart couldn't be here, but he would have to describe it board by board to Brown.

Their plan had Steinhart approaching from the rear of the property. From Newell's present angle, he could see that almost all the houses on the east side of the street were shrouded with trees and bushes and protected from four-footed and two-footed predators by a high chain-link fence along the reservoir property. Brown had gone even further and erected a cement-block wall *inside* the steel mesh barrier. A ridiculous barrier. A man with any vestige of muscle could easily heave himself over both the fence and the wall and into the backyard.

Newell cased the property from where he stood. The second home in the compound, the guesthouse that Brown had designed for his parents, had been almost completely invisible from the front. It was big enough to house a separate family. Most of the backyard space was taken up with a pool, and the rest with cement paving. Two white statues of Grecian maidens in togas stood beside the pool, glowing in the moonlight. California cyprus trees grew close to yet another fence, this one ensuring privacy from the street side of the property. He could make out tables with umbrellas, faded flowers in brick planters.

The place seemed abandoned, vacant. The lights were off in the guesthouse, and he could perceive only a dim glow deep inside the big house. Newell had to estimate how accessible this place might be for an arsonist. He had to find a way in, and a speedy way out, for the torch. There would be no second chance if his information didn't ring true. Brown was so cunning that he would catch Steinhart if he faltered in his descriptions.

Despite the property's abandoned appearance, Newell was sure that Manuela and Arthur still lived there with Krystal, and maybe with Heather too. He grimaced to think of what tragedy might result if he came away with flawed information. Brown would find himself another firebug, one Newell didn't know about. He saw that the expensive new motor home was parked snug against the guesthouse. If it went up, its carpeted walls soaked with gasoline, it would take the guesthouse, the main house, and maybe half the street with it. The resulting inferno would make all those cars on Ball Road and the Orange Freeway rear-end each other as the drivers braked to gawk.

Total destruction wasn't really what Brown had in mind; he had indicated on the tapes with Steinhart that he wanted the houses intact. The insurance payoff on the motor home would be adequate for the first payments to his "hit man."

But if it all went, Brown wouldn't be that upset. All of it was insured. The whole shebang. If the fire burned out of control, he would simply come into a great deal of cash from property that was no longer of any use to him. The money would only add to the wild time Brown planned to have cruising Australia with "Goldie" Steinhart.

A chill flicker of wind picked at the water of the reservoir, and Newell accelerated his survey, shivering. Okay, it was possible for the big blue house to be approached initially from the front; in the dark, if he was quiet and careful, "the arsonist" could slide past the palm trees growing close to the north side of the house. But he would have to be able to get out fast by vaulting the two fences and dashing around the reservoir. The neighbors were curious too. Strangers stood out. Newell made a mental note to remind Steinhart to mention the nosy neighbors.

He counted two cars, but there were supposed to be three. Did that mean the house was empty now? Or did it mean that only Arthur was out? Newell wondered if Brown really cared if the fire he planned took more with it than the motor home and the two houses, perhaps even his mother and father, and his two small daughters. The insurance money seemed all-important to him. It would provide professional fees; premium pay for the most dangerous crime of all.

Murder for hire.

It grew late. Even the cars on the freeway were few and far between. Newell retraced his own path, back through the dried-up oleanders, past the spill of broken concrete, close along Ball Road to the spot where his car waited. He would report back to Steinhart, and in the morning Steinhart would wait for another collect call from David Brown.

Newell looked back at the blue house and was seized with a grim vision of what could have happened. If Cully hadn't snitched Steinhart off, it might well have been Steinhart himself here now. Maybe only the motor home would have burned. Maybe the whole compound of blue buildings would have gone up like a pile of creosoted logs, the

Grecian maidens cracking and tumbling into the lonely pool. A total loss.

As he picked foxtails off his socks and pants legs, Newell felt a slight tightening in his gut. When he was in this mode, he did not often allow himself to think about any of it with emotion. He was far too caught up in the layers and twists necessary to make his own plans work. But sometimes it got so intricate, so convoluted, that the players blurred and changed. He was dealing with people he had no reason to trust. He was spending most of his time with an avowed hit man. All it would take would be one misstep to invoke disaster.

He shook his head sharply. He didn't let it get to him often. But now he did. The bleak irony of it caught Jay Newell unawares as he drove home too late to say good-night to his kids. If this had all worked out the way David Brown planned, Newell himself would have been right there on top of David's list, slated to be the first to get blown away when he least expected it.

Number one to get a bullet in the back of his head.

Richard Steinhart had been given no promises by the DA's office. He had only exchanged one jail cell for another. He had *used* people for years, but he had never set out to destroy them totally. For Steinhart, the frustration of David's killing plans became a kind of crusade. He did it all with words, using the details Newell had given him.

Steinhart proved to be a superb actor. He had lived by his wits for years, and he was good at it. Although he talked on the phone with David Brown from the Huntington Beach Jail, he sounded, always, as free as the wind. Sometimes Steinhart pretended that he was just coming in from a hot date; sometimes he pretended to be eating— pizza, of course. David missed pizza most of all the foods he was denied in jail. Steinhart yawned during some calls, as if he were talking in bed, and he pretended to trail the phone after him as he walked to the "kitchen" to get a beer out of his imaginary refrigerator.

And all the time he was in jail, surrounded by cops, working with Jay Newell to thwart David Brown David called collect to the "cold phone," and Steinhart or one of his "buddies" or "girlfriends" always accepted the calls. Every word was recorded.

David was anxious without Steinhart to talk to. He called him the day after he "got out"—February 3, 1989. He recognized the exchange as Huntington Beach and that worried him. He hadn't expected Steinhart to be in that area. "Who was that who answered the phone?" he asked suspiciously.

"Huh? That's Animal's old lady—I'm at Animal's house. He's good people."

"Had me kind of nervous to tell ya the truth," David said.

"Oh, you jerk—you stoop—you getting dumb on me or what? It's Animal's house—ah, Jackie's son. So what's happening, man?"

David had a tale of woe. The "district" guy was tormenting him. Now, there was going to be a custody hearing on Krystal.

"Well," Steinhart commiserated, "do you want me to do anything special to him? Give him an extra one for you . . . ?"

"No, no. I just—I'm starting to smile at the thought."

The tapes of the conversations between David and Steinhart revealed a paradox. For a man who had achieved a miraculous success in the business world, David Brown had not the slightest clue how to carry on repartee with another man. His world before jail had been dependent young women, family, and sycophants. They had all danced to whatever tune he played, and David seemed to have truly believed that he was larger than life. He still did—but he came across as a computer nerd bantering with a popular, macho man.

Almost. There was a sinuous stream of undiluted evil in David's conversation.

David boasted continually about what a funny guy he was—what "a ham," if given half a chance. "The life of the party, man." But his jokes, his attempts at bonding, *all* revolved around pizza and beer, with an occasional perverse reference to oral sex. This man who was such a card in his own domain demonstrated no more wit than the wife he was so determinedly trying to kill.

Steinhart laughed at the feeble pizza jokes, and then he asked how the "monies" were coming along. David assured him he was working on it.

"I ran into a snag," Steinhart explained. "I was out doing my homework. . . . It appears that the motor home you have—that, er, you're going to 'lend' me? It's really close up against the house."

Steinhart was playing it well, letting David think they had to talk in code. He, of course, had not been out to look at the motor home or the Chantilly Street house, or anything else the night before. Jay Newell had. Now, Steinhart sounded as if he knew the place by heart.

The guesthouse and the big blue house were only forty feet apart, he said, sounding just a touch concerned. "You're talking pretty high intensity fire there, boss."

David assured Steinhart he would have his parents stay away from the house the next day. Steinhart sounded relieved and described more of what he had "seen" the night before. "I was standing right across from the reservoir . . . went over that little chain-link fence."

"Right." David relaxed. Steinhart was taking care of business.

David listed the cars that should be parked in front. "There's a silver station wagon—a Nissan Maxima, and a black-tinted-window Taurus. . . . That's my newest toy. If one or the other of them is gone, they're not home."

"Okay. Now who all lives there?"

"Just my mom and dad are staying there, watching my shit, and taking care of my kid at my house."

Jay Newell, monitoring the calls, saw how clumsily David Brown planned. He could envision how it must have been with Cinnamon and Patti; David was always in a tearing hurry to have "things" happen, but he didn't track very well. Steinhart was smooth—mostly agreeing to everything, assuring David he was "cool."

Steinhart *did* bring up a vital area that David had completely overlooked. "I thought about this the other night," he said. "I don't have a fucking idea what they look like—your two buddies?"

"Well," David began slowly, "I don't know if you've ever done it before or not—but there's an old professional thing that I've seen in the movies, where you go to the library—and look up old newspaper clippings?"

David referred to Jay Newell as "the little guy—not *physically*— but I mean the least important."

Steinhart covered the mouthpiece and grinned at Newell.

However, David had seen an article in the *Orange County Register* about Newell's being named "California DA's Investigator of the Year." There had been a picture with that.

"What about the other guy?" Steinhart asked.

That was easy. The other guy—Jeoff Robinson—was in the paper continuously, David said. Every week, at least, with a picture too. Steinhart shouldn't have any trouble spotting him.

Steinhart pushed for physical descriptions, and David struggled to remember what his preferred targets looked like. Both of the "two cops" he wanted dead were over six feet tall. "The first one is brown eyes, mustache, well-groomed, ex–football player—but he's getting a bit of a tummy. You can tell he hasn't played for ages."

(In fact, Robinson's eyes were blue-green, and his stomach was flat as a board.)

Jay Newell got shorter shrift. "The other one is older," David began. ". . . Ugly as sin. Looks like a giant rat. Late forties, early fifties. Ugly mustache. Not as smart a dresser as the other one."

Newell was forty-two, and a good-looking man. But not to David Brown.

David suggested that Steinhart look in the yellow pages for their addresses. Steinhart rolled his eyes; David had much to learn in the murder-for-hire game.

David described his wife, Patti. "She's in K-14. They moved her. Bubble nose—"

"Bubble nose?" Steinhart asked, mystified.

"Yeah. It looks like two ball bearings stuck on the end of her nose. . . . You know, one of those real bony, gristly type noses . . . real dishwater blonde . . . Ah, her most gracing feature is her big lips . . . skinny . . . ah, blue eyes—"

"How much does she weigh?"

"From what I understand now, she's right at a hundred, maybe hundred and five tops."

Patti Bailey was a pretty woman. But she had become totally dispensable to her husband. He wanted her gone, as soon as possible, and had nothing kind to say about her.

She was as good as dead.

38

THE PLANS grew more precise, the phone calls more frequent. Steinhart, under heavy surveillance, went outside a jail cell for a short time on February 4. He met Tom Brown in back of Bennigan's restaurant in Westminster and collected the $1,700 David promised him for expenses and to buy two "throwaway guns."

And then he went back to jail.

David called Steinhart—collect—three times on February 3, four times on February 4, and twice on February 6. His goals never varied; he seemed to enjoy fine-tuning the details. Robinson and Newell were to be shot in the back of the head. As soon as that news reached the newspapers, Patti was to be killed. Steinhart assured David that he had arranged to put a woman into the Orange County Jail women's section who would kill Patti.

"Will it be self-inflicted?" David asked.

"No, I think she's going to back up on a knife."

"Okay! That's good, good! That's what I want!" David's voice was jubilant.

Steinhart explained that he had to have $10,000 right away. It would serve a double purpose. First, all he had to do was *show* the female hit-person the money, so that she would know it was waiting for her when she got out of jail after murdering Patti. Then he would use the same $10,000 to pay off Animal (who was played by Huntington Beach detective Bob Moran) and a second "hired killer" after they shot Robinson and Newell.

David arranged for his brother Tom to get another check from Joel Baruch. Baruch was allegedly told it was needed to buy rare coins for David's collection. David was working frantically to get the money freed up, and he was immensely frustrated. He was a man who had once had three phone lines at his right hand constantly. Now, he had to wait in the day room for a free phone and worry about the guards listening in. The logistics of keeping in touch with Steinhart and Tom Brown *and* his attorney were exhausting. He was used to being able to snap his fingers and have any amount of money he needed in hand.

"I hate having my life controlled by other people," he complained to Steinhart.

David didn't want to alienate Steinhart. He loved the guy, and he needed him. Steinhart with his "Plan A" 's and "Plan B" 's. Hell, Steinhart was even telling him that his biker buddies were making fun of him, calling him soft because he was doing so much for David— for nothing. David had to give him something back.

So he gave Steinhart *half* of the directions to his desert treasure. He had lied to Steinhart before about where the money was. "I tell everyone, you know, that it's out by Barstow?"

"Right," Steinhart said, waiting.

"It's not—it's only *up* that way. Do you know where Yucca Valley is?"

"Sure."

"Okay. Are you familiar with the road up the hill that you take to get to Yucca Valley? Do you go the Palm Springs route?"

"Yes."

David went into specifics. Steinhart was to follow Flat Land close to the windmill generators. After he passed the K Mart, he was to look for a bowling alley on the left, and then a "monument thing" that was either marked "29 Palms" or "Joshua Tree." "That's where you turn left—and that's where my property is."

Steinhart waited for the rest, but that was all David was going to give him for the moment.

Newell and Borris decided it was time to think seriously of getting Steinhart out of jail. He was being held as a material witness only. Newell didn't think that Steinhart was going to run on them, or on Rick King's case. He had kept all his promises so far. By now, Newell doubted that Steinhart had ever killed anyone. "He had a core of good in him all the time, but he tried to hide it."

On February 7, Steinhart appeared again before Judge David Carter. With Deputy DA Rick King's approval, he was released on his own recognizance. He was out of jail, under the California protected-witness program.

David Brown remained *in* jail, but he did not expect to be there long. He was smug in his faith in Steinhart. In fact, he felt that Steinhart was deferring to him more, that his ability to plan had impressed the hell out of him. Every time he got to feeling antsy, he reminded himself of that.

Things were dovetailing beautifully. They were almost ready. But Steinhart and David had to have two women to wipe out Patti as a witness—one to kill her, of course, and one to refute any of her taped statements and the transcripts of her preliminary testimony against David. In essence, even dead, Patti might still be a threat.

David waited eagerly for a visit from the woman Irv Cully called Smiley and Happy Face. She would pretend she had been in jail with Patti and testify that Patti was a liar.

On February 8, things really started moving. Even from jail, David felt that his executive ability was getting the job done.

First of all, David's brother Tom delivered $10,000 to Steinhart and "Animal" in the parking lot of Bennigan's at five minutes after three in the afternoon. Tom Brown, who worked as a foreman at All West Plastics, huddled behind the steering wheel as the big detective and the martial arts veteran approached his car. Animal leaned in to talk to him, while the guy with the ponytail and the biker's vest counted the money.

The transaction was recorded by hidden video cameras.

And at six-thirty that evening, David had a visit from Smiley. He marveled that Cully's girl had found him the perfect witness. In reality, the "Smiley" Newell had selected was a policewoman, an undercover narcotics agent, with a wire transmitter tucked in her bra. She smiled shyly as she told David that she had *already* been in jail with Patti, that she knew Patti slightly. That was great as far as David was concerned. There was no need for her to lie about being with Patti!

Smiley thanked David profusely for the $500 and said it had really helped with her rent. (In truth, Irv Cully's girlfriend had kept it.)

David was thrilled to see that Smiley was a looker. In fact—as Smiley asked him for details of how she was supposed to testify—he kept interrupting her with suggestive comments. He casually dropped the information that he was worth over five million dollars. "Every million of it is in cash right now. . . . The thing is, I didn't want to remarry until I find somebody I like. That's one of the things I like about you. What I heard—okay—is that your *preference* is a lot like my wife's were."

"Oh, really?"

"We had a dynamite marriage, I'll tell you."

He was speaking of Linda, his dead wife, not Patti—whom he denied ever marrying. "*She's* deceitful. She forced my real daughter to kill my wife . . . her little shtick was that *I* told them to. I *didn't* tell them to. I loved my wife."

Smiley played it dumb. Even her grammar was that of a woman who'd spent more time in jail than in school. She asked again and

again for David to explain exactly what she was to do. Slowly, it
seemed to dawn on her. "Okay," she repeated. "I tell them that when
I was in jail, I talked to Patti and she told me that you're innocent
and that she lied?"

That was it. David asked Smiley to repeat certain details, to expand
on her "friendship" with Patti. He didn't want her to lie really, but
he told her she would be saving an innocent man and returning him
to his child. He would be so grateful if she would talk to his attorney
soon and arrange to testify on his behalf.

"And there's no way that they could trace it back to me at all?"
Smiley asked. "How about if they want to put me on a lie detector?"

"It is not admissible in court," David said confidently. "Tell them,
'Fuck off, fella!' "

Smiley was worried about being recorded. She wondered if there
were little wires in the phones they talked on as they looked at each
other through plate glass. David laughed and shook his head. "No,
they can't. I hope they don't have a reason to—because that's why I
arranged to have my kid here." He gestured to where Krystal was
waiting with Manuela to visit him.

"*Why* did you have your kid here?"

God, the woman was dumb, he thought. That was okay. She was
the best-looking thing he had seen in months. "Because, hopefully,
they won't record me talking to my kid—you know, 'I love you,
Dada, I love you, Dada, come home, Dada,' and that."

Krystal was only four; already her father was using her.

And then, business over with Smiley, David turned on the charm.
"You're beautiful. . . . If you want to get to know me a little better,
I could take care of you for the rest of your life. I take care of people;
that's how I've managed to get ahead."

Smiley pretended to say a reluctant good-bye, letting David believe
she would be back. She left the visiting booth and went immediately
to have her hidden wire removed.

The net was tightening around David Arnold Brown.

He didn't know. Instead, David was elated. He had a new woman.
He was convinced she found him attractive and that she had been
interested when he mentioned the extent of his fortune. The next
day, he called Steinhart to crow: "I have a woman interested in me,
real interested." He seemed more excited about that than he was about
using Smiley to destroy Patti's credibility.

Steinhart feigned enthusiasm and told David that the second female,
the hit person, had been dropped off at the Orange County Jail. She

was, at that very moment, in Patti's module, ready to carry out her hit—just as soon as "the two cops" were killed. "Fortunately, this girl's done this—on the professional side . . . she's got a track record."

Patti Bailey's death was a fait accompli to David, almost old news to him now. He wanted to talk more about his new woman. "She's a good-looking gal."

"Right on." Steinhart laughed.

"She's got a mouth that God designed for blow jobs," David whispered.

Steinhart laughed. "Right on. Well, hey, we'll have to go out on a date when we all get out."

In his conversations with David, Steinhart sounded as laid-back and cool as ever. But in truth, he was not faring well on the street. His old weaknesses were tripping him up. Within twenty-four hours of his release, he was back with his woman, a woman who was beautiful—but heartbreakingly addicted to speedballs, a deadly combination of heroin and cocaine.

Steinhart stayed with her for three days and nights, all the while keeping up his wired phone calls to David, and his reports to Jay Newell. But he was losing ground. The woman was out of control, and Steinhart could feel himself slipping back. Moreover, Hessian bikers had located him, and they roared past the motel where he was staying, their engines a loud warning.

Newell shook his head remembering. "We were halfway through our phone trap with David Brown. We had to move Richard out of the first motel in the middle of the night because the Hessians who were looking for him had located him. Then he called us from the new place and said he needed help. When we got there, there was blood all over the walls, in the bathroom, in the bedroom. Steinhart's girlfriend was mainlining.

"He turned her in to save her life. It just about killed him. I spent a whole day either sitting in my car or in a coffee shop, with Richard crying and me trying to convince him he'd done the right thing."

And yet, talking to David, Steinhart sounded as controlled and happy-go-lucky as always. He missed only part of one long, bad day. Animal had to take his calls from David. Detective Moran—as Animal—growled at David, leaving him convinced that Steinhart truly had hired a killing machine.

By February 10, Steinhart had a new motel, and two new roommates, Newell and Tom Borris, who moved into a motel on the Pacific Coast Highway in Newport Beach with him.

It was almost time to trip the net release.

Newell, Borris, and Steinhart had a two-room suite. The hotel was instructed to accept collect calls from David Brown and put them on Steinhart's bill. When David called, his voice sounding more and more elated, Newell and Borris were listening in and taping his calls.

David Brown, the master manipulator, could never have imagined that his great and good friend Goldie was sharing a motel suite with his archenemies. But then Jay Newell had never imagined that he would be voluntarily sharing accommodations with the man who held a contract on his life. The hunted and the hunter had become friends, a friendship forged in the middle of a grueling investigation. Now, they slept in connecting rooms. Newell never had a nightmare.

Tom Borris did. Or rather, he would have had he been *able* to get to sleep. He woke Newell just before dawn the first morning and said he hadn't slept all night. He pointed to a figure standing in the open doorway between the two rooms, a figure silently watching them. "It was spooky the way he stood there," Newell recalled. "We figured either Steinhart had flipped or someone had managed to get into our suite."

One hand on his gun, Newell turned on the light.

The "assassin" was only their suit jackets hanging there in the doorway.

Officially, Newell and Borris had to be sure that Steinhart didn't disappear on them, while at the same time protecting him from a number of people who stalked him. Unofficially, the three men got along amazingly well. "I gave him a pair of shoes," Newell remembered. "All Richard had was thongs, and it was cold—our feet were the same size."

Steinhart was a fascinating roommate. "His stories were great," Newell recalled. "We didn't buy them all, but they kept us entertained. He'd told us he worked as Jerry Lewis's bodyguard, and we kind of doubted that one. And then, sure enough, we were waiting for Sunday brunch in the hotel and Richard sees some guy in line and waves him over. The guy's diamond-studded, and he greets Richard like an old buddy. *Then* he pulls out pictures of Richard and Jerry Lewis!"

Borris and Newell wore "soft clothes" and blended easily into Steinhart's lifestyle. So well, in fact, that Deputy DA Tom Borris was offered a chance to buy the "best Thai sticks you've ever had" by a man who sat on a stool down the bar. Newell, head of the Narcotics Enforcement Team, choked on that one, but he let it go by.

"We had a good time, considering," Newell remembered. "But it was time to close it down. I wanted to be home with my family, and David was demanding action on his 'hits.' "

It was Friday, February 10, 1989.

Steinhart assured David that it was all coming down on Monday, the 13th, or Tuesday. Tom Brown was to deliver the final payment of $11,000 *after* David got word that the first part of the "job" was done. Animal would then head off on his own, and Steinhart would start working on passports and ID for David.

"That's cool," Steinhart promised David. "I'm ready . . . we're ready."

"Okay."

"I miss you," Steinhart threw out.

"I miss the hell out of you, Richard. God damn it. I don't believe how much I love you!"

". . . I don't think we'll be needing that other five grand—for the escape," Steinhart said. "I think if we get rid of Patti and the two cops, and all your problems, you're going to beat this thing and walk anyway."

"That's what I'm counting on . . . we can do everything, no hiding man—that's what I'm so fucking excited about. . . . I don't know if I can love you any more except for cruising on a bike ought to give me a new feeling. . . . I really do miss you, Fat Bo."

"Fat Bo?" Steinhart laughed. "Okay. You're Hip Bo, Irv's Rat Bo, I'm Fat Bo—the Bo Brothers."

For a moment there, Newell sensed that David Brown was having more fun being one of the boys in jail than he had ever had in his life. But there was a yawning hole where David should have had some vestige of conscience. He had none at all. He was having such a great time as he awaited news of at least three cold-blooded murders.

Patti Bailey, his wife, the mother of his infant child, the woman who had given up everything for the love of him, was about to "back up on a knife."

At least, David believed she was.

David chafed at the wait over the weekend. He called Steinhart every time he got a free phone. On Monday, he called Steinhart at eight-thirty in the morning. "Hello," he said quietly, waiting.

"Hey, David!" Steinhart crowed. "David, it's *done!*"

"Say what?"

"I'm done. We're done. We're fucking done. Animal is in the garage right now—torching the pieces; he's melting the fuckers down right now. How did we do, huh?"

"You did great. . . ." David's voice was somehow hollow.

"Is that hot, or what?"

"Yeah, it's hot."

"Hey, man, how did we do, huh?"

"Wonderful. You're a good man."

"Wonderful? Is that all?"

David whispered that he was in a crowded area; people could be listening. His voice was flat as he listened to Steinhart describe the "murders" of Jay Newell and Jeoff Robinson. Steinhart said he even had Polaroids to show David. That frightened David. He wanted the Polaroids burned.

"Ah, man, we just walked in—I can't believe your timing."

"Shit, buy yourself an extra pizza on me!" David said.

". . . It went like clockwork. Bang! Bang! Right in the back of the head—both of them. Capped 'em both. I didn't have a chance to give them any last words from you though."

". . , That's all right," David stammered.

Steinhart thought the news should hit the papers soon—since the "hits" had happened right out in public. As soon as he and Animal collected the $11,000 from Tom, they would give the word on Patti.

"This is so fucking good, man, you won't believe it. They went so good."

"I love you," David said wanly.

And now, Steinhart needed the rest of the directions to the desert treasure. Hadn't he proved how loyal he could be?

Apparently so.

"You know where the left turn is?" David began.

"Yeah."

"You can only go left unless they've dumped some more development out there in the last couple of years. Turn left on that street at the landmark. You will pass the wash. It's less visible on the left than it is on the right. You're going to be headed north, okay? On the far side of the wash—on the right—it's like five, six foot high. Okay, you want to take the north side of the wash. Find a path up there. You will go exactly—on my odometer on a Nissan pickup—one and three-quarter miles. Okay. Then you head exactly north again. You may want a small compass for that because I made sure I was heading due north."

"Exactly north?"

"Exactly one and three-quarter miles. Okay, three-eighths of a mile or thereabouts, you'll see a boulder and a yucca tree. I call it a boulder because it's a heavy motherfucker, probably three—maximum four—feet around."

"Okay."

"Um—it's exactly under the boulder. . . . It's on property I owned at one time, but I made sure it's near a survey marker so if anybody was going to fence it in, they wouldn't have any reason to dig or move that boulder."

"Is your property close by this landmark?"

"It's on the other side of the street that you use to get to the wash."

"What's your address?"

David didn't remember the street name, nor did he remember the numbers. "It's five digits long. It's eight eight eight . . . something." The property address didn't matter; the yucca tree and the boulder did.

David Brown's fortune was buried beneath that boulder. He was willing to share it now with Richard Steinhart. "God, I love you, Richard."

"I love you, too. Anything else I need to know?"

"I did think of something last night that I was going to warn you about."

"Which was what?"

"But apparently you didn't need it."

"Well, what was it anyway?"

"The investigator was armed."

Now David told him. Had David ever intended for Steinhart to survive the two hits? He had forgotten a fairly vital piece of information.

Steinhart's answer was unruffled. "Oh, yeah—they both were. One had one in his briefcase, and one had one on him."

"I never noticed on the attorney."

"Well, I'll tell you what," Steinhart said sardonically. "It don't matter now, does it?"

It was raining and hailing and the parking lot at Bennigan's in Westminster was almost empty as Richard Steinhart and Det. Bob "Animal" Moran waited in their Camaro for Tom Brown's blue Ford Escort to turn in. At ten-twenty A.M., David's older brother arrived. He remained seated behind the wheel as he handed over the last payment $11,000 of David's money for whatever it was David was buying. David had him running all over the place on one errand or another.

Suddenly, seemingly from out of nowhere, the lot was alive with uniformed and undercover cops—all pointing guns at Tom Brown, Richard Steinhart, and Bob "Animal" Moran. Bewildered, Tom stag gered out of his car and was bent over the hood and handcuffed.

"You're all under arrest for murder," a Huntington Beach officer barked.

"For *what?*" Tom asked.

"For first-degree murder."

Animal Moran and Richard Steinhart, the two "hired killers" were also cuffed and hauled away. For all Tom Brown knew, David had ordered him into a nest of vipers, and he had been caught with the worst of them. He didn't know what in hell this was all about. He was both frightened and furious.

David Brown had now paid $23,400 for three murders that never happened. The "Bo Brothers" were out of business. But David didn't know that yet.

Tom Brown was transported to an interview room at the Huntington Beach Police Department. He sat alone, handcuffed, with a look of total bewilderment on his face for more than half an hour until Jay Newell and Fred McLean arrived to talk with him.

Tom Brown asked repeatedly, "What's going on?"

But Newell could not explain until he had read Tom Brown his Miranda rights.

Then he said slowly, "You're under arrest for murder—"

"For *who?*"

"Some people got killed," Newell said slowly, "and one of them—it looks like—was the wrong person."

Newell could be forgiven this fib. He suspected the news of a foul-up would get back to David, who had been having a wonderful time for weeks orchestrating Jay Newell's sudden death.

Tom Brown now looked both incredulous and panicked. All he knew about the two men at Bennigan's was that they were supposed to be protecting David. "David called me last week and told me to take eleven thousand dollars to them today."

Tom explained that he and his father always went to the office of Joel Baruch, David's attorney, to get checks from David's trust account. "He wouldn't tell me nothing. He just said that his life and Krystal's were in danger and he needed protection."

Tom recalled bringing the two beefy "bodyguards" $10,000 a week before. He remembered too, with some prompting from Newell, that he had delivered $1,700 before that—"to show good faith." David had given the orders. Tom had asked no questions. He knew nothing about murders. Nothing. He would have had no part in it. He shouted at Newell and McLean in his rage and fear.

"What would you say if I told you two people got killed—and one of them is the wrong person?" Newell asked.

"Nothing. I don't know anything about it."

Tom Brown was held for four hours and released. Clearly, he had been his brother's dupe and had no idea that he was delivering money intended—at least by David—to pay for three murders. Newell asked him not to tell anyone about what had happened, knowing that Tom *would* tell, and that it would get back to David.

Newell now had twenty-six audio and/or video tapes that tied David Brown irrevocably to solicitation to commit murder. In David's own words. In David's own voice.

When Tom Brown was dismissed after questioning, still confused and angry at the mess David had dumped him into, he apparently went right to his parents, who called Joel Baruch's office. They didn't know much. They knew only that someone had been killed, and that *it was the wrong person*. . . .

Later that afternoon, Tom Borris received a breathless call from Joel Baruch's partner, Jack Early. *"Is Jeoff Robinson dead?"*

"I can't discuss it," Borris answered tensely. "You've called right in the middle of our investigation."

Actually, Robinson was alive and well and working in the office next to Borris. But until all the pieces came together, Borris preferred not to announce that.

At nine-thirty on the night of February 13, David Brown had an official visit from his attorney, Joel Baruch. Deputy Dan Vazquez could not hear what the two were saying, but he saw Baruch wave his arms emphatically, and he could tell that the discussion was an extremely emotional one. David lit one cigarette after another, heedless that he was in a no-smoking area.

Vazquez caught fragments of sentences: ". . . just got the most terrible news . . ."

When David's attorney left, David headed down toward Irv Cully's cell. He was shouting, "Cully! Cully! Goldie fucked up! Goldie fucked up."

David had been nervous as a cat all day, and now he had just learned that the plan hadn't gone down smoothly after all. That damn Richard must have gone and shot the wrong guy!

39

D A V I D learned far worse news on Valentine's Day, February 14, 1989. Goldie *hadn't* shot the wrong man. He hadn't shot anybody. His beloved Goldie had set him up—had even cooperated with his bitterest enemies. Jeoff Robinson and Jay Newell—*and* Patti Bailey— were all quite alive. David, who considered himself the maestro of exploitation, had fallen completely for Richard Steinhart's gift of gab.

Without Steinhart's help, it was likely that all of David's designated victims *would* have been dead. But Steinhart had stalled David long enough for Newell and Borris to get solid evidence that a murder plot did, indeed, exist.

When David frantically tried to call his attorney, he found no comfort in that direction. Joel Baruch had left for Florida that morning to celebrate his wedding anniversary.

On February 15, David was charged with three counts of conspiracy to commit murder, three counts of solicitation to commit murder, solicitation to commit perjury, subornation of perjury, and conspiracy to commit arson. Jack Early, one of David's attorneys, described him as "surprised, shocked, and distraught."

An understatement perhaps.

No more shocked than Patti Bailey. When she learned that her husband had thoroughly intended that she would be dead by sundown on Valentine's Day, she told reporters that she figured, "Oh, come on."

But the next day, Jay Newell filled her in on all the details. She began to cry and to shake uncontrollably. "I'm hurt," she finally whispered. "But it's to be expected. *Anything* is to be expected. I believe it. I guess he likes to repeat history."

There was a new brittleness about Patti. She had seen all of her dreams evaporate. She had read her fifty letters from David and found he could no longer make her believe. They were full of lies, designed only to persuade her to protect him. She had no one. Rather than expecting *anything*, Patti expected nothing. Her family had cut her off. "But I understand—killing my own sister. I still have to live with that."

Paradoxically, Patti bravely told reporters she was experiencing a kind of freedom. She had been bound to David for so many years.

Jail let her be more her own person. Patti, who had been forced to drop out of high school, passed her GED test while she was in the Orange County Jail. "I feel a lot freer. I'm in jail, but I can do what I want."

Not really. Patti tried to hang herself in jail.

Irv Cully was moved to a different jail location and so was David Brown. The man without a home was Richard Steinhart. He needed a secure location. Not only was he waiting to testify in one trial, he would now be a witness in David Brown's trail. He was a target. His enemies branded him a "jailhouse snitch," which was not precisely accurate. *He* had been snitched off and then had agreed to cooperate with the District Attorney's Office because he deplored David Brown's morals and methods.

Steinhart had gained nothing and lost a good deal. He had no place to go, and he was not safe on the street. David was enraged, and the Hessians were still looking for him.

"I found him a place," Newell recalled with a wry smile. "The one thing you might say about it is that it was secure. Apartments and motels were expensive and vulnerable. So I rented him a bank vault. It wasn't fancy, but it had a window and it only cost six hundred dollars a month—including breakfast."

The vault was in a defunct bank. Steinhart decorated it to suit himself and for the moment, called it home.

With spring burgeoning in the desert, Steinhart headed out one day, seeking a certain monument that said either "29 Palms" or "Joshua Tree." He took a buddy with him, a borrowed pickup truck, and digging tools. David had told him repeatedly that there was a fortune buried up there, much of it in small bills, a fortune hidden from the IRS. It might be as little as $300,000 or it might be $5 million.

They found the left turn and they found the wash, and they followed their compasses due north as David had instructed. And they found a boulder next to a yucca tree.

"We dug, and we dug." Steinhart grimaced, remembering. "It was hot. We got a spot hollowed underneath, and my buddy was holding the boulder up, kind of, with wrecking bars. I was digging under it."

The wrecking bars gave way in the sand and the boulder came crashing down, catching one of Steinhart's middle fingers beneath it. "It squashed that finger like an empty banana peel," he said, holding it up to show scars. "And then it plain took it off. My buddy was all gung ho to keep digging, and I was trying to hold my finger on by a shred of flesh. I told him I didn't think we should pursue the project—at least not then."

Emergency room surgeons were able to reattach Steinhart's flattened finger, but his enthusiasm for treasure hunting was vastly diminished.

Richard Steinhart had never really beaten his addiction to cocaine. On May 14, 1989, Officer R. Reinhart of the Huntington Beach Police Department was staked out on Commodore Circle, a notorious area for drug dealing. He had made at least fifty drug arrests there. He spotted a slow-moving pickup truck driven by a young woman. As the officer observed the two occupants wheel around on Commodore Circle, he saw a young Hispanic man walk up to the truck and show the male passenger two plastic bags with white powder in them. The bearded passenger gave the man some money and accepted the Baggies. The officer didn't know Richard Steinhart, but he recognized a drug deal when he saw one going down.

Steinhart was busted again.

He went back to the Orange County Jail, but this time his life changed completely. "I was in total sep [separation]." He had his reputation as a physically powerful man, but that was all he had. He saw that "Charles Manson and mass murderers are heroes in prison." But he didn't want that.

Steinhart found what he wanted at chapel call on the evening of June 22, 1989. There are scores of men behind bars who "find God" because it is expedient. No one who talked to Richard Steinhart believed that he was among them; he became a man totally committed to his religion. "I'd been going three times a week to chapel call when some of it began to sink in," he said. In chapel that night, he experienced a jolting spiritual awakening. It never left him.

Indeed, he wasn't even *in* chapel for religious reasons. "I was only going to find out what was happening in the mods—'cause I was in total sep, or maybe to bully the kids out of their candy bars, their commissary packs, their peanuts and stuff, bully them to put money on my books and stuff. But the Holy Spirit came upon me. The Reverend Win Barr asked if anyone wanted to accept Jesus Christ. My hand just shot up, and I didn't realize it was *up*. Everybody's going, 'Steinhart's tryin' something—look!' They figured I had an escape plan, 'cause they *knew* me, and they asked me afterward how

I was going to do it, 'cause they wanted to ride on my coattails. . . .

"I went back to my cell—three concrete walls with a glass front, and a twenty-four-hour guard—and I tried to find the smallest corner of my cell so the bull in the bubble couldn't see me, and I got on my hands and knees and I started crying and I begged God for mercy . . . and forgiveness. I got off my knees a new creature."

At breakfast the next day, Steinhart suggested that his fellow prisoners say grace. Bewildered, they did. And then he led them around the table, singing "Amazing Grace." Most of them thought he was crazy, and some believed this was all part of a master escape plan.

There was no escape plan. Steinhart was, for ever after, a changed man.

He still worried, however, about his power to control his addiction when he was on the street again. He called Jay Newell for help. Newell found Set Free, a drug rehabilitation program that would waive its long waiting list—*only* if the patient came directly from jail. The day Steinhart was released, Newell picked him up and took him to the program. After that, he went to a church-sponsored rehabilitation program at Lake Elsinore, California.

Steinhart no longer cared about David Brown's elusive treasure. It was quite possible that the half million dollars, even 5 million—if it did indeed exist—still waited under some boulder, near some yucca tree on the way to Barstow, California.

Patti Bailey believed that David had a hidden cache of money in the desert. Although she never went with him, she saw him leave the house with bags of money many times. He told her he was going to bury it so that the tax men wouldn't find it.

There was no trial for David Brown in March 1989. The new charges virtually demanded a postponement. His case was becoming more and more complicated. It seemed likely that it would be autumn before a trial could get under way.

During the second week of May, Patti Bailey was allowed to plead guilty to her sister's murder in an Orange County juvenile courtroom. On June 2, she sobbed as Superior Court judge C. Robert Jameson sentenced her to the California Youth Authority until her twenty-fifth birthday.

Patti was now one of the key witnesses against David. She had barely turned twenty-one. If she had been tried as an adult, she would have faced twenty-seven years to life in prison. As a juvenile, she would probably be released when she was twenty-five. Patti didn't really understand that. Even as she pleaded guilty, and when she was sentenced, she believed that she would go to the California Youth Authority prison for four years, *then* be transferred to an adult facility where she would stay for the rest of her life.

"I pleaded guilty," she said, "because I know that what I did was wrong—real wrong. . . . I'm just sorry it ever happened. I just wish I could make it all go away. You never realize how much you miss someone until she's gone, and I'd give anything in the world to have her back now. I have to live with this the rest of my life. I don't think I'm getting off easy."

"There were no deals for Patti Bailey," Jeoff Robinson told the press. He explained that the case was heard in Juvenile Court because Patti was only seventeen at the time of the murder, because she did not pull the trigger, and probably most significantly, because she had been sexually abused and brainwashed during all the years she had lived with David Brown.

Joel Baruch sniped at Robinson. "That's the way the DA operates. They just bought themselves a witness." Baruch contended that he would prove at David's murder trial that he never wanted Linda dead, and that he was presently the unwitting target of lies told by his sixth wife, Patti, and his daughter, Cinnamon.

Ironically, Patti would now be locked up in Ventura, the prison school where Cinnamon had already spent four years. They would be housed in separate "cottages" far apart—but they would come in contact occasionally.

Arthur and Manuela, David's parents, would raise Krystal. Patti's little girl, Heather Nicole Bailey, was in the care of Mary Bailey, Rick's wife. Even if Patti should be released from prison in four years, she would miss her baby's vital, growing-up years.

When Patti was transferred to the Ventura School in Camarillo, David continued to write to her. His trial lay ahead. He needed Patti's support. He asked her if she was "woman enough" to drop her story and warned her to "watch her back" because she was "trusting the wrong people."

That wasn't true. Patti didn't trust anyone. Her heart beat too fast, she perspired, her chin shook, and sometimes she felt as if she could get no air at all.

No, Patti Ann Bailey Brown did not get "a deal."

• • •

Cinnamon and Patti were in prison, and David Brown was in jail, awaiting what should have been a speedy trial. But justice rumbled along as sluggishly as an overloaded mule. There was no closure. No one connected with the case could make plans.

On June 19, 1989, Joel Baruch filed a second recusal motion on behalf of his client. He sought to have the Orange County District Attorney's Office removed from the case. Since David Brown now stood accused of conspiring and soliciting the murder of two Orange County staff members—Jeoff Robinson and Jay Newell—Baruch suggested there would be a "conflict of interest."

Should Baruch be successful in removing the DA's office—or only Robinson and Newell—he would accomplish what David had clumsily tried to achieve with his murder plots. A new prosecuting team would be brought in. It was unlikely that *any* team from the California State Attorney General's Office could learn as much about David Brown as Newell and Robinson knew. His life was so intricate, his plans so devious. What had been written down was voluminous; the sheer experience that Newell and Robinson shared was vital to the prosecution's case.

Deputy District Attorney Tom Borris countered the recusal motion. "We are looking at Baruch very closely." After the DA's office realized that the money for the planned "hits" had been released in two checks from Baruch's office to Tom Brown, Baruch's possible involvement in the assassination plot became a question too. However, Borris said his office could find no evidence that the defense lawyer had *known* that the money was allegedly to be used as a murder payoff. One $10,000 check had a notation that it was to buy "rare coins."

"What difference does it make where the money comes from?" Baruch snapped. His statement in the recusal motion summed up his argument: "The maneuvering by the District Attorney's Office to keep Deputy District Attorney Robinson on the case poignantly demonstrates how that office has lost all objectivity and impartiality in making critical decisions."

Jim Enright, chief deputy district attorney, said that evidence of the murder-for-hire plan would be introduced to support a death sentence verdict if the death penalty *was* sought. Since Robinson was one of the intended *victims*, he would be replaced in the trial at that point by Tom Borris.

Baruch contended that Robinson would already have won the jury's sympathy by then; it would be too late for them not to think of him as the victim-to-be. "No juror should be permitted to make a life-or-death judgment in a case where he knows and likes the victim."

What a complicated legal situation it had become. Enright suggested that, by the time the jurors reached a penalty phase—if they should find David Brown guilty in the first phase of the trial—an entire new jury could be selected. Enright announced flatly that there was no question of removing Robinson. Robinson had established rapport with the key witnesses, and he knew the case inside and out.

Baruch was scathing. "We have to go through all this just to keep Robinson on the case? I mean—is Jeoff Robinson the only talented prosecutor they have?"

Underlying all the argument, there was the fact that death penalty cases are excruciatingly difficult to prove. Most jurors-to-be are uneasy with the concept of finding a defendant guilty if it means he—or she—will die. The Brown case was especially difficult to prove; Newell and Robinson now believed that David Brown had not actually pulled the trigger the night his wife died. Although he was just as culpable—if not *more* culpable—as the actual shooter, under the law, would jurors grasp that?

Robinson had prosecuted a number of exacting homicide cases; he suspected this one was destined to be *the* most memorable, no matter what the verdict. His three chief witnesses were convicts—or ex-convicts. Two convicted murderesses, and a born-again strong-arm drug dealer. The prosecutor had not exactly been tossed into a field of daisies.

The defendant, on the other hand, had, as yet, no criminal record and would be presented by the defense as a conscientious businessman who had saved lives with his computer skill. The newspapers always referred to David as an "executive."

Nothing was black-and-white, and an intelligent jury would know that. But this case was no sure thing. Robinson would never give up the prosecution of David Brown to a new team, nor would any of the brass at the Orange County DA's office.

Both Robinson and Newell had, quite literally, risked their lives on this one.

The defense and the prosecution wrangled sporadically as full summer came to Orange County. The actual trial seemed no closer than it ever had. The official date was August 2, 1989, but no one involved seemed to feel it would begin then. It seemed sometimes as if David Arnold Brown would forever be suspended in limbo in the county jail.

Then on July 29, 1989, Joel Baruch abruptly resigned as David Brown's attorney, citing a "conflict of interest" that he refused to discuss. Now, David had no lawyer of record. Any further proceedings were delayed until August 11. The motion to remove Jeoffrey Robinson as prosecutor was taken off the court calendar.

Verbal fisticuffs between attorneys continued when David Brown hired a new lawyer: Richard Schwartzberg. Baruch had one final go-round associated with the Brown case. He brought a civil lawsuit against Schwartzberg, claiming that David Brown's new attorney had slandered him in court. Baruch charged that Schwartzberg had told other attorneys in court that Baruch had taken part in the plot to have members of the Orange County prosecution team killed.

Schwartzberg, who had been joking, agreed to make a $500 donation to a charity benefiting cystic fibrosis to settle the suit. "It isn't worth the time and money to fight this," he explained. ". . . It was a way for both sides to save face. Schwartzberg also agreed to apologize to Baruch.

Schwartzberg, a brilliant legal mind, would soon be joined by Gary M. Pohlson, one of the three or four top defense attorneys in Orange County. Schwartzberg was a walking law library, and Pohlson had a warm, friendly style that jurors responded to. David Brown had now hired himself a dynamite defense team—which did not come cheap.

Indeed, it was necessary for Jay Newell to photocopy all the payoff money from the murder plot so that the *actual* money could be removed from evidence and given to Brown's new lawyers. The buried money apparently was not tapped, but David did have a safe in a storage shed in Orange. He gave the combination to a defense investigator. The lock would not click open. When a locksmith easily flicked the dial and the heavy door swung open, there was nothing inside.

The mystery of just how much money David Brown had access to remained unanswered.

The new guard for the defense took over. David Brown had had three laywers, and now he had two more. His legal expenses were nudging up toward the half-million-dollar mark, according to educated guesses, and he had yet to go to trial.

He was a demanding client, calling Gary Pohlson at his office or at home with suggestions and complaints. Gary Pohlson was not yet forty, a stocky, muscular man with an open, Irish-looking face. He described himself to juries as "fat and bald," and he was neither, although there was an encroaching sparse spot on the top of his head. His suits were impeccably tailored, and his silk ties perfectly matched his socks. He could take no credit at all for that. His wife bought his clothes.

Gary Pohlson was a good man and looked it. He could represent Attila the Hun, and the jury and gallery would still like him for himself. In 1989, he tried six difficult cases, won four—and lost two. Pohlson usually "fell in love with" his client, finding the positive and bringing it out in court.

A career as a criminal defense attorney was far afield from Gary Pohlson's original goal. He attended St. John's Seminary in Camarillo, preparing for the priesthood. He met his wife-to-be's brother there, and eventually they both entered the secular world. Pohlson met his wife on a blind date—set up by her brother. They had been married eighteen years and had three children.

Pohlson was active in his church and community, an avid basketball player, and the consummate father. He played basketball with his boys every night and drove them sixty miles round trip three times a week so they could play basketball on one of the best junior teams in southern California. "I want to win," he admitted. "Everything. Even if I'm playing basketball with my kids in the backyard, I want to beat them!"

The David Brown trial would be Pohlson's sixth time up against Jeoff Robinson. He had lost the first five. Nevertheless, they were friends. Not close friends—but they often played basketball together over the noon hour with other attorneys and deputy DAs, and they socialized occasionally. They more than respected one another in the courtroom, which in no way precluded the possibility of explosive reactions in the trial to come.

With the change of attorneys, it was obvious that David Brown would not have his day in court until the spring of 1990. However, the DA's office announced that it would not seek the death penalty. Spokesmen refused to disclose the reasons for dropping the death penalty. But Bryan Brown, who headed the DA's Homicide Unit, said, "I'm not really comfortable going into the details, but we heard about a number of factors we weren't aware of. This caused us to reverse our decision to seek the death penalty against him."

• • •

Patti had just begun her sentence. Cinnamon remained in prison. It seemed a bleak twist that, had she not come forward with the truth, she might have hoped to win a parole at her 1989 winter review with the parole board. For now, she was placing her trust in Jay Newell and Jeoff Robinson. She waited.

She had been waiting for almost five years. She was no longer a child, and within six months, she would no longer be a teenager. All those years had been swallowed up by her sentence.

David Brown's spirits rose. Things seemed to be coming around his way again. He had a great team of attorneys. The battered phoenix stirred and began to come alive.

PART FOUR

• • •

The Trial

40

T H E R E was a possibility that David Brown would face not one but two trials: the first on the murder charge in his fifth wife's death, and the second on the charges evolving from the plot to have the prosecution team and his *sixth* wife killed. But the murder trial came first. It was to begin February 20, 1990, in Superior Court judge Donald A. McCartin's courtroom—Department 30, on the eighth floor of the Orange County Courthouse.

The defense asked for a delay, which was granted. The new trial date was scheduled for March 28. David Brown asked for more time. If his request was not granted, he threatened smugly to fire his attorneys, confident that that would force another long wait before he faced a jury. But McCartin would have none of it. Brown could fire his attorneys if he chose, but he was not getting more than a month's delay; the Court was prepared to proceed on April 25.

And so it would.

But before Brown's trial started, there was another blighted spring on Ocean Breeze Drive. Back in the old neighborhood in Garden Grove, four days of violence again shocked neighbors who had been jolted five years earlier—almost five years to the day—by Linda Brown's murder. On March 30, 1990, the woman who lived in the house directly behind the former Brown residence—on Jane Drive—broke into television star Sharon Gless's home. Joni Leigh Penn, thirty, had been obsessed with Gless for four years. Armed with a .22 semiautomatic rifle, she barricaded herself in Gless's San Fernando Valley home and held off police for seven hours before a female police negotiator talked her out.

Four days later, Garden Grove firefighters responded to a fully involved fire in the house directly across the street from the house where Linda Brown died. It was the house with the fountain and the colored lights, and it had just been remodeled. When the fire was tapped, firefighters discovered the body of a middle-aged man in the master bedroom. Identified as that of the homeowner, the badly charred body proved to be that of a murder victim. And once again, yellow police ribbons surrounded a house on Ocean Breeze Drive.

The 1990 incidents had, of course, no connection to the Brown murder case, but the location of the homes of those involved—all three—were in a perfectly straight line from east to west, almost a fault line of evil.

Judge Donald A. McCartin was a pilot for both the navy and the Marines in the Second World War, landing on the impossibly small decks of aircraft carriers. In his early sixties, he was a handsome, tall, lean man. He could be formidable as he gazed down from his bench at trial participants. He was alternately witty and scathing, a benevolent father figure and an irascible curmudgeon. If he appeared to be asleep, he was not; he was listening. He was completely unpredictable and kept young lawyers a degree off-balance. As the David Brown trial began, McCartin was dealing with a bad back, the result of a recent athletic injury.

Department 30 was a highly individual courtroom, reflecting many of McCartin's moods and interests. Actually, it was a wild and crazy courtroom, slyly decorated with humorous touches that helped the mind glance away from time to time when the testimony became bitter and tragic.

A narrow shelf protruded from McCartin's bench, supporting a statuette of a bewigged judge who was covering his mouth with his hand. He was either gagging or laughing at justice. On McCartin's right, facing the witness box, there were three little figures made of flat stones and painted in bright colors. They may have been Speak No Evil, See No Evil, Hear No Evil, but it was hard to tell. They may only have been there, as the box of Kleenex was, to comfort the witness.

On the right wall, behind Deputy Marshal "Mitch" Miller's desk, there was a selection of drawings and photographs. One was of a ferocious stubbly-bearded face; beneath the face were the words "Good Morning." Most of the other pictures were of McCartin family dogs. Some were grinning and wearing nightgowns. All looked happy and healthy. The judge was a dog lover. He once spent $4,000 to replace a beloved golden retriever's hips with prostheses. McCartin discussed dogs affectionately and pointed out that his preference for them summed up "what I think of the human race." He may have been kidding.

Judge Donald McCartin was also a man with four sons and three stepdaughters who enjoyed the comparative peace of a lake cabin north of Orange County whenever possible.

Miller had been McCartin's bailiff for eight years. Gail Carpenter, McCartin's clerk, had occupied the small desk below the bench for five. She was unfailingly cheerful, and nothing ruffled her. Sandra Wingerd was the pretty red-haired court stenographer. The year-long Randy Craft serial-murder trial was held in Judge McCartin's courtroom; his staff was used to television cameras and anchormen, to newspaper reporters and book writers, to Hollywood "producers."

The jury box was on the left side of the courtroom; the seal of California, flanked by the American and the California flags, was behind Judge McCartin.

By most states' standards, Department 30 was a huge courtroom, with comfortable cushioned seating for two hundred or more potential jurors or members of the gallery. The seats squeaked and whined, however, when a court watcher took even too deep a breath or reached down to search for a pen or legal pad.

The attorneys and the jurors had more comfortable, less creaky chairs; the defendant would sit in a chair without casters. A good solid wooden chair allowed for few quick movements and was a precaution that evoked a silly mental picture of the accused making a break for freedom in a fast-moving chair.

But David Arnold Brown had already demonstrated a penchant for escape. He would be brought up from the basement—usually by Miller and Deputy Marshal Glenn Hoopingarner—in handcuffs and ankle chains. During breaks, he would wait in a holding cell just outside the courtroom. He could smoke there.

The pretrial motions and McCartin's decisions were damaging to the defense. Gary Pohlson argued that he could not "conceive of a more damaging piece of evidence" than the Steinhart tapes, the tapes that substantiated a plot to kill Jeoff Robinson, Jay Newell, and Patti Bailey. He wanted them out. "There are other things that this plot could show besides consciousness of guilt."

"There was an attempt to thwart the prosecution of this case," Jeoff Robinson argued. "It's a tough case for both sides. . . . When David Brown takes part in that kind of activity, we should have the right to bring it before the jury."

"If this comes in, we roll over—the jury's going to roll over us," Pohlson retorted.

McCartin acknowledged that the tapes *were* damaging, but he ruled against the defense. "I don't see it as a tight call. I don't see any way I can rule it out, unless I lost my sanity."

David Brown himself took the stand. Pohlson questioned him about the interview he gave to Jay Newell and Fred McLean on the morning he was arrested. That interview was damning, and the defense wanted it gone. David recalled that he was tired and groggy from prescription medicine during that interview. "I never understood until the end of the interview that I was under arrest. I had nothing to hide. I still don't."

McCartin watched part of that three-hour tape. It was patently clear that Newell advised Brown of his rights under Miranda and told him up front that he was under arrest.

That tape too was in.

Gary Pohlson and Richard Schwartzberg had a hard row to hoe. A trial, *any* trial, was theater. *This* trial promised high drama.

At nine-thirty A.M. on Monday, April 30, 1990, Department 30 was empty, save for Bailiff Miller. It was cool and quiet, and its windows—a rarity in a courtroom—provided a panoramic view of miles of flat land that spread out below—until it disappeared into a blur of smog.

The lawyers arrived; both Robinson and Pohlson wore gray, lightly striped suits, first-day-of-trial suits. For the next few days, they would pick similar suits, as if there were an unwritten guide to courtroom clothing.

And there was a changing of the guard here. Jay Newell had carried this case with him for more than five years. Now, it was in Jeoff Robinson's hands, and Newell would stay in the background, except for his moments on the stand. Newell was, for the moment, the support system.

Fred McLean sat in the back of the courtroom. "If all three of us were at the prosecution table," he explained, "it might look like we're ganging up on the defendant. I can see fine from here."

The press was in the front row, just behind the prosecution table and the defense team. Eric Lichtblau from the *Los Angeles Times* had written dozens of articles about the Brown murder case. Although recently transferred out of the Orange County bureau of the *Times*, he had asked to see this one through to the end. Jeff Collins, of the *Orange County Register*, was back home again after working for a Texas paper; he was playing catch-up with an entirely new case to him. Barney Morris of Channel 7, the ABC affiliate in Los Angeles, was present with a cameraman; Dave Lopez of CBS's Channel 2 was there too. California courts allow cameras and tape recorders in the courtroom—with special permission; cameramen had to stand eighteen feet back from the bar and use no strobes or flashes.

With the sound of clanking chains, the gallery hushed. David Arnold Brown himself was about to enter the courtroom for the first time in this trial. The papers had touted the computer genius, the executive, the millionaire. Photographs had been only head shots, and some of those when Brown was six years younger than he was now. This was the man who collected beautiful women. *Five* of them had married him, one twice.

The courtroom was quiet, waiting. . . .

David Brown entered. *He was a pear-shaped man with a humped back.* There was a barely audible gasp as the gallery realized that the man shuffling to the plain wooden chair was one and the same as the consummate ladies' man they had read about. How could this be? The defendant was very short and very fat, and his face was pockmarked and the pale green-white of jailhouse pallor. David Brown had lank dark-brown hair, with no trace of gray. He had lost a great deal of it in the year and a half since his arrest. He wore a white dress shirt over a T-shirt, and gray polyester pants without a belt (forbidden). The threads from the pants' label were still visible.

David Brown was now thirty-seven; he could easily have been fifty.

The way David looked made his reputation even more incredible. He was the embodiment of the nightmare blind date. A daughter would love her father no matter how he looked. But all the other women who reputedly adored David Brown? If he looked the part of a seducer, yes—but this man had to be more adept at mind games than anyone had imagined.

A huge jury pool filed in. Judge McCartin immediately dismissed those who were due to go off jury duty at the end of April, explaining that the case was expected to extend at least until the middle of June.

Jury selection was full of good-natured banter. Pohlson announced he favored "bald buys—especially pudgy bald guys." Robinson commented that "in Judge McCartin's court, you enter never-never land in some time warp."

McCartin joked about Robinson's "competence," the deputy DA objected, and Pohlson "sustained." The gallery laughed. McCartin said, "We sometimes change places in this courtroom. I may come down and be the defense or the prosecutor."

Robinson pointed out that the defense had two attorneys, and he was all by himself. "We'll allow Mr. Robinson to have his mother sit next to him," McCartin decreed.

"His mother doesn't like him," Pohlson stipulated.

The gallery roared again. People are nervous in courtrooms; humor relaxes them. It did not relax David Brown. He was confused by the laughter and obviously concerned that his attorney was joking with the prosecutor. His "dynamite life-of-the-party" sense of humor had deserted him.

Potential jurors moved into the jury box to be questioned. Jury selection is done on a gut-feeling level or with experience or with time-honored rules of thumb. Selecting a ringer is always possible. Jurors have been known to hold back information or to lie to be selected.

Each time the lineup seemed perfect to the observer, it was as if the defense and prosecution were playing musical chairs. Jurors, often bewildered, were asked to step down. Four hours. Six hours, and most of them were gone. Robinson and Pohlson started again. The voir dire (direct questioning of prospective jurors) was hilarious, and the courtroom erupted with laughter again and again. It took close to three days before twelve jurors and three alternates were seated.

It was 1:47 P.M. on May 2. No one would really know what they were thinking. Not until the end.

There were housewives, an executive secretary, a telephone line-man, an electronics technician, an assistant purchasing agent, a teacher of the developmentally disabled, engineers. Seven women and five men. The three alternates were two women and one man. Almost all of them had children, teenagers or young adults.

They did not know David Brown. If they had heard of him at all, it was long ago in a hastily read newspaper article, and they remembered no details. His notoriety had, to date, come in short media bursts—gone by the next day.

On May 5, 1990, Cinco de Mayo weekend in Santa Ana, California, the weather was clear and hot, and the city full of the sounds of celebration: a parade down Main Street, firecrackers *and* gunshots far into the night. In two days, David Brown's trial would, at long last, truly begin. The prosecution felt good; the September 22 arrest-interview tape was in, and the Steinhart conspiracy tapes were in. If the jury believed Cinnamon and Patti and Steinhart, there would be no acquittal.

If the defense had no surprises in store . . .

There was, however, a potentially nasty surprise waiting for them in the wings. On May 4, Jay Newell had received an absorbing phone call from someone he had not spoken to for a year, Dan Coston*, an inmate in the Orange County Jail. Intelligent, verbal, and inventive, Coston was a petty crook who took great pride in his two-decade career as a snitch.

In his first meeting with Coston, Newell had found him less than credible. Coston had told a rambling story about David Brown's being "set up" by Irv Cully. But he waffled at most of Newell's questions despite Newell's insistence that "there's something you're not telling me."

At that time Coston stonewalled. He said he "always explored his possibilities." He hinted that he could work for the DA's office, but Newell failed to bite. When he asked Coston outright if he was being paid by one of Brown's attorneys, Coston would not answer. But as soon as Newell left, Coston went scurrying to a private investigator working for David Brown with the news that he thought he could entrap Jay Newell.

A bad judgment call.

Newell figured the meeting was a "fishing trip" for Coston. He taped it and made notes, but rarely thought of Coston in the period between May of 1989 and May of 1990.

Orange County jails of late had spawned a virtual cottage industry for snitches who specialized in complicated machinations that were designed to win them favor, and in the best of circumstances, financial gain.

Dan Coston had not told Jay Newell even 10 percent of what he knew about David Brown. Coston had observed David Brown for some time. He had watched Cully and Steinhart. In his estimation, Cully was a dummy, and so was Steinhart, who had gotten absolutely nothing for all his dealings with "Thurston."

Around March of 1989, Dan Coston moved into David Brown's life. Disappointed at his betrayal by Steinhart, David had needed another strong man to look out for his interests. And Coston saw his association with Brown as beneficial to himself in many ways. Brown was a millionaire—reportedly many times over—and there was money to be made. Brown was newsworthy, and Coston had always fancied himself a media entrepreneur. And then, once he had bled

Brown for all he could get, there was the "double agent" part of the game. Dan Coston would simply go to the DA and snitch David off; that way, he might be able to bargain for a sentence reduction for himself. Beyond that, Coston loved the games. Playing each side against the middle and rarely telling the whole truth to anyone . . . As he admitted once to a private investigator, "I do in some way get a kick playing these little mental games and stuff with these people."

David Brown was a real challenge. Both Coston and Brown had manipulated other people for as long as they could remember. It was a balancing act. As far as David knew, Coston was completely loyal to him; he paid him to be.

On June 12, 1989, as David Brown dictated, Dan Coston wrote a letter. He later "released" the letter to *Time, Playboy, Penthouse, Esquire, Life, Newsweek, People, U.S. News and World Report, A Current Affair, 60 Minutes, Oprah Winfrey, Donahue,* and *Geraldo,* along with all major newspapers and television stations in Los Angeles and San Francisco, *and* to both national and local bar associations. He also sent it to the editors of prison newspapers all over America.

David particularly wanted the *Los Angeles Times* editors to see the letter. He detested Eric Lichtblau, the young reporter who was always writing unfavorable articles about him. He had given Lichtblau an exclusive interview, and yet he felt the *L.A. Times* reporter had misconstrued everything he had said, and David was furious. He hoped his letter might cost Lichtblau his job.

David paid for the stamps and the typists needed to get the letter out. It read:

Dear Sirs:

I write this letter today to inform you of an event soon to take place which I believe you and the parties you represent—be it your organizations or simply the readers of your periodical or newspaper—should be very interested in hearing about.

The event of which I speak is the criminal trial of a prominent individual, millionaire enterpreneur Mr. David Brown, who is being tried unjustly on charges of *solicitation of murder* which witnesses will prove, were in fact, concocted through the combined cooperation of the Orange County District Attorney's Office, the Orange County Sheriff's Department, and agents of theirs—two jailhouse informants.

The prosecution will attempt to prove, through the use of these jailhouse informants, that Mr. Brown conspired to kill the prosecutors involved with his original ongoing trial on charges of murder.

The defense will attempt to prove through rebuttal testimony from witnesses, themselves jailhouse informants of previous experience with knowledge directly relating to the charges against Mr. Brown, that not only is the prosecution witnesses' testimony of a false and perjured nature, but that this testimony is a concoction conceived and executed with the full knowledge and assistance of the District Attorney's Office, under the direction of the Sheriff's Department. . . .

The reason I believe this trial will be newsworthy . . . is due to my knowledge of defense intent to not only show a concerted effort of conspiracy to enter false and perjured testimony in this trial, but the defense also intends to show that this is a practice which has been used in a number of high profile criminal trials. . . .

To me, a *police informant* myself for over 18 years, with my first hand knowledge of the unethical practices used by prosecutors and their agents, the question of whether or not jailhouse informant testimony, and hence reliability should be used and relied upon without collaboration [*sic*] is possibly the single most important legal question due to be raised.

A *defense witness* myself for Mr. Brown in his upcoming trial, the single and most important question to *me* must be the possible miscarriage of justice . . . .

Should you care to hear more or become involved in one form or another, be it through caring to relate pertinent information, or perhaps wanting to set up personal interviews with me and/or other witnesses . . . please contact my attorney. . . ."

Evidently, Coston's credentials as an eighteen-year jailhouse informant, and David Brown's rhetoric, failed to impress the media; no one courted either of them for an interview.

Next, Dan Coston painstakenly printed "legal" documents through the fall and winter of 1989, saying what David Brown asked him to say—that the entire plot against the DA's men had originated in the mind of Irv Cully, and that he, Dan Coston, would get up in court and say so.

Coston squeezed everything he figured he could get out of David Brown, and when the well was dry, he put on a different face. On May 4, 1990, when Dan Coston called Newell, he apologized in his most obsequious, buddy-buddy manner for having been so vague in their last meeting. "I didn't want to tell you what was going on because, if you knew, then I would have become an agent for the DA. I had to get close to David and get evidence."

With Robinson listening on an extension, Newell gave his finest performance as a slow-witted detective, asking Coston to repeat his story again and again. The more confused he sounded, the more information Coston offered, all the while trying to establish himself as a great and good friend of the DA, only working for the good of mankind.

"From the beginning," Coston said, "when David first came into our tank—when he got transferred from the IRC to the main jail after he got charged with the conspiracy to kill you and Robinson and Patricia—David asked me to say to his investigator that *I* knew about the conspiracy all along. He said he'd pay me to say what he wanted, and I'd never have to work for the rest of my life. . . . I have a contract here that me and David drew up—he'll pay me a million dollars. . . . He says he doesn't have a chance in hell without me. . . . I thought, well, okay, beautiful. This will be good—he's continuing to finagle. David says, 'Here's what I need, Dan. You say that Irv Cully *approached you.*' "

Newell kept up his dumb act. "I'm kind of slow—you'll have to run that by me again. Why would you turn down a million dollars?"

Coston was vague on that one.

Coston said that David figured that if he could make it look as if he had been seduced, enticed, *entrapped* into the idea of killing his enemies, he would not be guilty of solicitation and conspiracy. Dan Coston had become his new man. "He said it would discredit the prosecution's case," Coston explained. "He also wanted me to say Steinhart approached *David* and assaulted him and threatened his family if David didn't go through with the hits."

David was apparently grateful for Coston's promises of help. According to Coston, in August of 1989, David gave him $1,800—in money orders, signed by K.M.B. (Krystal M. Brown). Shortly thereafter, David arranged for five one-thousand-dollar money orders to be paid to a female relative of Coston's "for ten oil paintings." There really *were* paintings. Manuela and Arthur had ceremoniously loaded them into their car outside the Orange County Jail after giving the money orders to Coston's relative.

"She took a sponge," Coston explained, laughing. "She dipped it in a bunch of oil paint and kind of threw it at the canvas. But there were 'paintings.' And David's parents gave her a receipt for five thousand dollars plus the eighteen hundred dollars already paid to me, and the money David had them pay to Billy Calixo*." (Another inmate David had approached to be a witness.) David's parents never knew the reasons behind his orders to give money to the other prisoners; they followed his instructions to the letter and never asked questions.

David also promised Coston a job in San Diego, an apartment, and a 1989 Mustang, upon his release from jail. "But when I got out, I couldn't locate the car."

Coston said there were, perhaps, a half dozen Orange County Jail inmates who had received the *promise* of money from David—if they would testify that he had been forced into the murder plot against Robinson and Newell.

Great. Now the trial had begun. Newell was working twelve to eighteen hours a day backing up Robinson, planning strategy. If Coston was telling the truth, fine. If he was playing games again, Newell had no time for him. "You have nothing written from David, nothing in his handwriting?" he asked Coston.

"I have receipts. I have a picture of a diamond ring—David's writing of what he's going to give me in advance—one hundred thousand dollars . . . I believe he has a million dollars. He's stashed away a bundle of money." That was not news to Newell. Finally, to prove his claims, Coston burst out with, "I have a forty-nine-thousand-dollar diamond ring—I've had it appraised—an emerald-cut diamond."

"You do? Why?"

"He gave it to me," Coston said excitedly. "He gave it to me as a down payment for when I testify. At the end of my testimony, I get the rest of the million dollars."

Dan Coston was, in fact, scheduled to testify in the trial at hand. Gary Pohlson was counting on him. No, neither Pohlson nor Schwartzberg had any idea that David had bribed him to testify.

Newell smiled slightly to think that David Brown, who had been burned so often, was still frantically devising plots and promising fortunes to cover up his former plots.

And now, with his trial drawing closer, he was prepared to pay much more. "Here's the plan right now," Coston said. "Robinson's going to put on your case. And then Gary Pohlson's going to take a two-week vacation."

"Right. I know about that. We're going to be in recess."

"Then they're going to put me on the stand as the key witness, with purposes of creating an impression of an elaborate plot by you and Robinson and Vazquez and the Sheriff's department . . . that you're incorporating the second case 'cause you don't have anything on the first case—that that's the length the DA's office will go to actually convict somebody. . . . I'm going to discuss conversations with Cully, and that I warned David of a plot that Cully was going to set Brown up. . . . I really never did—but I'm supposed to testify to that."

"What's your reason for stopping now?"

"My whole intent was to go to court and answer Mr. Pohlson's question about 'Have you ever been paid for your testimony?' and then I was going to say, 'Yeah—I got about fifty grand.' "

But Dan Coston insisted, "Hey, I've been on your side all along, Jay." He wasn't sure he could trust David Brown, even though David had been paying him $200 a month since August of 1989—and had promised to do so forever.

"Do you feel safe with all your books and receipts there?" Newell asked. "You're not afraid David will have someone take it away from you?"

"Nobody knows."

"It's probably better you don't spook David with this."

"I know. In so many words, he's indicated this is his last chance. If it doesn't work, he doesn't care anymore. He paid me the money and said, 'Don't fuck me.' . . . But he's fine. He loves me. His whole life depends on me."

"Who started this?" Newell asked.

"David did—when he came up on the tier. He says, 'You'll never have to work the rest of your life. . . . if you get me those statements.' "

Newell warned Coston that, from this point on, he was not to do any more "investigating." Whatever Coston had planned to do—without Newell's suggestion—was okay. If he testified as he had planned to do, if he told the truth, that was up to Coston.

And then Dan Coston hinted that he had selfish reasons for his massive betrayal of David Brown. He was coming up for sentencing himself on May 16.

No promises. No deals. Newell would not budge. He had to digest the information that Coston had just spent two hours telling him. "Don't do anything," Newell warned Coston. "Don't actively change your plans. Call me tomorrow at two P.M."

Robinson and Newell had just been handed a most valuable gift. *He* didn't know it, but Coston had just blown the defense case out of the water, without ever testifying.

Dan Coston had copies of everything. And through discovery, Gary Pohlson had a right to see what evidence the DA's office had against his client, David Brown. Coston turned over the picture of David's familiar emerald-cut diamond ring, and David's note that accompanied it:

	Important Facts	
Color	Weight/Size	Specifics
F?	4.2 Cts.	VS2
	Emerald Cut	
	PREMIUM	

David wrote instructions to Coston's relative about what she was to say when she took the ring to be appraised: "This is her Dad's—she wants to have one made just like it or similar. Please tell me how much it will cost?"

The ring was appraised at $40,500. David Brown's down payment on freedom. The million-dollar contract was dated May 4, 1990, written in David Brown's own hand.

To Dan Willard Coston,

As per your request, here is what I've agreed to provide:

$40,500.—paid on demand to date.

$949,500.—to be paid on demand after completion of all current criminal trials. This balance is to be provided directly to Dan Willard Coston or his designated agent on his demand with the understanding that I must be free from jail and charges before the funds can be accessed.

I do hereby promise to provide Coston with the balance of $949,500. due him on his demand in U.S. Currency/Legal Tender. This is a requirement imposed on him and agreed to by me as there is no alternative for services or inconveniences imposed on him by O.C. Judicial practices.

This is no confession on my part to any illegal practice nor is it an accusation to recipient for illegal practices, it is simply an agreement to reimburse recipient for services and inconveniences imposed on him

I swear to the above on this date:

May 4, 1990
DAB

An identical contract, save for the dollar amount, was written to Billy Calixo: $2,600 already paid, $97,400 when David was free.

David Brown had hired a competent, ethical, honorable pair of attorneys. He had tried to circumvent them with his own devious plans. He could not hand his life over to anyone; he needed to be in control. Unfortunately for the defense, Pohlson and Schwartzberg did not seek discovery on Dan Coston's double-agent role until after Gary Pohlson made his opening statement. When Pohlson found out what David had done, he never considered calling Dan Coston.

Coston kept the ring.

41

T H E   T H R E E days of jury selection were fun. But the tone of the trial changed dramatically as Jeoff Robinson rose to make his opening statement. He would tell the jury what he was going to prove to them. And then he would present witnesses to substantiate his opening statement. At the end of what threatened to be a long, long trial, he would remind them of the facts.

Robinson had been waiting for this moment for almost two years. He had gone over each minute aspect of the case many times. There was so much that had to be woven together, all the frayed ends of the sad lives of four people: Linda, David, Cinnamon, and Patti. Robinson scarcely glanced at his notes as he spoke steadily for more than two hours; this story was caught in his memory, probably irrevocably.

The easel behind Robinson held four large blowups—photographs of the principals: David Brown on top, and below him his daughter and the sisters he married. The prosecution had been careful to present photos that showed them as they were in the spring of 1985. This was important—because the jury was about to relive the last five years.

Robinson's opening statement was not filled with dramatic gestures; there was no need. The facts themselves offered more than enough pathos and drama.

"No more laughs now," Robinson began. "We will be a lot more serious than last week. This will be kind of like a road map or a jigsaw puzzle. This was basically how you treat this opening statement. Once you've seen the whole picture, you'll have some idea where the pieces fit.

"The story I'm about to tell you is a modern-day tragedy. Sit back, be comfortable. I'm going to take you back to March nineteenth, 1985. This will take time."

And then, in a remarkably concise, step-by-step way, Robinson began to relate to the jurors a horrific sequence of events. "The first police officer responds to 'a woman shot' at approximately three A.M., a call to respond to Ocean Breeze Drive in Garden Grove. . . ."

How many, many times had Robinson, Newell, and McLean gone over this scenario? For them, it was like, "Once upon a time, there were three bears. . . ." Had David Brown himself ever thought about the inconsistencies in his stories or his reprehensible behavior? Did he now recognize the glaring flaws as Robinson related his complicated, tangled history? Perhaps not. He listened nervously, his eyes darting, as Robinson revealed him to the light.

Robinson's memory and sense of story were incredible. He moved through 1985, 1986, 1987. "David Brown is extremely bright," he said. "He is gifted. He is no dummy. He is adept at being manipulative and devious. He sometimes lacks common sense, but he has an uncanny ability to get other people to do his bidding."

Robinson gave the jury two simple motives that David Brown had to kill his wife, Linda:

"One—to have Patti instead of Linda.

"Two—to have a whole lot of money.

". . . David denies sex with Patti. 'We only hold each other to ease the pain.' "

Robinson knew full well that Patti and Cinnamon would not be great witnesses, and he prepared the jury. "Patti has . . . not a great background. Not extremely bright—nor is Cinnamon. Patti's very much a follower—a weak person . . . authorities wonder if one *strong* person didn't orchestrate this—using little people.

"Patti shakes, chatters. . . . Patti had a very unique relationship with David Brown. He told her at eleven or twelve that he would marry her. He was her alpha and omega. David was her father, her provider, her friend. . . . David won out over her sister when it came down to a choice. . . .

"There's more," Robinson said as he saw incredulous looks on jurors' faces. Some of them, to this moment, had led lives where they had never encountered such things as murder and molestation. Their eyes widened, even as they managed to keep their faces calm.

". . . In jail, after the preliminary hearing—to avoid the hammer that was going to fall—the plan was to have Patti killed . . . he arranged with a jail inmate to have someone arrested to go into Patti's tank and have her 'shanked' [knifed]."

This jury did not know that the "prosecutor" and "investigator" that David Brown sought to have killed were Jeoff Robinson and Jay Newell. Their names would never be mentioned in this courtroom as potential victims. All the tapes to be played had been edited so that Robinson's and Newell's names would not come through.

"He wasn't set up or pressured," Robinson explained. A calm voice speaking of uncalm motivation. "He *wanted* it done. He had a lot of money to subsidize the plan. Steinhart thought Brown was kind of crazy—but the money was good."

Robinson pointed out the inconsistencies in David Brown's reasons for ordering the hits. "I'm doing this because I'm *innocent?* . . . And when David Brown hears from Steinhart that the prosecutor and the investigator are dead, he says, 'I love you, buddy. I'd get more excited but there's too many people in the tank.' "

There was so much for the jurors to absorb in one hearing. Newell, McLean, and Robinson had constructed this case as painstakingly as a skyscraper made of toothpicks. It was just as complicated: five years of lies and plots and killing games.

Robinson left the jury with "buzz words," David Brown's phrases that the investigators had learned to recognize, words that had telegraphed lies, words that demonstrated the defendant's cowardice: "Honest to God" . . . "Leave me out" . . . "Don't give me up!" . . . "I'm not involved" . . . "Don't mention my name."

"The bottom line," Robinson summed up. "This case belies David Brown's righteous indignation. He was a diabolical manipulator. Linda was older, getting a mind of her own. He wanted a new robot, and he did it for eight hundred and thirty-five thousand dollars. He did it to kill the DA and the investigator to weaken the case.

"He did it to get away with murder!"

How could a defense attorney, even one as talented as Gary Pohlson, stand up now and present a believable opening statement? Robinson had deliberately brought out all the weak spots in his own case. It was a sly—and time-worn—tactic meant to reduce the impact of information that would surely come from the defense. Robinson had even mentioned the minute amount of cocaine found in Linda Brown's blood in postmortem tests. Pohlson expected all this. The two attorneys knew each other well. They had had ample opportunity to study each other's style and technique.

Pohlson rose and spoke to the jury of unnamed witnesses who would come forward to substantiate the natural panic of an innocent man. Only a desperate man would agree to a murder plot, and Pohlson hinted that David Brown's reason had become unhinged. Pohlson's only other avenue of defense would be to attack Cinnamon Brown and Patti Bailey.

Throwaway girls.

Pohlson explained that he usually reserved his opening statement until the defense portion of the trial began. "I figure this case opens with the prosecution's case." He said he agreed with the facts as stated, but he did not agree with what the facts meant. He suggested that the evidence showed something entirely different. "These two girls had their own agenda, their own problems. . . . Cinnamon and Patti are going to lie as they have lied before—over and over and over again. They have motives."

Pohlson outlined the motivations behind Cinnamon Brown and Patti Bailey, the reasons he submitted that they killed Linda Brown all on their own. "Cinnamon Brown killed Linda. She'd been expelled from Brenda's house—again. Things were not going well. She told the medical student, the police, the psychiatrist, about the problems. Three months prior to the murder, she was upset, she had problems with Linda. The day before, Linda said Cinnamon would be gone. Again, Linda allegedly said she would kill Cinnamon if she didn't leave. . . . She's nineteen. Is she *really* young and immature? How was she five years ago? Depressed. Upset. Impressionable. She told people, 'Linda was the cause of all my problems.' She thinks, 'I may lose my dad. She's giving me and my dad a hard time.' "

And Patti. Pohlson took a chance here. Like Robinson, he laid out the worst news for his side. "Patti is also having problems with Linda. Patti had been in love with David for a long time. As early as eleven, sexual molestation; at fifteen, they started intercourse. Patti was very jealous of Linda. She wants to supplant Linda. She wants what he can give her. Linda had lots of jewelry—cars. Both girls wanted what Linda had."

One by one, Pohlson pointed out the lies Cinnamon and Patti had told. And there *were* many lies. Why would both these young women turn on David Brown at this point? "Cinnamon's motive is to get out of prison. She wants to lay it on David and Patti. Patti? Patti isn't sure her sister is really dead. Is Linda in the car with her when she drives? Patti's state of mind? What would help *her* as she comes forward November seventh, 1988? She has something—a *great deal*—to gain. Instead of twenty-seven years to life in prison, she gets out when she's only twenty-five."

And now Pohlson tackled a most worrisome area. Until the day before trail, Pohlson had fought to keep the 1989 murder plot out of this trial. But Judge McCartin had allowed it in, and Pohlson had to put out the brush fires of doubt that it would surely start.

If David Brown was innocent, why would he plot to have Patti and the "prosecutor" and the "investigator" killed? "We'll hear from Joel Baruch," Pohlson said. "You will hear that David Brown got panicked by Baruch. Baruch asked to be excused because Jeoff Robinson intimidates him."

Pohlson's point was that if Joel Baruch was intimidated by Robinson, then David Brown, an avowed coward, was totally panicked.

"An innocent man believes he's being railroaded by a prosecutor on a vendetta. He kind of lost it. [The murder plot] was Irv Cully's idea—and he's a longtime snitch." His client, Pohlson explained, was confused. He quoted David: "I don't know what was going through my mind. I was innocent. I didn't know how to get out of this."

"The prosecutor scared him," Pohlson said, and then he summed up the thrust of his case. "We won't differ on the facts. But we'll argue and fight on what they mean. Keep in mind 'reasonable doubt.'

" 'Lies' is the operative word."

If Pohlson's viewpoint was to be believed, then the jury would have to see Cinnamon and Patti as wicked, scheming teenagers who would kill to get what they wanted. Jewelry and cars and presents, and for Patti, sex with David, undeterred by her older sister.

David Brown relaxed. His attorney had revealed the girls as the treacherous little liars they were.

Robinson and Newell had *expected* Gary Pohlson to go after their main witnesses. There had been no surprises.

It was time to let the jury relive the case through the eyes of those who were there five years ago.

"Call Officer Alan Day."

42

A PARADE of police witnesses took the stand first, consulting their notepads, although their memories of the early hours of March 19, 1985, were crystalline. This case had disturbed them from the beginning.

"Mr. Brown looked haggard," Officer Day testified, describing David's demeanor on the murder night. "Chain-smoking—his hands trembled lighting cigarettes. He looked older than he was. He was very lucid, but vague on specific times he was certain places. He broke into a sweat."

Day repeated what David had told him of his whereabouts at the time of the murder and what he had done after he returned home to find Patti Bailey near hysteria. "He said he saw Linda in an 'unusual' position—with her arm over the side of the bed, and she never lay like that." But David had told Day he was afraid to go into the master bedroom. He made sure Patti was okay, then called his father and told him that Cinnamon had killed Linda.

Gary Pohlson cross-examined Day briefly. "Where did you think Cinnamon would be?" he asked.

"The trailer is the only place I can think of."

Fred McLean followed Day to the witness stand, testifying in his laconic Kansas drawl. His memory of the green stucco house was photographic. He could close his eyes and see the .38 revolver lying on the shaggy yellow carpet of the master bedroom.

Robinson asked McLean to describe how he found Cinnamon.

"Mr. Brown said he believed Cinnamon was maybe at her mother's or at a friend's. I went back out to the backyard, even though the other officers had searched and found no one. The area behind the garage is not visible from the back door. You have to go back there."

Robinson introduced photographs of two red doghouses; the floor of the larger one was covered with vomit.

"Why did you go back there?"

"It was the only possible place where the suspect might be. There were three small, excited dogs in the kennel area. I realized they weren't dangerous, so I went in. I looked into the door of the large doghouse and saw a crouched figure. I called, 'Cinnamon?' Her answer was unintelligible. I put my hand in and said, 'Come out.' "

"Did she?"

"She did. She was not really coherent. She was sluggish and clutching a cardboard note—she was covered with vomit."

"What did the note say?"

" 'Dear God' "—McLean's voice softened as he remembered—" 'Dear God, please forgive me. I didn't mean to hurt her.' "

On cross-examination, Pohlson asked if the empty medicine vials were fingerprinted.

"No. I had already handled them getting them to the hospital. The glass was fingerprinted."

But the prints wouldn't really have mattered; all the suspects *lived* in the house.

"Call Cinnamon Brown!"

This was the prosecution witness that those watching had been waiting to see and hear. A few days before, Jay Newell and Fred McLean had driven Cinnamon and Patti Bailey down from Ventura and lodged them in separate wings under tight security in Juvenile Hall. "We didn't dare risk their safety by putting them into the county jail," Newell explained. "David might have found a way to get to them before they testified."

All eyes fixed on the door to the left of Judge McCartin.

Newell and McLean led Cinnamon Brown to the witness stand. She was small, still only a shade over five feet tall, a girl-woman who had become quite beautiful in her years of captivity. Her now-blond hair was thick and wavy and tumbled in shiny twists to her waist. She wore very little makeup, and her dress was pale peach and high necked. She wore cream-colored pumps with high heels.

Cinnamon looked at Jeoff Robinson and pursed her lips nervously. She did not glance toward the defense table. Her father focused on the table in front of him. The gallery would learn to gauge his emotional responses chiefly by the tinge of scarlet that occasionally crept up his neck, or—when he was intensely disturbed—by the lack of any color at all. Then, even his ears were stark white.

Robinson stood far back from his witness, but his body language was sheltering. He was going to have to pull Cinnamon along through hell now—hoping it would somehow save her from worse battering when she was cross-examined.

"Cinnamon, did you ever tell some lies before you came into court? Did you tell lies on the subject of Linda's death?"

"Yes."

"Objection!"

"Sustained."

"Cinnamon, did you tell more than ten lies?"

"No." Cinnamon Brown's voice was childlike and very faint.

"Are you going to lie today?"

"No."

"Objection!"

Robinson and Pohlson approached the bench, conferred with Judge McCartin, and appeared to have come to some kind of agreement.

"Where do you live?"

"Ventura School."

"Is that a prison?"

"Yes."

"How long have you lived there?"

"Four and a half years."

"Why are you living in a prison?"

"Because I killed Linda."

There it was. Robinson had gone to the heart of what the jury was surely wondering. If Cinnamon had lied in the past, she had admitted it. She admitted the biggest lie of all—that she lied about killing Linda.

"Who was Linda?"

"My stepmom."

"Cinnamon, let's go back to March of 1985. Remember the night the crime occurred?"

"Yes."

"Who was living at the house?"

"Me, Linda, my father, Patti, Krystal—my little sister."

"How old was Krystal?"

"I'm not sure. She was an infant. Small."

"Cinnamon, how was it that Patti Bailey was living at your home?"

"I think it was because their house wasn't suitable—so she came to live with us. I'm not sure. . . ."

"Cinnamon, going back six or seven months before, was it the same group living in your house?"

"Yes."

". . . Did you overhear something between Patti Bailey and your dad?"

Over objections, she was allowed to answer only "Yes, I did."

"On March nineteenth, 1985, were you suffering mental problems?"

"No."

"Were you suicidal?"

"No."

"Do you know what being depressed means?"

"Yes."

"*Were* you depressed?"

"No."

Cinnamon's answers came in monosyllables. She offered nothing more. It didn't matter. Robinson would gradually draw the true story from her. There was no hurry. He occasionally used vocabulary that was common to most, but a shade beyond what Cinnamon was familiar with. The technique enhanced the picture of a fourteen-year-old girl still caught in time.

Pohlson studied the witness carefully. If he was going to free *his* client, he would have to lean hard on Cinnamon and on Patti.

"Cinnamon, how old were you in 1985?" Robinson continued.

"Fourteen."

"How old are you today?"

"Nineteen."

"Six or seven months before March nineteenth, did you get along with your dad—did you love your dad?"

"Yes."

"Did you love Linda?"

"Yes."

"Did you have problems with her?"

"Everyday—typical problems—like doing the dishes, cleaning the doghouse."

"Did you hate her?"

"No."

In response to Robinson's questions, Cinnamon described the odd household that existed in 1985. She got along with everyone; she thought of Patti Bailey as a sister. Yes, they argued, but they loved each other. They fought over silly things such as who was going to sit in the front seat. Patti was sixteen, almost seventeen. Cinnamon had only argued with her father about typical things—"Like, 'Cinny, go wash the car,' and I didn't want to."

Cinnamon's answers came so softly that it was difficult to evaluate her emotions, but she looked desperately uncomfortable as she discussed getting along with her father. Tears filled her eyes and trailed down her cheeks.

"Do you feel bad talking about your dad?"

She wiped her eyes. "Yes." Cinnamon bowed her head like a penitent. She was such a small figure sitting in the witness box, no bigger than a twelve-year-old.

"Cinnamon," Robinson asked gently, "Do you still love your dad?"

"*Yes.*"

Her answer was much more terrible to hear than if she had said, "No." Cinnamon accepted a tissue, but declined a break. She would continue.

Robinson changed the topic. Cinnamon said she didn't *like* CYA, but she had gotten used to it. Of course she would like to be free someday.

"Cinnamon, simply because you want to get out of prison, are you making things up about your dad?"

"No—if I wanted—"

Pohlson objected, and Judge McCartin struck everything after "no."

"Cinnamon," Robinson asked once more—so that there would be no question. "Did you do the killing?"

"Yeah . . . yes."

Under further questioning, Cinnamon told the jury about the terror she felt as she was drawn into the plans to kill her stepmother. She had been repeatedly told by both David and Patti that Linda and Alan were planning to take over David's business—Data Recovery—and they were going to kill him to do it. "He said we have to get rid of her. He could move away or he would kill himself before he'd let her kill him. He would leave. I said, 'Why don't you divorce her?' and he said it wouldn't work. . . ."

"What was your feeling when your dad told you he would have to leave you guys?"

"I was scared . . . crying."

"Did you believe him?"

"Yes."

She had believed it all. Over and over, her father had said, "Get rid of Linda . . . we have to kill her." She had heard it so many times on so many different drives that she could no longer remember how many. It was always her father, Patti, and herself. Linda was never around when they discussed the predicament they were in, and how to solve it.

At this fragile moment, the door of the courtroom opened, and unbelievably, unthinkably, a class of a hundred or more junior high school students filed in noisily. They were on a field trip. Cinnamon, stricken, stared past Robinson at the sea of young faces.

Robinson and Pohlson both approached the bench. Surely, the

students should not stay. They were very young, and this trip was only a lark for them. Their chairs creaked and their feet sounded like thunder at this tense moment.

Despite Robinson's urgent request, Judge McCartin shook his head. This was a public courtroom. The students could stay. As they realized what they were listening to, even the fourteen-year-olds in the group became quiet. Did they know they were listening to a young woman who was *their* age when she committed the crime of murder?

The questioning continued, and Cinnamon's voice was so faint that even the judge next to her could not hear her. McCartin startled her when he said gruffly, "Put the mike on the witness."

"Cinnamon, do you recall specific occasions . . . discussions?"

"Yes . . . several . . . on the beach, my father told me to go down the beach. When I got back, we left. The topic came up of what was to be done to Linda."

"What was to be done?"

"Ways to kill her . . ."

Yes, she remembered some of the ways. They could shoot Linda or electrocute her in the bathtub. Cinnamon thought that was her idea.

"Were you serious?"

"Yes."

"Why did you *seriously* suggest a way to kill Linda?"

"Because I wanted her dead. I didn't want to lose my father."

". . . Did your dad suggest *who*, if anybody, should do it?"

"Yes . . . he said one of us girls would have to do it. He didn't have the stomach to do it."

". . . Did he ever complain about a weak stomach before?"

"He was always sick."

Robinson pelted his witness with questions. He knew Pohlson would do the same tomorrow or the next day on cross-examination. He had to get all the truth out of Cinnamon *now*. Yes, David told them repeatedly that she should do it, that one of the girls had to. Cinnamon began to sob again. "I was willing to do it because I loved him, and I didn't want to lose him."

Listening intently, Pohlson was poised. He objected to what he construed to be leading questions from Robinson. Robinson was trying to show that there was no benefit at all for Cinnamon in Linda's death, but he could not phrase a question that pleased either Pohlson or Judge McCartin.

After three objections, McCartin bristled and growled at Robinson,

"You want to be sworn—take the stand? No more argument. No more leading questions!"

Finally, Robinson got a full question out. "On your own, did you ever plan to do something to Linda?"

"No."

The death plan had evolved from a constant drumming in of the principles of family and staying together and most of all, *love*. Unless Linda died, all of those things would be lost.

"He said, 'If you loved me, you would do this for me.' "

With all the scheming and talking and plotting and persuasion, it always came down to *love*. Always. Once the murder script was in motion, someone would have to perform. And it was Cinnamon who was selected.

"Did your dad ever say, 'Cinnamon, don't do it?' "

She shook her head slightly. "He said, 'If you love me, you'll do it. If you don't, I'll have to go away.' I felt guilty."

"Did you ever feel he said things to *make* you feel guilty?"

"Yes."

"*Were* you jealous of Linda?"

"No."

"Her jewelry?"

"I wasn't interested in her jewelry. I wanted to go to the beach. He gave me the things I wanted—my radio and my Walkman."

Some of the jurors watched Jeoff Robinson. Others looked down at their laps. Only a very few looked at Cinnamon. It was as if they found her so delicate and so sad that it would be cruel to stare at her. *She* kept her eyes fastened on the prosecutor. Clearly, she had come to trust him.

Cinnamon had a solid memory of all the crucial events five or six years before. She had become a little more relaxed on the witness stand. Now, ever so gradually, Robinson led her into disturbing details, as if she were slowly stepping into icy water.

"Did you think killing someone was all right?"

"Objection!"

"Sustained."

"*What* did you think about what you did?"

"I was doing the right thing . . . because my dad told me to." Cinnamon was crying again. "Why would he tell me to do something that wasn't right?" Clearly, she had asked herself this question many times before and had not come to terms with her father's depravity; emotionally, she was still in danger.

Robinson moved inexorably closer to the murder night.

They were on one of their many car trips when David turned to Cinnamon. "He said—since I'm the youngest—I was too young to get in trouble for it. They'd send me to a psychiatrist and send me home. He didn't mention going to jail. I said, yes, I would do it."

Cinnamon could not remember how long her father said she would be away. She thought only a few days.

"After the murder, he said I should try to kill myself—shoot myself in the head. I could just nick myself. I got scared. I said I didn't want to. I said I'd rather take the medicine. I believed it would just look like I *tried* to kill myself."

Pohlson asked for a sidebar conference. Robinson seemed tense. The presence of the platoon of teenagers in the courtroom had upset his witness and thrown off his rhythm.

For the first time, Cinnamon darted a quick sideways look at her father.

Robinson asked Cinnamon about the suicide note. There had been many of them.

"He told me to write a note to say I was sorry for what I did. I wrote them and showed them to my dad. . . . He picked one; I was to get rid of the others."

Robinson had drawn Cinnamon along with him—to the night of March 18. Each of her responses came as if she had been holding her breath; Robinson had to ask her the next detail in sequence before she could say it aloud.

"Before that night, were there discussions on who would do what?"

"He said he would be gone so he wouldn't have anything to do with it. I knew I was going to go to the doghouse, after I shot Linda."

The jury had never heard about the Uno game, the argument over putting the baby to sleep. Cinnamon relived the last day for them. "We were asleep already—I don't know how long. I heard a door opening. He walked in and said, 'Girls, get up. It has to be done tonight.' My dad told me to follow him. I followed him to his room and stood at the door. He told me to wait and be quiet. . . ."

Cinnamon's voice was thick with tears.

"I got a glass from the kitchen, and he took the pill bottles to the pantry. He told me to take more, and I said. 'I can't swallow any more.' But he kept telling me to take more. We left the bottles and the glass there."

"Did you ever feel that you would die as a result of these suggestions?"

"No."

But suddenly she did. A look of stunning shock and then ineffable sadness washed over Cinnamon's face. It was obvious that she had at long last acknowledged the truth in this one frozen moment. Her father had made her take the pills—not to give her an alibi or only to make her sick—but because he wanted her dead. This was the worst, the last thing Cinnamon had not faced, and she wept as it sunk in. And then, quickly, she darted a look at her father that seemed to say, "I know it all now. I *know*."

"Cinnamon," Robinson drew her back. "What happened then?"

"We went to the living room by his recliner. He grabbed a brown pillow from the recliner and told me to hold the pillow over the gun. I didn't know why. He said Patti would show me. There wasn't a gun, but I knew I'd see one soon. Patti was standing with us. My father was getting ready to leave 'cause he had his keys and everything with him and he was right by the door. Then he said, 'We can do this another time if you want, but if you love me, let's do it now.'

"I went to our room. Patti was wiping off the gun that she had sitting on the bed with a towel. She handed it to me. She told me, 'You know what you have to go do.' . . . I asked how to work it. . . . I was very scared, very nervous. I took the gun to my dad's room—it was very dark. I fired the gun toward where Linda would be 'cause I knew she slept on that side of the bed. . . ."

Tears streamed down Cinnamon's face.

"Linda was sleeping. I knew I was pointing the gun right at her. I knew it was going to hit her. I pulled the trigger. There was a loud noise and a jolt. I got scared, and the pillow got caught in the gun, and I ran to Patti's room and told her, 'I broke the gun!' I took the baby and gave Patti the gun. The gun went off. . . . And we could hear Linda crying. . . . Patti said I had to go finish, so I took the gun. . . ."

The courtroom was very quiet, suspended in this moment. The jurors were finally all looking at Cinnamon, their faces empty, listening.

"I went back because Linda was still alive and I'd been told to go back and finish. I wanted her dead too. I went back to make sure she was dead. I walked in and fired the gun again. I just walked in and pointed it toward her. I knew she was there. I was going to shoot her."

"And then what did you do?"

"I dropped the gun. I was dizzy. I ran outside through the kitchen and I got the note I was supposed to get from the trailer. I ran to the doghouse 'cause that's where I was supposed to go. That's what I was supposed to do."

"Did you know what you had done?"

"Yes."

"How did you feel?"

"Cold and scared. The dogs came in. I remember getting sick in the doghouse. The police found me and took me out and took me to the police station."

Cinnamon remembered the detectives' questions, and she remembered vomiting into the trash can. She remembered telling the police things that weren't true. She kept in her mind that she had to say she didn't like Linda, and that she had done it all by herself.

"Hadn't you just taken a human life? Didn't you know that was wrong?" Robinson asked softly, incredulously.

"Yes—but my dad told me it was all right."

"All right?"

"Under these circumstances, it was all right."

Cinnamon remembered talking to the psychologists and the psychiatrists, but her father had come to see her and told her that she must tell *everyone* that she had no memory of the murder at all. She had lied for him for more than three years.

"My dad said I wouldn't be there very long. I'd be let out. He'd hire an attorney—that it would take a little time."

"Did your father continue to say that?"

"For a long time."

Every time she went before the parole board, she lied.

"I told them, 'I don't remember,' and they said I wasn't telling them the truth, and I'd stay there until I did remember."

"Why did you keep telling that lie?" Robinson asked.

Pohlson objected. "He's arguing with his own witness, Your Honor."

"Overruled."

"I thought my father was going to get me out."

"At some point, did you feel your dad wasn't truthful with you?"

"Yes. He kept telling me he'd get me out. I'd call home and he'd say he was sick, but my grandma said he was out shopping."

Cinnamon described the time she caught her father kissing Patti. The seed of doubt planted then had never really gone away. "When my dad came to CYA, I questioned him about Patti, and he said there was nothing going on—that she was just there to take care of Krystal. . . ."

Did your dad ever say anything about insurance?"

"No."

"When is the first time you heard about insurance?"

"When the board brought it up."

"Why didn't you come forward? Why didn't you get *mad?*"

"I thought I was being loyal to my dad, but I found out he was lying."

Robinson asked the questions he knew Gary Pohlson would. "Does it help your chance of parole to tell the truth . . . ?"

"Yes."

"Do you think because you testified that you'll get out?"

". . . No. I still have to go to Board, and they can hold me to 1992 or 1995 if they want to."

"Have you said anything that's untrue?"

"No. I've lied before, but never on the stand."

"You lied to Jay Newell?"

"Yes. I told the truth except that I shot Linda. I was ashamed to admit that I was the one who actually pulled the trigger."

"Why?"

"Because I loved Linda."

"Did you ever actually *hate* Linda?"

"No."

"Why *did* you tell the truth?"

"Because I felt more ashamed not telling the truth."

"Do you know what perjury is?"

"Yes—not telling the truth on the stand."

"Does it bother you to tell your story with your dad here?"

Cinnamon glanced at her father, whose body was silently poised for her response. The look on her face obviated an answer.

Without realizing it, Cinnamon Brown shuddered, ever so slightly.

43

I T   W A S late in the second day of trial, but Cinnamon's ordeal was far from over. She now had to face cross-examination by her father's attorneys. Richard Schwartzberg, co-counsel for the defense, asked for written notice if the Orange County District Attorney's Office intended to help Cinnamon gain a parole.

Robinson was annoyed. He was a mercurial man whose emotions showed in his face and posture, much as a landscape changes when clouds sweep over. "I won't dignify that," he said shortly, angered that Schwartzberg would try to bootstrap this motion into the case.

McCartin looked at Schwartzberg and snapped, "It ain't close— let's go to work."

Gary Pohlson had an unenviable job before him. Cross-examining children, the elderly, the pitiable, and the victims was often a necessary part of defense law. There was a fine line to be walked. If he went easy on Cinnamon, he would elicit no telling outbursts. If he came down too hard, the jury would turn away his arguments and want to save her.

But Cinnamon and Patti were the two accusing witnesses. Pohlson had to knock the foundation out of their credibility.

He asked Cinnamon first about her feelings on finding herself in prison, about her hopes for freedom. Cinnamon looked straight into Pohlson's eyes, her gaze steady. She held her body very still, like a little animal caught in the open. Of course she longed to get out. She had pinned her early hopes on her father. She realized, finally, that he would not help her.

David Brown stared at his daughter fixedly, almost bemused that she would say these things about him. He expected his attorney to turn her around.

Pohlson could not shake Cinnamon about her hopes for an early release. She had none.

"I was surprised—not upset—when I got up to CYA. The board told me I'd be out by the time I was twenty-five. Each time you go up—and you're good—you get a time cut, but you have to deal with your offense to get a time cut. . . . Dealing with my offense is accepting what I've done to Linda."

"*Did* you accept what you've done to Linda?"

"Yes—in the past year and a half."

"Was that before or after you first spoke to Jay Newell?"

"After."

Pohlson chipped away at Cinnamon's lies. Yes, she lied to Jay Newell about who did the shooting. No, she wasn't trying to implicate Patti; she just could not say out loud that she was the shooter.

Pohlson's tone was only a shade mocking. He would lead Cinnamon again through her life with her father and Linda. She thought of Linda, she said, as a mother. She was not jealous of Linda. Linda was her father's wife.

The day wound down to an end. Tomorrow, Cinnamon would face three more hours of cross-examination. . . .

On the second day, Cinnamon seemed a bit more at ease. She wore a royal-blue dress with a tiny peplum, the skirt shorter than Robinson would have liked. Pohlson wanted to unmask a wicked stepdaughter, and such creatures traditionally wear too much makeup and dress too seductively. Cinnamon's voice was so tiny that it made up for her dress.

"Did you prepare to testify . . . read your transcript from the preliminary hearing . . . listen to any videotapes?"

She answered yes. Of course she prepared. Anyone would. It was a favorite ploy of defense attorneys to make preparation by witnesses appear suspect.

Pohlson's aggression built as the morning progressed. "Were you ashamed in 1985 of having killed Linda?"

"When I first did it, no—but it was a couple of years ago when I realized I'd taken somebody's life—"

"You thought you'd get off?"

Pohlson got rough, but Cinnamon dug in. She admitted every lie. If she didn't remember, she said so.

"You *loved* Linda Brown?"

"Yes."

"But you wanted to *kill* her?" Pohlson was full of disbelief.

"I was more loyal to my dad than I was to her."

". . . The night of the murder—how many different versions have you given? Let's go through the different versions, Cinnamon. We can count them, or we can do a summation."

Cinnamon counted. "One, I did it myself; two, I don't remember; three, I lied when I said I was outside. I guess that's three."

Pohlson came up with seven—Cinnamon's stories to Fred McLean, Pam French, Dr. Seawright Anderson, Kim Hicks, different versions to Jay Newell. She did not argue with him.

The defense attorney's intent was obvious. He wanted to solidify the murder plans and discussions in the jurors' minds. The most damning testimony for the prosecution came when Pohlson asked Cinnamon to be specific about times and methods of murder.

It began gradually, Cinnamon recalled. The first time in the living room, the second on the way to the chiropractor. "I wasn't quite sure it was a serious plan. . . . Another time, we were in the van. I think Patti said that Linda was going to kill my father and what were we going to do about it . . . it was sometime in the seven months before the murder. . . . Most of the time, we said 'get rid of'—that means kill."

Yes, Cinnamon admitted suggesting ways to kill Linda.

"What?" Pohlson pounced. "What ways?"

"Electrocuting her . . . in the bathtub, throwing an appliance in. We were laughing and joking around, and we said, 'No, she only takes showers—' "

"You *laughed?* About killing her?"

"No—we laughed about getting Linda into the bathtub."

"I mean," Pohlson breathed, "it's kind of a big deal, isn't it—killing someone?"

The words hung in the courtroom; they were headline words. "Daughter Jokes About Murder Plot."

There was no sound in the courtroom. Pohlson whirled suddenly and asked, "Who's *Maynard?* Who's *Oscar?*" He spat out the names as if he expected them to trigger some intense reaction from Cinnamon. The gallery perked up, fascinated. But Cinnamon visibly relaxed.

For the first—and only—time, Cinnamon smiled, remembering better days. "Me and my dad joked about it. If I was clumsy, or if I dropped something, we'd say, 'Maynard did it.' It was just teasing."

Robinson questioned Cinnamon once more, briefly.

"*Do* you have imaginary friends?" he asked.

"No. We were just joking about Maynard and Oscar."

When it was finally over, despite all the ugliness that Cinnamon spoke of in her soft childlike voice, one thing shone through: she had told the unflinching, unvarnished truth. "I didn't want to lose my dad," she cried, sobbing. "Killing my stepmother showed that I loved him."

For the first time, Cinnamon deliberately turned her head toward her father and talked of her discovery of the insurance payoff, and of her father's secret marriage to Patti. "I was mad and angry because they didn't tell me. And I felt hurt that they just left me there. And it seemed like I was not important to them anymore. They were just as involved as I was. . . . They killed Linda just as much as I did!"

At seven minutes to three on Thursday afternoon, May 10, Cinnamon Brown was finally allowed to step down.

Jay Newell took the stand the next morning—to introduce the first of the tapes made in the summer of 1988. Robinson submitted the surveillance photographs taken of Cinnamon and her unsuspecting father on August 13 as they sat on the lawn at the CYA prison.

David Brown's own words came back to haunt him, as they would frequently during the trial. The jury followed the long tape with transcripts. David's voice, deep and rumbly, counterpointed Cinnamon's high, light voice. She had an atonal emphasis that made her questions end in a whine. He sounded so confident on the tape as he worked to damn up the leaks that had suddenly threatened his safe jetty.

"You can tell the truth if you don't tell the whole truth," the taped David told his daughter. "If there was knowledge . . . in advance of what was going to happen, then we'll all go to jail. . . . Do you see any reason for five people's lives to be ruined . . . for all of us to go to jail because we knew what was going to happen beforehand? *I* can't survive in jail. . . . I would kill myself before I'd let myself die a slow and painful death in a cell."

It was hard to know what the jurors thought of the tapes. Their eyes were locked tight on their transcripts as they tried to follow each word. David Brown used profanity often, and a woman juror suppressed a nervous giggle at words she had never said.

On Monday, May 14, 1990, Cinnamon had returned to prison, and Patti Bailey would take her place on the stand. Like Cinnamon, she was escorted in by Fred McLean and Jay Newell.

She looked so much like her dead sister. Pretty because she was young and wide-eyed. Patti wore an almost matronly wine-and-white patterned dress. She was full breasted and had a tiny waist. Her husband had once described her weight to his "hired killer" as "about a hundred pounds." She weighed 143 pounds. Her blond hair was long and wavy, and she had a pouf of curly bangs. Her overall impression was sweet and modest.

She was very nervous. She trembled constantly, a subtle vibration as if she might break and fly apart in pieces at any moment. Some of her sisters were in the gallery, but the defense wanted them out. Robinson asked that only Mary Bailey, who was caring for Patti's child and who offered Patti emotional support, be allowed to stay, but all the Baileys were banned to the hallway, and Patti was left, alone, to testify.

Robinson elicited the story of Patti's short, sad life.

"At home, we were poor. We were lucky if we had food on the table. . . . I had trouble with my brothers 'trying things' in my room at night. My mom is an alcoholic. I don't know my father. I thought David was great. I loved the idea of moving in with David and Linda."

Patti told the courtroom of her initiation into sex with David Brown. At eleven, she was "physically contacted" and engaged in touching and fondling, and soon in oral sex with her sister's husband/boyfriend.

"Where did these things take place?"

". . . On the way to the restaurant, in the car. I wanted his attention. I cared about David."

The sexual contacts continued after Patti moved from her mother's home. At fifteen, she began having sexual intercourse with David.

Patti's voice was husky as she relived her adolescence. "I loved living there. I got everything I wanted. I didn't have to worry where food was coming from."

David had promised he would marry her one day. "At first, when he talked about getting married, I thought he was kidding. . . . I loved him. He was everything to me. *He was my life support system.* . . ."

"Patti," Robinson asked, "are you still in love with David?"

"Objection!"

"Overruled—you may answer."

"*Yes.*"

It was impossible to doubt Patti Bailey, or to ignore the chilling similarity to Brenda Sands's memory of her early life with David. She too had depended on David Brown utterly. She too talked of the miracle of having enough to eat. She was the oldest of eleven children of a single mother; Patti was the youngest. David's money was very important to Patti. She had never had any.

But she loved him too. "I cared about him. He was warm and loving and sensitive when I needed somebody. . . . I was confused about it

[sex]." Because there had been molestation in her mother's house, and then with David, Patti said she believed "that was the way a house went."

Patti seemed old, and very weary. There was a bitter acceptance about her. She did not smile.

"How many houses did you live in with David?"

"Five or six."

"Where?"

"Two in Anaheim, Brea, Yorba Linda, Yucca Valley—I can't remember them all."

"Did your life with David progress?"

"There was more physical contact. I was around him more."

"How was your relationship with Linda?"

"It was good. She was like a mother to me. She was like my best friend. You could confide in her about anything."

It was obvious that Patti could not see the dichotomy here; she *meant* what she was saying. Robinson asked her how she felt, then, about having sexual relations with her sister's husband.

"Guilty. I knew it was Linda and David—it wasn't supposed to be me . . . and I wanted David."

Robinson asked how the lovemaking was managed when they all lived in the same house.

"Linda would go to the store, or we'd get up in the middle of the night."

And then, in 1983, David had begun his constant drumming about Linda's moods, about how she had changed. About how "scared" he was of his wife. Patti too thought Linda seemed distant, not the same "as she used to be."

"Were you looking for changes?"

"Yes . . . I was looking for anything I could. . . ."

"How long before Linda's death did Cinnamon know of the 'plot to kill David'?"

"Three to six months."

Patti Bailey slipped her glasses on and instantly became a plain, stolid, blank woman who was not in the least pretty. The glasses were so scratched that she could barely see out of them.

"Did you ever actually hear Linda plot?"

"No."

Patti recalled David's continual warnings that the family would break up if something happened to him. "I wouldn't have a place to go. I never had a family. David was my family. He was everything to me. . . . It was always, 'She's going to break up *the family*,' if we didn't do something first."

"Did you help?"

"Yes."

"Did you want her dead?"

". . . Yes . . ."

"Did you love your sister?"

"Yes—but I loved David more. He gave me love . . . material things . . . everything."

"Between the two—if you could only have one—who wins?"

"David."

Why had Cinnamon become involved? Patti explained that she herself couldn't kill Linda, and Cinnamon would probably only get a few months.

"Six months prior to Linda's death, were there active suggestions?"

"Yes, several. . . ."

"What were they?"

"Stabbing, suffocating, putting cyanide in her Coca-Cola. David would say what would be a 'good' or a 'bad' idea."

"Did you talk about paralyzing Linda?"

"That was my idea. Have David work on a car—up on the rack—and have Linda get under. . . . He said it wouldn't stop her from wanting him dead. He asked me to be the one."

"Why you?"

"He couldn't take to see it. He couldn't stand to see it. He didn't *want* to see it."

Robinson's questions continued, each one leading to the next. David Brown sat slightly forward, watching his wife with steady eyes, his lips slightly parted. He looked like a lizard sitting on a rock, waiting for a bug to come into his line of sight. Patti never glanced at him. Without her glasses, she could not see him across the courtroom. *With* her glasses, she could barely see through the scratched lenses.

"Did you ever compete with Cinnamon to prove your love?"

"Yes—"

"Objection!"

"Sustained," McCartin said. "The answer is stricken."

Robinson rephrased the question and Patti was allowed to answer. "We'd try to outdo each other, to see who could come up with the best idea that David would approve of."

"Did you have to prove yourself?"

"Yes."

"Before Linda's actual death, were you awakened at night?"

"Yes. David woke me up about a month before that and said Linda had to be taken care of. We went down the hall to the bedroom. I took a pillow from the end of the bed. He gave me the gun. He told me to use the pillow to muffle the noise so the neighbors wouldn't hear it. I had no warning when I went to bed. He kept saying that I had to kill her before she killed him. It was after midnight—Linda was sleeping when I went in her room. I put the gun to her back and stood there for a few minutes. I couldn't do it."

"What did he say?"

"He wasn't mad—he said, 'It's okay.' "

One blazing truth became increasingly apparent as Patti Bailey testified. Although she had had no opportunity to talk with Cinnamon Brown alone in more than *five* years, her memory absolutely corroborated Cinnamon's.

After midnight on that cold March night, David *had* awakened both of them and told them it had to be done. He *had* given Cinnamon some "medicine. . . . He left about five minutes later. He said. 'It doesn't have to be done, but if you girls love me, you'll do it.' "

"Did he ever say, 'Don't do it'?" Robinson asked.

"No. . . ."

Just as Cinnamon had done, Patti began to choke up with tears as the questions focused in on the actual murder. Again, her recall was the same as Cinnamon's.

"Did you murder your sister?" Robinson asked quietly.

"In my mind, I did." Patti Bailey wiped her eyes.

Jeoff Robinson held out a picture of a smiling Linda Brown and asked if this was Patti's sister.

She was sobbing. "Yes . . ."

Patti explained that she dealt with the murder for several years simply by putting it out of her mind. But the memory bubbled up to the surface. She had tried to kill herself three times.

"How?"

". . . By slicing my wrists, taking sleeping pills—'cause I couldn't live with what I did."

"Did you lie?"

"Yes."

Patti talked of the moment David returned from his "drive" to the beach. He was gone for an hour and forty-five minutes. "I told him Cinnamon had shot Linda. I told him not to go back to her room, and he said, 'Oh, my God.' He seemed kind of surprised, but relieved to have it over with. He didn't cry. He was calm. He told me to check the trailer for Cinnamon. . . . I was scared and upset, and I didn't understand why he sent me to look in the trailer when I *knew* she was supposed to be in the doghouse."

Patti explained that David was very concerned that the police suspected him. He instructed her, if they were arrested too, that *she* was to take the blame and keep him out of it.

"He would have to go to jail. In the first thirty days, he was always afraid he was being followed, that someone was around. . . . He was afraid to go to Cinnamon's trial. He was afraid that Cinnamon would tell on both of us during the trial."

"Did you lie at Cinnamon's trial?"

"He told me to say that Cinnamon was crazy, and to give short answers. He said Linda and Cinnamon had reasons for not getting along, and to make up stories of arguments and say Cinnamon was depressed. I was told to make Cinnamon sound 'a little bad and half-crazy.' I was to report to David during the trial and get instructions."

David had apparently told Patti to imply that Cinnamon had tried to shoot *her*, too. Robinson questioned Patti vigorously about lying. She had lied at Cinnamon's trial. Was she lying now?

"No."

With Cinnamon safely in prison, David forbade Patti to see her family, checked on her with a beeper system, and moved his parents in. He had married her, finally, "because he said he was dying and Krystal needed a legal stepmother."

After Cinnamon summoned David to the Ventura School twice in the summer of 1988, David had panicked. "[At home] we talked about getting arrested. . . . David said for me to take the blame. He'd get a lawyer for me, take care of Heather, and make sure I had everything I needed or wanted while I was in jail or prison. We were afraid. . . . David thought the house was bugged."

In the squad car on the way to the Orange County Courthouse on the morning of their arrest, Patti testified that David pointed at the floor and mouthed that they were bugged. "He said untrue things. He asked me, 'Who is the father of the baby?' I told him that he was."

In the courthouse, Patti had waited for hours while David was being interviewed by Jay Newell and Fred McLean. "When I was interviewed, I tried to cover up again."

"At some point, did you hear the tape of David's interview that day?"

"Yes."

"Were you upset?"

"Yes."

"Why?"

"Because I couldn't believe the things he said about me."

Patti Bailey responded to questions about where she thought she was going after she pleaded guilty, and how long she thought her sentence would be.

"I thought I was going to the women's prison in Frontera, but I went to CYA instead."

It was apparent that Patti was still confused. She seemed to think she was serving life in prison, that she would be moved from Ventura to Frontera when she was twenty-five.

Robinson found himself between a rock and a hard place. His witness was nonverbal, terrified, and depressed. She was not forthcoming, but she answered honestly. Even more than Cinnamon, Patti was a difficult witness. She needed the questions to help her focus. When Robinson tried to explain, McCartin, seemingly furious because Robinson was asking leading questions, excused the jury.

The judge turned to Pohlson. "Do you want a mistrial?"

A bit startled at first, Pohlson was on his feet, asking for a motion for mistrial because of Robinson's leading questions.

McCartin ordered Robinson to stop calling his witnesses by their first names. He denied the mistrial. "For now."

"No more questions," Robinson said angrily.

Many in the courtroom understood the need for his technique. The jurors, as all jurors are, were inscrutable.

After a recess, Pohlson rose to cross-examine Patti Bailey. "Mrs. Brown or Miss Bailey?" he asked.

"Miss Bailey."

Once again, Patti related the sordid sexual connection she had had to David Brown. In 1983, two years before she died, Linda had ordered David to take Patti back home.

"David came back and got me and said if Linda said no, they'd get a divorce."

"How did you feel?"

"I was grateful."

Patti recalled that she had "normal teenage problems" with her sister. "David told me that Linda was always threatening to throw me out."

Pohlson asked her to describe when she began having intercourse with her brother-in-law.

". . . The beginning of 1983."

"How often . . . ?"

"Weekly, sometimes twice a week, sometimes every other week."

Patti still evaded reality. She testified that she was sure Linda never suspected anything. Yes, she felt guilty, and she had asked David to stop—but then *he* made her feel guilty for asking. She had had sex with one of her brothers before moving in with David and Linda.

"Did you feel guilty about that?"

"No—my brother was forcing me."

"Did you resent it?"

"Yes. Sometimes."

David had been the first—before her brother. Even with David she sometimes felt forced to have sex. She had never told anyone about David—not until the preliminary hearing to this long-delayed trial.

As Patti spoke, she twisted rhythmically in her chair from side to side, and her body trembled more.

Was she in love with David Brown when she moved into her sister's home?

"I was as in love as an eleven-year-old can be."

"Were you jealous of Linda?"

"Yes. . . . He was giving her attention he wasn't giving me. Holding her, touching her, being affectionate."

"Were you jealous in 1980, 1981?"

Patti testified that she envied Linda her possessions, the *things* David gave his wife. "[Otherwise] David tried to be equal with all his girls—with me and Cinnamon."

But not like Linda. By 1982, Patti insisted that she had learned to accept things the way they were. She was the little sister who engaged in oral sex with her brother-in-law every time Linda wasn't around. David never forced her—physically.

Patti seemed to have no guile. She was a phlegmatic young woman who had yawning gaps in her education and socialization. She was David Brown's "product," his collector's prize. Her inflection was sometimes sardonic, very like David's. He had been her only model. It may have been difficult to *like* Patti—but not to pity her. Pohlson's questions drove her to retreat into a certain toughness.

She talked of Linda's second wedding to David.

"Did it bother you?"

"Yeah, it bothered me."

"You wished you could take her place?"

"Sure. I wanted to be David's wife."

The sexual contacts, of course, continued. "He was nice to me, but he was only affectionate when Linda left the room. He'd wink at me, blow me a kiss, give me a hug. We'd hold hands. She never caught us."

Patti still hoped to marry David. But her hopes had dimmed when Linda got pregnant a year after her second wedding. However, when Krystal was born on July 20, 1984, Patti felt David seemed very distant to Linda.

"I was scared that it would break up the family."

"Wasn't that what you wanted?" Pohlson asked.

"No."

"It *never* occurred to you that you could take her place?"

"No."

He wouldn't let her slide on that one. Finally, Patti answered, "Well, once or twice, but that wasn't the reason she was killed. It was to save David."

Pohlson relentlessly questioned Patti on the methods of murder considered. Each time Cinnamon or Patti talked about this, there were more ways. Patti remembered suggesting, when they lived in Yucca Valley, that the television could fall on Linda and hit her on the head.

"And another plan?"

"Garden Grove was the 'paralyzing plan.' "

"Did you ever think that it was wrong to paralyze a newborn baby's mother?"

"What do you mean?" Patti asked dully.

"Did you ever think it was wrong to paralyze a newborn baby's mother?"

Clearly, Patti saw in Pohlson a failure to understand. He was talking apples, and the subject was oranges.

"There was *always* a discussion about how to kill Linda—when she wasn't around . . . stabbing, suffocating. The day before we talked about pushing her off a cliff—me or Cinnamon."

"How . . . ?"

"She was supposed to be out looking at the view and one of us was supposed to take a running jump and push her over."

Who was to have done the stabbing? Pohlson's questions had lulled Patti into even flatter affect.

"Cinnamon."

". . . Suffocation?"

"I don't remember who was going to do it."[1]

"Were you willing to suffocate her?"

"Yes, I was."

There were two constant themes portending that Linda Bailey Brown would die. Cinnamon could not bear to lose her father. And Patti?

"I didn't want nothing to happen to David. David was everything to me."

No one in the gallery doubted that that was true.

Pohlson was occasionally brutal in his cross-examination of Patti Bailey. He accused her of telling the truth because she thought it would help her case to cooperate with the prosecution. Didn't she think that being a witness against David Brown would help her?

"I didn't know I'd be a witness until the end of December. . . . I asked Mr. Rubright if I could talk to the district attorneys. We agreed it would be best if I talked to them. . . ."

"You thought you'd get a better deal?"

"No."

"Did you have any hope that it would help?"

"Yeah, I hoped it would help— but I was going to plead guilty either way."

"Were you angry—upset with David Brown?"

"I was upset."

"When?"

"Sometime in October, over a statement he made to the police . . . that he was *scared* of me. . . . I was angry and upset with everyone at that point."

". . . When did you decide to do the 'right thing'?" Pohlson asked, his voice full of scorn.

"When I realized I couldn't live with myself. . . . I was having a difficult time. I was blocking it until November seventh. I still couldn't remember details. It's hard for me to believe my sister was dead. When I was in a car, it seemed like she was still there. I went to her funeral, but I didn't believe she was dead."

Each lie that Patti told—every one—was brought out and analyzed in this grueling cross-examination. Patti replied that she had not lied; she was "confused. I didn't want to remember that I'd been so involved in my sister's murder."

Patti Bailey Brown, swiveling in her chair, quivering like a leaf in the wind, her hands nervously touching her face, was questioned on redirect, recross. She had exposed all that she was, everything she thought.

It left her with nothing.

44

J E O F F Robinson, with help from Jay Newell and Fred McLean, had choreographed this trial so that the living witnesses were followed by audio or video tapes that either confirmed or refuted their testimony. The audiotape made at the Ventura School on August 27, 1988, played now in the courtroom, David and Patti and Cinnamon talking together two weeks after David's first taped visit. David is offering Patti in exchange for Cinnamon in prison. David Brown's ethnic slurs, his raunchy sexual jokes, his easy explanation that incest was normal, "that a lot of fathers have sex with their daughters," were heard in this courtroom.

It was a very long tape, and the jury and gallery listened again on Wednesday morning, May 16. There would be many more tapes, so many that Judge McCartin suggested that popcorn be provided.

Even if David Brown chose not to testify, his voice and his opinions were now familiar in this courtroom. When the jurors finished hearing what was *actually* said during David's visits to his daughter in prison, the *videotape* of the interview just after David Brown's and Patti Bailey's arrest was played. He was talking to Jay Newell and Fred McLean. David's face was on a large television screen, and the jurors were afforded a viewpoint never imagined before such technical advances. David leaned forward, fascinated by his own image.

It was once again nine o'clock on the morning of September 22, 1988, and for three hours, the two investigators and the suspect jousted in the tiny yellow interview room. At the beginning, David Brown, sipping Perrier and smoking, was the confident millionaire computer genius, tossing out his familiar claims to fame: he and Linda—"Mr. and Mrs. Coca-Cola"—his Pentagon contacts, the *Challenger*, the Stealth bomber, the MGM hotel. He bragged of his "dynamite" sex life with his late wife: Linda's "quirks," her desire to please him with her hands. It was too dimly lit in Department 30 to see what effect these intimate revelations had on the jurors.

When this interview took place, it had been only four weeks since Cinnamon's body wire caught every word of her father's visits. Even so, David's memory of those visits was vague. Newell even had to help him remember *when* he visited.

David's recall of the reason Cinnamon summoned him up to CYA was that she wanted his blessing on a crush she had on an Asian boy. She was afraid he would be prejudiced because of the jokes he made about the Vietnamese in Garden Grove. But of course, David told Newell and McLean, he had no feelings against "Orientals." "If he was black, of course I'd want to meet him."

Minute by minute, David Brown wove himself a trap of words. He had no notion that the visits with Cinnamon were on tape. He manufactured a different story. He did discuss Cinnamon's confusion, her desire to know "the truth" about the murder. But he molded the story to suit himself. Newell allowed him to dig a deeper hole.

"The board told her *I* killed Linda for the insurance money. . . . She said, 'Daddy, I know you didn't do it,' and I said. 'Well, tell me, honestly—did you do it?' and she says, 'No, Daddy, I was outside. . . . I remember being outside and hearing the gunshots.' "

He re-reconstructed his last visit to Ventura—on August 27, 1988. "Cinnamon said, 'One way or another, I want out of here now!' and I told her I was as anxious as she was to find out who did it."

The long tape was remarkable. It was almost possible to see wheels working inside David Brown's head. He dodged, feinted, created, and ran from any connection to Linda's murder. His voice was confident. Every answer was complicated and started another trail away from Newell's questions. David presented himself as the complete father, the long-suffering martyr who only wanted to find out the truth and put the real shooter behind bars.

He pointed always away from himself.

Twenty-two minutes after he hinted that Patti or Cinnamon *may* have been guilty of murder, David changed his mind. It may well have been Patti and Linda's brothers. Perhaps Alan. Perhaps Larry. "I've been shot at when I was driving."

Newell asked a blunt question about the conversations at Ventura School. "Did you and Cinnamon discuss—at that meeting—about you being involved *with* Cinnamon and Patti in a plan to kill Linda?"

"That's what I'm leading up to—"

"Well, yes or no . . . ?" Newell pressed.

"Her understanding that there was a conspiracy—I told her I knew of no such conspiracy for anyone to hurt me."

"Who brought that up?"

"That's the hard part—"

"Who brought it up?"

". . . Cinnamon . . ."

"Did you, prior to Linda being killed, have discussions about killing Linda?"

"*They* had suggested it, and I had told them, 'No. I would rather die.' *Cinnamon and Patti both said they would kill Linda—before they would let anyone hurt me.* I told them I've had threats on my life so many times that it makes no difference to me."

Another five minutes, and David then announced that he had had threats on his life that had nothing at all to do with Linda and her family, sinister forces waiting on the streets to shoot him.

"How much money did you get from Linda's death?"

"I don't honestly know—it went into savings. . . ."

"How much?"

"Maybe five or six hundred thousand . . ."

"Would it be closer to eight hundred thousand?" Newell prodded.

"I honestly don't know."

Nor was David Brown sure how many insurance companies he had with policies on Linda. Or how many paid off. One insurance company didn't want to pay off, and he didn't really care. David thought they settled for about $10,000. (*In truth, he had demanded—and received—$75,000.*)

"Did you ever have a physical relationship with Patti Bailey?" It sounded like a throwaway question, but each time David Brown was asked about either insurance or his relationship with Patti, he tensed, and Newell was obviously using that. "Hell, no . . . ," David said. His words had no expression, nor did his follow up-question: "Why would you ask that?"

David was not even sure where Cinnamon was found the night of the murder. He thought "in the backyard."

"Did you have anything to do with giving Cinnamon drugs that night?" Newell asked.

"God, no . . ." The same flat emphasis.

"Did you prepare some drugs for Cinnamon to take to make it look like she was committing suicide?"

"God, no . . ."

"Okay." Newell pressed. "Did you that night that Linda was killed have Cinnamon get a suicide note to have in her possession?"

"No, I would never have been a party to anything like that."

"Did you have Cinnamon do some practice notes to have handy that night?"

"For what reason . . . ? I'm not a stupid person. . . . If I was going to stage something, it would be a lot more sophisticated than this. I've even got books at home that I've started writing—my imagination was extremely vivid. . . . That's why I'm good at the business I'm in."

"Books that—" Newell began to ask.

"Science fiction . . . My imagination was strong enough to—God, even from watching TV, you can get a million ideas of how to stage something," David insisted. ". . . If I was to prepare her [for suicide], I would have given her very large quantities of tranquilizers and muscle relaxers."

"Did you ever talk to Cinnamon at Ventura School about giving her the drugs that night?"

"No way . . . I would have told her she was out of her mind."

"You *would* have?" Newell's doubt was thick in his voice. "One last question—and it's a yes or no question—are you actually the one who pulled the trigger of the gun that killed Linda?"

"Absolutely not." Again, the flat answer. David Brown was not annoyed or surprised or indignant.

And that, in itself, was damning.

An hour and forty-five minutes into this interview, David seemed slightly distracted, but still confident. His voice had a new hollowness in it, and he drew out his words, syllable by syllable. And then, casually, Newell opened a manila envelope and removed four eight-by-ten surveillance photos. One by one, he set them down on the table in front of David Brown. He became absolutely motionless. He froze, stunned.

"Hey, David," Newell said easily, "we have pictures of you during your visit to Ventura School, and we have tape recordings of that conversation, and you're not telling me the truth right now, because you discussed *all* those things with her in very great detail."

For the first time in almost two hours, David Brown had nothing to say.

Newell said repeatedly, "David, I believe you when you say you didn't pull the trigger. I believe that. Up until today, I had doubts—but I believe you."

"I couldn't hurt anybody. . . ."

"I believe you didn't pull the trigger."

Each time Jay Newell confirmed his "belief" in David Brown, he opened the door wider for David to give someone else up in this most heinous crime. If he had read him correctly, David would turn in his mother or his father or *Krystal* to save himself.

The jury was seeing a police interrogation, not testimony about what went on, but the actual interrogation. They would be able to judge for themselves what they believed was true. David Arnold Brown was *testifying* on this flickering television screen.

Jay Newell asked him for the truth. David backpedaled eight years, admitting to illegal sex with fifteen-year-old Linda, discussing The Process and embellishing the assassination attempts on his life.

"What does this have to do with Linda dying?"

"I'm getting to that."

McLean, who had been silent, gruffly reminded David that he and Newell were only looking for the truth. "We are capable of disproving any lies."

Pushed into a corner, David once again sacrificed Patti Bailey. She had been his devoted slave for almost fifteen years. She would die for him, or kill for him. It didn't matter.

"I need to know if I need to be afraid anymore—for Krystal and myself," he said shakily. "I need to know if I'm going to be protected."

"Protected from whom?" McLean asked.

". . . From Patti."

Two hours and six minutes into this interview, David gave up Patti Bailey as the probable killer. He confided that he had lived in constant terror of Patti, afraid that she would kill him or Krystal. To Newell's suggestion that Patti be asked to move out, David explained she would be even *more* dangerous then. There was no telling what she might do. No, it was safer to let her live in his house, safer not to set her off. "I'm scared to death of that girl."

"Who do you believe killed Linda?" Newell asked.

"There's no doubt in my mind—Patti."

In this utterly fascinating study of psychopathy, David Brown completely reversed himself on everything he had emphatically stated at the beginning of the interrogation. He had assessed the damage to himself and "erased" what he had said before.

Now, he remembered telling Cinnamon to say she did it so she would get less time.

Now, he remembered telling Cinnamon to say she had lost her memory.

Now, he remembered that he went to his fourteen-year-old daughter and asked her to lie—to protect Patti.

Now, he recalled preparing medication for Cinnamon to drink to make it look as if she were trying to commit suicide. But he didn't want to hurt her. He had mixed up Tylenol, Bayer aspirin, and baking soda, "just something to make her sick to her stomach." He would not admit that he gave Cinnamon any medication that would kill her, or even hurt her.

Now, David admitted that he knew about the plot to kill Linda, but he was helpless to stop it. Patti promoted it. David could not control Cinnamon. "She was headstrong just like her mother. . . .

"This is the honest-to-God truth. . . . I didn't think they were going to do it. I told them, 'Absolutely no way.' I said, 'Cinny, I hope this is a game. . . .' She said, 'No, Daddy, it's no game.' "

And then David had driven away from the house where his beloved wife slept, fully aware of the wicked girls' plot to murder her. The concoction he had made for Cinnamon was, he insisted, only something that would foam up and "maybe make her numb for a while."

But he reminded the detectives he had told them not to do it.

"Who got the gun out, David?" Newell asked.

"I believe it was in Linda's nightstand."

"Who got the gun out?"

". . . Either Patti or Cinnamon.

"I *told* Cinnamon if she was to go through with this thing, no matter what I said, I didn't want to be there. If she was to go through with this thing, she should leave the note somewhere like in the kitchen where everyone would see it, and she was to go hide in her trailer."

David Brown actually sounded relieved. He seemed to believe that he was in the clear. He had given up Patti. He had given up Cinnamon. He embroidered a little more on Patti's guilt. He thought he had heard her confess in her dreams. Not, of course, because they were sleeping together, but because Patti was given to "nap attacks."

If that was not enough, he offered more. At the end of November of 1985, he said he had asked Patti directly if she was the one who killed Linda. "She said, 'You really don't want to know.' "

"Why, then," Newell asked incredulously, "why at the end of November 1985—you have a daughter in *prison*—why didn't you bring that forward?"

"What could I do?"

". . . This is September of 1988, David."

"She didn't really confess. . . . I only heard her reliving it. Is that proof?"

For just a moment, Newell—who never betrayed emotion during interrogation—had disgust in his voice. His own daughters meant everything to him.

"Do you have a sexual relationship with Patti?"

". . . God, no . . ."

"Did you *ever* have a sexual relationship with Patti?"

"We hold each other . . . because it gets to me real bad over what's happened. It just tears me up—"

"Wait a minute," McLean's voice broke in. "You're telling me and Jay that you embrace—for support—the woman that you believe killed your wife, who you told us earlier you were so deeply in love with?"

David could not come up with an answer to that one before the next question.

"Is Patti in love with you?" Newell asked.

"That's the most confusing part."

"Yes or no."

"I don't know."

David Brown had tripped himself up again and again, and now he accused McLean and Newell of playing word games with him. He could not explain why he had left Cinnamon in prison while he lived with the woman he had just said murdered his "beloved wife." He could not explain why he continued to live with that woman he called a murderess. He could not explain why he would bring his parents to live with a murderess. He was not even sure if he had had "love" or "sex" with Patti.

Newell and McLean had spun the spinner, and he had lost his balance.

The screen went fuzzy. The interview was over.

45

T H E   T A P E that Gary Pohlson feared lingered in the minds of everyone who had seen and heard it. The courtroom was quiet, save for the sound of David Brown scuffling his feet nervously beneath his chair.

The Steinhart tapes were next. The jurors were handed new transcripts. David Brown now had to listen to his good friend "Goldie" and himself as they plotted the deaths of an unnamed prosecutor and an unnamed prosecutor's investigator, as well as the murder of the "girl upstairs."

From the "Birdcage" tape to maneuverings to get money to fund the "hits" to the last tape where Steinhart assured David Brown that his enemies were dead, the jurors and gallery scarcely shifted in their squeaking chairs.

Tapes 12A and B, 13A and B, 14A and B, 15A and B. Hours of cunning plans.

From time to time, David shook his head slightly or wrote on the yellow pad in front of him. The jurors heard of his escape plan, of his belief that it didn't matter if two deputies died because David figured he was "worth more than they are." And when he got the word on the day before Valentine's Day that the DA's men were dead, the jurors heard David Brown say, "You did great . . . wonderful, you're a good man. . . . God, I love you, Richard."

As the tapes played, Jeoff Robinson sat with his back to the jury and Jay Newell looked down at the table in front of him. Neither knew if the jurors realized that David's designated targets were, at this moment, in the courtroom. Their names were carefully "whited out" of the transcripts. The men David wanted dead might well have been *any* prosecutor, and *any* investigator.

The descriptions David gave to Steinhart were way off anyway. And Newell, for this trial, had shaved his mustache. He smiled faintly as he heard himself described as "looks like a big ugly rat—has an ugly mustache; yeah, we'll call him Ugly Mustache."

And through this long afternoon of listening to tapes about murder for hire, Steinhart emerged as something of a comedian. David had never detected it, but the jurors and the gallery did. Steinhart's breezy style, his deft manipulation of the "boss," were, at times, hilarious.

Suddenly, there was a great gap in the continuity of the trial. A year ago, Gary Pohlson and his wife had bought tickets for a Hawaiian vacation—to begin on May 20, 1990. David Brown's trial has been delayed so often, at his own request, that his new attorney's vacation now coincided with his court dates. Everyone concerned had waited for the defendant; now Brown would have to wait for eleven days while Pohlson went on vacation.

No one familiar with California trials seemed surprised. Department 30 would be "dark" until the day after Memorial Day.

The trial began again on May 29 with more tapes featuring Steinhart and David Brown. And finally, on May 30, Robinson announced, "There are no more tapes." A witness more familiar to a murder trial took the stand. Martin Harry Breen, a criminalist, did the toxicological examination of the blood sample drawn from Cinnamon Brown on March 19, 1985. He testified that a blood screen for alcohol proved negative—as did analysis for barbiturates, sedatives, hypnotics, PCP, opiates, cocaine or its metabolites. Breen explained that he found propoxyphene—"an analgesic used in Darvon or Darvocet. It's a mild painkiller."

"Can it be toxic?" Robinson asked.

"It can be lethal."

"What was the quantity in Cinnamon Brown?"

"Six-tenths of a microgram per milliliter."

"Was this a therapeutic dose?"

"Generally, it is not. It is above the therapeutic level, which would normally be one one-hundredth to three-tenths micrograms per milliliter."

"What would six-tenths mean?"

". . . It would be either toxic or lethal."

"Call Richard Steinhart!"

Richard Steinhart, larger than life, filled the courtroom with his presence. He wore a black T-shirt, jeans, and a black leather vest, and his long hair, goatee, and mustache were all black and luxuriant. His tattoos were the only touch of color.

Steinhart stood at attention, shoulders back, to be sworn, then swung himself into the witness chair with one powerful arm. There was a crackling vibrancy about him, this witness so familiar already because his *voice* had filled the courtroom for days.

"How many times have you been in the Orange County Jail?" Robinson asked.

"Two or three times."

"What was the nature of your offense?"

"Probation violation on a drug charge."

"Was Christmas Eve, 1988, your first time in jail?"

"That was the first time."

Steinhart explained that he had used cocaine, eventually a thousand-dollar-a-day habit, for twelve years.

"You stopped?"

"Yes, sir . . . a little over a year ago. Since May 14, 1989, I have had no drugs or alcohol."

Steinhart explained that he rode with an "outlaw" motorcycle club and became privy to information on a triple murder in 1980. The FBI approached him in 1983 about being a witness. He agreed. He was now waiting to testify in that trial—also in Orange County.

"Why did you go into jail on Christmas Eve, 1988?" Robinson never attempted to paint Steinhart as less than notorious.

"My girlfriend and I were visiting her mother. She didn't think I was appropriate for the young lady, so she called the cops."

"Did you look like you look now?" Robinson asked with a grin.

"Worse—I cleaned up today."

Steinhart, at Robinson's urging, described meeting David Brown in the Orange County Jail. David was absolutely fascinated. He showed more interest in Steinhart's testimony than he had in any other thus far in the trial.

Steinhart recalled David's awe at his impromptu martial arts demonstration. "He said, 'That was really great. How did you *do* that?' We'd sit alone at the table, and we started talking—about my war stories, my past. . . . He told me he was being railroaded; he wanted to know how you get someone out of jail. . . . He was quite well-off. He told me about his coin collection, his stamp collection, his jewelry, his safes, his monies. . . . He said, 'In case things go sour, what would it cost me to get out of jail? . . . How much hits would cost . . .'"

Even though the subject was chilling, Steinhart was funny. "I'd get uncomfortable talking about it," he said. "I didn't need no witnesses. The other inmates were a bunch of rats, looking for a way to make a deal. Also, we were in a PC [protective custody] tank. I was supposed to be testifying against the Hessians. . . ."

"Ever avoid the DA?" Robinson asked.

"Every chance I got."

"Did you intend to testify?"

"No way."

"Why?"

"I'm breathing, aren't I? . . . I was being held as a material witness so I wouldn't fly. I'm in that PC tank with homos, child abusers, molesters, and snitches—the cream of the crop."

"What's a snitch?"

"A person who gathers information to help *their* case. See, there's two kinds of rats. Number one is people who make stuff up, and number two is the vulture type who preys on the weak, depressed guys after they've been in jail about two or three days. You want your mommy and you tell what you've done."

Steinhart explained that he meant to keep to himself, but that he had become involved with David Brown because of the promise of a half a million dollars.

"What did you intend to do for that?"

"I was to help him escape for fifty thousand dollars. I fully intended to do so. If he'd given me the half million dollars up front, I would have let him rot. . . . If he gave it to me in bits and pieces, I'd have done it. . . . He asked me to terminate Bailey. He came to be quite concerned that Patti had given some damaging testimony at some other trial [the preliminary hearing]. . . . He went to court quite often—he told me Bailey damaged him. He had no problem with Cinnamon's testimony, but he was afraid Bailey's would give him the gas chamber. . . . Bailey had to be terminated, and I told him I could have it done."

Robinson asked if there were other requests, and Steinhart nodded.

"To terminate the investigators. David's case was deteriorating all around him. He told me the DA was really trying to screw him and fuck with him. He thought . . . if he got rid of the DA and the investigator, their replacements wouldn't be able to catch up 'cause these two had been in on it from the beginning."

Steinhart was enjoying his own ferocious act. He had the usually enigmatic jury enthralled. *He* thought, he said, that he was getting out of jail when he left the Orange County Jail, but he had found himself in another jail. "I expected to get out and go live in Brown's house and have a car with monies in it—six hundred dollars for two drop guns for the escape. Great bunch of guys you are!" He teased Robinson about the "fine accommodations you folks set up for me."

He testified about how the tapes with David were made, beginning with the body wire in the Birdcage. David looked embarrassed and annoyed.

And then, suddenly, when Steinhart had been on the stand for about an hour, he seemed to have trouble tracking Robinson's questions. He threw up his arms and tossed his head. It appeared, at first, that the testimony had distressed him.

Was this another act?

But Robinson called for a recess so that Steinhart could take his medication. A pretty blond woman who wore a headband of feathers and a jean jacket came from the gallery to help him. He was very ill, and it was not an act.

With Steinhart's permission, Robinson asked him about his condition when the trial resumed. "I've been up at Lake Elsinore, at the Lincoln Christian Fellowship. I've been praising Jesus. I got married on April twentieth, and then I got sicker and sicker. I found out four weeks ago that I was HIV positive. Nine days ago, I found out that I have full-blown AIDS. I take AZT—the docs just doubled my dose."

There was a real sense of loss in the room. So far in the trial, this bombastic biker was the runaway favorite. After a lunch break, a more subdued Steinhart took the stand.

It was difficult for Pohlson to cross-examine Steinhart because he agreed amiably to every negative thrown his way. Yes, David had felt the "DA was screwing him."

"Which hit was first discussed?"

"I believe Patti. . . . He said Patti lied. She framed him. David was upset with the way the DA was treating him. I believe first the escape, then Patti, then the two—the DA and the investigator."

"Was Mr. Brown scared—nervous?" Pohlson asked.

"Very much so."

"He thinks he's going to get the gas chamber for something he didn't do?"

"Yes."

Pohlson wanted to show that Steinhart got "favors" from the DA for his cooperation with them. He read through a rap sheet showing that Steinhart was arrested in 1986 and released, and again in 1987 when he *did* some jail time—both times for possession of cocaine.

"Oh, yeah . . . I pleaded guilty to a felony. I got three years probation and seven days in jail."

"Any other conditions?"

"I must testify in the other case. Truthfully. So I lied to them and said I would. I had a habit of not showing up. I just wanted out. The only thing on my mind was to get more drugs."

"Did you get—or expect—favors for helping the authorities?"

". . . It worked before—I got out. This time, it didn't work. . . ."

On redirect, Robinson asked if David wanted to get rid of Patti's testimony, get rid of the "two gentlemen," to keep the case from going sour. "Was Mr. Brown desperate?"

"Yes."

"Was he in control?"

"He had his faculties."

". . . You lied [before] to get out and get dope?"

"That's right," Steinhart agreed readily.

"You have any reason to lie now? Any charges pending?"

"No."

Pohlson had another crack at Steinhart, but questioning him was akin to wrestling a teddy bear. He wouldn't disagree and he wouldn't fight back.

Steinhart was passed back and forth between direct and cross several times. He was self-deprecating and open. When Judge McCartin finally excused Steinhart, he waved at the bench and said, "God bless you," as he left the stand.

The jury clearly hated to see him go.

Dr. Richard Fukomoto testified to the postmortem examination he had performed on Linda Brown five years before. "Two gunshot wounds of entry in the chest wall from a large-caliber weapon."

The toxicological screen had shown only one drug: cocaine. "There was no cocaine in the blood. There was a very small quantity in the brain and liver. Benzoylecgonine—BE, the metabolite of cocaine—was also found. These levels are on the lower spectrum . . . at the low end of recreational use."

Cross-examined by Richard Schwartzberg, Dr. Fukomoto said that he could not tell when the drug was either ingested or injected. Nor could he determine in what amount. His best guess was that the cocaine got into Linda's system within hours of her death.

This would continue to be a question mark. No one would ever know how the cocaine got into Linda Brown's system. The day she died, she played Uno, cooked a huge meal, took care of her baby, and entertained her in-laws. *When* did she have time to use cocaine?

"Call Dillard Veal!"

Dillard Veal, the consummate insurance man, took the stand. It was Veal who gave Fred McLean a crash course in life insurance and underwriting. He was a short, dapper man who laughed easily.

Testifying in a gentlemanly Southern drawl, Veal explained why he had occasion to review David Brown's insurance history. It was his company, Liberty Life, that paid off on a policy that had not even been accepted. Linda had applied on February 21, 1985. Only one premium had been paid—the one that accompanied her application: $113.34. "A tentative agreement was made with Mr. Brown to settle his claim for fifty thousand dollars. On my next visit to Orange County, that was not acceptable. I was referred to his lawyer, Mr. Phillips, and we agreed to a payment of seventy-three thousand seven hundred and fifty dollars."

David's application for insurance with Liberty Life, like all his other applications, had been perused closely by underwriters. He listed hypertension and colitis under health concerns. When he sought payment on Linda's policy, Dillard Veal had researched any other policies extant and applied for and found Linda had *four* policies, all issued within the thirteen months prior to her death. David had none.

She had not mentioned the other three on her application to Liberty. "That would have mattered to Liberty," Veal explained. "You wouldn't want someone to be overinsured—far beyond their expected needs. We get suspicious the higher it gets." He pointed out that a housewife with limited training and education would probably not be approved to buy a million-dollar insurance policy. "She would be overinsured."

On each of the policies the Browns applied for, David's occupation was listed as either "computer expert" or "computer specialist"; Linda was listed as a "housewife." On the Liberty Life application, she had added, "Help husband in his work."

The defense position was that Linda Brown had been a "key man" in Data Recovery, and that her death would have been expected to cripple the company. Obviously, it had not. Data Recovery had continued without a ripple when Linda died.

The jury now knew that David Brown had collected $843,626.68 on claims he submitted after Linda died.

Robinson entered into evidence a certified copy of a marriage license—issued to David A. Brown and Patricia Bailey.

After eleven days, the prosecution was winding down.

At 11:22 A.M. on the last day of May 1990, the prosecution rested its case. It was Thursday, and Judge McCartin's courtroom was always "dark" on Fridays. The bulk of David Brown's defense would wait for three more days.

46

T H E R E had been a few hints of the direction that the defense would go. Pohlson and Schwartzberg had lost their best witness. Dan Coston, who now had David's $40,000 emerald-cut diamond ring, would not, of course, testify that David had been enticed and en-trapped into murder-for-hire plots by Irv Cully and Richard Steinhart. And he most assuredly would not be allowed to testify that David had promised him a million dollars to lie on the stand. The double-agent snitch's name would never be mentioned in this courtroom.

The loss had been rough on the defense case. David *wanted* to testify, but it would be against Pohlson's good judgment. David had no ability at all to see himself as others saw him. He had viewed the September 22 arrest interview and felt he had handled himself very well. He could not *see* that he had completely changed his story from beginning to end. He could not *see* that the sexual details about his dead wife were in bad taste and inappropriate. If David got on the stand, he would have to face cross-examination from Robinson, and Pohlson knew that Robinson would skewer his client.

It had been obvious for some time that David Brown was not happy with the way his case was going. He whispered continually to Pohlson or tugged at his sleeve. No one could hear his words, but his expression was petulant.

If they would just let him tell it, he could straighten everything out.

Pamela French, the Garden Grove policewoman who had accom-panied Cinnamon to the hospital the morning of Linda's murder, was the first defense witness. She had heard Cinnamon Brown's second confession as she sat with her in the hospital room. Officer French did not agree with Robinson that Cinnamon's statements had sounded "preprogrammed."

On Monday morning, June 4, the defense case went into high gear. Before the jury was brought in, Richard Schwartzberg argued against the inclusion of "special circumstances" in his client's charges. He insisted there had been no proof that the motive for Linda's murder was for insurance. Robinson argued that insurance can be "incidental" and need not be the primary reason for murder for special circumstances to attach.

"Why would David Brown not have waited to kill Linda then," Schwartzberg asked, "until the last policy took effect?" It was an important area for the defense. Special circumstances would undoubtedly bring a sentence of life without possibility of parole.

The television cameras were back. Barney Morris and Dave Lopez would have today's testimony on the five-o'clock news in Los Angeles.

Jay Newell was the first witness for the *defense*.

Of course. Pohlson would try to show through Newell how many times Cinnamon and Patti had lied to him. Newell was a calm and experienced witness. He was friendly and responsive, but he could not be tripped up. The girls had already testified to their lies; the jury could count them.

There were no deals. There were no threats. Newell had only given them a layman's explanation of perjury before both Cinnamon and Patti testified in the preliminary hearing. Newell acknowledged that he had believed either David or Patti was the shooter when he first talked to Cinnamon at Ventura in August of 1988. He just didn't know which one. On October 29, he returned Cinnamon's call and she admitted that *she* was the shooter.

Robinson cross-examined his own investigator. Not surprisingly, they had no disagreements.

"Have you ever heard me say one word—or have *you* said one word about a deal?"

"No."

"We purposely avoided that?"

"Yes."

Dr. Seawright Anderson testified to his examination of Cinnamon Brown five years before, to her confession to him in his first consultation, and to her complete loss of memory in the second. Anderson had never talked to David Brown or to Patti Bailey Brown. It was difficult now for Pohlson to undermine Cinnamon's and Patti's testimony. They had told the truth, and Dr. Anderson was testifying to a distant, flawed reality.

David Brown would not testify; his witnesses became, instead, a flying buttress of defense attorneys. First, Alex Forgette, Cinnamon's attorney. Forgette testified that he did, indeed, tell David Brown that he represented Cinnamon, and only Cinnamon. David had not de-

murred when Forgette warned him that he would go after anyone—
even Brown—to protect Cinnamon. The defendant had continued to
retain Forgette. "Mr. Brown kept paying me and he cooperated in
every way."

"Call Joel Baruch!"

Those who remembered the last courtroom meeting between Robinson and Baruch tensed. For those who did not, it was rapidly
apparent that Baruch and Robinson were full-blown adversaries.

Pohlson wanted to show that David Brown had good reason to
believe he was being railroaded, sacrificed on the altar of the ambitions
of the DA's office. Baruch was quite willing to oblige. He explained
that he was David Brown's attorney from about October 1, 1988,
until after the preliminary hearing—held to determine if there was
enough evidence to hold Brown over for trial. The preliminary hearing
had taken from December 19 through January.

Since this procedure had taken place *before* the murder-for-hire
schemes between the defendant and Richard Steinhart, it was essential
that Baruch did not name either the prosecutor *or* the investigator
then working on the case. Would Baruch protect their anonymity?

Asked what he had told his client about "the prosecutor," Joel
Baruch answered, "I conveyed to him that the prosecutor did not like
me and that he was going to go after Mr. Brown a little bit
harder. . . ."

"Did you to convey this to 'the investigator'?"

"Yes."

"And what was his response?"

"The investigator would stop at nothing to get his point across. He
didn't pay attention to rules. There *are* rules."

Baruch appeared to be a cold, almost supercilious, man. Any resentment he had for Robinson had scarcely diminished. The feeling
was mutual, and apparent to even those who didn't know the history.

"How long was the preliminary hearing?" Pohlson asked.

"A month or two. It wasn't continuous."

"What was the tenor or tone of the interaction between the prosecutor and yourself?"

"It was chaotic." Baruch half-smiled. "It invaded the preliminary
hearing."

Richard Schwartzberg read from transcripts of that hearing and
inadvertently spoke Jeoff Robinson's name aloud. Now, the jury knew
who "the prosecutor" was who was meant to die. It was the prosecutor
who was trying this case. Jeoff Robinson.

There was a sudden, almost panicky, sidebar conference. The jury was fascinated. They were told nothing more. Baruch remained on the stand.

Yes, Baruch recalled, answering Pohlson, there had been a recusal hearing and there were confrontations in the hallway. No, Mr. Baruch did not care for "the prosecutor."

Finally, Robinson rose to cross-examine the man who had once called him a "buffoon." "Do you have any bias to help out Mr. Brown?"

"No."

"You were paid three hundred thousand dollars to represent Mr. Brown?"

"No."

"How much?"

"Prior to February 1989?"

"The total amount." Robinson dug in.

"About two hundred and fifty thousand dollars—but we refunded some of the money."

"How *much?*"

Pohlson objected.

"Sustained."

"In the preliminary hearing, you told Mr. Brown that he'd get nailed," Robinson continued, "because 'the prosecutor' didn't like you, didn't you?"

"I told him that it was a consideration—that our previous battles would make it hard on Mr. Brown."

"And you said 'the investigator' would stop at nothing to get Mr. Brown?"

"Yes . . . I gave examples in this case. . . . I definitely indicated my participation in the case could affect him. . . . I told him this several times over a period of time, over the entire preliminary hearing."

Robinson was scathing. ". . . The investigator and the prosecutor are going after your client because they don't like *you?* That they lost some reason, some objectivity—that they'd convict him *just because they didn't like you?*"

"No, I didn't say that."

Robinson read the decision of Judge Schwenk, who had found no merit in Joel Baruch's recusal motion against "the prosecutor." He now accused Baruch of trying "to buy the case in the press—of *trying* the case in the press."

"No! It was to try to stop an unethical prosecutor from steamrolling David Brown. . . . Some cases need to be tried in the press. You let your client go naked. Jurors read, and they need to know both sides. . . . I wanted the press to know our position."

"Were you worried about what would follow after you told Mr. Brown [about 'the prosecutor']."

"No—"

"You didn't think the situation was serious?"

"Certainly serious for Mr. Brown."

"Why didn't you make a motion against the prosecutor *before* the preliminary hearing?"

"You know you can't do that. Some prosecutors play fair with the defense—some play a game."

". . . Did you think your client was going to do something bad?" Robinson moved carefully for Baruch's jugular, and McCartin sat alert, watching. "Why write checks for over twenty thousand dollars for his brother?"

"It was for rare coins.'

"You think—"

"Exactly," Baruch cut in smoothly. "Mr. Brown was a coin collector . . . he asked me to write a check for coins so I wrote a check for coins."

"The morning after two people were supposedly killed, *you* leave and go to Florida?"

"Yes . . . for an anniversary with my—then wife."

"On the night before, were you in the jail in a heated conversation with Mr. Brown?"

Baruch glared at Robinson. The jury may have been lost. The intensity of the feud between these two attorneys was white-hot. Robinson seemed to believe that Baruch had some knowledge of the murder plots, and he had stopped just short of accusing him of that.

The jury was excused and McCartin roared at Robinson, "I love you, but our romance is ending. I'm getting upset, goddammit. Hear my voice change? I do things. Like kill attorneys. . . . You're pursuing crap. I don't know what the hell you're getting into. . . . Goddammit, let's get the show on the road!"

Pohlson soothed the waters. He let Joel Baruch explain that it was necessary for a defense attorney to establish a relationship of personal rapport with his client.

"You gave him instances of dealing with the prosecutor and the investigator?" Pohlson asked.

"Several."

"Were you concerned it would cause him to do something?"

"No," Baruch insisted. "I wouldn't have told him if I thought it would."

Surely the jurors realized now that Robinson and Newell were "the prosecutor" and "the investigator," but everyone pretended that Schwartzberg had not slipped. The code names continued.

It was Tuesday, June 5. The weather was bright and sunny, but the weather was always bright and sunny in Santa Ana. The fountain outside the courthouse had not been turned on for months because of the drought. But for some reason, this morning, it spouted and arced twenty feet in the air. The brides leaving their courthouse weddings laughed as they ran by.

The last witness for the defense was yet another attorney: Donald Rubright, who represented Patti Bailey. The defense obviously wanted to imply that Patti Bailey was offered a "deal" to testify against her husband—that she would be tried in juvenile court instead of adult court. The prosecution was just as determined to show that she had not.

It was a wash.

"Did the 'district attorney' tell you he didn't want Patti Bailey to testify thinking she had some kind of a deal?" Robinson asked Rubright.

"Yes."

"My advice," Rubright said to Gary Pohlson's similar question, "was for her to testify. I believed it would benefit her. There would be advantages."

"How many times did you see her?"

"Maybe seventy-five to a hundred times, counting phone conversations."

"Did she trust you?"

"Ultimately, yes."

David Brown's 1099 forms from 1981 through 1985 were offered and accepted as evidence.

Dr. Kim Hicks was supposed to have testified against Cinnamon. A stipulation was offered and accepted as to what her testimony would have been. Like Dr. Anderson, she would have testified as to Cinnamon's statements just after Linda's murder.

But Cinnamon herself had already told the jury about that in this courtroom.

The defense rested at eleven minutes after eleven. A good omen for David Brown, the inveterate Las Vegas gambler?

47

W E D N E S D A Y , June 6, was taken up with the ponderous, but necessary, debate between the prosecution, the defense, and Judge McCartin over jury instructions. David Brown asked to be excused from court during this part of his trial. He had apparently come to detest this courtroom, his uncomfortable and ultimately stationary chair, and the eyes that burned into his back from the gallery. The Bailey sisters and brothers were there, always watching. They did not wish him well.

Final arguments would not begin until Tuesday morning, June 12. For those caught up in the emotion of this trial, the week yawned ahead, empty. As in all trials that last for weeks, there was a sense of impending loss for the regulars in the gallery—for the jury too. This tight group would soon disband and scatter in all directions. A number of friendships had taken root and would continue, but they would never again be together in this particular fashion. Every day in Department 30 had promised drama and revelation.

The rest of life was never so dependably bizarre.

Jeoff Robinson ran marathons; even during the Brown trial, he ran the Long Beach Marathon on one blazing-hot, smoggy Sunday. He thought of quitting when he "hit the wall" after nineteen miles, his lungs burning from bad air and heat. But then, like most of those who fear stepping on cracks for fear of damage to their mothers' backs, he kept going—afraid of jinxing the trial's outcome. Irrational? Of course. Normal human superstition? Of course.

After half a hundred felony trials, Robinson might well have become blasé by now and overconfident. He never had. The Brown verdict mattered a great deal to him, and not simply because he liked to win. Keeping David Brown inside was, for Robinson, damage control. Like Jay Newell and Fred McLean, Robinson walked with a gnawing worry that something vital might have been overlooked, that some piddling legal nicety might rear its head and let David Arnold Brown go free.

Robinson could not let that happen. His final, most important task was before him now; in his closing arguments, he had to give the jury everything he and Newell and McLean had turned up in their long investigation. He had to tie all the major facts and the incidental—but meaningful—trivia into one blockbuster of a package that would leave no doubts at all in the jurors' minds.

The fact that Robinson had committed this case to automatic memory wasn't enough. Robinson now went into "heavy training" in these last days before the big fight.

The three protagonists for the State met on Thursday in a conference room deep in the belly of the Orange County Courthouse to go over the most salient prosecution points once again. Fortunately, Robinson was not a prima donna; he accepted advice and suggestions with grace. McLean and Newell laid out *their* perceptions of what had to be included in Robinson's closing arguments. Robinson jotted down notes in his jagged left-handed script. And then they listened as he argued—not his own case—but *the defense's* case. Robinson tried to second-guess what Pohlson would say and be prepared to beat him to it, to defuse the defense's case before it happened.

For almost a day, the three men discussed "What if . . ." and "Hit that area hard . . ." and "Don't forget to include . . ." And then Robinson holed up with his notes and his yellow legal pads. For days—and nights—he wrote and thought and rethought and rehearsed what he would say. He slept little. Four days to go.

The courtroom had been three-quarters empty for much of this long trial, but this morning, Tuesday, June 12, 1990, it was packed with spectators—courthouse employees, relatives of the attorneys, the curious drawn by increased media coverage, the media themselves, relatives of the defendant and the deceased.

Manuela Brown, David's mother, was in the fourth row behind the defense table. David's sister Susan was with her, and Manuela had also brought five-year-old Krystal. She was a chubby little girl in a ruffled, flowery dress and white Mary Jane shoes. She looked bewildered, and she was obviously there to point up what a fine family man her father was. It seemed a frail ploy, given the testimony of Cinnamon, his oldest daughter, and his complete denial of Heather, his youngest.

David Brown entered with the familiar clanking of chains. He wore a pink dress shirt and tie and gray polyester slacks. He turned around, spotted Krystal, and grinned and waved to her with his small star-shaped hand. She waved back; she plainly adored her daddy—just as Cinnamon had once adored him.

Whatever the verdict would be, it could not have been wise or sensitive to bring Krystal here on this day to hear words recalling her mother's violent death and words condemning her father. She had already lost enough.

It was 9:20 A.M. and everything was ready—save for one alternate juror whose seat was empty. The trial had come this far, and everyone was nervous that the young woman was missing. Gail Carpenter was picking up her phone to call the tardy juror just as she scurried in at 9:23, complaining about the freeway gridlock. The jurors, who had sometimes worn shorts and sundresses on hot June days, had dressed more formally today.

Judge McCartin explained to the jury how they must listen to closing arguments. "Argument is not evidence, and the displays are not part of evidence, so don't expect to get them. Don't treat closing arguments as evidence. . . . If the attorneys start to argue, rely on your own memory."

The courtroom was hushed as Jeoff Robinson rose to speak. He wore his "serious" navy-blue suit. "Good morning," he addressed the jury.

"Morning," they chorused. There was a pronounced air of expectancy. This was the Super Bowl part of the trial, and everyone knew it.

"I will speak twice . . . ," Robinson explained. "Because we have the burden of proof . . . The buck has to stop somewhere."

Robinson thanked the jury for their patience and attention and asked only that they *would* give him a verdict. "I don't care if it takes five minutes or five hours or five days—or *ten* days."

The jurors were so solemn, so absorbed, that Robinson caught them off guard when he grinned suddenly and said, "I'm only going to talk long enough until I've convinced you that I'm right. As I convince you, I'd ask you to raise your hands. When I've convinced you all, I'll stop talking."

The jurors and the gallery laughed, albeit nervously—the last laugh of the day. But the tension was eased.

"The primary question is," Robinson began, "*why* are we here? The answer is what I told you in my opening statement—I told you you were going to hear a modern-day tragedy, and [during this trial] you couldn't have heard a more atrocious set of facts that displays that this *is* a modern-day tragedy. . . . This can't happen, but it did. . . . This *isn't* a fantasy. . . . This man—at the end of the counsel's table, David Arnold Brown—in what the People will characterize as a very deviate and depraved manner, orchestrated the murder of his twenty-three-year-old wife—a woman he professed to *love*. . . . How more depraved an act is there than to take the life of the person that you *at least* espouse most to care for and trust . . . to kill the one you've shared vows with . . . to kill the one you've shared your most inner darkest secrets with? And probably the person who would be the least suspecting that you would do this. There probably can be no more serious breach of trust. There's probably a hierarchy of trust. You kill a stranger—an acquaintance—maybe a family member. But the *wife*—the person you hold all this commonality with? It is really significant, and that's why we're here.

"To further aggravate . . . we have the fact that Mr. Brown enlisted and encouraged his own flesh and blood—a fourteen-year-old girl— Cinnamon. That was a fourteen-year-old child any way you want to look at it . . . who was corrupted and tainted and *twisted* by her father. . . . Is it fair for this little girl to have been placed in the situation she was . . . ?"

". . . By his own admission, Mr. Brown's a coward. . . . There's no question that this man has others do his bidding because he is the *ultimate* coward. He's a person that wants, wants, wants, but he doesn't want to put himself on the line. As he says over and over, 'Leave *me* out of it.' Per his own words, he 'didn't have the stomach for it.'

"We further have that, in preparation for this atrocious act, Mr. Brown sweetened the pot a little bit . . . by overinsuring his beloved—the one he has said over and over he would rather die in her place. He overinsures her to the point that it makes the act well, well worth it. After that . . . Mr. Brown comes into a huge windfall. . . . There's no question but that Mr. Brown knew exactly what he was going to gain. . . .

"If that weren't enough—after collecting eight hundred and forty-two thousand dollars, we have another act by Mr. Brown. In the preparation of this murder—actually long before—Mr. Brown preyed upon a young, vulnerable girl from less than fortunate circumstances. Regardless of what you think of Patti Bailey, we all are the products of our environment. . . . Mr. Brown preyed upon . . . Patti Bailey. In preying upon her, he promised her a new life. . . . Mr. Brown knew about her problems with family members, with clothing. Money. Food. What kid wouldn't want out of that hell she was in— to come with Mr. Brown?

"She didn't grow up to be Shirley Temple. You saw her—almost 'zombielike,' but was that because she's just an innately cold person, or was that because she's not that far removed from the hold that's been placed on her for several years? Even adults can be brainwashed by other adults. Imagine what vulnerable children in the right situation would do—what can happen.

". . . Mr. Brown, for his own perverted and selfish indulgences, prepares Patti Bailey to the point that she views him as her sole sense of support. . . . She told you, 'He was my life support.' He was the cure-all for her . . . and Mr. Brown was very adept at insuring that he remained that way, by sequestering these girls. . . . He gets her to the point where she is willing to take the life of her own flesh and blood—*her sister*."

The courtroom was silent except for Jeoff Robinson's voice. It was not that he had given the jurors new information; it was more that they were hearing a litany of "atrocious acts" so packed into the same time frame that they became more unthinkable.

During these long months, they had heard all the tapes, they had heard David Brown's voice cajoling, denying, explaining (although never from the witness stand), and they had seen the young girls that the DA was talking about. In the beginning of this trial, all of it was akin to viewing a television drama.

Now, it was real.

"After the murder," Robinson continued, "the atrocious acts don't stop. As time goes by, things seem to get worse and worse. We have Cinnamon Brown's own life jeopardized by her father. . . . What would have happened if Cinnamon didn't vomit? There's no question what would have happened. You would have had the perfect murder. You would have had the act you wanted done—the murder of your wife—you would have had her sister there in her place, someone still young enough to mold, not twenty-three and independent. You would have had a suicide note that would have extricated *you*. And then— if the stomach [Cinnamon's] doesn't vomit—you've got no witnesses.

"If that stomach doesn't vomit"—he nodded to the jury—"*you're* driving your car or *you're* at work [today] and I'm down in my office. We're not here. To think that a father could jeopardize his own flesh and blood in that fashion is scary. . . .

"Mr. Brown knew that his daughter might not live to tell about it. His other alternative was that if she did, she's prepared with a story. . . . This fourteen-year-old girl—because she loves her father so much—is prepared to go through with it. . . . The defense is going to tell you Mr. Brown hasn't done any of this—it's those girls—those 'crazy girls'; they've done this on their own. Well, if you're convinced that that's how it happened, then so be it. Walk him out of here."

Robinson reminded the jury that the thrust of this case came through most forcefully in the three-and-a-half-hour interview that David Brown had with Jay Newell and Fred McLean on the morning of his arrest on September 22, 1988. "After he lies for a couple of hours, the walls finally start tumbling in. He can only plug up so many holes, and finally, like water, the truth starts coming through. He kills himself. That videotape is his end. That's what this case is all about."

Robinson pointed out that Ventura was *not* a school; it was a prison. "Cinnamon Brown's been put on hold since she was fourteen. Mr. Brown's trying so hard to keep her incarcerated and keep himself out of it. How far can this guy go?

"This man doesn't have a conscience. None. This man is the typical sociopathic personality. All he thinks about is *me*. Everybody else in his life is just a pawn. He can justify whatever he does by always saying that *he's worth it*."

A major factor in proving David Brown guilty of murder had been to establish his "consciousness of guilt." Was he, indeed, aware that *he* was guilty of murder in the death of his wife, even though he was miles away when the shots were fired? Robinson stressed that Brown's actions *after* the crime showed a great deal of conscious knowledge of his own guilt.

"He plans to eliminate and/or kill the obstacles to his freedom—the prosecutor and the investigator that know the case so well—get them out so the new people can get in. Is that not the conscience of a guilty man?

"And then the ultimate was—to kill this woman he's married to—Patti Bailey—you'll see the marriage certificate. He was *willing* to kill *this* wife because she could testify against him."

Robinson spoke next of Linda Bailey. Linda was the forgotten woman. She had been dead for more than five years. Dead so long that it was easy to forget that her death began this long tumbling down into utter evil. Linda's little girl sat in the courtroom fidgeting, unable to understand what the man in front was talking about. Krystal Brown rubbed her eyes and leaned her head on her grandmother's ample shoulder.

It fell to Robinson to explain the legal rituals attendant to murder. Count I was for the murder of Linda Brown. Count II was for conspiracy to murder. Was it necessary to explain murder? For the record, perhaps. "Every person who kills a human being with malice afore-thought is guilty of violating Section 187 of the penal code. . . ."

The case before the jury was, Robinson said, "all or nothing." (Jury instructions agreed upon earlier had eliminated the possibility of sec-ond-degree murder or manslaughter charges.) "Mr. Brown is either guilty of first-degree murder or he is not guilty. . . . The defendant has the right to have a lesser offense included in the charge. In this case . . . we'll go to accessory after the fact. Mr. Brown would like very much for you to find him guilty of this. . . . He would shake your hand fifty times over if you gave him one of those. That would be a *gift!*" Robinson pointed to the display board with the definition of first-degree murder. "The facts of this case are a *textbook* first-degree murder case."

If the jurors had agreed with Robinson's case thus far, they had accepted that David Brown planned the killing of Linda Brown, *pre-meditated* the killing of Linda Brown for a long time—*years*—before she was eventually killed. Her murder was not the result of a sudden, rash impulse. "A cold, calculated judgment and decision. . . . It can only be first-degree murder," Robinson said succinctly.

The next explanation of the law was more important to the layman, most of whom assume that it is necessary to actually pull the trigger or place one's hands around the throat of a victim to qualify as a killer. Not necessarily. "When two or more people gather to plan a crime, it's more likely that that crime will be pulled off," Robinson explained. "The legislature wanted to thwart that problem by making this—the actual planning—a separate crime. That's conspiracy."

How could a person—not the actual perpetrator of the crime—be guilty? The legal concept was one of "vicarious liability." "This says," Robinson explained, "that there can be many players in a particular crime. There can be the 'hands-on' slayer—but if you aid and abet, you can be as guilty as the actual perpetrator. . . . *Mr. Brown is equally guilty, even though he's not the actual perpetrator.*"

Robinson was doing a good job of explaining rather difficult legal sticking points to a lay jury. This case was quite different from tele-vision murder trials. David Brown's hands were not stained with any victim's blood—not literally. But if Robinson was to be believed, they dripped scarlet.

The defense had stressed—and surely would continue to stress—that their client had attempted to withdraw from the plan, that David Brown had told the girls not to go through with killing Linda. And that too brought up a fine legal area. There was simple "withdrawal" and then there was "effective withdrawal." Had David Brown truly tried to terminate all of his liability in the alleged plot to kill his wife? *Had* he intended to remove himself totally from the situation?

"One area Mr. Brown seemed very enamored of—in his tapes at Ventura and in his interview with Mr. Newell," Robinson reminded the jury. "He seemed to repeat and to make it a point—even in a nonresponsive fashion—he'd say to Cinnamon [at CYA], 'But I told you not to do it!' 'Remember I told you, "Don't do it!" ' and then Cinnamon says, 'But that wasn't until the end.' And then he said—according to testimony from the girls in court—'Well, you girls don't have to do it, but if you love me . . .' Well, Mr. Brown's *got* to say he withdrew from the plan."

Robinson pointed out that Brown was caught unaware by the existence of the tape made during his visits at Ventura. He had to concede something—but he would only concede what Newell already knew. "As he gets pressed against the wall . . . he concedes, 'Well, I did mix up some medication—but I didn't try to kill her.' 'Yeah, I did help her with some suicide notes, but . . .'

"You have viable proof out of Mr. Brown's own mouth that he aided and abetted. . . . Mr. Brown now has to prove to you that he withdrew. . . . And there's a rule of law that addresses that. ". . . Termination of liability of one who has aided and abetted a crime—he may end his responsibility by notifying the other parties of his intention to withdraw, *and* by doing everything in his power to prevent its commission."

Robinson's voice had only a slight sarcastic edge as he listed the steps David Brown claimed to have taken to stop the murder of his wife. He quoted Brown's grudging admissions as he asked if the jurors believed that the defendant *effectively* withdrew from the killing plans. " 'If you do it against my will, I'm going to leave.' . . . 'Okay, girls, I brought you up to this point, I told you how it's going to go down, I screened your notes for you—I showed you the best suicide note, I mixed the concoction for you—I got you all prepped, but now I'm saying, "I'm heading out. *Don't do it.*" '

"Is *that* everything in his power to prevent its commission? That's ridiculous. That's crazy. Would you leave the home of the woman you loved—the woman that he has said over and over how much he loved and cared for, how he would rather have died himself—and yet he's going to leave and not do a thing, knowing these girls are going to kill her, and *let* them do that? 'Hey, girls! Wake up, wake up, girls—I'm leaving—don't shoot anybody.' Is that an effective withdrawal? No."

The courtroom, if possible, was even quieter. It was 10:10 A.M., and Krystal Brown had, thank God, fallen sound asleep.

Robinson now went patiently over the "special circumstances" finding. The death concerned had to be intentional, and it had to be carried out for financial gain. Linda Brown's murder fit both these criteria. "It doesn't have to be the *prime* motive—just as long as money was one of them," Robinson said. "What was his mind-set at the time of the killing? . . . Did he expect to collect insurance? It's pretty clear. Mr. Brown had had several contacts with insurance agents. Within two years of her [Linda's] death, there were four policies totaling *gross* overinsurance—over a million dollars . . . but he had policies on her before, the defense will say, and he let those lapse. Why did he? We'll never know. But we do know that Patti Bailey testified he was talking about killing Linda as early as 1983.

"Then, in Brea, Patti says they really didn't talk about it for an extended time. Maybe things were going okay for a while. . . . The bottom line is that, within *one month* of her death, on February twenty-first, he gets her to sign up for a *new* policy—for four hundred grand. You don't have to be an insurance broker to know what that means. This is a classic case of a spouse taking insurance on the other spouse in the hope of gaining a windfall."

The morning break rolled around. The jurors could not see the clock; it was behind them. The rest of the listeners had not noticed the time.

Twenty minutes later, Robinson struck at the very heart of the conspiracy. "In the case in 1985, you have to remember something. When all the parties . . . live in the same home such as we have in Ocean Breeze, if you have to go beyond physical evidence—fingerprints, fibers—which are not apropos here, you have to ask, "*Who would be the one most plausible? . . . Who had the most compelling reasons to want Linda dead? Who had control over this peculiar family . . . ? Who made the ultimate decisions as to the methodology of murder? Who was bright enough to master that?* I think you know the answer to that. *"Who ultimately gained the most?*

"I think if you answer all four of those questions, you have your man. . . .

"Mr. Brown's got no problem with grabbing whoever he can and using them as a shield to keep the heat off himself. . . . He's going to blame it on Cinnamon. . . . You read the letters he wrote to Patti while he was in jail. You're going to see David flip-flop all over the place. . . . In that interview with Cinnamon, he's saying he's 'scared to death' to live with *Patti* . . . and with Jay Newell, David says he's even scared to throw Patti out . . . now, he's arrested and Patti *has* to be his friend, and so you'll see in the letters an attempt to brainwash Patti. "These girls are dependent on him. . . . Can these girls control David Brown? It's like Edgar Bergen saying, 'Charlie McCarthy's running me all over. Look at these puppets. Look what they're doing to me.' "

Robinson asked the jury to remember everything they knew about the defendant. Given that knowledge, would it seem out of character to them that he would solicit murder? "Look at his degradation of women. He refers to them as various body parts. Look at his description of Patti Bailey. This was his *wife*. . . . He became Patti's *life support*. He had to be there, she thought, in order for her to live. . . . When a man takes liberties with a child at an age as young and tender as that, over and over, would a girl not go to hell and back for him?

"This was the kingdom of Brown, his own little fiefdom! Some kingdom. Their family outings—they talked about killing Linda. This man—he's had one hell of a reign. He's juvenile and he's a genius."

But, Robinson pointed out, David Brown always had a "noble" reason for what he wanted done. He wanted to be out of jail because "Krystal needs him . . . I'm doing it because I'm innocent . . . I'm doing it because the DA is screwing me . . . I'm doing it because Linda's going to kill me . . . I'm doing it because the Mafia's after me."

Robinson was building to a grand finish, even as he systematically tore down David Brown's alibis for the times of all his crimes. He stressed that it did not matter how the tapes with Richard Steinhart were orchestrated; all that mattered was what David Brown believed and said on those murder-for-hire tapes. Even if David Brown truly believed he was being "railroaded," would an *innocent* man respond in this way?

David Brown was furious; a brick-red flush crawled up the back of his neck, and he frequently whispered urgently to Pohlson. When Robinson referred to him as "the Love God—David Brown," he smiled slightly, then realized as the gallery stifled giggles that he was being satirized. He was angry anyway because he had never had the chance to take the stand.

"What kind of man," Robinson continued, "leaves Cinnamon to languish, while *he's* living it up? A real creep—and that's being nice. He told Cinnamon, 'It's much harder on grown men in prison,' and he said to Patti, 'Just leave me out. Back me up and leave me out . . . like we'll do jail in shifts—when Krystal's old enough, we'll get her up here [to Ventura].

"The coup de grace [was] on September 22, 1988—Jay Newell's interrogation. It's beyond all doubt. You get the true flavor of what Mr. Brown is all about. This is the pinnacle of truth. This *decent* human being who's running a home for wayward girls and they turned around and bit him . . . the facade falls away. He's not dealing with little girls anymore—he's with streetwise investigators."

Robinson pointed out how Brown had given ground slowly to Jay Newell. He denied of course, giving Cinnamon a fatal potion, substituting a harmless concoction in his recall. "Look at page eighty-six," Robinson said, pointing to a transcript of that interview, " 'No, sir, I was not there at all. There was a glass—you guys probably found it . . . it was Bayer aspirin . . . and soda.' And Mr. Newell asked him, 'You know what kind of pills would kill her, and how much, don't you?' And he says, 'I would think so by how my pills make me feel—yes. And I said, "Cinny, if you are half-serious—okay, fine." I mixed some Tylenol, some aspirin, and some baking soda because the baking soda—if you get enough in you—it will make you sick and I said, "It will look like someone your age tried to kill themselves," . . . and I said, "Cinny, I hope this is really a joke," and she said, "No, Daddy, it's no joke." '

". . . So he says," Robinson sneered, " 'Okay—well, I gotta get out of here.' "

"If you knew it [the 'potion'] had been made because she was going to kill Linda, and you say this would help carry that out and make it look like she was going to commit suicide afterward . . . Look at page eighty-seven—'I told her if she was going to go through with this thing, regardless of what I said or what I did, I didn't want to be there.' Okay, if you're going through with this murder, I don't want to be here—I want to be gone.

"Is that an *innocent* man?

". . . He doesn't want it to happen, but, 'Here, honey—leave the note in the kitchen.' "

David Brown had admitted to every incriminating fact. Robinson reminded the jury that David always said "God, no" to questions about a sexual relationship with Patti, and how he slipped and told Newell that she talked in her sleep. He had to find a way to explain that goof to Newell, so he discussed the "Garfield nap attack" syndrome that Patti was prone to.

"They just held each other—because 'it gets to me real bad. It just tears me up.' " Robinson quoted. "It tears me up so much that . . . I've got this eight hundred and fifty thousand dollars, but it tears me up. It tears me up so bad I have to have sexual relations with Patti— but it tears me up about Linda. Boy, I miss her."

Robinson wound to a close with a searing look at Brown's consciousness of guilt.

"He's self-indulgent. It's *me. Me. I. I. Money. Sex. Protection*. . . . The plot to kill the prosecutor and the investigator, and all the tapes that are entered, show David Brown's consciousness of guilt. Innocent people don't go out in a premeditated fashion and take human lives. You tell me an innocent man would be involved in a horrendous act to murder his wife!"

Just as David Brown seemed about to burst with rage and frustration, Robinson sat down. He would have another chance with the jury. He had already answered every possible defense he thought Gary Pohlson might bring up. He looked at the jurors and tried to guess what they were thinking.

They gave him no clue at all.

48

F E W   I N the courtroom envied Gary Pohlson the job before him. The jury had *heard* his client on tape as he admitted participation in one murder (his own wife's) and as he cold-bloodedly planned at least three more. How could Pohlson explain all that away? Still, the defense attorney smiled expansively as he strode to the lectern to begin his final arguments. Everyone in the courtroom—including Robinson—liked Pohlson; could he now rub some of those warm responses off on David Brown?

Pohlson fired his shotgun approach around the courtroom. The concepts flowed, but did not necessarily connect. It was difficult to grasp one argument before he moved on to the next, leaving his listeners to grapple with shades of meaning.

"I am concerned that *feelings* will overwhelm truth. . . . On one side we have the two girls . . . on the other side we have David Brown—who is obviously not as sympathetic a character," Pohlson began earnestly. "Because of that and because of all the tears we've had, and the laughter we've had, and the anger we've had, it's my fear that we'll get a little bit off the truth . . . the facts. Maybe we'll be overwhelmed by the emotions, by the sympathies for these young girls, by their tears. . . . Every case is important to the person sitting over there in the defendant's chair. Sometimes we lose track. We go through these things and we laugh and we make jokes. And I am obviously the worst offender—maybe the second worst." He nodded in Jeoff Robinson's direction. The jury smiled nervously.

"It's not just Cinnamon and Patti Bailey who are sympathetic characters," Pohlson continued. He said he had approached the case from a "very human point of view" and found that it divided itself up easily into five areas: feelings, special circumstances, persons (Patti, Cinnamon, and David), lies, and motives—motives both to lie and to kill. He wrote his designated areas on the display easel. And from those scribbles, he promised that the truth would emerge.

"The last thing I want to talk to you about is the truth."

It was an unfortunate phrase, perhaps even a Freudian slip.

Pohlson urged the jury to look at the evidence, and to realize that each side viewed it differently. "There's somebody who's not going to be right. If you think the defendant's actions were because he was conscious of being guilty, then you can use that. For two and a half days of these horrendous tapes—they're talking about killing some people, about evil things. What about the reasons behind it? What about consciousness of *innocence?* Joel Baruch called the prosecutor names and fought and fought and fought [with him] in court. *Yes*, he went back to David Brown and said that the prosecutor and the investigator were unethical and were out to get him."

Astoundingly, Pohlson urged the jury to replay the arrest tape of September 22, and to *listen*—listen to what was really said. The Steinhart tapes too were "oppressive . . . Mr. Brown tried to participate in a very bad thing. But he was desperate. He felt he didn't have a chance—because [he thought] 'The prosecutor is lying . . .' "

"Look at the September 22 tape and see what a frightened, wimpy guy he is. Brown was panicked! . . . You ever see two more different men than Richard Steinhart and David Brown? Steinhart's strong and David Brown's weak. Steinhart? He played David Brown like a fish. . . . He preyed on David Brown's weakness. . . . He saw Brown was upset and scared and he was afraid he'd be put away by Patti's testimony. He told Richard Steinhart he was a desperate person—he doesn't have a chance. . . .

"That doesn't mean he's guilty."

Pohlson had to stress reasonable doubt; it was all he had. His own client had lied to him about bribing witnesses. Pohlson was doing the best any man could under the suffocating restraints he labored against. "Listen to all the tapes again and get a *feeling* and get *beyond* the feeling, and then take it [further] regarding reasonable doubt."

Pohlson said he could not see that the simple buying of insurance indicated that special circumstances should attach to his client. "Was there too much insurance? Mr. Robinson thinks so. What else? I don't know—maybe I missed something."

David Brown gazed at his attorney as if he truly expected that Pohlson could pull him out of this mire he was in. For those who understood, it was obvious that Pohlson could have only faint hope for an acquittal. He had predicted that the arrest tape would "roll over us," and the September 22 interview had flattened his case like a road kill. He wanted the special circumstances out. If he didn't cut that loose and let it drift behind, his client could not only be convicted; he could be "L-WOPPed"—life without possibility of parole.

Distasteful as it was, Pohlson had to attack Cinnamon and Patti and undermine their calamitous testimony. "The prosecution would have you believe that [Mr.Brown] is a genius who came up with a clever plot to kill Linda. Does that *sound* like a clever plan . . . these emotional, young, depressed, *greedy* girls? . . . These are not two little angels who got led astray and manipulated by Mr. Brown. First of all, Cinnamon Brown did the killing and Patti helped her. Cinnamon went back in at Patti's instructions and finished her [Linda] off. She fires between six and fifteen inches, the gun gets jammed in the pillow. She was going to fire again . . . shoot this woman that they testified, *in tears*, how much they loved. . . ."

Pohlson was caustic. "We're talking a disturbed, upset, fourteen-year-old girl. *Manipulated* by David Brown?" Pohlson shook his head. "The reason she's upset is she's finally where she wants to be. Her father makes a lot of money. She has nice things. *Linda* was the threat. Cinnamon told a lot of people Linda was going to kick her out. She'd lose all that."

In restrospect, it was quite possible that Gary Pohlson might have felt the most antipathy toward this phase of his closing arguments. But he plunged ahead, describing Patti as a Lolita-like child who lusted after her sister's husband, an eleven-year-old who forced herself on David Brown as they rode in his truck. "Is this just a poor, little manipulated girl?"

For only an instant, the female jurors' eyes betrayed their resistance to this argument. Pohlson had gone over the line. Eleven-year-olds do not force fellatio upon twenty-seven-year-old men.

Pohlson returned to his pounding theme. "Look at all the lies these girls have told. They've been lying for years."

True. Indeed, they had been. Pohlson painstakingly went over each spate of lying. There was no argument on this from the prosecution. It would have been foolhardy of Robinson to deny the girls lied. It was up to the jury to discern *why* they lied and if they were lying *now*.

"Think about all the times Cinnamon Brown and Patti Bailey talked about, 'We never took him serious.' I'm suggesting they *didn't* take him serious. . . . Maybe David Brown was negligent there. Maybe he should have put his foot down. There is a lot of evidence of nonserious talk . . . until the girls actually did it. . . . So what is his reaction to this—*as a father?* 'Oh, my God, my daughter killed my wife!' . . . He asked Patti Bailey, 'What's the matter?' [when he comes home on the night of the killing] and she says, 'Something did happen,' and he says, '*Oh, my God!*' . . . That speaks volumes. . . .

"*The girls did it!*"

Final arguments took all of June 12. Robinson began his rebuttal the next morning. The personalities of both the prosecution and the defense were so strong, so likable, so much a factor in this long trial, that it *was*—as Robinson pointed out—sometimes difficult to extricate feelings from the facts.

"Mr. Brown had the resources to do it, and he went out and got a great attorney who made a great argument. . . . Every time I hear Mr. Pohlson, I think he's great . . . he's a *good* lawyer—but good lawyers *don't* make facts good; they make them sound good. . . . It's almost like cotton candy. It looked good, it tasted great, but then it dissipates. . . .

"The point is the facts are the facts are the facts."

Rebuttal was rhetoric and reminding. Robinson was earnest and competent. He steered the jury back to the place where their feelings were relevant. "You're not just a computer where we put the testimony in and you spit out credible/not credible. . . . That's why we have juries—because you trade upon your life experience."

David Brown, Robinson said, had killed for lust and for money. "Is that so difficult to believe?" If anything, Robinson was even more convincing on rebuttal than he had been during his final arguments. He was relaxed and confident, a marathon runner who had caught his second wind.

David Brown's ego had surely suffered at the hands of the prosecutor *and* his own attorney; Pohlson had called him a coward and wimpy; Robinson had dubbed him the "Love God." Now he scoffed at the picture of Brown as a terrified, desperate man. "This is no innocent man—this is a diabolical man; this is no victim . . . the kids aren't running that home. . . . Mr. Brown knows what the carrot is for different individuals; for adults, for people he doesn't know—it's money. For kids—for his child—for Patti Bailey, it's family. He always has something that somebody needs or wants."

David Brown stared at Jeoff Robinson as if he were watching a snake. His body was stiff with shock. He looked concerned—no, stricken. Pohlson requested a sidebar conference.

No one in the gallery knew what was said. Robinson continued as if there had been no interruption, quoting the defendant from more of the endless tapes. To "Smiley," the undercover policewoman who pretended to be a paid snitch: "Nobody can prove anything. . . . Promise that you won't give me up. You don't have to worry about me—I believe in people—I take care of people. That's how I've managed to get ahead—but I've got a long way to go."

To Richard Steinhart, who had said that Patti would back up on a knife: "Good. Good. That's what I want." Robinson quoted Bob Dylan: "You don't need a weatherman to know which way the wind's blowing."

He ended on a triumphant note. After two hours of rebuttal, he felt good. These were the last words the jury would hear before they retired to deliberate David Brown's innocence or guilt: "Justice has waited since March of 1985. He's had a long and evil reign—the kingdom of David Brown. . . . Cinnamon and Patti have had their just rewards. I'm asking you to give David Brown the same.

"Thank you."

And then, incredibly, Judge McCartin turned to Gary Pohlson and asked if the defense would like another shot at argument. Would the defense care to speak again? Robinson was stunned, and Pohlson was caught off guard. McCartin decreed that each of the attorneys would have another fifteen minutes, since the Court thought Pohlson's final arguments might have suffered because a night had passed since the jury had heard them.

There were two ways to view McCartin's move. He may have been bending over backward to be sure this trial was fair and just. He had made controversial rulings before for that very reason. Or Judge McCartin may have been deliberately slapping down Robinson, defusing his all-inclusive rebuttal. McCartin had displayed ambivalence toward Robinson during this trial—the old lion cuffing the energetic young cub. McCartin was an inscrutable, unpredictable man, a dour jurist—but engaging when he doffed his black robes and revealed blue jeans.

Now, McCartin had frustrated and angered Robinson to the point that he could not hide his rage. Pohlson had not asked for more time and seemed as surprised as Robinson was furious.

Robinson objected.

"You lost," McCartin said implacably.

"So what's new?" Robinson asked irreverently.

"So what's new," said the judge.

The two abbreviated rebuttals were stilted and repetitive. Each side had already finished. It was over at eleven-thirty A.M. on June 13, 1990. This afternoon, Judge McCartin would read the jury instructions, and then they would debate the legal fate of David Arnold Brown.

49

T H E   J U R Y retired at twelve minutes to three on June 13. McCartin instructed that they would deliberate only between the hours of nine and four-thirty. There would be no midnight watches in this trial.

The longer a jury stays out, the more nervous the prosecution becomes. Nothing was ever a sure thing. And this case, of all cases, *was* based on feelings and individual perceptions. If the jurors had expected David Brown's fingerprints on his dead wife's body, or even on the gun, they had been disappointed. If they believed that "once a liar, always a liar," they would toss out Patti's and Cinnamon's testimony. The baby—and the People's case—would go out with the bathwater.

Nobody knew.

The jury was not sequestered. Judge McCartin had not sequestered a jury in a dozen years. Word was that they debated for two hours that first afternoon, then went home. The next day, June 14, passed with no word.

June 15, the third day—it was too long. Nobody who cared about this case wanted to stray very far from the Orange County Courthouse. It was Friday; if the jury didn't come in with a verdict, they would not meet again to deliberate until Monday. It would be a very long weekend.

Robinson put on his running gear and circled nearby streets.

Newell tried to work.

McLean *did* work. "I figured my part was over. I couldn't change anything—I might as well go back to work. They could beep me if anything happened."

None of them relished solid food. This was the time of wondering what would happen *if*. If the jury acquitted David Brown, the men who had dogged his trail for five years pondered what he had meant when he told "Smiley," "I still have a long way to go." If the jury acquitted, David would walk away. Maybe the jury *would* "walk him out of here" as Robinson had invited a hundred years ago during his closing argument. Maybe he would dig up his $5 million, collect Krystal, and continue on his merry way.

It was a daunting picture.

"Mitch" Miller and Gail Carpenter only hinted at the arrival and departure times of the elusive jurors. They hadn't actually been *deliberating* all this time. Many had high school and college graduations to attend as June hit midstream; Judge McCartin allowed for that. How many actual hours had they deliberated? It might have been fifteen; it might have been many less. It was hard to figure for those outside the locked courtroom. The longer the jurors stayed out, the more semi-comforting explanations emerged.

Even so, a conviction began to seem unlikely.

A little before two, Jay Newell and Jeoff Robinson reluctantly left the courthouse and headed for the little shop where they routinely ate frozen yogurt instead of lunch. Yogurt they could get down. They were like nervous expectant fathers, however, gulping the stuff so fast that it hit their sinuses with a blast of pain.

Then they headed back toward the courthouse. As they circled the juniper island and walked past the reflecting pond, they caught the buzz of excitement, a palpable feeling.

"They've got a verdict," someone called, but Newell and Robinson figured it was a joke.

The buzz became a roar. Attorneys on the escalator coming down from the second-floor DA's office grinned and confirmed.

They had a verdict.

It was 2:45 P.M. on the longest Friday of 1990.

Department 30 was jam-packed with people, the first time it had been that full since jury selection. There were virtually every employee of the Orange County District Attorney's Office, a number of the Bailey siblings, the press and their microphones and cameras and notebooks. Everyone who had ever dropped in during the two-month trial seemed to be back; strange faces who had never been here before were there now.

All waited for the defendant. At 3:16 David Brown shed his chains and walked to his wooden chair. He was pale green and dewy with perspiration. In all of his life, he had never had to answer for even one sin.

Would he now?

As the jury filed in, they were all half-smiling. No one watching had the vaguest clue whether this was good or bad. Stephen M. Lopez was the jury foreman. He handed the verdict to Bailiff Miller, who passed it to Judge McCartin.

McCartin, the great poker face, read it silently.

David Brown appeared to be fascinated, curious—as if he too were only an enthralled spectator.

Gail Carpenter, McCartin's usually ebullient clerk, stood to read the verdict in her high, clear voice. "Count I . . . C-71791—first-degree murder, a felony, to wit: violation of Section 187 of the Penal Code of the State of California, in that on or about March 19, 1985, in the County of Orange, State of California, the said defendant did willfully, unlawfully, and feloniously, and with malice aforethought, kill Linda Brown, a human being . . .

"*Guilty.*"

No one breathed. The verdict floated in the courtroom.

"Count II—in Orange County, California, the crime of felony, to wit: violation of Section 182.1/187, conspiracy to commit murder . . . *Guilty.*"

Whispers. One to go.

". . . Special circumstances—that the aforesaid crimes were committed with the hope and expectation of financial gain . . . *Guilty.*"

David Arnold Brown had just been L-WOPPed.

Judge McCartin set the sentencing date: August 22, at nine A.M. After so long, it was over so quickly.

David Brown did not change expression, but a red flush stained his face. He took a sip of water, then was led away by Bailiff "Mitch" Miller and Deputy Marshal Glenn Hoopingarner. As the verdict began to sink in, he shook his head in surprise. It wasn't supposed to be this way.

In the corridor outside Department 30, the pickings were ripe for the television and still cameras. The Bailey brothers and sisters came dangerously close to hysteria as they celebrated the verdict, sobbing and shouting, screaming out their victory.

Alan Bailey hyperventilated and sank to the floor, crying, "Guilty! Guilty! There's no way he'll get out of prison. He's evil to the core. At one time, I thought he was my best friend. I'm just glad he's away forever and ever and ever. He destroyed, he manipulated, but justice prevailed!"

Mary Bailey sobbed in her husband's arms, while Terry Blanchard, one of the jurors, stared, dumbfounded, at the bedlam.

Brenda Sands looked shyly into the television cameras. Did she think Cinnamon would be able to live a normal life now? She looked bewildered and murmured, "I don't know."

Jay Newell, as always, vanished down the back stairs before he could be caught in a camera lens.

But Jeoff Robinson explained to the press, "Had it not been for Jay Newell, we wouldn't be here. It was a case already closed, but this guy never gave up."

Sadly, this day of triumph was also a day of tragedy for Jay Newell; his father, "J. D.," had suddenly become critically ill and was dying. The man who would have been proudest of his son's finest hour would not live to share all the accolades.

Robinson had one task that came before all others. Ignoring clamoring reporters, he hurried to his office and placed a call to the Ventura School, asking to have Cinnamon Brown call him collect.

When the call came in, Robinson spoke earnestly into the phone. "Cinnamon, it's over. The jury found him guilty. I want you to remember that, starting right now, this is the first day of the rest of *your* life."

The David Brown jury, finally allowed to talk, explained that they had actually deliberated only a short time. "The first afternoon, we elected our foreman—Steve Lopez," one juror recalled. "Our first vote was eight guilties and four undecided. On the second day, we watched the arrest tape. And on the third day, we watched more tape. We ony deliberated seven hours. That tape convinced us—we watched David Brown completely turn around from what he said at the beginning of his interview with Newell."

One of the female jurors admitted that she had been shocked at the extent of the sexual perversion discussed: "I've never been exposed to anything like that." Another, more worldly, juror said, "Oral sex? I cannot imagine allowing that man to even touch my arm."

Several women jurors had caught David's easy explanation to Patti and Cinnamon (on the CYA tape) that fathers often had sex with their daughters—that it was no big deal. That did not make him guilty of murder, they stressed, but it demonstrated the way his mind worked and made it easier for them to see how he could manipulate the teenagers.

Their most believable witness? Unanimously—Richard Steinhart. "Richard Steinhart was a breath of fresh air," a heretofore shy woman juror exclaimed. "We had no trouble believing him. He had nothing to gain by lying—and nothing to lose."

Asked why they had smiled as they walked into the courtroom on that last day, several jurors said it had nothing to do with whether they had voted innocent or guilty. "We were surprised to see so many people out in the gallery—we had stage fright, and if we were smiling, it was because we were nervous!"

50

THE PHOENIX remained inert in the ashes of his life. On Monday, July 23, David Brown pleaded guilty to charges that he conspired to have Jeoff Robinson, Jay Newell, and Patti Bailey murdered. Five lesser charges were dismissed. In essence, this was a plea bargain; Brown was given six years—to run concurrent with whatever sentence Judge McCartin would hand down on August 22.

Two years apiece for plotting to take three lives. It rankled those who cared about the would-be victims, but the time meant nothing. It might help to keep David Brown inside prison walls longer if he should ever come up for parole.

On July 18, Jay Newell interrupted his family's vacation trip, and Jeoff Robinson joined him in Sacramento. In an unusual move, the two appeared before the Juvenile Parole Board. They wanted the board to know that *they* were responsible for Cinnamon's recent reticence in talking about her offense. In order to convict David Brown, it had been necessary for Cinnamon to remain silent. Newell and Robinson asked that she not be penalized for this.

Cinnamon had already done more time than most juvenile homicide offenders. Given the revelation of her father's murder plans, Newell and Robinson urged the board to consider Cinnamon's next appearance before the board—probably in early 1991—in a favorable light.

There had been no deal at all. But both Robinson and Newell felt it was high time Cinnamon had someone on her side.

August 22 came and went without a sentence for Brown on the murder charges. The new sentencing date would be September 17. David Brown said that he would produce a number of letters on his behalf from huge corporations—even from the Pentagon. Letters that would support probation. None came.

Deputy Probation Officer Bruce B. Carel did, however, receive a number of letters condemning the convicted man, letters from Linda and Patti's sisters and brothers, from their mother. The messages were all full of regret and fear.

"Please make the sentence where he can *never* get out and do harm to anyone else—because I believe if he gets out, *he will*."

"He messed up so many people's lives, all for his own selfish reasons. . . . I feel he should never be able to see the light of day or night."

"This kind of person doesn't belong out with the human race, where he may do this again to someone else's family."

"What he has done is just plain sick and I don't feel there is enough punishment too hard for him, and I hope he has to do some of the suffering the family has done over the past five years."

There were highly literate letters and near-illiterate letters, but the message was all the same. Lock him up forever, and then watch him closely.

Newell added his own warning. "I feel David A. Brown should not only remain in prison for the rest of his natural life, but that it should not be forgotten that he will use and manipulate whoever he can to do his bidding. He should be closely monitored."

On September 17, 1990, the major players gathered for the last time in Judge Donald McCartin's courtroom. Everything was the same; only the jury box was empty—although several of the jurors sat in the gallery now to watch David Brown's sentencing.

Brown wore a huge neck brace. One explanation said he had fallen in the shower; another that he had fallen out of his bunk. The neck brace was possibly only a last bid for sympathy. Since Judge McCartin had suffered continual severe neck and back pain throughout the trial, Brown's ploy was so ill advised as to be utterly stupid—if it was a ploy.

McCartin gazed down at the man convicted in his courtroom three months earlier, and the television cameras caught his image. He had refused to set aside the special circumstances, feeling that the excessive insurance on Linda Brown's life was certainly an equal motive in her killing. "I won't strike that.

". . . This started out as a death-penalty case," McCartin said, moving into the most serious conviction. He looked directly at David Brown for the first time. "Somewhere it was struck. . . . Maybe because you had no prior record."

McCartin spoke to Pohlson and Schwartzberg. "If this had gone to the jury as a death-penalty case, I'd have no problem sentencing your client to either life without possibility of parole or to death. I drove

Mr. Robinson into the ground on this one, and Mr. Pohlson is one of the best—if not *the* best [criminal defense attorney]."

McCartin took a deep breath and turned again to David Brown.

"The trouble is, Mr. Brown—you're a scary person. . . . I have some concerns for my *own* safety. You don't *look* like Charlie Manson—he's crazy to look at, but you look a lot saner than your own defense attorney—but look what you did from jail. Look what you did to your own children, to your sister-in-law. It's scary to think you can manipulate people and do all this and not bat an eye. Even *Charlie Manson* didn't use *family*. . . . You're a master manipulator. I think the circumstances of this case are unbelievable. . . . You [seem to] have a pleasant personality, but you had no concern for your daughter, for your sister-in-law, for your wife. If Cinnamon had gone under, you would have walked away."

"Mr. Brown, you make Charlie Manson look like a piker."

With that said, Judge Donald McCartin sentenced David Arnold Brown to life without possibility of parole and added a $10,000 fine. "With six years to run concurrent already on case C-80475."

The brace hid David's neck, but the tips of his ears were blanched white. Whatever he had expected, it was not this. He twisted in the wind while McCartin lambasted him with words.

David Arnold Brown had been in custody over seven hundred days, and he would get credit for that. Probation was denied. He had sixty days to file an appeal.

"Do you have any questions, Mr. Brown?" McCartin asked.

Mr. Brown did not, but he complained to his guards on the way out of the courtroom that the judge had had no reason to be so mean about it all. "He didn't have to say that about Manson."

51

O N S E P T E M B E R 20, 1990, I went to see David Brown. With the gracious help of Judge Donald McCartin, Gail Carpenter, and "Mitch" Miller, I was armed with a piece of paper that entitled me to one official visit. David's parents still visited faithfully, and he didn't want to miss a regular visit—but my "official" status allowed me to visit David once during any time he agreed to see me and to stay as long as I wanted.

The street scene outside the Orange County Jail looked like a small-scale fiesta. Vendors sold fast food and watermelon to visitors. Inside, there was no sense of fun. It has always saddened me to see jail visitors waiting to see someone they love. The waiting room of the IRC was vast and furnished with bright-turquoise molded couches and chairs— "Barbie" furniture, blocklike and legless; it wasn't very comfortable, but appeared totally indestructible.

Mothers and fathers and children and babies and pregnant teenagers and friends and baby-sitters either crowded into line to talk to the desk officers or perched fretfully on the unyielding plastic blocks. Jail visitors get little respect, and they always seem burdened with worry and anxiety.

My piece of paper carried little weight with the desk officers, and I languished with the rest of the visitors. Finally, at length, I was directed to an elevator that went to J Module. I walked down a long, long windowless hall. It could have been a cattle ramp—if it had not been for the surveillance cameras mounted high on the corners. There was not a soul in sight. The hall smelled like a zoo, a smell that blossomed as I walked farther down toward the visitors' cubicles.

I had interviewed so many prisoners in so many jails and prisons, but I had never shaken the claustrophobic feeling that now gripped me as I moved farther and farther into the bowels of a custodial facility.

I had been given number nine. Cubicles one and nine were reserved for attorneys, the clergy, and other official visitors. They were more than cubicles; they were little rooms with doors that closed, with pale-yellow cinder-block walls and one little steel jump seat in front of a glass partition.

There air was hot and still, fetid.

David Brown, wearing a voluminous mustard-colored jumpsuit, sat down on the other side of the glass and picked up his phone receiver. How strange it was to look at the front of him when I had spent the spring looking at the back of his head!

At first glance, David's eyes were dark; on closer perusal, they were silver, hazel, gray, and yet none of these; they reflected light like a pool with many-colored leaves adrift. He rarely blinked. His acne-scarred face was a mask. He was wary of me, so cautious that he had no spontaneity. He had apparently recovered from his neck injury; the collar he wore in court three days before was gone.

I asked if I might tape our conversation, and he refused. He had been badly burned by hidden tapes; he apparently didn't realize that a tape made in full view would only substantiate what he said to me. No matter. I had taken notes for years. Fingers before ears. Where I came from, tape recorders were not allowed in courtrooms or jails, and I had a permanent callus on one finger from clutching a pen through scores of interviews and trials.

David Brown had things to get off his chest. He would, of course, appeal. "They're scared to death of me, you know—afraid I'll kill the judge. I think McCartin was just making a show at sentencing. He pounded on his chest like Tarzan so he can go home and tell his wife. I found him totally unprofessional."

Brown wanted to know where I stood on Jeoff Robinson—did I not agree that he was a "dishonest man, a manipulator," who was given to temper tantrums?

At the risk of alienating my subject, I shook my head.

"No," I murmured. "I found him very competent. He's charismatic in the courtroom."

Brown disagreed. He viewed Jeoff Robinson—*and* Jay Newell—as men with overweening political ambitions. "They are dishonest men. Robinson's manipulative. *I* have always tried to do right by people." He mentioned other interests—newspaper sales, for instance—that were profiting from his own misfortune. He hastened to explain, however, that he was not unused to media coverage. "I was famous *before* Linda was murdered."

Once again he listed his credits, the lives he had saved, the corporations that would have perished without him. He told me about his fame, his money, the MGM fire, the Pentagon connection, the "towering inferno" Los Angeles bank fire. "I've been in almost every magazine you can name. Robinson can bring down a millionaire and he gets people's attention." David assured me he didn't need all this notoriety. Fame had courted him on his own merits. He was after all

"Mr. Coca-Cola," and the man who had extricated the *Challenger* secrets.

I commented that he had been lucky to be in the right place at the right time in the booming world of computers. He corrected me. "I like to think it was *my* skill and intelligence."

David assured me that he had made a fortune, although he had always been unusually fair in billing his clients. He explained his modest billing approach. "I recovered data for one bank that located three hundred and eighty million dollars for them! If I charged even one percent of what I saved them, I'd have got more than three million dollars." He smiled slightly, enjoying the tease. "Maybe I *did*. But I always kept a low profile. I didn't pay taxes on it—*if* I got it."

Undeterred by my positive comments about Robinson, he warned me nevertheless, "You're going to have to keep an open mind." I must understand, he stressed, that I was talking to a man who had always tried to play fair with people.

He castigated Brenda, his first wife, and recalled how that divorce "tore me up." He took much pleasure in his millions because he knew Brenda regretted losing him. He explained that *he* had been faithful; his second wife, Lori, had been only a friend until he found himself dumped by a "cheating wife."

David was anxious to know if I had talked to Brenda. I nodded. "A little."

"She lied about me, I'll bet."

"No." I told him the truth. "She told me how good you were to her when she was fifteen, how you took care of her, and how much she loved you then."

David was put off by my answers; he had not yet been able to get a fix on me. I could sense David Brown sizing me up. What would work with me? Where were my weaknesses? My vanities? This was a man who enjoyed word games and keeping his opponent off-balance. He tried another tack with me. "You're one of the smartest women I've met in a long time," he commented. "Most of the people in here are grapefruits."

". . . Thanks a lot."

Then David Brown wanted to talk about his betrayers. Patti's defection was uppermost in his mind. "I believed her when she said she didn't do it."

"*Who* did do it?" I asked.

"I don't know," he said impatiently. "I'm not a police detective.

Linda was saying, 'It hurts—it hurts. Help me. Help me!' Anyone who could do that has to be pretty cold."

David burned with the memory of seeing Newell and Robinson talking to Patti before an early pretrial hearing. "I swear it was an emotional conversation; I couldn't hear what they were saying, but their hands were moving. I swear they were coaching her." Indeed, he insisted that both girls had been coached to say what they did.

David had nothing at all good to say about his own attorneys. "Pohlson didn't put on one-tenth of the defense I wanted, not one-tenth of the witnesses. He's a spoiled brat, very egotistical. He's the one that wouldn't let me question him—he'd get real angry, *real angry*. I fired Pohlson. McCartin wouldn't let me. I still would have been allowed to have a Marsden hearing, but when you hire an attorney, you can fire him."

David was convinced that Jeoff Robinson and Gary Pohlson were such close friends that Pohlson deliberately lost his case. He wished now that he had been allowed to hire C. Thomas McDonald (Randy Craft's attorney) or Milton Grimes.

As for witnesses, Brown thought all of the Baileys should have been called by the defense. His perceptions were fatally flawed. The Baileys had not only voiced their hatred for him, they had shouted it to the media and rejoiced in his conviction, but he skimmed over that. "The Baileys swore by me. We had no problems."

His views of Cinnamon were also skewed. "Cinnamon was a violent and abusive teenager. Patti was unstable; she tended to like a lot of guys. I felt Patti was a little bit infatuated with me."

He gave this information to me confidentially, as if I had not heard Patti's damning testimony on his sexual abuse and the stolen episodes of sexual activity between them whenever Linda's back was turned.

David Brown labored to convince me of Cinnamon's violence. "Cinny was verbally abusive to me—more than you'd want a teenager to be. Brenda called and said, 'She hit me! My mouth is bleeding. I never want her back!'" Long suffering, he had rescued Brenda, he explained, and had taken the "vicious" teenager into his own home. He allowed that he didn't have to face the brunt of the problems with Cinnamon. "I wasn't around her and Patti; Linda was home with them all day."

David then revealed a new scenario to me about March 19, 1985. "They were both going home to their mothers that day—Patti and Linda were constantly butting heads, Patti disobeyed Linda, tried to borrow her jewelry and clothes, tried to run the house. . . . Cinnamon had reasons for resentment and being upset. Her mother kept yelling, 'Get out of my house—I never want to see you again!' "

David sighed as he recalled his decision. "Linda said, 'Either she goes or I go!' It was a horrible thing for me to choose—since Cinny was nine or ten, she got on my nerves too—she was such an unusual kid. She made both Brenda and Linda hate her, and I did too. Can you understand that?"

I didn't answer—because I *couldn't* understand that.

"They killed her because they were going home that day. Patti had to eliminate Linda to take her place. Cinnamon wanted to be in a loving home. They both had motives. It may sound weird, but I wish to God Linda was here to testify."

Why would that sound weird . . . ?

I asked, "How do you feel about Cinnamon now?"

"It's rough." He sighed, lighting a cigarette. "Coming to terms. She killed my wife. What's it matter to kill me too? She knew I faced the death penalty at the time she changed her story. Her father could die, and she didn't care. She's cold . . . and evil."

David attributed Cinnamon's treachery to the fact that she was in love with a boy at Ventura School. "She was in a whirlwind of love . . . she was desperate to get out. She's proved what a liar she is."

I asked Brown about the four insurance policies. Just as he had in the interview with Newell and McLean, he tensed up at the mention of insurance. I noted that, when he was hard-pressed for an answer to a difficult question, his eyes slid right while he constructed his response. "I never spent the insurance money. I don't need that money."

"You didn't?"

"I cashed the checks," he answered cagily.

"What did you do with the money?"

"Let's just say it's invested."

"Where?"

"I can't say. I don't want Patti and Cinny to know how that money was invested. I don't want the Baileys to know where it's invested."

Ten minutes before, David had told me he got along fine with the Baileys, and now he denigrated them as criminals, drug users, whose decadence shocked him. He reminded me of his many, many beneficences to the Baileys, all unappreciated. "I'm not guilty—that family was. Ethel was greedy," David said. "She wanted to *sell* Patti to Linda for twenty-five hundred dollars, and Linda just told her she was crazy! I think Ethel was planning to put Patti out for prostitution, and she thought she'd lose money if Patti came to live with us. We were willing to go to court to keep Patti."

"But you took Patti back home—at Linda's insistence—didn't you?" I asked.

David explained that was true, but that it was *he* who had decided Patti couldn't live with them any longer. "Frankly, she was coming on to me, and I couldn't have that, so I took her home to Riverside. Then she called up and said that one of her brothers had raped her, so we went to get her. We had her checked at Martin Luther King Hospital, and there was no sign of rape. But we brought her back home."

Once on the subject of the Bailey family, David was reminded of more of their vices. "It's true I didn't like to visit the Baileys," he said. "Ethel would sit there and go through a six-pack in an hour. They did drugs in front of us. I don't believe in drinking or doing drugs or abusing your children," he finished.

David Brown was a fascinating interview. He was expansive and generous with details in areas that had no particular bearing on his case, and cryptically stingy when I probed too close to perilous aspects of the case or asked questions he had no canned answers for.

He described his hardscrabble childhood. He was Horatio Alger reborn, a boy who struggled to survive and now helped others less fortunate. There was the sense that I was hearing a memorized spiel. Many of the anecdotes were familiar. I had heard them on tape, *seen* him on videotape saying the same words.

I asked him if his childhood had been happy, and he quickly reversed the question. "Was *yours?* . . . What's happy?"

David Brown clearly did not like direct questions. I asked him, just to change the direction of the conversation—and because I had found it to be a good interviewing technique to relax subjects—"If you could go anywhere in the world, where would you choose?"

He froze. "Why would you want to know that?"

"No reason. I'm trying to get to know you."

Then I realized that he suspected I was seeking information about some eventual escape destination. I had no doubt at all that, even as we talked in this totally secure jial, the man on the other side of the glass *was* devising schemes once again.

When I asked him what was wrong with his heart, David looked wary again. "It's a physical problem," he said shortly.

"I imagined it was. What are your symptoms?"

His eyes slid to the right, and there was a long silence.

"Do you have an irregular heartbeat?" I pushed.

"No."

"Do you have tightness in your chest?"

"No."

"Do you feel pain?"

"No."

"Do you have shortness of breath?"

Finally he nodded. "And I have numbness. I can't feel my arms sometimes."

It was obvious even to a layman that David Brown's heart was fine; he suffered from the classic symptoms of panic attacks. But for once, he didn't want to talk about his many ailments; he wanted to talk about how he was seduced and threatened into the murder-for-hire plot by Irv Cully and Richard Steinhart.

"I was being strong-armed by those guys; they had pictures of the Chantilly Street house. They would have killed my mom and dad and children—one by one. They told Newell and Robinson that they could lock me in a cell and *get* me. The DA said, 'If you can, *do it*.'"

Brown studied my face to see if I was buying this, and I stared back at him.

He tried harder. "Listen, there were tons of message slips [between Cully and Steinhart and the Orange County DA's Office] that disappeared. Irv gets pizza, juice, burritos. *We* don't get that stuff in here."

David had apparently perused items taken in discovery from the prosecution by his attorney Gary Pohlson. One was a scrawled note from Irv Cully: "During the discussion with Newell, Myself and 'Goldie' Steinhart would APPRECIATE two styrofoam cups and a BIG can of pineapple juice, as a token of good faith."

Food was obviously very important in David Brown's life. He mentioned it often. Being denied his favorite foods was apparently symbolic of his loss of power in jail. He seized on Cully's modest request to show me the DA's office was crooked. There was nothing in evidence to indicate that Cully ever *got* his pineapple juice.

And Steinhart, of course, never got any pizza; he only put on such a good act from his phone in the Huntington Beach Jail that David still *thought* he had. If the stakes in David's games had less potential for tragedy, his petulance about food would have been laughable.

David suggested that I read the September 22 interview again and again. "Act out the parts," he urged. He still believed that he deported himself very well the morning of his arrest in that devastating interview with Jay Newell.

I *had* read the transcript ten times; I had viewed the videotape a dozen times, alone and with others, and perceived a man who revealed his sociopathy completely. It was significant that David saw himself—and Newell—in reversed roles.

From David's point of view, it was Jay Newell who lied. "As naive as I might sound," he said, deliberately ingenuous, "I didn't think an officer of the law could *lie*. I've never been arrested in my life. He caught me with a right hook, and I believed him. He flat-out lied to me. He made it sound like I admitted I was guilty! I was scared to death, Ann. He caught me with my shorts down! It *shocked* me to see the pictures [taken by the surveillance camera in Ventura]. I didn't know it was Cinnamon. Would I deny it—if I knew I'd done it? Wouldn't that just make her mad?"

David Brown confided to me that he feared prison. "The cons will go after me because they think I'm rich, or they'll blackmail me."

"Couldn't you use your money inside to buy an easier life?" I asked.
"No way."

I asked David if he was, indeed, still wealthy. He contemplated me and then said earnestly, "Honest to God, I'm flat broke."

There it was again, "honest to God" as a preamble to a flat-out lie.

I asked another blunt question. "Is Heather your child?"

"No! . . . Patti's a slut. Patti was going out since junior high school. She was dating a contractor. A DNA test would show I'm not Heather's father. I've asked for a blood test."

"Why did you marry Patti then?"

"That's a hard one to explain." David's eyes moved again to the right as he formulated an explanation. The marriage was only a dummy marriage, never meant to be real, he assured me. "Hell, I won't deny that during some real lonely and emotional times, I did have some 'encounters' with Patti—she wasn't unattractive—but trust me, she couldn't have gotten pregnant. How shall I say it—she couldn't have gotten pregnant with the *kind* of encounter we had. I had emotional problems and physical problems that precluded—ah, sexual intercourse."

But apparently did not preclude oral copulation, as Brown subtlely suggested, as he watched my face to see my reaction. I said nothing.

"And then," he continued, "my folks were there, and Krystal, and Alan lived there. I was having a relationship with Betsy Stubbs right up to the arrest."

Betsy Stubbs, the daughter of David's insurance agent, more recently the baby-sitter. Betsy Stubbs, who at nineteen, still believed she could miscarry by "throwing up a baby." Jay Newell had interviewed Betsy and learned of her affair with David—even while he was married to Patti. "I didn't have boyfriends," she had said to Newell, sobbing. "He was the first guy who made me feel attractive and a little bit important."

Betsy clearly mattered little to David; he mentioned her only to bolster his indictment of Patti. He expanded on Patti's black desire for him. "Patti killed Linda to get to me. I was scared to death of Patti. I thought she *was* the one who killed Linda. That's why my parents lived there. We were *that close* to having her move out when we were arrested. Patti was looking into buying property in Oregon. . . . I hated Patti. I wouldn't have minded if something happened to her."

There was a loathsome kind of fascination here. David Brown blamed *everything* on someone else. In the three hours we had talked, he blamed Patti, Brenda, Cinnamon, the Baileys, Gary Pohlson, Jeoff Robinson, Jay Newell, Richard Steinhart, Irv Cully, *and* the justice system for his misfortunes.

He added Joel Baruch, his ex-attorney. "I was forced into PC [the protective custody wing] and they planted Irv Cully and Richard Steinhart in there to entrap me. Baruch said, 'Pay them. They're just criminals. They won't really kill Robinson.' I told Baruch to warn Robinson. I *believed* Baruch and he was gone to Florida." This was typical David Brown rhetoric; whatever served him best at the moment was that day's truth.

I had a creeping sense of déjà vu. How many times had I listened to convicted killers deflect blame before it ever touched them? In a sense, I think they all came to a place where they *believed* what they were saying. David Brown looked sincere, and he sounded genuinely aggrieved; I believed that, for that space in time, he believed. He actually saw himself as a victim.

He was impatient with those who kept harping on the old truths. "Robinson says I brainwashed Cinny and Patti," he said with a laugh. "How could that be?"

"Do you understand the steps in brainwashing?" I asked.

He shook his head, but David was curious.

"I wrote a book about it once," I said. "In order to brainwash someone, four criteria must be met. First of all, the victim has to suffer a profound psychic shock—"

"They never had that."

"They thought their home was being broken up," I said. "They depended on you completely. They didn't think they could get along without you."

"Naw—that doesn't fit. What else?"

"The victim must be removed from everything and everyone that makes her feel safe," I offered. "The girls weren't in school—all they had was home. They thought Linda was going to kill you, that the 'family' would be gone, and there would be no home."

Already, David Brown was shaking his head. ". . . Doesn't fit."

"The third thing is that the subject is 'programmed'—told what the brainwasher wants her to believe, over and over and over again."

This time, David said nothing.

"Fourth," I said, "the victim is promised a reward. Usually her very life. Patti said you were her 'life support.' "

"No way. It doesn't fit. I didn't brainwash those girls. They did it all on their own."

David enjoyed the mental jousting. I could tell he rather liked the idea of being a successful Svengali, but he would not, of course, admit that to me.

He changed the subject. I had come too close to reality for him. He wanted me to know how very, very much he had loved Linda. He had treated her like a queen, never letting the romance go out of their perfect marriage. "I had an account with a special florist—for Linda," he recalled, his eyes actually misting. "I ordered only expensive, unusual arrangements, and I insisted on crystal vases. I had that florist scouring Nordstrom's and I. Magnin's looking for just the right crystal vases."

David described his meticulous attention to the details of Linda's inurnment, repeating to me, as he had to anyone who would listen, how important it was to him that her ashes had a pleasant resting place. He told me how lovingly he composed the inscription for the plaque to mark her place in the "twenty-four-hour-a-day fountain."

"What did you write?" I asked, pen poised.

David only repeated that he had grappled to find the right words to write on the plaque that covered Linda's niche in the fountain. And yet, urged to remember, he could not.

"The words—the words that you wrote?" I asked again.

He looked blank and shook his head. "I don't remember. Go look at the plaque—you'll see how much I loved her."

David said he still felt close to Linda, that they had shared an interest in communication between the real world and the other world beyond, in ghosts and psychic phenomena. "Linda and I believed in that kind of stuff," he said. "We went to psychics. We only went to the best. They told me I would be very, very successful in business, and that I would live to an old age. But Linda—well, two of them just turned white when she asked about her future. They didn't want to talk about it. The third finally came right out and told her she would die very young. I'm afraid she believed them. It troubled her, and I guess it scared her more when Krystal was born—because they'd all told her she would give birth to a daughter, and that part had come true."

After three hours, I was beginning to hear David Brown's explanations for the second time. Obviously, he believed that he had won me over with his arguments. He urged me to begin work at once as an investigator for *him* and suggested that I start with his parents. "They will tell you what kind of person I am. . . . I've never hurt anybody. I'm not violent. . . . *"I divorce women. I don't kill them."*

I had already spent twenty months investigating the death of Linda Brown, and the crimes for which David Brown was convicted. Nothing he said had convinced me of his innocence.

But I had wanted to give him a chance to speak. And so once again, I had looked into the chillingly blank eyes of a sociopath—the antisocial personality. Empty eyes, reflecting nothing, even as the brain that controlled them skittered frantically around for new excuses, new plans, new plots. I had hoped that David Brown might offer me some definitive key to unlock the reasons behind his conscienceless life. I was disappointed. Perhaps he didn't know himself why he was the way he was.

David Brown had thought he could manipulate me, as he had always tried to manipulate others. But I had been to school. And suddenly I could not get away fast enough—out of the airless cubicle, down the blank hall and into the waiting room whose Barbie chairs were now filled with a whole different platoon of visitors.

Afterword

THE HARDEST concept for most laymen to understand is that criminals such as David Brown are quite sane. When we encounter or read about individuals who commit heinous and ugly crimes, it is easier to write them off as "crazy." Deliberate cruelty is hard to accept so we tend to say, "You'd have to be crazy to do that."

No.

Sociopathy may be the most intriguing of all mental aberrations. To greater and lesser degrees, the vast majority of human beings empathize with each other. Even two-year-olds understand that other creatures feel pain and cry. "If it hurts me, then it must hurt you too." The sociopath (or antisocial personality or psychopath; the terms are interchangeable) *understands* the concept of empathy only intellectually. Indeed, he uses it to further his own aims. But he does not, apparently *cannot*, understand it emotionally. He cannot put himself in another human's shoes; the concept is utterly foreign to him. As Jeoff Robinson said in his closing arguments, David Brown *"wants, wants, wants."*

David Brown wanted sex and money and respect and *things*. He betrayed women, his brother, his parents, his children, all of his wives, to get what he wanted. After midnight on March 19, 1985, he drove away in the night, knowing that his sleeping wife would be dead when he returned. He let his daughter take the rap for it. He married Patti Bailey, impregnated her, and blithely offered her up as the next sacrifice. I have no doubt that, as Robinson suggested, David Brown would renounce Krystal to stay free.

He will offer up *anyone* to benefit himself. And as he does so, he will feel completely within his rights.

"I'm worth it."

Whether he truly believes he is "worth it," or whether he is only trying to pad an almost nonexistent sense of self-esteem, is an absorbing question.

In talking to psychiatrists and psychologists, David had given, I suspect, a "safe" version of his early life. He claimed sexual molestation by "an old man in the park." I have no doubt he was molested; the molester is far more likely to have been someone quite familiar to him. Child molestation is a cyclical crime, running through families like an incurable virus.

Still a child, David Brown viewed suicide attempts of a close relative. Still a child, he worked all alone through the night in a gas station. He speaks proudly of his accomplishment, but how lonely it must have been at four A.M. on a dark desert morning for an eleven-year-old.

David Brown had an aggressive mother and a meek father. He had no money for clothes or school supplies. A school picture of the young David—perhaps eight years old—looks like Beaver Cleaver. He needs braces, the buttons on his shirt don't match, his pocket is torn—but his eyes seem clear and trusting. It is well nigh impossible to connect this child of 1960 to the overweight manipulator of 1990.

And yet the seeds would have been there.

Even then.

David Brown, the poor teenager, the welfare recipient, sought sex and wealth to cover up his inadequacies, and he *used* sex and wealth to control others. He hit puberty obsessed with sex. Throughout his life, he vacillated between periods of inhibited sexual desire and intense sexual activity. He freely voices his preferred sexual activity—fellatio—to fellow prisoners, detectives, and the young women he attempts to seduce.

They are all young women—girls, really. Brenda Kurges Brown Sands is unarguably the personification of David's ideal female. Or at least she was once. When she was fourteen or fifteen, poor, dependent, trusting, and adoring, he rescued her. When she became even slightly independent, the relationship began to erode.

Lori, his second wife, was sweet, kind, and trusting. But she was nineteen when David married her. Too old.

Linda, who was both his third and fifth wife, was perfect. So like Brenda when the teenage David chose *her*. But Linda too grew up. Like Brenda, she bore David's child, and he was no longer her only love.

Patti shared Linda's abysmal background. Like Brenda and Linda, she was running from an unhappy home when David "saved" her. From eleven to twenty-one, Patti remained David's perfect sex slave. But she too grew up and became a mother, and in doing so, she lost the only man she had ever loved.

With Patti, his wife, down the hall, Betsy Stubbs shared David's bed the week he was arrested. Betsy was a plain girl who used too much makeup and wore her skirts too short. She was a "little slow" and had no self-confidence at all. She engaged in oral sex with David, she told Jay Newell, because she thought no one else would want her.

All of them were David's kind of women. They allowed him to maintain absolute control. David was in charge. Cindy, his fourth wife, was the only aberration. She had two children when he married her, and she was older. That marriage, of course, lasted only six months.

Had David Brown not been arrested and convicted, this man who was married *six* times by the time he was thirty-three would surely have continued his search for "Brenda." The young Brenda. He might have grown old, but his women would have continued to be teenagers. In truth, I suspect David Brown detests women. He teased his mother sadistically, and he characterizes women by their body parts—never by their minds or souls.

Jeoff Robinson gave two primary motives for Linda Bailey Brown's murder: lust and greed. Those are the concepts, the goals, that shaped David Brown's life.

He is the complete sociopath.

He is also narcissistic and a hypochondriac. The person who suffers from the narcissistic personality disorder feels a sense of entitlement; he believes that he deserves everything he wants—because he is *special*. The hypochondriac revels in the attention he gets for all his imaginary illnesses. David has convinced others he is dying of colon cancer for twenty years!

Even the most brilliant forensic psychiatrists do not *know* what factors cause sociopathy. Every sadistic sociopathic killer I have ever written about suffered abuse in early childhood—under the age of five. Abandonment, physical abuse, sexual abuse, humiliation, rejection. The developing conscience, which should have blossomed around two or three, was smothered aborning. These children fought to survive; they had neither time nor energy to grow a conscience. They learned, instead, to look out for number one, for if they did not, who would? Therapists cannot go back a dozen or more years later and *insert* a conscience; it is far too late.

But every child who is abused, abandoned, rejected, humiliated, under the age of five does not grow up to be antisocial. What makes the difference? After two decades of examining the sociopathic killer, I have come to believe that there are genetic, predisposing factors that come into play. The very intelligent, very sensitive child—abused—seems most likely to adjust, to *survive* at all costs. And the cost is the complete loss of ability to empathize and to feel regret and guilt.

A growing school among psychiatrists espouses the "bad seed" theory. Some experts believe that a certain percentage of infants are born *evil*, and that no amount of nurturing can overcome a bad seed's natural tendencies.

Others cite *physiological* causes. We share with animals the limbic system in the brain. The limbic system tells us what we *want*. Animals take what they want and have no control system. Human beings have the prefrontal lobe that gives us feelings and reasoning power. That, in essence, gives us brakes. One school of thought suggests that some infants *are* born with a breakdown in the pathways between the prefrontal lobe and the limbic system and lack the ability to control their desires. Like animals, they simply take what they want—congenitally crippled villains.

I reject the bad seed and the limbic breakdown theories—possibly because I don't want to believe that any child is born with his fate already sealed. Rather, I think genetic predisposition *combines* with the way a child is raised to shape what he will become. The search for a definitive answer to the cause of sociopathy continues.

Something over three percent of all males in America fall within the parameters of the antisocial personality. One percent of females fit that mold. They are, fortunately, not all murderers. These are the people all of us interact with at some point in our lives, usually to our regret. These are the people who cheat in business, who steal from us, who break our hearts and move on without looking back—and without remorse.

These are the politicians who ignore the rules, get caught, and appear on television to explain why the rules the rest of us live by were not meant for *them*. And if we do not believe them, they are genuinely shocked.

These are the "preachers" who solicit money in the name of God and spend it on themselves. Who break the commandments, while telling us not to. Caught, they cry real tears and beg for forgiveness. Forgiven, they do not change.

And then there are the David Browns. The antisocial personalities who easily cross over the boundary lines that separate cheaters, con artists, and predators of the lonely hearts from murderers.

The antisocial personality has no conscience. This is a concept as foreign to most of us—and as difficult to understand—as truly visualizing infinity. Our minds shut down. We cannot imagine what it must be like to distance ourselves totally from another creature's pain.

Those without the baggage of conscience can step into new rooms in their lives and close the door of the past tightly behind them so that no wisp of odor or sound penetrates. No guilt. No bad dreams. No looking back at all. For them, yesterday never really happened. For most of us, the future is the only unknown; we remember the past, and it often haunts us. The sociopath lets the past die behind a series of locked mental doors.

The *sadistic* sociopaths, the killers, seem to have, however, a curious sense of ritual for the dead. It does not matter that a sociopath has caused the death in question; he—or she—will go to great lengths to tie up loose ends neatly.

A lovely funeral service. A red rose in a coffin. A poem of remembrance. An engraved statue or headstone or plaque. The symbolic gesture seems to make it easier to close the doors.

Yes, I killed you—it was necessary—but I gave you a great funeral.

Yes, I killed you—but I engraved your name so no one will forget you.

Yes, I killed you—but I always carry your picture in my wallet.

After David's conviction, Jay Newell went to the cemetery where Linda Brown's ashes were interred, curious about what her niche plaque actually said. Linda *was* in a fountain, as David described. David had given her two niche plaques. The upper plaque read simply, "Linda Marie Brown," and beneath that, "1961–1985," the dates separated by a dove. The lower plaque bore the words David had forgotten:

"Your love, kindness, caring, and beauty will shine forever. Love, Krystal and David."

Because antisocial personalities are missing something as vital as true feelings of concern, they often substitute symbolism. They need touchstones to help bridge the gap between themselves and humans who can feel. They may identify with astrology or mysticism or unicorns or—as in David Brown's case—the phoenix.

The day after Linda was shot, David asked Officer Alan Day to bring him his cross, but I suspect it was his phoenix pendant that he clung to. The dove dies but the phoenix lives forever.

David Brown is the ultimate survivor, indeed a phoenix, always gathering shape and energy in the ashes of his failures. He accepts no blame and therefore cannot change. He truly can see no *reason* to change. All guilt detaches and slips away from him like ice in a warm rain. He has no bad dreams. He plans only for the future. Even now, if his captors are not vigilant, he will fly free, victorious once again.

On November 28, 1990, David was moved from the prison facility at Chino, California—where he was undergoing tests and evaluation—to New Folsom Prison in Sacramento. Now, and for the rest of his life, he will be known as prisoner E-70756. New Folsom has the most modern security devices in the California penal system. He has been segregated for his own protection.

Data Recovery is still in business. A Chicago office answers phone calls, and apparently David Brown still receives profits.

Patti Bailey remains a prisoner at the Ventura facility in Camarillo. She will probably be there until she is twenty-five years old. The daughter she bore David lives with Mary and Rick Bailey.

David has begun to write to Patti again, clever, beguiling letters—designed to draw her back to him. No one can predict what Patti's future holds. Her only model has been David; her ethics, her education, her sexual orientation, her morality. He caught her in a box with invisible walls for more than a decade. Whether she can ever truly escape him is questionable.

Richard Steinhart and his wife, Pat, have placed their faith in God. Richard now goes by the name of Liberty. He has undergone a near-miraculous remission from AIDS and works on a crisis line at Melody Lane Center in Anaheim fielding calls from those whose lives have been blighted by drugs. He also speaks frequently to high school and youth groups in his campaign to save them from the mistakes he once made. He gives them Bibles, which he pays for himself or with donations. Liberty is a dynamic speaker, full of bluster and humor—and love.

Eighteen months after "Goldie" Steinhart plotted with David Brown to get rid of Jeoff Robinson and Jay Newell, Newell's wife—Betty Jo—went with me to meet Liberty. When we asked for Richard Steinhart at Melody Lane, we got blank looks. They knew only "Liberty."

After talking with Liberty for an hour or so, Betty Jo felt comfortable enough to ask, "You weren't *really* going to shoot my husband, were you?"

"The way I was then?" he answered. "Yes . . . right in the back of the head."

It was a searing moment. In the telephone room of a drug clinic, Jay Newell's wife and I joined hands with Liberty and said a prayer of thanks for a tragedy that didn't happen.

Liberty has no illusions about David Brown. "He'll always be dangerous—he'll always be able to get somebody to do what he wants if he has money—of if he can convince some con he has money."

Jeoff Robinson has several more felony trials behind him now, but he will remember the David Brown case as the most memorable of many memorable murder cases. Someday—but not quite yet—Robinson may accept his father and brother's invitation to join their law firm. He loves his family devotedly, but he eats, sleeps, and breathes the prosecution of felons.

With Jay Newell, Robinson joined the Brown jury for a reunion after David Brown's sentencing. They chose Bennigan's—the restaurant whose parking lot was the site of the payoffs made by Tom Brown, the payoffs that David Brown believed would result in Robinson's and Newell's executions.

Jay Newell still heads the Narcotics Enforcement Team for the Orange County District Attorney's Office. He and his wife contribute to the Orange County chapter of Child Help U.S.A., an organization open to all kids in trouble—no questions asked.

Fred McLean is training for a hundred-mile marathon. He and his wife, Bernie, have a grandson now, but that hasn't slowed Fred—or Bernie—down. After the trial, it was Fred McLean who noticed Patti Bailey's scratched glasses, took her prescription, and bought her a pair that she could see out of.

Cinnamon Brown is still in prison as this is written. She has been moved to "M.C.," an adult cottage, and shares her room with another girl. She sleeps in the top bunk. "I appreciated having my own room over the years—but I can manage having a roommate."

"Wards" are offered a chance to learn dog grooming and that tempted Cinnamon, but she chose to continue to work for TWA on the reservations lines instead. She is one of their five top-rated employees at Ventura.

She has earned twenty-four hours in college credits and maintains a 3.33 GPA (B+). She is currently studying cultural anthropology, American democracy, and art appreciation. She is very busy working, going to college, and with therapy groups.

Still, Cinnamon is always aware that she is locked up. Although she has "free movement" to the TWA offices (inside the CYA campus), it is easy to receive a behavior report. There are so many rules to remember.

Cinnamon has both dreams and fears for her future. She has many regrets about the past. She thinks she is, in many ways, *more* mature at twenty than she would be had she never been locked up. She gained a great deal of self-respect when she told the truth in 1988, and she shows concern for the younger wards at Ventura School.

"My friend came to me in confidence once and explained that our counselor was molesting her. I told her to tell someone in authority, and she said we would have no way to prove what was going on. So I gave her my tape recorder and told her to record it. So she taped it to her body and got it recorded. I got this idea from Jay recording my father and me. I knew the counselor would have no idea it was there and continue on. It worked. I'm proud that I was able to help her out of that awful situation.

"Jay Newell helped me the most while I've been in Ventura. He gave me strength, and he believes in me. Jeoff has helped too and so has Fred. I appreciate them for all they've done."

Cinnamon realizes and accepts that she will probably never see her father again. Even today, however, she is ambivalent. The little girl who trusted her daddy cannot quite let him go.

"My dad was a challenge," she remembers. "Especially as I grew, things became more complicated. I had to struggle to show him I loved him. I was very dependent on him. I needed his approval on *everything*. He was tops then—I had full trust in him. . . .

"I feel sorry for my father. He's done very bad things to people, and I feel sorry for him because it doesn't matter to him. I love him still. But I will not forgive him for the awful mistakes I've made because of him. It bothers me knowing he's most likely not going to change himself. He'll feel at home in prison. He can have people tend to his needs. He'll never be alone and he'll have people to manipulate. Prison will be comfortable for him. He'll get the attention he needs. I regret having to turn him in, because now my little sister will not know her dad or ever know her mom. I feel totally responsible. I pray my father changes. I love our memories and fun. I'll not agree with the things my father does, but I'll always have that love there. I'll never see him again and I can live with that."

After his conviction, Cinnamon sent her father the Lord's Prayer and the Catholic confession prayer. Her note read:

DADDY,
   I sure hope you will read these and remember who they're from. I took time to do this for you 'cause I love you. And I think they will bring some hope into your life.

LOVE ALWAYS,
CINNY 1990

Cinnamon, finally able to participate in counseling now that she has no secrets, knows that she has to let her father go, to forgive him for what he did to her. If she harbors resentment, she knows it will only destroy her. Cinnamon refers to her mother, Brenda, as "my backbone—she believes in me and she shares herself with me . . . we communicate fine now and I love her with all my being."

Cinnamon and Patti are not close even though they are locked in the same prison. "She wants me to act like nothing ever happened and start over," Cinnamon says. "I can't. I can't just not remember the hurt and pain. Here in Ventura, she goes out of her way to be where I am. I need space from her. She acts like she needs my approval, but talks bad about me to someone else. I don't understand why she plays games with my emotions—talking about her baby, Heather, and her and my dad's marriage or about letters she gets from my dad. She hurts me but smiles in my face, saying she loves me. I'm fine by myself . . . I'm moving on with my life."

Cinnamon has learned not to expect too much. Even so, she cannot repress that bubble of hope that maybe her next parole hearing will set her free after six years in jail and prison. Although she might be expected to be bitter, she is not. She struggles still with the regret her father cannot feel, but she wants so much to return to the world outside one day.

"I miss my family. I miss seeing my two younger sisters grow. I also miss the beach and being around people who are happy. I miss riding my bike. I miss having people there for me. I miss food. I really miss having a dog. Maybe another Chihuahua—they're faithful dogs. I miss being creative; we're limited to what we can do here—such as making crafts.

"When I go home, I want to go to Disneyland—the happiest place on earth—Sea World, the zoo in San Diego. I love animals. I really want to learn how to drive and buy a car. I've always felt insecure about driving. I thought I'd never have a chance.

"I want to find a job and start living within the community, learn about environmental problems around me so I can be aware and help the community. I would eventually like finding the things my father has that are mine. All those memories in pictures and personal items. I truly want my personal property.

"After quite some time and I feel comfortable, I would like to get in contact with Krystal, my little sister. . . . My dad's side of the family disowned me after my father was arrested. So I no longer exist to them, which really hurts."

Even as Cinnamon strives to be free, she is frightened of the world outside Ventura School. At twenty, she has never been allowed any contact with boys beyond holding hands. The world has moved on without her for six years.

"I'm comfortable here," she explains. "Sometimes I get so caught up here, I forget there's out there. I worry about my safety from my dad. I worry about not learning how to drive. I worry I won't have a chance to catch up on the things I haven't got to do yet. Like I'll only have a while to catch up—before something awful happens. I wonder if I'll live longer in here than out there, because of my father. So many changes since I've been here; I'm nervous that I'll be lost out there.

"I'll be different than the others. I grew up in jail. How will people see me? Will they treat me like a criminal? Will they trust me?

"I haven't let Ventura change me in any negative ways. I observed everything. I'm still very young at heart. I love to laugh and make people laugh. I'm mature, but I kept my innocence—meaning Ventura didn't harden me because I wouldn't let it. So will people stereotype me and judge me? Or will I be given another chance totally? Will I seem like a threat to people because I shamefully killed Linda?"

David Brown continues to saddle his oldest daughter with fear and pain, even though he never writes to her. How lamentable that Cinnamon must walk with the specter of "something awful" cutting off her life.

Her dreams are modest. "I want a comfortable, normal job, and I want to someday marry and have children. I want a family and maybe a job as a travel agent or in social services or in education. I want to earn my AA [associate degree] and attend some courses on travel.

"I want a simple life; I want to focus on myself and bringing happiness to myself. [In Ventura,] I learned how to be assertive. I learned to appreciate others' values. I learned patience. I basically learned people skills. I learned how to adjust with many different personalities.

"I learned not to give up hope."

Last of all, Cinnamon Brown at twenty vows never to forget Linda. It might be better for her if she could let go just a little, but she cannot.

"It's important to me that people know I feel very ashamed of what I did to Linda. It's very painful knowing I took her life and she'll never have a chance again. I took the law into my own hands, and I think constantly of what I've done to Linda. I cry and pray for her often, because I loved her.

"That's what hurts more than anything. *I loved her, and still believed my father's lies . . . and I killed her!* None of it was true. Linda wasn't the person my father made her out to be. I think it's okay for me to love her and miss her. If there was one wish given to me, and it could be anything, I'd wish Linda her life back. Not because of the consequences but because I hate living with the pain of Linda being dead because of me. She trusted me and loved me, and I was selfish and took her life. I'll never forget those emotions at all. I'll never forget Linda. She'll always be there to remind me of what I've done.

"I never want the pain to go away. I deserve to live with the painful truth. . . ."

"I've learned to appreciate all that we're given—good or bad. I picked the positive things and kept them and formed an understanding of the bad. I couldn't change them, so I learned to accept them and not forget them.

"It took a while for me to trust again. But it was well worth it. Not everyone is a bad seed.

"Unfortunately, my father was. . . ."

On January 15, 1991, Cinnamon Brown faced the California Youthful Offender Parole Board for the sixth time. She had already been incarcerated longer than the five-and-a-half-year average sentence served by convicted juvenile murderers in California. Even high-profile teenage killers whose crimes had been totally reprehensible had been released. But not Cinnamon. Her mother and grandmother and Jeoff Robinson and Jay Newell had reason to be optimistic that she was, at last, close to freedom. Indeed, they were more hopeful than Cinnamon herself, who had long since grown used to disappointment.

Robinson and Newell asked for a chance to speak to the parole board before Cinnamon was ushered in. They explained that Cinnamon had declined to talk to the board alone since late 1988 at their express request, that it had been vital that she remain silent until her father was convicted. Robinson asserted that she had been given this directive after her father's defense attorneys got hold of a private psychological report that they used to attack her character.

Cinnamon Brown had been truly between a rock and a hard place; she had to place her faith in someone, and she had trusted Jay Newell and Jeoff Robinson. She had ached to tell the whole story to the parole board but she'd kept quiet, even though she had known it would prolong her time in prison into late 1990 or early 1991, at the very least. Knowing the risk she was taking, Cinnamon had kept all the promises she'd made.

The Orange County district attorneys had, in return, made her no promises. They could not. But Jeoff Robinson had told the David Brown jury that he believed Cinnamon should now be free. Many of the jurors felt the same way, and they had written letters to the parole board on her behalf.

For two agonizing hours, Cinnamon answered the board's questions, and listened to their characterizations of her. Victor Weishart, chairman of the parole board, was clearly not impressed with Cinnamon's prior refusal to open up to the board. He had encountered Cinnamon at parole hearings before and apparently did not find that she had grown in any way.

The three-member board issued a statement after the closed hearing. They had ruled that Cinnamon's "testimony against her father should not be considered in determining Cinnamon's parole readiness." By a two-to-one vote, the panel chose not to change the date she would be eligible for parole. Her current parole date was now set for March 1992. The dissenting board member, Fred Bautista, favored a CYA staff recommendation that *one month* be cut from her sentence, "time off for good behavior," which would allow her to be released in *February* 1992.

"[Cinnamon Brown] still needs to make much more progress in addressing the reasons why she became involved in this calculated crime," the board concluded. "[She] is manipulative and [her psychologist] describes her as customarily flippant in therapy." Comparing her to David Brown, the board stressed that being "manipulative" was "a trait employed to perfection by her father."

Cinnamon, who had endured prison for a half-dozen years while her father and Patti Bailey lived in luxury, and then while they fought conviction, was given little hope that she would get out before she was 25 years old. Although she had been brought into the killing plot *years* after her father and Patti began discussing it, Cinnamon had apparently come to be seen as the prime instigator in the board's mind. She had kept silent first to protect her father, and later to protect the State's case.

She was not angry; she was crushed. Jeoff Robinson said she had not really expected to get out, but the board's refusal to give her even 30 days of good time negated everything she had done to try to improve herself. "She did not expect to be paroled," Robinson told Christopher Pummer of the *Los Angeles Times*, "But it upset her to be labeled a manipulative, cold-blooded, murderess. . . . She has acknowledged her culpability, she has admitted pulling the trigger and she has expressed remorse. . . ."

Robinson and Jay Newell were convinced that Cinnamon had long ago broken free of her father's hold over her, although the board apparently did not agree with that view. "At this point in her life," Robinson commented, "I think she has broken free. She loves her father, but she is not under the influence of David Brown."

Both Robinson and Newell were stunned by the parole board's assessment of Cinnamon Brown. Newell said little, but his jaw tightened with the strain of *not* speaking. Robinson told Jeff Collins of the Orange County Register, "As an observer and not an advocate, I don't believe that Cinnamon was treated completely fairly. . . . They were very harsh and very myopic, in my view."

The two Orange County DA's men had gone to CYA because they believed the board labored under false assumptions. "At least one member of the board thought she had done this for insurance money," Robinson said. "We wanted to explain that this wasn't the case. We offered no specific recommendations for shortening Cinnamon's sentence."

Newell's and Robinson's presence and information made no difference at all. The girl who had gone into prison at fifteen, and who was now close to twenty-one, returned to her cell with little hope. Ironically, Patti Bailey will probably be released from prison before Cinnamon. If each is held until her twenty-fifth birthday—as the law allows—Patti will be eligible for release in 1993, while Cinnamon will not be twenty-five until 1995. The parole board, of course, has it within its power to schedule a parole hearing at any time.

In the meantime, Cinnamon continues to work and study inside prison. Although Patti's company brings back excruciatingly painful memories, Patti was moved first into Cinnamon's cottage, and then into the room right next door to her.

Cinnamon does not write to her father or hear from him. Patti receives daily mail from David Brown.

There are never neat, clean endings to murder cases. There are certainly never happy endings, but there is, in the best of cases, a certain justice.

For Cinnamon Brown, justice has proved to be as hard to grasp as a bit of dandelion fluff in the wind. She holds on to her faith in God, and to the few friends who continue to support her.

Her story is far from over.

Acknowledgments

MORE THAN most authors, true crime writers are dependent upon the memories, perceptions, insights, and knowledge of those who have lived through the real story. More than most authors, true crime writers also seem to need buffering and kind words while we are immersed in the black intricacies of the sociopathic mind. I am grateful for those who knew the truth and shared it with me, and for those who helped me deal with those realities. My appreciation goes to the scores of Orange County, California, residents who graciously gave me their time and shared their personal impressions. And as always, I thank my own motley support system, which saw me through the unraveling of a tragic and shocking story. Thank you to:

Garden Grove Police Department: Chief John Robertson, Detective Fred McLean, Detective William Morrissey, Detective Ron Shave, Forensic Specialist Marsha MacWillie.

Orange County deputy coroner Bernice Mazuca.

Orange County District Attorney's Office: District Attorney Michael Capizzi, Deputy District Attorney Jeoffrey Robinson, Senior Attorney's Investigator Jay Newell, Deputy District Attorney Tom Borris (now in private practice), Chief, District Attorney's Bureau of Investigation, Loren "Duke" DuChesne, Assistant Chief, District Attorney's Bureau of Investigation, Vince Vasil and his wife, Lou Vasil, Supervising Attorneys' Investigator Jim Aumond, Chief Deputy District Attorney Jim Enright, Assistant District Attorney Ed Freeman, Technical Service Adviser Greg Gulen. Support staff: Annabelle Roberts, Anne Leonard, Debbie Jackson, Karen Keyes, LaVonne Campbell, Edna Selleck, and Roxanne McDonald.

Orange County Superior Court, Department 30: Superior Court Judge Donald A. McCartin, Court Clerk Gail Carpenter, Court Reporter Sandra Wingerd, Bailiff "Mitch" Miller, Deputy Marshal Glenn "Hoop" Hoopingarner.

Defense attorneys: Gary M. Pohlson, Richard Schwartzberg.

Eric Lichtblau and Jerry Hicks, *Los Angeles Times;* Jeff Collins, *Orange County Register;* Dave Lopez, CBS–Channel 2, Los Angeles; Barney Morris, ABC, Channel 7, Los Angeles.

With special thanks to: Brenda Sands, Doris Smith, Janell Wheeler, Anita Sands, Gary Miller, Otis and Cecil Fox, Betty Jo Newell, Rita and Mark Robinson, Sr., Derek Johnson, Sandy and Gene Walsh, Katie, Brad, Torrie and Chrissie Walsh, Cheryl Goodman, Teri Blanchard, Rita Nugent, Fred Land, Don Lasseter, Courtney Michelle, Jan E. Elinsky, Larry T. Nakashima, Meghann Shane, Deborah Duke, Virginia Newell, Beatrice Munoz, Ebba "Sunny" Cole, Joey Moscatiello and all the family at Pepino's Restaurant in El Toro, Jimmy Buffett, Stephen M. Lopez, Rick Watkins, Pamela Starns, David Miller, Donna Nichol, Mary Bailey, Rick Bailey, Alan Bailey, Valerie Bailey, Ethel Bailey, Child Help of Orange County.

My reconstruction of the ambiance, detail, and testimony in the long trial in Department 30 was helped immeasurably by the efforts of my trial assistants, Donna Anders and Leslie Rule. Leslie also served as my photographer and took several hundred photographs, both during the trial and around Orange County.

Northwest support included: Marlene Price, Mike Rule, Jennifer A. Gladwell, Cheri Luxa, Gerry Brittingham, Mike Prezbindowski, Tina Abeel, Laura Harris, Becca Harris, Brian Halquist, David Coughlan, Luke and Nancy Fiorante, Mildred Yoacham, Eilene Schultz, Lars and Debb Larson, Maureen and Bill Woodcock, Ruth and Vernon Cornelius, Dr. Peter J. Modde, Austin and Charlotte Seth, Dr. Carl Berner and staff, Andy Rule, S. Bruce Sherles, Forrest Schultz, Anne and Chris Jaeger, *and* Ms. Haleigh Jean Jaeger, who was born the day this book was finished.

Thank you to my mother, Sophie Hansen Stackhouse, who always let me explore and "research" and never clipped my wings. And to the rest of the clan of Michigan Danes who helped to shape my life: the late Montcalm County, Michigan, sheriff Chris Hansen; the late Anna Hansen; the late Amelia Hansen Mills; the late Montcalm County, Michigan, sheriff Elton Sampson; Emma Hansen McKenney; Montcalm County coroner Dr. Carl M. Hansen; Freda Hansen Sampson Grunwald; Donna Hansen Basom; Montcalm County prosecuting attorney Bruce Basom; Jan Basom Schubert; Calhoun County, Michigan, judicial clerk Sara Jane Plushnik; Chris L. McKenney; Karen Hudson; Jim Sampson; Christa Hansen; Terry Hansen. The love of the law, and most of all, the search for justice, courses through all our veins.

In New York, I was fortunate indeed to have a brilliant, patient, and incisive editor, Frederic W. Hills; his cheerful and competent assistant, Daphne Bien; and a no-nonsense manuscript editor, Burton Beals. This book also marks two decades with the best agents an author ever had: Joan and Joe Foley.

Last of all, my deep gratitude goes to a very practical helper—Matthew Noel Harris—who single-handedly rescued Chapter 24 from my computer's secret vault.

TRUE CRIME DIARY

James Bland

One hundred and eighty real-life murder stories, quirky, gory, ingenious, bungled, or just plain horrifying, arranged in diary form for the fascination of all true crime addicts.

4 January 1964: The Boston Strangler's last victim found naked, trussed, raped and strangled with a New Year greetings card against her right foot.

25 April 1935: a shark in an Australian aquarium brought up a human arm – and started a murder hunt.

11 May 1916: a Hungarian blacksmith bought a house at an auction. He found the bodies of seven women in the adjoining workshop.

23 November 1910: Dr Crippen hanged at Pentonville Prison for the murder of his second wife. He had poisoned her, and concealed her dismembered remains beneath the cellar floor of their home.

29 December 1969: Muriel McKay abducted from her London home. The body was never found, but two Trinidadian brothers, Arthur and Nizamodeen Hosein, were convicted of her murder – it is believed that she was fed to the pigs on Arthur Hosein's farm.

TRUE CRIME DIARY

'A splendid collection of true stories'
True Crime Monthly

Also available:
TRUE CRIME DIARY VOLUME 2

NON-FICTION/CRIME